THE PEOPLE THEMSELVES

★★★★ THE PEOPLE THEMSELVES

POPULAR CONSTITUTIONALISM

AND JUDICIAL REVIEW ★★★★★

LARRY D. KRAMER

OXFORD

UNIVERSITY PRESS

2004

OXFORD

UNIVERSITY PRESS

Oxford   New York
Auckland   Bangkok   Buenos Aires   Cape Town   Chennai
Dar es Salaam   Delhi   Hong Kong   Istanbul   Karachi   Kolkata
Kuala Lumpur   Madrid   Melbourne   Mexico City   Mumbai   Nairobi
São Paulo   Shanghai   Taipei   Tokyo   Toronto

Copyright © 2004 by Oxford University Press, Inc.

Published by Oxford University Press, Inc.
198 Madison Avenue, New York, New York 10016

www.oup.com

Oxford is a registered trademark of Oxford University Press

Library of Congress Cataloging-in-Publication Data
Kramer, Larry, 1958–
The people themselves : popular constitutionalism and judicial review /
by Larry D. Kramer.
p. cm.
Includes bibliographical references and index.
ISBN-13 978-0-19-530645-3
ISBN 0-19-530645-7
ISBN 0-19-516918-2
1. People (Constitutional law)—United States. 2. Constituent power—United States.
3. Judicial review—United States. I. Title.
KF4881 .K73 2004
342.73—dc22   2003020734

Printed in the United States of America
on acid-free paper

★ *To Sarah and Kiki* ★

Who Are the Best Keepers of the People's Liberties?

Republican.—The People themselves. The sacred trust can be no where so safe as in the hands most interested in preserving it.

Anti-republican.—The people are stupid, suspicious, licentious. They cannot safely trust themselves. When they have established government they should think of nothing but obedience, leaving the care of their liberties to their wiser rulers.

James Madison
National Gazette, December 22, 1792

Acknowledgments

★ ★ ★

In the course of working on this project, I have received useful advice and challenging criticism from countless friends, colleagues, and students. I would especially like to thank Akhil Amar, John Baker, Rachel Barkow, Richard B. Bernstein, Saul Cornell, Ronald Dworkin, Noah Feldman, John Ferejohn, Martin Flaherty, Barry Friedman, David Golove, Mark Graber, Don Herzog, Daryl Levinson, Sandy Levinson, Joyce Malcolm, Liam Murphy, Pasquale Pasquino, Steven Perry, Rick Pildes, Peter Schuck, Geoffrey Stone, William Stuntz, and Mark Tushnet. I also received insightful feedback from participants in the N.Y.U. Legal History Colloquium and from faculty workshops at the law schools of Columbia, Cornell, North Carolina, N.Y.U., Ohio State, Stanford, and Yale. I would also like to thank Jay Shuman for his always invaluable research assistance and amazing detective abilities and Laura Russo and Christopher Bradley for help in producing the text.

Certain friends and colleagues deserve special mention. In addition to feedback in the form of comments, Jack Rakove, John Reid, and William Nelson have helped to educate me generally, offering a ridiculously undeserved amount of their own time over the years. Many of the ideas in here were first developed in long conversations with William Treanor, who disagrees with much of what I have to say but was willing to put that aside and help me make it better anyway. I have also been wonderfully helped by my compatriots in crime, Reva Siegel, Robert Post, and especially Willy Forbath, whose insights and encouragement kept me going when I sometimes doubted the value of what we were doing. I want to thank Bill Miller and Don Herzog for pushing me to try something that went just a bit beyond what I thought I could do: whether or not I succeeded, it was worth the effort. Above all, I owe thanks to my wife, Sarah Delson, for her endless willingness to listen and talk things over, for her cheer and encouragement, for her patience in suffering through my moods when things weren't going well, for her willingness to let me work long hours, for herself, and (above all) for Kiki.

This project could not have been completed without generous research support from the New York University School of Law. A first cut at the argument in this book, much revised here, was published as an article, "We the Court," 115 *Harvard Law Review* 4 (2001). In addition, parts of chapter four are drawn from "Putting the Politics Back into the Political Safeguards of Federalism," 100 *Columbia Law Review* 215 (2000). I am grateful to the editors of both journals for their initial help in producing these pieces.

Contents

CONTENTS

THE PEOPLE THEMSELVES

Introduction

POPULAR CONSTITUTIONALISM

Some snapshots from the early American Republic:

Monday, July 29, 1793. A jury acquitted Gideon Henfield of charges that he violated the law of nations by serving aboard a French privateer.[1] The facts of Henfield's case were uncontested, and his defense turned on a point of law. Henfield argued that it was unconstitutional to prosecute him because his actions were not proscribed by any existing statute or law of the United States. The court—consisting of Supreme Court Justices James Wilson and James Iredell and District Court Judge Richard Peters—instructed jurors that Henfield's defense was legally frivolous. It was the "joint and unanimous opinion of the court," Wilson told them, that Henfield's acts might be culpable as common law offenses against the United States.[2] The jury disagreed, and its verdict triggered celebrations throughout the nation. John Marshall reports that Henfield's acquittal was greeted with "extravagant marks of joy and exultation" by a public that doubted the administration's position.[3] Bonfires were lit and feasts held in cities and towns from Maine to Georgia. In Charleston, South Carolina, a "number of respectable citizens" followed an evening of "great hilarity and harmony" by toasting "[t]he patriotic jury of Philadelphia who acquitted Gideon Henfield, and supported the rights of man. (*Three cheers*)."[4] The *National Gazette* praised Henfield's jury for

3

upholding the Constitution against a court and an Administration whose views had been corrupted by "motives of policy":

> When the seven bishops (good and celebrated men) were tried for petitioning James the Second, a similar difference of opinion arose between the bench and the jury, the people then as the people now exulted in the verdict of acquittal; and our posterity will, probably, venerate this as we venerate that jury, for adding to the security of the rights and liberties of mankind.[5]

* * *

Saturday, July 18, 1795. At least 5,000 people gathered in front of Federal Hall in New York City to protest the Jay Treaty.[6] Planned for weeks by Republicans anxious to see the treaty condemned, the crowd of mostly tradesmen and laborers was unexpectedly joined by some of the city's elite, hastily assembled by Federalist merchants under the leadership of Alexander Hamilton. The determined Federalists tried to take over the rally. As the meeting was about to commence, Hamilton mounted the steps of a nearby building surrounded by supporters and began to speak. Republican leaders asked him to yield, which Hamilton haughtily refused to do. The crowd reacted angrily, drowning Hamilton out with "hissings, coughings, and hootings."[7] Hamilton offered a written resolution, which he urged be adopted as reflecting the true sense of the city. The crowd paused to listen, but exploded in fury upon hearing that it was "unnecessary to give an opinion on the treaty" because the people had "full confidence in the wisdom and virtue of the President of the United States, to whom, in conjunction with the Senate, the discussion of the question constitutionally belongs."[8] Hamilton and his companions were driven away amidst shouts of "we'll hear no more of it" and "tear it up."[9] Someone in the crowd allegedly threw a rock that hit Hamilton in the head. Similar scenes were repeated around the country.

* * *

July 2, 1798. During a debate in Congress over whether to adopt the Alien Act—which gave the President unilateral power to imprison or deport aliens, even in peacetime—New York's Edward Livingston reproached the bill's supporters. "If we are ready to violate the constitution we have sworn to defend," he warned, "will the people submit to our unauthorized acts? Will the states sanction our usurped powers? Sir, they ought not to submit. They would deserve the chains which these measures are for them if they did not resist."[10] Responses to Livingston's admonition were immediate and widespread. Public meetings in Kentucky, Virginia, and throughout the Middle Atlantic states denounced the Alien and Sedition Acts and declared them null and void.[11] A militia company in one Virginia county announced that it would not assist in enforcing the laws, while a regiment in Madison County, Kentucky, resolved that such acts "are infringements of the Constitution and of natural rights, and . . . we cannot approve or submit to them."[12] Federalists responded to these and similar declarations by pleading that judgments of constitutionality be left for courts to make, a position their opponents fiercely denied. To say that "a decision as to the constitutionality of all legislative acts, lies solely with the judiciary," wrote a correspondent in the *Albany Register*, "is removing the cornerstone on which our federal compact rests; it is taking from the people the ultimate sovereignty."[13]

* * *

In these and countless similar scenes, Americans of the Founding era reveal how they understood their role in popular government in ways that we, who take so much for granted, do not. The United States was then the only country in the world with a government founded explicitly on the consent of its people, given in a distinct and identifiable act, and the people who gave that consent were intensely, profoundly conscious of the fact. And proud. This pride, this awareness of the fragility and importance of their venture in popular government, informed everything the Founding generation did. It was, as Gordon Wood has said, "the deeply felt meaning of the Revolution."[14]

Modern commentators, especially legal commentators, read the Founders' letters and speeches anachronistically, giving too much weight, or the wrong kind of weight, to complaints about "the excess of democracy."[15] We depict the men who framed and ratified the Constitution as striving to create a self-correcting system of checks and balances whose fundamental operations could all take place from within the government itself, with minimal involvement or interference from the people. Our political grammar is saturated with this reading of the Founding, which sees the movement to write a new Constitution almost exclusively in antidemocratic terms. Our Constitution on this view—a view that pervades both legal and historical scholarship on the subject—was adopted first and foremost to put a check on the people, to minimize their role in governing, to shove them as far offstage as possible without technically abandoning republicanism.

There is, of course, an element of truth to this characterization. Having overvalued the capacity of an unchecked legislature to govern during the wave of romantic enthusiasm that swept the country with the Declaration of Independence, America's leadership relearned the hard way in the 1780s why it was necessary to fragment and separate power within the government. Yet we must be careful, lest we exaggerate the extent and nature of the reaction by focusing too narrowly on its direction.

Equally important, we must not judge the words and actions of men of the eighteenth century by our own standards of what it means to be a "democrat." The views of even the most "anti" of Anti-Federalists would be reactionary today, very far outside the political mainstream in most respects. In their own time, however, and especially against the background of the greater Atlantic world, America's Founders were at the other end of the political spectrum: wild-eyed radicals taking a risky gamble on popular rule. The debate between Federalists and Anti-Federalists was, in effect, an argument between factions on the democratic left; even "high-toned" Federalists were populist under prevailing views, which deemed stable government without a monarch or formal aristocracy out of the question. America's Founding generation, in daring contrast, embraced a political ideology that celebrated the central role of "the people" in supplying government with its energy and direction, an ideal that remained at all times in the forefront of their thinking—Federalist and Anti-Federalist alike. Preserving liberty demanded a constitution whose internal architecture was carefully arranged to check power, just as it demanded leaders of sufficient "character" and "virtue." But structural innovations and virtuous leadership were "auxiliary devices" to channel and control popular politics, not to isolate or eliminate it. The people themselves remained responsible for making things work.

This was especially true when it came to a constitution, the most direct expression of the people's voice. Listen to St. George Tucker, in the appendix to his 1803 edition of *Blackstone's Commentaries:*

> [T]he American Revolution has formed a new epoch in the history of civil institutions, by reducing to practice, what, before, had been supposed to exist only in the visionary speculations of theoretical writers. . . . The world, for the first time since the annals of its inhabitants began, saw an original written compact formed by the free and deliberate voices of the individuals disposed to unite in the same social bonds; thus exhibiting a political phenomenon unknown to former ages. . . . [T]he powers of the several branches of government are defined, and

the excess of them, as well in the *legislature,* as in the *other* branches, finds limits, which cannot be transgressed without offending against the greater power from whom all authority, among us, is derived; to wit, the PEOPLE.[16]

When Tucker and his contemporaries invoked "the people," moreover, they were not conjuring an empty abstraction or describing a mythic philosophical justification for government. "The people" they knew could speak, and had done so. "The people" they knew had fought a revolution, expressed dissatisfaction with the first fruits of independence, and debated and adopted a new charter to govern themselves. Certainly the Founders were concerned about the dangers of popular government, some of them obsessively so. But they were also captivated by its possibilities and in awe of its importance. Their Constitution remained, fundamentally, an act of popular will: the people's charter, made by the people. And, as we shall see, it was "the people themselves"—working through and responding to their agents in the government—who were responsible for seeing that it was properly interpreted and implemented. The idea of turning this responsibility over to judges was simply unthinkable.

A practice of judicial review did emerge, and early on—well before *Marbury v. Madison,* which mostly repeated arguments already developed by others. Among the objectives of this book is to elucidate the nature of this early practice, which bore little resemblance to judicial review today. But the story that follows is more than a revisionist history of the origins of judicial review (though it is certainly that). For efforts to define a role for courts have been part of a larger and more fundamental struggle to maintain the authority of ordinary citizens over their Constitution. Time and again, the Founding generation and its successors responded to evolving social, political, and cultural conditions by improvising institutional and intellectual solutions to preserve popular control over the course of constitutional law—a kind of control we seem to have lost, or surrendered, today.

We in the twenty-first century tend to divide the world into two distinct domains: a domain of politics and a domain of law. In politics, the people rule. But not in law. Law is set aside for a trained elite of judges and lawyers whose professional task is to implement the formal decisions produced in and by politics. The Constitution, in this modern understanding, is a species of law—special only inasmuch as it sets the boundaries within which politics takes place. As law, the Constitution is set aside for this same elite to handle, subject to paramount supervision from the U.S. Supreme Court. Constitutional politics, in which the people have a role, is the process by which new constitutional law is made. It is distinguished from interpreting and enforcing existing constitutional law—tasks ultimately and authoritatively done for us in courts and by judges. Gerald Leonard puts the point nicely in observing how we are inclined today "to see politics as *working within* a constitutional order rather than *working out* that constitutional order."[17]

This modern understanding is, as we shall see, of surprisingly recent vintage. It reflects neither the original conception of constitutionalism nor its course over most of American history. Both in its origins and for most of our history, American constitutionalism assigned ordinary citizens a central and pivotal role in implementing their Constitution. Final interpretive authority rested with "the people themselves," and courts no less than elected representatives were subordinate to their judgments. It is the story of this practice of "popular constitutionalism" that emerges through our study of judicial review. Many, perhaps most, scholars today believe that "popular sovereignty" is and can be expressed only at rare moments, that "the people" are otherwise either absent or present only as an abstraction. Such was the belief of neither our Founding Fathers nor of their children nor of their children's children, and in charting how they constructed an idea of judicial review we will also be charting their efforts to explain and preserve the active sovereignty of the people over the Constitution. And along the way, perhaps, we may find some reasons to reawaken our own seemingly deadened sensibilities in this respect.

1

In Substance, and in Principle, the Same as It Was Heretofore

THE CUSTOMARY CONSTITUTION

The idea of a "constitution" was not new in 1787 or even in 1776. Americans had a concept of constitutional law and well-developed ideas about the nature of a constitution long before they sat down to write any of their own. From a historian's perspective, this concept reached back at least as far as the struggles between James I and Parliament,[1] though men of the seventeenth and eighteenth centuries liked to speak of an "Ancient Constitution" whose practices had been followed since "time out of mind."[2] Colonial Americans were wedded to the principles of this constitution, intimately familiar with its terms and convinced of its essential rightness and wisdom.[3] The patterns of thought and action formed by this experience naturally shaped their understanding of the task of writing new constitutions after the Revolution and thus provide a necessary starting point in recovering the original Constitution.

"What, But Immemorial Usage"

The word "constitution" had several meanings in the seventeenth and eighteenth centuries, not all of which correspond to modern understandings. According to one usage, a "constitution" was simply the arrangement of existing laws and practices that, literally, constituted the government; it was neither anterior nor superior to government or ordinary law, making it possible to speak of a law being unconstitutional without it also being illegal.[4] To just the opposite effect, another usage paired the constitution with ordinary law and constitutionality with legality. Writing in 1788, William Paley described the constitution as nothing more than "one principal division, head, section, or title of the code of publick laws."[5] "The terms *constitutional* and *unconstitutional*, mean *legal* and *illegal*," he explained, for constitutional law is "founded in the same authority with the law of the land upon any other subject; and to be ascertained by the same inquiries."

Still a third usage, and the one most pertinent here because acted upon by American revolutionaries, equated the constitution with "fundamental law." Yet the phrase fundamental law itself was not always used consistently.[6] In some instances, fundamental law was used interchangeably with old and valued customs, customs that might or might not be capable of controlling the sovereign. In other instances, it described rules setting forth the procedures for exercising legislative power, such as the requirement that all three estates—King, Lords, and Commons—consent before a bill could become law. Most commonly, however, the term fundamental law was used as a synonym for what we still think of today as constitutional law: a body of immutable principles beyond the reach of any institution of government.

Compounding our confusion over the meaning of fundamental law was its (to modern eyes) muddled relationship with common law, the body of customary rules and principles that governed most ordinary legal affairs in a time before legislatures were active. Fundamental law drew upon and shared many of the abiding principles of the common law. Much fundamental law was, in fact, derived from common law—the right to trial by jury being an obvious and outstanding example. Yet not all common law constituted fundamental law, while much of what was recognized as fundamental law was not derived from the common law. Despite substantial overlap, then, fundamental law formed a conceptually distinct body of principles and customs. Its precise boundaries vis-à-vis the common law may have been hazy, even to writers and speakers of the time, but boundaries nevertheless existed, and participants seemed capable of understanding one another and knowing when someone meant to invoke fundamental law in its strong sense.

More complex than the relationship of fundamental law to common law was that of fundamental law to natural law. That there was a "law of nature" (or, as some in the eighteenth century preferred to have it, a "law of reason") was taken for granted, as was the natural law's transcendence and superiority to the positive law enacted by human institutions.[7] Statements to this effect were virtual boilerplate in contemporary works of legal and political theory. Even Sir William Blackstone, the great positivist himself, began his *Commentaries* by recognizing a law of nature that "is of course superior in obligation to any other. It is binding all over the globe, in all countries, and at all times: no human laws are of any validity, if contrary to this; and such of them as are valid derive all their force, and all their authority, mediately or immediately, from this original."[8] Yet the significance of natural law's preeminence was less clear in practice because human law somehow managed always to offer an acceptable solution.[9] As one sixteenth- century judge explained:

> [W]e ought not to think that the founders of our laws were remiss in searching after the law of nature, or that they were ignorant of it. Nor have we any reason, from the laws which they have made, to conceive so low an opinion of them, for their laws argue to the contrary, and shew that they who made them were men of the greatest and most profound judgement, and acquainted as well with the law of nature as with the law of reason, and the law of God also. For there is nothing ordained in our law contrary to nature or reason or the law of God, but our law is agreeable to them all.[10]

Interpretive slippage of this sort was common when it came to fundamental law. For while fundamental and natural law may have been distinct, the generality and openness of their respective contents drained the distinction of its practical significance. Writers could (and did) presume that fundamental law conformed to the law of nature and so could (and did) draw interchangeably on both in making arguments. Fundamental law was, in part, an embodiment or expression of nature and reason in positive law. As one anonymous seventeenth-century pamphleteer put it, fundamental law was "a settling of the laws of nature and common equity (by common consent) in such a form of polity and government as that they may be administered among us with honour and safety."[11]

The eighteenth-century constitutional law tradition thus blended arguments from natural law with arguments from morality, from custom, and from common and statutory law in ways that blurred distinctions a modern lawyer assumes must be sharply articulated.[12] Nagging concern for precision about hierarchies and sources of law emerged later to become a hallmark of nineteenth- and twentieth-century legal thinking. Lawyers in the eighteenth century were aware of these distinctions, but in a manner that was seldom formulated with exactitude because a sharing and concordance of principles made it unnecessary to emphasize purely conceptual differences. So while the borders may have been murky, still they existed, and a positive notion of fundamental law provided the hub around which constitutional argument was organized. Both before and after the Revolution, in short, American Whigs believed there existed a fundamental or constitutional law whose terms "mark[ed] out and fix[ed] the chief lines and boundaries between the authority of rulers, and the liberties and privileges of the people."[13]

What were the characteristics or properties of this law? First and foremost, it rested on consent: the consent of the governed. The British constitution embodied a contract between the people and their rulers, whereby the people conferred certain powers, reserved certain privileges, and generally laid out the terms on which they agreed to be governed.[14] This agreement was "the very essence of . . . Jurisdiction," for authority to govern could be derived only through a "Compact" whose commencement "carried with it . . . the Consent of all Parties."[15] It was, necessarily, an agreement by implication, for no identifiable act marked the formal commencement of constitutional government. But this in no way diminished its popular basis, which rested on prescription. "However the historical fact may be of a social contract," explained Richard Wooddeson in 1792,

> government ought to be, and is generally *considered* as founded on consent, tacit or express, on a real, or *quasi*, compact. This theory is a material basis of political rights; and as a theoretical point is not difficult to be maintained. For what gives any legislature a right to act, where no express consent can be shewn? what, but immemorial usage? and what is the intrinsic force of immemorial usage, in establishing this fundamental or any other law, but that it is evidence of common acquiescence and consent?[16]

Wooddeson's invocation of "immemorial usage" is important for another reason, as it points to a second significant aspect of English constitutionalism. Rather than being located in a single text or identified with a particular enactment, the content and authority of the British constitution derived from principles long-enshrined in English legal culture and practice. We can, in other words, describe the body of fundamental law that in the eyes of eighteenth-century Englishmen formed their constitution as a *customary* constitution.

We should be careful in using the term "customary," for as we have already seen, sources of constitutional authority were not confined to custom. The convention of referring to England's constitution as "unwritten" is, in this sense, anachronistic, and it reflects a distinctly modern need to distinguish our own neatly written texts. Custom and practice were, of course, central sources of authority for fundamental law in the seventeenth and eighteenth centuries. But so, too, were a variety of written materials—including Magna Carta; the Bible; key statutes like the Declaration of Rights of 1689 and Act of Settlement of 1701; prominent treatises, particularly those by Vattel, Pufendorf, and Grotius; and certain philosophical works, of which John Locke's were probably the most important.[17]

These textual sources were not themselves fundamental law, any more than were the principles of natural law regularly cited for support by disputants. The constitution consisted of immutable principles of English liberty that were derived from "custom immemorial," a bounded and very real canon whose roots were said to be lost in the distant Saxon past. Subsequent enactments, later developed practices, learned treatises, and arguments drawn from natural law were all useful in helping to illuminate, translate, and make sense of these ancient principles. Constitutional polemicists employed these diverse sources to articulate and apply the enduring precepts of fundamental law, often claiming implausible gothic roots for practices in a way that maddened both contemporary and subsequent historians.[18] But, then, as John Reid has convincingly demonstrated, the lawyers, politicians, and pamphleteers who invoked the principles of the British constitution were not doing history.[19] They were employing a methodology that lawyers today typically associate with the common law: constructing arguments based on analogy, principle, and what Reid calls "forensic history" (which is to say law office history, which is to say not history at all). Fundamental law was distinct from common law, inasmuch as its rules, its principles, and its sources were different, albeit with some overlap. Methodologically, however, the fundamental law and the common law were siblings. This is what we mean by calling the British constitution a form of customary law. It was, as Reid urges, not a fixed or identifiable program, but rather "a constitutional apparatus of forensic advocacy to propagate anew traditional forms of restraint upon the current sovereign."[20] Put more simply, the customary constitution was a framework for argument, in which historical accuracy was less important than analogical persuasiveness in maintaining over time an established balance between liberty and power despite new or changed circumstances.

Like other forms of customary law, the content of this constitution was uncertain and open-ended. Indeed, the requirements of fundamental law were considerably less clear even than those of the common law, which after the fifteenth century had become centralized in the royal courts, and thus rested less on societal custom and practice than on formal judicial precedent and the opinion of legal professionals.[21] No similar development took place with respect to fundamental law, and courts had no special role in settling disputes over the meaning of the constitution.[22] Between its diverse sources, fluid nature, and the absence of any centralized forum for resolving conflict, fundamental law tended to be "whatever could be plausibly argued and forcibly maintained."[23] Yet this in no way reduced its status or significance. "Fundamental law contemplated unresolved controversy over contending legitimate interpretations, and unlike ordinary law did not need authoritative resolution of this controversy in order to maintain its efficacy. In the absence of authoritative determination of fundamental law's meaning, challenged governmental action stood, debate continued, and constitutional principles retained all their vitality."[24]

It did not follow that nothing was fixed. On the contrary, there was consensus about a great deal of fundamental law, particularly in the eighteenth century, after its most controversial features (the scope of the Crown's prerogative and the relationship between church and state) had been stabilized in the Glorious Revolution and its aftermath. These settled principles included both the existence of certain inalienable rights, such as the right to a jury or to petition the government, and matters of procedure and the exercise of executive or legislative power, such as the requirement that Parliament consent to legislation. Constitutional disputes might arise respecting the precise meaning or application of these principles in particular contexts, but there was general agreement as to their existence and even as to their application in a fairly broad range of circumstances.

The British constitution was, again like other forms of customary law, simultaneously immutable and evolving, unchanging yet always different. If this sounds paradoxical, think of Coke's timeless aphorism "out of the old Fields must spring and grow the new Corn."[25] Better still is Matthew Hale's famous analogy to the Argonauts: "As the Argonauts Ship was the same when it returned home, as it was when it went out, tho' in that long Voyage it had successive Amendments, and scarce came back with any of its former Materials."[26] Details, applications, even institutions might change, but the fundamental law itself remained constant and retained its essential substance as a bulwark protecting liberty from power. This capacity to improve without changing was regularly singled out as one of the British constitution's cardinal virtues. Speaking at the end of the eighteenth century, legal scholar John Reeves observed:

> That our Constitution is not precisely the same that it was in the Reign of Ja[mes] I, I am the last man to deny; because it is one of the strongest persuasions I have, about its excellence, that it is capable of, and is continually receiving, improvements, either by the accession of new benefits, or by the attainment of new securities to protect original rights. Many of these have accrued since the time of James I. There was the Petition of Right, which rather secured old Rights than gave new ones; the abolition of the star Chamber was a new benefit; the Habeas Corpus Act was a new benefit; the Bill of Rights was rather a new security to old Rights. . . . All these, without enumerating others, were improvements in the Constitution, and nothing can be clearer, than that the Constitution is not now, in all its circumstances, though it is in substance, and in principle, the same as it was heretofore.[27]

Change in the customary constitution occurred chiefly through two mechanisms, corresponding to the two principles on which its authority rested, consent and prescription. Consistent with Whig theories of the contractual basis of fundamental law, the constitution could be altered by clear, convulsive expressions of popular will. The theoretical basis for this sort of change had been worked out during the exclusion crisis of 1678–81[28] and put to the test in the Revolution of 1688—which in the eighteenth century epitomized the potential for constitutional change through popular action. Later historians have belittled virtually every claim made for the Glorious Revolution: that it reflected popular will, that it brought about sweeping reform, indeed, that it "settled" much of anything at all. But men and women of the time did not doubt the significance of what had been accomplished.[29] As they saw it, the people of England had summoned a convention, removed one monarch from the throne, replaced him with another (actually two others), drafted a Declaration of Rights, and settled the succession on a Protestant line. Extend one's view a few years more, and this same people had provided for elections every three years, ensured that the legislature would meet annually, made the judiciary independent, and ejected placemen from Parliament.

Nor was the significance of these developments lost in the colonies. Americans, too, had suffered under Stuart oppression, and upheaval in the mother country triggered simultaneous rebellions in New England, New

York, and Maryland.[30] The colonists believed themselves equal participants in a revolutionary moment, and they interpreted the Revolution of 1688 as confirming their entitlement to the same rights and liberties as their countrymen across the Atlantic.[31] Their efforts to mimic the Glorious Revolution in the New World nevertheless produced mixed results. The Dominion of New England disappeared, and new governments were established (or old governments reestablished) both there and in New York and Maryland. But the efforts of various colonial legislatures to enact further measures imitating those adopted by Parliament were quashed in England. Remarkably, this seemed neither to dampen American enthusiasm for the Glorious Revolution nor to upset the colonists' belief that 1688 represented a triumph of Whig ideals on both sides of the Atlantic. The colonies continued to press for change and gradually achieved most of their goals in practice, if not formally enacted law.[32] Later, Americans would learn that they and the English had derived very different lessons from the Glorious Revolution, but no one on either side of the Atlantic (no Whig, at least) ever doubted that it had significantly, and legitimately, altered the content of fundamental law.

The second method of constitutional change—modification by prescription—was more common. Precisely because the British constitution was rooted in custom, it could be amended by usage: by the inauguration of new practices that, once they had achieved a degree of acceptance, could be cited as "precedents." Preserving the customary constitution called for vigilance, as everything was potentially up for grabs. By "such tacit agreement as this of prescription," explained Cambridge legal theorist Thomas Rutherforth in the mid-1750s, "[l]aws may be repealed, customs may be established into laws, civil constitutions of government may be altered, subjects may enlarge their privileges, governors may extend their prerogative."[33] Nothing was fixed, nothing permanently settled. "[W]hatever constitution . . . might appear from former usage to have been established in any civil society," Rutherforth continued, "a different or contrary usage, after it obtains, will afford the same evidence, that the governors and the people have mutually agreed to change the constitution." This principle may look familiar: courts today frequently give weight to established practices. But appearances can be misleading, for the eighteenth-century understanding was different and stronger, with each instance of acquiescence to a formerly unconstitutional practice carrying weight roughly akin to that accorded lower court judicial precedent today.

By way of illustration, consider the debate of the 1760s between the American colonists and imperial authorities over the significance of Britain's navigation laws. Parliament had enacted a great many such laws to regulate colonial trade in the century before the Revolution; some had been ignored, but there were at least ten to fifteen that had not—more than enough to sustain a constitutional argument under prevailing standards.[34] Given American acquiescence to these laws, Massachusetts Attorney General (and loyalist) Jonathan Sewall argued, Britain's authority to exercise legislative jurisdiction over the colonies could no longer be challenged. Its claim was both old and established, having been "made, openly and expressly, before the grant of the charter [in 1691], and [having] ever since been uniformly exercised by them, and acknowledged by us."[35]

This was not an argument to be lightly dismissed. Whig leaders responded by trying to distinguish the navigation laws in ways that would confine the effect of the precedent. John Adams argued that the first navigation act "was not executed as an act of parliament, but as a law of the colony, to which the king agreed."[36] By reenacting the law on its own, the Massachusetts assembly had deprived Parliament of a precedent supporting its authority to legislate without assent from the colonial legislature. Of course, Adams's response failed to answer the many subsequently enacted laws, not to mention the needs of other colonies whose legislatures had acceded to the English law. A better answer—from the American viewpoint, at least—was offered by John Dickinson in his famous *Letters from a Farmer in Pennsylvania*. According to Dickinson, the navigation laws "were all intended solely as regulations of trade," not for raising revenue or regulating internal colonial affairs.[37] They established Parliament's authority to enact a comprehensive scheme of imperial trade regulation, which the colonists were prepared to accept, but they could not be cited as precedent for anything more. Certainly they could not sustain either a power to tax for revenue without consent or a power to legislate colonial affairs generally.

Anxiety about allowing precedent to become established was a pervasive feature of eighteenth-century constitutional practice, which helps to explain the extravagant reactions of American dissidents even to Parliament's most modest interventions. The Townsend Acts imposed very light duties on glass, paper, paints, and tea, but colonial leaders understood that Parliament's real objective was to generate a precedent supporting its claim to bind the colonies by internal legislation. Hence, voters in one Rhode Island town charged the British with acting for "the express purpose" of introducing "arbitrary power and slavery,"[38] while the Connecticut Assembly protested the "manner in and by which" the Acts were made, alleging not only that they "most undeniably deprive[d] the Colonists of their essential rights as Englishmen," but also that, if left unopposed, the legislation threatened to "strip them of all that is good and valuable in life."[39] When Lord North offered to repeal three of the Acts, leaving only the impost on tea, colonial agents scoffed "this will signify nothing."[40] As the Virginia House of Burgesses explained in its petition to the king, Americans could not accept even the tax upon tea because it was still being retained "for the avowed purpose of establishing a precedent against us."[41]

A still better illustration of the role of precedent is the American response to the Tea Act of 1773, which actually reduced the price of tea, but in a way that implied Parliament's power to impose duties for the purpose of raising revenue and so compelled colonial rebels to destroy the tea rather than permit it to be landed. Under existing trade rules, tea was deemed "imported" once it had arrived in a colonial port. If the tea were not offloaded within twenty days, it would be seized by customs officials who would retain a portion to satisfy import duties. Once in harbor, moreover, a ship bearing tea could not leave without obtaining a pass from Crown officials and could not return to England without violating laws against colonial re-exportation. This put the colonists in a bind. If a ship bearing tea had entered a colonial port, it would not be permitted to leave without offloading its cargo. If the ship did offload, a duty would be paid. If it did not, customs officials would seize the tea and, once again, a duty would be paid. Either way, London would get its precedent. It might be a flawed precedent, but from the Americans' perspective, even a tarnished precedent was to be avoided. Most colonies sidestepped the dilemma by warning pilots to anchor their ships outside the legal limits of the harbor. But the captain of the *Dartmouth* ignored this advice and led several ships into Boston harbor anyway, leading to the Boston Tea Party. The Whigs of Boston had not wanted to destroy the tea, and they negotiated frantically to find another solution. But time ran out, and on the nineteenth day after the ships reached Boston—the day before its cargo would become forfeit and entered in customs house records—they concluded that they had no choice but to destroy the goods.[42]

"And Adjudge Such Act to be Void"

Consent and prescription were devices for changing the constitution. But what about its day-to-day enforcement? How, or rather, by whom was this customary constitution, with its varied sources and uncertain terms, interpreted and enforced? Conventional wisdom long held that the British constitution rested on and recognized the supremacy of Parliament. But the doctrine of legislative supremacy began to gain momentum only in the second decade of the eighteenth century, after Parliament extended its term from three to seven years in the Septennial Act of 1716.[43] Parliamentary supremacy was not fully established even in England before the nineteenth century, and it never achieved acceptance in the American colonies.[44] Yet the concept of a constitution existed and was taken seriously and debated on both sides of the Atlantic throughout the seventeenth and eighteenth centuries. The unceasing struggles between Crown and Parliament were *constitutional* struggles; they were, moreover, struggles about what the constitution required or commanded, not about which institution could "make" it. The existence of extant fundamental or constitutional law binding on the whole government, in other words, was taken for granted by all involved, with no sense whatever that its creation or interpretation was an exclusively legislative prerogative.

Nor did the customary constitution contain anything even remotely like the modern concept of judicial review, which is to say a practice of regularly submitting constitutional disputes to judges for resolution in the context of ordinary litigation. Indeed, it is doubtful that the customary constitution made room for any form of judicial review of legislation at all.

This last point requires a bit more explanation given Sir Edward Coke's famously enigmatic opinion in *Dr. Bonham's Case*, which some historians and legal scholars have credited with inventing a doctrine akin to our modern practice. Thomas Bonham sued leading members of the Royal College of Physicians in London for having fined and imprisoned him without legal authority. In the course of upholding Bonham's action, the newly appointed Chief Justice Coke wrote in 1610: "And it appears in our books, that in many cases, the common law will controul acts of parliament, and sometimes adjudge them to be utterly void: for when an act of parliament is against common right and reason, or repugnant, or impossible to be performed, the common law will controul it, and adjudge such act to be void."[45]

The amount of ink spilled by many of our greatest legal scholars in the effort to make sense of this little passage is nothing short of astonishing—though not so astonishing, perhaps, as the fact that we are still less than completely sure what Coke meant to say. The prevailing understanding today, first proposed by Samuel Thorne in 1938, is that Coke was making a straightforward point based on "ordinary common law rules of statutory interpretation," to wit, that a court could (and should) refuse to follow a statute absurd on its face.[46] Although this might at first seem an unobvious reading of Coke's language, other historians have shown how Thorne's reading is consistent with the issues in the case and the overall structure of Coke's opinion, as well as with Coke's other writings and the broader intellectual context of early seventeenth-century political thought.[47] That said, there remain many excellent scholars who continue to believe that Coke meant to establish the authority of the courts and the common law over Parliament and legislation.

We need not rehash these arguments here, for what Coke thought he was saying matters less than how he came to be understood, and here the evidence points strongly toward Thorne's statutory reading. *Dr. Bonham's Case* was never an especially important precedent. It made sporadic appearances during the controversies surrounding the English Civil War, where it proved useful to royalists defending the king's prerogative because it supported their claim that Parliament's powers were limited.[48] It also showed up as dictum in one or two judicial decisions.[49] But after the Glorious Revolution and Acts of Settlement, *Dr. Bonham's Case* largely disappeared from the courts. The opinion was still read by those who studied Coke, of course, and Coke's language was included essentially verbatim in various eighteenth-century treatises and digests.[50] But for lawyers who may have thought to use it in court, *Dr. Bonham's Case* appears to have come through only as a doctrine of statutory interpretation. That, at least, is how Blackstone restated the holding in the first volume of his *Commentaries*. Indeed, Blackstone sought to narrow Coke's position still further by limiting it to statutes that were "impossible to be performed" or to "collateral consequences" of other laws if these consequences were not clearly spelled out in the statute's language and were "manifestly contradictory to common sense."[51]

Some scholars respond that, whatever the case may have been in England, things in America were different. Whether rightly or wrongly, they say, the American colonists did read *Dr. Bonham's Case* as authority for "a judicially enforceable higher law," and Coke's argument was the immediate source and direct forerunner of judicial review.[52] In fact, there is little basis for this belief.

To begin with, the only known seventeenth-century case on this side of the Atlantic to discuss Coke's doctrine rather clearly reflects the statutory interpretation view. The issue in *Giddings v. Browne*, decided in 1657, was whether the Ipswich Town Meeting could vote a gift of a hundred pounds to build a house for a minister. Magistrate Symonds ruled that the town had exceeded its authority under colonial law. Noting that the statute on which the town relied would be inconsistent with fundamental law (by authorizing a confiscation of property) were it construed to permit the gift, Symonds stated: "I conceive that it is an extreme dishonour cast upon the [colonial legislature], to make such a construction of their positive laws as doth infringe the fundamentall law of mine and thine; for it must needs be void, if it should indeed be necessarily construed against the right or liberty of the subject. But the law in its true sense is good."[53] Later in the opinion, Symonds added "a little about interpretation of lawes and of rules to be attended therein"—his first rule being "that where a law is such as that, by wresting, a man may give such an interpretation as will overthrow it, when it might be construed to be good; this is a corrupt interpretation. So holy scripture may be wrested."[54] The analogy to Scripture is revealing. Obviously, no one could "overthrow" the Bible, much less find it void; the argument was that a construction that created such tension must be wrong.

Indeed, practically the only evidence ever cited to prove that Coke's statement "became a rallying cry for Americans"[55] is James Otis's argument in the *Writs of Assistance Case*. Known also as *Petition of Lechmere* or *Paxton v. Gray*, the case was never formally reported and comes to us mainly through notes taken by John Adams and Josiah Quincy, who were in the courtroom to hear the arguments. In 1760 customs officials asked the Massachusetts Superior Court to issue general writs of assistance permitting them to command help from ordinary citizens in carrying out searches or seizures without individualized grounds for suspicion or any other cause. Unsure whether issuing such writs would be proper, the court set the matter down for argument. The question turned on whether there existed any source of authority for a colonial court, and in particular, for the Superior Court, to issue a general writ of assistance.

Jeremiah Gridley, arguing for the Crown, maintained that the power to issue such writs could be inferred as a matter of general principles from the "necessity" of the case, relying secondarily and for additional support on § 5(2) of the Act of Frauds of 1662.[56] Otis contested both grounds. With respect to the former, he charged that general writs were contrary to fundamental principles of law and not supported by precedent. Turning to Gridley's statutory argument, Otis asserted, as recorded by John Adams: "As to Acts of Parliament. an Act against the Constitution is void: an Act against natural Equity is void: and if an Act of Parliament should be made, in the very Words of this Petition, it would be void. The Executive Courts must pass such Acts into disuse . . . Reason of the Com^n Law to control an Act of Parliament."[57]

Was Otis calling for judicial review or was he making a more conventional argument to construe a statute narrowly? Commentators who champion the former view frequently rely on a much later description of the case provided by Adams.[58] In letters written to William Tudor in 1817–18, the aged ex-President re-created the circumstances surrounding the case while breathlessly proclaiming that "the child Independence was born" the day Otis challenged the writs.[59] But it is hard to swallow Adams's report, written some fifty-six years after the fact, regarding the importance of Otis's speech to the American cause—particularly since, as other historians have noted, Otis's now-famous oratory received scant attention at the time.[60] It seems clear that Adams was using his correspondence with Tudor (who was collecting material for a biography of Otis) to indulge in a bit of late-life romanticizing: seeking to secure the place in history he thought due his old companion, his native state, and, of course, himself.[61] More damning for our purposes, Adams pursued this goal by "mak[ing] fairly free with literal fact" and "put[ting] into Otis's mouth as eloquent and impressive a discourse as could be thought up"—going so far as to depict Otis making arguments not yet imagined in 1761 and thus leading the chief historian of the *Writs of Assistance Case* to dismiss these letters as "all but valueless" in revealing what happened.[62]

Nor do Adams's contemporaneous notes provide more or better support for the conclusion that Otis argued for judicial review, as opposed to urging that the statute could be narrowly construed. Adams records Otis essentially restating the Cokean position that an act against fundamental or natural law would be void and that the common law would therefore "control" it. But why should we infer from this that Otis was arguing anything other than statutory interpretation? We have already seen how this narrower understanding of Coke was the most plausible one in the seventeenth and early eighteenth centuries, and we have no reason to believe this had changed by 1761. Why assume that a reading accessible to Coke's contemporaries and to us was not similarly accessible to Americans in the middle of the eighteenth century? Where, after all, did Blackstone get it from? Or the Massachusetts court that decided *Giddings v. Browne*? If the statutory reading seems a stretch to us today—or, to put it differently, if the judicial review reading seems more natural—could this not be because our own familiarity with judicial review makes it so? And would not the opposite have been true for Otis? Would not the narrower reading have been more natural?

There is, moreover, an additional reason for thinking that Otis, like Blackstone only a few years later, probably relied on Coke as authority for reading the statute narrowly: namely, Otis did not need to push Coke's authority farther than this because the "less sweeping" understanding of Coke "suited [his] purpose exactly."[63] The statute on which Gridley relied for the court's authority to issue a general writ, § 5(2) of the Act of Frauds, provided that "it shall be lawful to or for any Person or Persons authorized by Writ of Assistance under the Seal of his Majesty's Court of Exchequer, to take a Constable, Headborough or other Publick Officer inhabiting near unto the Place, and in the Day-time to enter, and go into any House." The statute refers only to a "Writ of Assistance," without specifying whether the writ can be general or must be specific. This ambiguity opened the way for Otis to argue that, since allowing general writs would contravene fundamental law, the court should construe the statute narrowly to require specific grounds. Indeed, this precise position had been taken in a recently published article in the *London Magazine* that was known to everyone in the case and on which Otis relied heavily in preparing his argument.[64]

If we put the *Writs of Assistance Case* aside, or even if we do not, the most telling fact is how *little* evidence supports the idea that Coke or *Dr. Bonham* were important to Americans in developing the principle of judicial review. There are, to be sure, one or two other suggestive references to the case—a baffling passage in a pamphlet authored by James Otis in 1764,[65] and an argument made by George Mason in an obscure 1772 case.[66] But whatever one makes of these, much more impressive is how seldom Coke's authority was invoked in connection with judicial review.[67] This is particularly striking in the 1780s, when the matter was first openly argued and debated.[68] The bottom line seems to be that even if there could have been an understanding of Coke that might theoretically have provided a foundation for judicial review, in fact Coke's writings were not important in its development—apparently because this was not how the case was understood. Instead, the concept of judicial review sprang from other intellectual and political sources: sources that were themselves not judicial in nature.

The same point is true for the assorted principles of hierarchical review that already existed in colonial America. English legal practice had for centuries recognized an idea of superior and inferior law according to which courts would enforce superior laws over inferior ones, such as statutes over municipal by-laws and charters over statutes. Some commentators have assumed that these forms of review were or would have been precedent for a principle like judicial review, apparently because they assume that a constitution would have been treated as nothing more than another, albeit higher form of ordinary law—an assumption that we shall see below is misplaced. Certainly the general notion that superior forms of law trump inferior ones had a part in the concept of judicial review that substantially emerged, but it is misleading to describe these antecedent practices as a nascent or immature form of constitutional review, which is why they were not invoked by anyone to explain or justify it.

Reconciling the existence in the eighteenth century of a constitution that was "law" with the absence of any notion that judges had a special role in determining its meaning has proved difficult for modern minds to grasp. In our world, there is law and there is politics, with nothing much in between. For us, the Constitution is a subset of law, and law is something presumptively and primarily, even if not exclusively, within the province of courts. How, then, could the customary constitution have been "law" and yet not a matter for judges routinely and specially to address? This seeming paradox has led some historians to dismiss the idea that eighteenth-century fundamental law really was law, as opposed to "ethics" or "a kind of moral inhibition or conscience existing in the minds of legislators and others."[69]

To say this, however, is to misunderstand the language and conceptual framework of eighteenth-century legal thought. Constitutional or fundamental law subsisted as an independent modality, distinct from both politics and from the ordinary law interpreted and enforced by courts. It was a special category of law. It possessed critical attributes of ordinary law: its obligations were meant to be binding, for example, and its content was not a matter of mere will or policy but reflected rules whose meaning was determined by argument based on precedent, analogy, and principle.[70] Yet constitutional law also purported to govern the sovereign itself, thus generating controversies that were inherently matters for resolution in a political domain.[71] Modern discourse has so thoroughly conflated the meaning of "constitution" with "law" and of "law" with "courts" that we no longer possess the language to describe a distinct category of this sort; the best way to capture its essence today may thus be (as one leading historian has done) to call it "political-legal."[72]

"Accountable to the Community"

Which still leaves the question: if neither judges nor legislators were responsible for interpreting and enforcing fundamental law, who was? The people themselves. Legislative power, it was said, is always "accountable to the *Community*," whose members could judge whether lawmakers had acted consistently with "the *Fundamental Rule of society*" and withhold support from measures that "Breach the *Constitution*."[73] John Dickinson expressed the basic assumption in his *Letters from a Farmer in Pennsylvania*: "Ought not the PEOPLE therefore to watch? to observe facts? to search into causes? to investigate designs? And have they not a right of JUDGING from the evidence before them, on no slighter points than their *liberty* and *happiness?*"[74]

This was not mere pabulum; nor was it a Lockean appeal to nature after a dissolution of government. It was, rather, the invocation of a specific set of legal remedies by which "the people"—conceived as a collective body capable of independent action—were empowered to enforce the constitution against errant rulers.[75] The community itself had both a right and a responsibility to act when the ordinary legal process failed, and unconstitutional laws could be resisted by community members who continued to profess loyalty to the government and to follow its other laws.

Means of correction and forms of resistance were well established and highly structured. First and foremost, was the right to vote,[76] though this was seldom discussed prior to American independence, because even in England most controversies involved the Crown, and because citizens in the colonies did not vote for Parliament and had to resort to other mechanisms. Next in importance, though perhaps not effectiveness, was the right to petition, together with what became its corollary, the newly emerging right of assembly.[77] Publicly denouncing unconstitutional acts, explaining why they were unconstitutional, and requesting or demanding that authorities retract them were rights of considerable significance in the eighteenth century—truly fundamental, because necessary to explain, defend, and secure other rights.[78] How else, urged one 1760s pamphleteer, can authorities learn "the *real* and the *universal* sense of the people"?[79] The first phase of American resistance to the Stamp Act consisted of petitions beseeching Parliament to reject the offending legislation. It was only after Parliament ignored these petitions—worse, after it failed even to consider them—that Americans turned to more aggressive forms of resistance.[80] The right of petition (transformed by the Revolution from the humble request of a subject into a citizen's right to remonstrate) nevertheless remained an important device for the public to express its views on constitutional issues, offering government officials an opportunity to measure popular opinion and, if necessary, to change their course of action. Anti-Federalists pressed for an amendment guaranteeing the privilege,[81] which was duly incorporated into the First Amendment, and petitioning remained a prominent feature of American politics throughout the early decades of the Republic.[82]

If petitioning and pamphleteering failed to elicit a repeal, more assertive forms of resistance were available, invoked in many instances only after a formal public notice had been issued and a public meeting held.[83] The process of governing in the eighteenth century was necessarily a local affair, and the instruments and institutions of local government were in the hands of the community. Law enforcement was practically impossible if community sympathies were strongly on the side of an alleged lawbreaker.[84] Professional police forces did not yet exist, and in most communities there was only a county sheriff and a handful of local magistrates. The ability to arrest lawbreakers depended on institutions like the "hue and cry" or, if greater force was needed, the *posse comitatus* or the militia. Even if an arrest could be made without such assistance, friends and neighbors might intervene and demand that the prisoner be released. The townspeople of Lanesborough, Massachusetts, for example, freed prisoners confined for resisting the Stamp Act and warned the sheriff against trying to apprehend anyone else. Attorney Joseph Hawley defended their action in a local newspaper, insisting that the sheriff "should have been resisted in his said exercise of arbitrary and unjust force."[85]

If a defendant could be brought to trial, successful prosecution still depended on the willingness of a grand jury to indict and a civil or criminal petit jury to find guilt. Conversely, these same juries could become a potent weapon with which to frustrate any local official foolish enough to enforce laws the community deemed unconstitutional. In 1769 a Suffolk County grand jury indicted General Thomas Gage, Governor Francis Bernard, the commissioners of the customs, and the collector and comptroller of the port of Boston "for writing certain letters to the secretary of state, and other [of] the king's ministers, and therein slandering the inhabitants of the town of Boston, and of the province of Massachusetts Bay."[86] The indictment came to naught because the prosecutor refused to proceed on instructions from London, but the same grand jury was more effective in other cases. In one instance, just as John Hancock was about to be tried and most likely convicted in a (juryless) vice-admiralty court, the Suffolk County grand jury indicted the prosecution's sole witness, who promptly fled the county, forcing the Crown prosecutor to drop the case.[87]

If, for some reason, control of local institutions was still not sufficient to bring about a change in the law, even more coercive means of popular opposition were available. Americans protested each round of British taxation by boycotting English goods; by 1768, America's Whig leadership was running a highly integrated intercolonial scheme of nonimportation agreements.[88] Imperial authorities searched in vain for arguments to declare these illegal. Even Thomas Hutchinson, the staunchly royalist governor of Massachusetts, at one point conceded that "[t]he Combinations against importing . . . are Subversive of government, and yet are justifiable as legal."[89]

And then there was the mob, or "crowd," as historians have relabeled it to capture its rediscovered respectability. Mobbing was an accepted, if not exactly admired, form of political action—common in England and on the Continent as well as in America.[90]

Crowd action represented a direct expression of popular sovereignty, justified as a last resort in the writings of Grotius, Pufendorf, and Locke, not to mention by long tradition.[91] Indeed, custom and ancient practice were more responsible than philosophy for shaping and legitimating crowd activity. The practice of "skimmington" or "charivari"—in which local townsfolk, typically in rural areas, enforced codes of law and morality by publicly humiliating offenders to the accompaniment of catcalls, beating drums, and clanging pots and pans—had deep roots in England and Europe.[92] Transplanted to the colonies through immigration, these rituals were absorbed and politicized by urban communities in the second half of the eighteenth century, becoming critical elements of colonial opposition to imperial policy.[93]

Whether enforcing morality or law, eighteenth-century Whig mobs were generally conservative: organized to uphold community values against indifferent or ineffective public officials and illegal or unconstitutional government action. They consisted not of criminals or gangs or drunks and other riff-raff, but of what contemporaries referred to as the "middling sorts"—shopkeepers, artisans, farmers, and laborers—sometimes led by one of their own, but often led by local gentry.[94] These mobs demonstrated a "remarkable single-mindedness and discriminating purposefulness" in selecting their targets and in taking care not to inflict collateral damage.[95] After the Boston Tea Party, an "Impartial Observer" reported that no cargo other than tea had been disturbed and boasted that "such attention to private property was observed that a small padlock belonging to the Captain of one of the Ships being broke, another was procured and sent to him."[96] Mob action followed implicit, customary rules about how much violence was appropriate and which targets were permissible, making it possible for contemporaries to distinguish constitutional mob action from a simple riot.[97] The crowd observed these rules with surprising (though obviously not perfect) faithfulness, and the blame for injuries or death, when these occurred, typically lay with constituted authorities.[98] Such consequences were rare in colonial and Revolutionary America, however, for imperial government was so weak that Crown officials usually could do little more than stand helplessly by.[99]

Bear in mind that these popular remedies were neither mutually exclusive nor necessarily invoked in a particular order. Opposition tended to begin nonviolently, with protests in the newspapers or organized conventions and petitions, and to become violent only if no redress was forthcoming. But this was not always true. Americans protested Parliament's abuses by simultaneously petitioning, mobbing, interfering with regular law enforcement, and running a nonimportation scheme. In American eyes, an unconstitutional law was void, "*a mere nullity.*"[100] Public officials who sought to enforce such laws were themselves outlaws who "ought to be deemed no better than a highwayman, and should be proceeded against in due course of law."[101] Resistance through any or all of these means was thus a "political-legal" duty, enjoined on everyone in the community concerned with maintaining liberty against arbitrary power.[102]

Note, too, that while fundamental law was not part of the ordinary business or responsibility of courts, it did sometimes find its way into judicial proceedings. Though constitutional challenges were infrequent, certain aspects of the constitution, such as the role of juries or of habeas corpus, dealt directly with courts and the judicial process, and action by the executive might be reviewed as well. But courts also occasionally confronted broader questions of fundamental law in relation to litigation. This happened in two ways, both suggested above. First, *Dr. Bonham's Case* had survived as a rule of statutory interpretation, albeit modified somewhat in Blackstone's hands. Infrequently employed, it nevertheless permitted judges to take fundamental law into account and to construe a statute narrowly if it conflicted with established principles, at least as to "collateral consequences" that were not spelled out clearly in the text. This is how James Duane used *Dr. Bonham* in *Rutgers v. Waddington,*[103] and the South Carolina court did something similar in *Ham v. McLaws.*[104]

Second, lawyers argued fundamental law to juries, which rendered verdicts based on their own interpretation and understanding of the constitution.[105] This was consistent with the broad power of the eighteenth-century jury to find law as well as fact and to decide every aspect of a case.[106] Judges might instruct juries, but it was, in the words of John Adams, "not only [every juror's] right but his Duty in that Case to find the Verdict according to his own best Understanding, Judgment and Conscience, tho in Direct opposition to the Direction of the Court."[107] Placing juries in this dominant position, Adams explained, introduced "a mixture of popular power" into the execution of the law and was thus an important protection of liberty.[108] This was particularly true when it came to fundamental law, for the jury was "the

Voice of the People,"[109] the community personified to render judgment in a particular case. Who better to ensure that fundamental law was respected? "The great Principles of the Constitution, are intimately known, they are sensibly felt by every Briton," Adams gushed, "it is scarcely extravagant to say, they are drawn in and imbibed with Nurse's Milk and first air."[110] Juries thus played an important role shaping or reshaping constitutional law, as happened, for example, in the famous trial of John Peter Zenger. Charged with seditious libel, Zenger argued that the nature of a publication as libelous was a jury question and that truthful statements could not be libelous—both arguments contrary to existing English precedent. The jury's subsequent verdict in Zenger's favor went against the court's instructions and was quickly incorporated into the Americans' understanding of fundamental law, becoming "staple elements of the colonial legal challenge."[111]

Popular Constitutionalism, circa 1765

The jury's power to address issues of fundamental law—along with voting, mobbing, petitioning, and the rest—reflects and manifests the overarching theme of the customary constitution, which was its essential character as what we might call "popular law." Fundamental law was different from ordinary law, or what we typically think of today as ordinary law, both in its conceptual underpinnings and in actual operation. It was law created by the people to regulate and restrain the government, as opposed to ordinary law, which is law enacted by the government to regulate and restrain the people. This inversion, in turn, inverted what today we take to be the usual assignment of authority to interpret and enforce. Government officials are our authoritative interpreters of ordinary law. We have indirect control over what laws the government promulgates by virtue of our ability to elect and remove most lawmakers. But once a law has been enacted, ordinary citizens assume a subordinate position relative to government officials in ascertaining its meaning and imposing sanctions. We must still decide what we think a law requires or commands—that is, we must still interpret the law to determine what obligations it enjoins. But our interpretations are mere projections, efforts to comply that lack formal legal significance or effect. If challenged, these interpretations are submitted to designated public officials (administrators, prosecutors, judges, and the like) who decide if we are right or wrong and arrange an appropriate punishment if the answer is wrong. When it comes to ordinary law, in other words, the government regulates us.

This relationship was, in effect, reversed when it came to fundamental law. "A *Constitution*," wrote Judge William Nelson of Virginia in the 1790s, "is to the *governors*, or rather to the departments of *government*, what a *law* is to individuals."[112] The object of fundamental law was to regulate public officials, who were thus in the position of ordinary citizens with respect to it and required to do their best to ascertain its meaning while going about the daily business of governing. But their interpretations were not authoritative. They were now the projections, subject to direct supervision and correction by the superior authority of "the people"—conceived in this context, it should be remembered, as a collective body capable of independent action and expression. It was this inversion of interpretive authority, this turning upside-down of the structure of legal interpretation that accounted for the various features of fundamental law described above: its uncertain content, its fluid modes of revision, and its varied popular enforcement mechanisms.

What emerges is a constitutional system that was self-consciously legal in nature, but in a manner foreign to modern sensibilities about the makeup of legality. For us, legality is crucially (though, of course, not solely) a matter of authority. We expect to find a rule of recognition that assigns someone the power to resolve controversies with a degree of certainty and finality: so at the end of the day we have something we can point to and say "yes, *that* is the law." Eighteenth-century constitutionalism was less concerned with quick, clear resolutions. Its notion of legality was less rigid and more diffuse—more willing to tolerate ongoing controversy over competing plausible interpretations of the constitution, more willing to ascribe authority to an idea as unfocused as "the people." It was, as Christine Desan has recently observed, a system "in which many actors participated in determining law," and in which processes we think of today as only and necessarily "political" were understood by participants "to produce *legality* as opposed to acts of will, power, or grace."[113]

This system of constitutionalism rested and relied on a culture in which public officials, community leaders, and ordinary citizens believed in a distinction between law and politics, shared a set of conventions about how to argue within each domain, and took seriously the role difference thus produced. Desan names this "the public faith" and describes it as a "commitment that bound members of a political community together," a commitment ultimately perpetuated and enforced in the public sphere through continued participation (or not) in the life of the community.[114] John Reid, who has done the most to help us recover this system's formal structure and language, refers to it as "Whig law"—a set of understandings and conventions about rights and liberty that, as we have seen, yielded a framework for argument rather than a fixed program of identifiable outcomes.[115]

What is most critical is understanding that participants in this culture took seriously the distinction between fundamental law and mere politics and responded to different arguments in each setting, giving the community at large a credible interpretive voice when it came to the constitution. Problems of fundamental law—what we would call questions of constitutional interpretation—were thought of as "legal" problems, but also as problems that could be authoritatively settled only by "the people" expressing themselves through the popular devices described above. Constitutional law in such a setting might sometimes be hard to identify, but this uncertainty seems not to have troubled anyone overmuch. Ultimately, the constitution was, as Reid argues, "whatever could be plausibly argued and forcibly maintained."[116]

To modern ears, it undoubtedly sounds paradoxical to speak of a system of law in which the law is nothing more than that which can be "plausibly argued and forcibly maintained." What kind of legal system is that, particularly coming from a people celebrated for its supposed commitment to "an empire of laws and not men"?[117] It is this tension that presumably lies behind the judgment of so many historians to disregard the insistence of eighteenth-century writers that this was law and to demote their constitution to the status of ethics or morality.

Yet this popular constitutionalism may be less foreign than it seems at first. Legal philosophers have long recognized, as lawyers and judges already knew instinctively, that determining the content and meaning of a functioning constitution—any constitution—inevitably presents problems of uncertainty.[118] And while such problems were potentially or theoretically widespread given the diverse sources of eighteenth-century constitutional law, in practice everything was hardly open or uncertain. On the contrary, as noted above, there was consensus on a wide range of issues. The customary constitution was, in this sense, neither better nor worse, neither more nor less settled, than other bodies of customary law whose status as law has seldom been questioned.

The real difference, it seems, is less the content of the customary constitution or the extent to which it was unsettled than the notion that constitutional interpretation and enforcement were left to the community. Most modern legal scholars and political commentators assume that leaving questions of constitutional law to the community as ultimate decision maker would destabilize a legal order. They might even be right, but this is an empirical rather than a theoretical claim. Those who make such an assumption presumably base it on the world with which they are familiar, our world, in which a constitutional system like that of seventeenth- and eighteenth-century Great Britain may seem almost fanciful. Yet this order existed and worked tolerably well for more than a century and a half before the American Revolution occurred. In saying this, we need not follow Burke by ignoring the bloody years of the Civil War and Interregnum. But one is hard put to point to another system, even in the modern era, that has worked longer or better, which is why the British constitution was so widely admired among enlightened eighteenth-century Europeans. And our own Civil War stands as a reminder of the need to avoid smugness.

A question nags: how did they do it? Certainly the modern assumption makes intuitive sense, and not only to us today. In *Federalist 49*, James Madison cautioned against "a frequent reference of constitutional questions, to the decision of the whole society," because he worried that such appeals could "deprive the government of that veneration . . . without which perhaps the wisest and freest governments would not possess the requisite stability."[119] We will see in the next chapter how America's Founders, including Madison, dealt with problems of constitutional interpretation and enforcement (though, without looking too far ahead, we can say that it was not by embracing a modern doctrine of judicial review). In the meantime, one wonders how the customary constitution lasted as long as it did.

Developing a complete answer to this question is a topic beyond the scope of the present inquiry. For our purposes, what matters most is that this system *did* last and that it provided the context within which American constitutionalism developed after the Revolution. A few, fairly obvious factors should be acknowledged, however, for they are relevant to what comes later.

First, opportunities for constitutional conflict were limited. The scope of the eighteenth-century British constitution was narrow, at least in comparison to modern constitutions. Its terms were spare (though not necessarily uncomplicated), and the space it purported to occupy was relatively uncrowded—again, by comparison to what came later. The main points of contention, the relationship of Crown to Parliament and of church to state, had been settled in compromises that were widely accepted. Plus, demands on government were modest, further reducing the number of controversies likely to arise. According to Whig theory, the main task of a representative assembly was defensive: checking arbitrary action by the Crown, rather than governing through legislation.[120] For most of the eighteenth century, Parliament did not do that much, especially at home.[121] What laws it passed were typically instigated by individual petitions seeking redress of a particular grievance or permission to undertake some local activity, meaning that "[t]he great mass of legislation was personal and local in scope, largely consisting of enclosure bills, turnpike and canal bills, and naturalization bills."[122] This inactivity was more pronounced and lasted longer in the colonies than in the mother country.[123] At the time of the American Revolution, the notion that lawmaking should be the chief activity of a representative assembly was just beginning to find acceptance.[124]

Second, social and political deference (not to mention economic dependence) of the masses to a relatively homogeneous elite helped to keep the number of disputes down; this same deference and dependence also worked to ensure that, when problems arose, things did not spin too far out of control.[125] We must be careful not to overstate either the extent of deference or the degree to which the ruling elite was homogeneous, for this was an exceedingly complex system.[126] Members of the laboring classes were hardly automatons, particularly in the colonies.[127] Officeholding may have been "securely in the hands of upper-class groups,"[128] but the conventions that secured their dominance rested on cultural and ideological understandings that limited as well as empowered.[129] There were, moreover, schisms and divisions within the aristocratic classes that controlled politics and government—divisions manifested in such ways as the persistence of Whig and Tory factions, the rise of competition for office, and the emergence of a radical critique bewailing constitutional "corruption" and decline.[130] Still, radicalism remained at the fringes, and the ruling aristocracy was generally effective when it came to protecting its broadly shared interests in keeping conflict to tolerable levels.[131]

Mainly, however, the customary constitution worked because people believed in it: because they accepted its premises and were willing to live up to the roles it assigned them. This was not an act of free will or self-conscious choice—no more, anyway, than our own belief in a very different kind of constitution was freely chosen. The customary constitution made sense to people in the eighteenth century. It made sense because it fit the world they had inherited and the world they experienced. It would not have occurred to them to question whether such a system was possible because it was all around them and because its very existence shaped their understanding of the possibilities. Edmund Morgan made essentially this point in *Inventing the People*:

> Government requires make believe. Make believe that the king is divine, make believe that he can do no wrong or make believe that the

voice of the people is the voice of God. Make believe that the people *have* a voice or make believe that the representatives of the people *are* the people. Make believe that governors are the servants of the people. Make believe that all men are equal or make believe that they are not.

The political world of make-believe mingles with the real world in strange ways, for the make-believe world may often mold the real one. In order to be viable, in order to serve its purpose, whatever that purpose may be, a fiction must bear some resemblance to fact. If it strays too far from fact, the willing suspension of disbelief collapses. And conversely it may collapse if facts stray too far from the fiction.[132]

Morgan's model is a familiar pragmatist one. The social world is constructed of and by a web of beliefs and practices. We choose our practices in light of beliefs about whether the practices are good or bad, yet we understand the content and meaning of these same beliefs only as refracted through the practices they purport to explain. The process is one of moving constantly back and forth, resolving whatever tensions we uncover on a piecemeal basis. As Don Herzog explains, "[w]e confront anomalies within our beliefs, within our practices, and most important in the relationships between the two. And our goal is always to make the broader web of beliefs and practices as coherent as we can."[133]

What may seem anomalous to us, however, did not seem so to people in eighteenth-century England and America. To them, belief in a customary constitution that limited the government and was enforced by the people themselves made sense. This belief was neither fact nor fiction. It was an interpretation: a strategy to explain the world they experienced, but one that, at the same time, helped shape that world. It was not until something about their practices or their beliefs, or both, had changed that they would have any reason to doubt.

2

A Rule Obligatory upon Every Department

THE ORIGINS OF JUDICIAL REVIEW

The foregoing description of eighteenth-century constitutionalism is misleading in one respect: it privileges a version embraced by American Whigs. Their understanding was at one time close to that held by Whigs in England, but Englishmen and Americans faced different problems and had to address their problems in different institutional settings. Not surprisingly, they came over time to see the customary constitution through different lenses.[1] The concept of fundamental law in the mother country and in the colonies diverged, evolving gradually in England into the system of legislative sovereignty so famously celebrated by Blackstone.[2] This development was by no means unheeded or unopposed, and pockets of resistance could be found even in London well into the nineteenth century.[3] But holdouts were few in number, and by the middle of the eighteenth century the orthodox view in England located sovereignty in Parliament rather than in the people out-of-doors. And with this development, the tradition of constitutionalism described earlier began to lose its grip, particularly the idea of "legal" resistance to unconstitutional legislative measures. This is why many in England were genuinely puzzled, and not merely angered, by the rebellion in America.[4]

Americans Whigs never accepted the idea of parliamentary sovereignty. For them, the Glorious Revolution was both a reaffirmation of popular sovereignty and a confirmation of the continuing viability of the customary constitution as a check on government.[5] The colonists were informed about events across the Atlantic, but conveniently inattentive to their potential significance. They managed, through impressively persistent and clever political maneuvering, to keep both king and Parliament at bay and so to avoid any major confrontations until the early 1760s.[6] By then, six decades of nearly continuous war had strained even the powerful British finance system, and Britain needed money.[7] Parliament cracked down on smuggling and tried to force the colonies to bear a reasonable share of the expenses of empire.[8] Americans awoke, startled and anxious, to discover that they could no longer ignore their differences with Britain. Within a decade, and much to their own amazement, they found themselves declaring independence.

"In Order to Support Its Fundamental, Constitutional Law"

We need note only two things about the controversies leading up to 1776. First, the period 1763–76 consisted of a series of disagreements about the meaning and proper interpretation of the customary constitution.[9] This does not mean that the Revolution was caused by these disagreements. An event this wrenching—one that shredded lifelong community bonds, that forced colonials to reconstitute their identities, to abandon their Britishness and become "Americans"—plainly had multiple and complex causes: social, cultural, economic, and political, as well as legal. But the triggering events in the eyes of the Americans themselves consisted of Great Britain's persistent and repeated efforts to deprive them of what they viewed as their constitutional rights. Writing in 1824, an aged Thomas Jefferson romantically credited the American Revolution to the laws of nature. "We had no occasion," he mused, "to search into musty records, to hunt up royal parchments, or to investigate the laws and institutions of a semi-barbarous ancestry."[10] Yet the influential *Summary View of the Rights of British America* that Jefferson penned in 1774 did precisely that, and it reads just like a lawyer's and a historian's brief asserting the legal and constitutional rights of Americans.[11] This is equally if not more true of the more famous Declaration that Jefferson authored two years later. John Reid rightly brands the claim that American independence was based on natural law "one of the most widely repeated errors of American history":

Anyone giving a reasonable reading to the entire Declaration of Independence, not just to the rhetorical preamble where "nature and nature's

God" are mentioned, will readily see that document accused the King of Great Britain of violating only the legal and constitutional rights of American colonists. It did not, in a single instance, accuse George III of violating a natural right. In fact, natural law was never cited by an official colonial governmental body to identify a right claimed, except rights that were also claimed as constitutional rights. Natural law simply was not a significant part of the American whig constitutional case; certainly not nearly as important as some twentieth-century writers have assumed.[12]

The colonists made their case and presented their grievances in legal and constitutional terms right up to and including the moment they declared independence, seeing themselves always as defenders of ancient liberties and the British constitution from the malefic scheming of corrupt imperial authorities. America became an independent nation, James Varnum observed a few years later, only "in order to support its fundamental, constitutional law, against the encroachments of Great Britain."[13] This matters, because it tells us what to look for in examining the constitutions Americans created after the Revolution. It was a rebellion in defense of a concept of constitutionalism, a concept Americans did not suddenly decide to abandon or repudiate upon achieving independence.

A second point to note about the Revolution is that American opposition to England was not only defended and justified in terms of the British constitution: it was also waged on such terms. What Americans did, as well as how they explained their actions, offers a detailed portrait of the eighteenth-century customary constitution in action. A crucial check was missing, inasmuch as Americans had no actual or even virtual representation in Parliament and so could not use elections or instructions to affect imperial policy.[14] Lacking the ability to change law peaceably from within, Americans resorted to the full array of alternatives—peaceable and otherwise—for combating unconstitutional government action. They were successful for a time, too. The Stamp Act was repealed, and Britain's every other effort to tax or regulate was either similarly withdrawn or effectively disabled by local opposition.

Unfortunately, because London viewed American resistance as illegitimate and illegal, it kept raising the stakes—culminating eventually in the Coercive Acts (or, as Americans called them, the Intolerable Acts), which led the colonies to invoke their ultimate right of revolution. Yet the Declaration of Independence was less a failure of constitutional process than evidence of genuinely irreconcilable differences: differences so little understood by the combatants on either side that their repeated efforts to bridge the gap only succeeded in making it wider. For our purposes, in any event, we need simply to observe that Americans saw themselves as having conducted a struggle to preserve constitutional rule through the use of constitutional forms of opposition.

We might also note that no one, at any time, seems ever to have considered bringing these constitutional disputes before a judge to have them settled—a point so obvious one would be embarrassed to mention it, but for the need to underscore the absence of anything resembling modern judicial review before the Declaration of Independence. Constitutional issues did crop up in a few court proceedings, usually as arguments to a jury.[15] Such arguments were an accepted feature of the customary constitution, an appeal to "the Voice of the People" and so an instance of the same "political-legal" opposition to unconstitutional laws as that engaged in by Whig mobs or by merchants enforcing nonimportation agreements.

In at least one instance, moreover, the call for resistance in the courtroom extended beyond jurors to include the judges as well. Most of the documents that required stamps under the Stamp Act were for use in legal proceedings. Whig mobs could (and did) ensure that stamped paper was unavailable, but the efficacy of their action would be blunted if the courts responded by shutting down, since this could be interpreted as signaling the judiciary's acceptance of the Act's constitutionality. "A suspense from business implies a tacit acquaintance [i.e., recognition] of the law," worried Charles Carroll of Carrollton, "or at least the right of the power of imposing such laws upon us."[16] Opposition leaders therefore urged judges to join their protest instead, by remaining open and conducting business without stamped paper.[17] Because the Stamp Act is "utterly void, and of no binding Force upon us," the Whigs of Boston reasoned, "therefore in a legal sense we know Nothing of it."[18] It followed that "therefore [the judges] should pay no Regard to it."[19] Similar entreaties were made throughout the colonies.[20]

The argument met with only limited success,[21] mainly because lawyers and judges feared that "if the Parliament of England should determine to force the Act down our Throats, they would immediately set Prosecutions on foot against the principal civil-officers who had ventured to risque the Penalties."[22] But lack of success in persuading judges to embrace civil disobedience and risk punishment at this early stage is less significant than what the argument portended for the future. For here we see the beginnings of something that would subsequently evolve into a first approximation of judicial review:

an argument that judges, *no less* than anyone else, should resist unconstitutional laws. This obligation did not arise from any special competence the judges possessed as judges, and it certainly was not based on the notion that constitutional law was ordinary law subject to judicial control. It was, rather, simply another instance of the right of every citizen to refuse to recognize the validity of unconstitutional laws—a "political-legal" duty and responsibility rather than a strictly legal one.

"The People Themselves . . . Can Alone Declare Its True Meaning"

Many things started to change after the colonies declared their independence. With respect to constitutional law, the most important turn was, of course, the drafting of new constitutions in the states. This was a legal as well as a practical necessity because, by proclaiming independence, Americans had abrogated their existing constitutions—not just the imperial constitution that governed relations with England, but also each individual colony's internal constitution, which was embodied in a charter granted by the Crown.[23]

Some Americans had begun to question the continued authority of royal government even before July 4. "The Continuing to Swear Allegiance to the power that is Cutting our throats is Certainly absurd," offered Caesar Rodney of Delaware.[24] In making American independence official, however, the Continental Congress left no doubt that every trace of imperial authority was to be effaced. On May 15, 1776, the delegates smoothed the way for their more famous declaration of July 4 with a resolution recommending the establishment of new state governments. The preamble declared that it was "necessary that the exercise of every kind of authority under the said crown should be totally suppressed, and all the powers of government, exerted under the authority of the people of the colonies."[25] The initial reason for preparing written constitutions was thus to fill a gap created by having renounced allegiance to the Crown.

It followed that the main order of business was to replace what had been abolished by reestablishing the basic structures needed to govern: new legislatures, new executives, and new judiciaries. A few states added Declarations of Rights, while others embedded rights in the text, the more clearly to establish and expand upon the fundamental liberties that Great Britain had tried to deny them.[26] At the level of structuring institutions, radical experiments were tried in "new-modeling" state government—mostly things that had been well-mooted in the Revolutionary and pre-Revolutionary pamphlet literature but never before tried in practice. The new states were all to be republican, of course; there would be no kings or nobles in the United States. The executive power was drastically limited, with most authority transferred to the popularly elected lower houses of the legislature (the body that, at the time, was thought most trustworthy in safeguarding liberty). Pennsylvania, followed for a short time by Georgia and Vermont, went so far as to eliminate an upper house altogether, establishing unicameral legislatures subject to frequent election. Other innovations were also tried, varying from state to state, but including such measures as a broadened suffrage, explicit guarantees of the right to instruct, required rotation in office, and a formal process for revising the constitution.

These were, beyond doubt, momentous changes. The various experiments in institutional form, not to mention ongoing debates about such issues as how to adopt and change a written constitution, testify to how earnestly Americans in this period wrestled with basic problems of constitutional formation and meaning. Historians disagree about how quickly they came to a robust and mature understanding of what it meant to create a written constitution, but all agree that the change thus produced in their thinking was profound.[27]

At the same time, and equally important though too often ignored, is what did *not* change. The men who crafted new state constitutions were building on an existing heritage: a theory and practice of constitutionalism many of whose fundamental premises were undisturbed. Far from being overturned, these premises continued to be taken for granted. Americans did not for the first time abruptly realize the benefits of having a constitution in 1776, nor did they write constitutions out of some newly discovered desire to have written charters or a sudden appreciation of the advantages of a central text. New constitutions were needed in the states to replace those parts of the old ones that had been abrogated, to substitute new institutions for institutions that no longer worked or did not fit republican ideals. But the texts were situated within an established constitutional tradition, and they took their place alongside existing practices and understandings, many of which remained viable.[28]

For this reason, Connecticut and Rhode Island concluded that they did not even need new constitutions, because their existing charters already provided for the popular election of statewide officers. Lacking any necessity to replace royal officials or fabricate new institutions, these former colonies needed only to establish that their existing governments rested on the consent of the people and not the authority of the Crown. This was achieved in Connecticut by means of an ordinary statute confirming that the charter was still in effect, while Rhode Island resolved to substitute the name of the state for that of the king on official documents.[29] That accomplished, the traditional constitutional practice was simply continued in both states, and not until well into the nineteenth century did either replace its charter.

Evidence abounds of the ongoing vitality of the customary constitution after the Declaration of Independence and drafting of new state constitutions. The most obvious indication of the viability of its substantive principles is, ironically, the lawyers' arguments and judges' opinions in some of the earliest cases purporting to exercise judicial review (to which we will return below). In the 1780 case of *Holmes v. Walton*, the New Jersey Supreme Court relied on seventeenth-century sources and traditions respecting the "Laws of the Land" in refusing to apply a state statute that required loyalists whose property had been seized to challenge the seizure before a six-person jury.[30] And in *Trevett v. Weeden*, James Varnum cited Norman precedent in urging the court to accept jurisdiction to decide whether a statute denying trial by jury altogether violated the state's constitution.[31] Responding to a claim that Rhode Island did not have a constitution, Varnum snarled, "Constitution!—We have none:—Who dares to say that?—None but a British emissary, or a traitor to his country."[32] Varnum cited a 1663 colonial statute providing for trial by jury and explained: "This act . . . was not creative of a new law, but declaratory of the rights of all the people, as derived through the Charter from their progenitors, time out of mind. It exhibited the most valuable part of their political constitution, and formed a sacred stipulation that it should never be violated."[33]

Additional examples abound. A series of South Carolina cases turned on Magna Carta, including one in 1792 that invalidated a land grant under its authority.[34] Oliver Ellsworth opposed a prohibition on ex post facto laws in the Federal Convention because "there was no lawyer, no civilian who would not say that ex post facto laws were void of themselves. It cannot be necessary to prohibit them."[35] James Wilson went a step further, saying that to include such a prohibition would "bring reflexions on the Constitution—and proclaim that we are ignorant of the first principles of Legislation, or are constituting a Government which will be so."[36] As William Treanor has shown, reasoning of this sort—extratextual and based on custom and tradition—was a pervasive feature of constitutional argument in the 1780s and 1790s.[37] Other scholars have traced the use of such reasoning well beyond that into the nineteenth century.[38]

Failure to appreciate the persistence of the customary constitution after the Revolution has led modern scholars to misunderstand or misinterpret important events of the Founding era. Consider the now-famous debate between Justices Chase and Iredell in the 1798 case of *Calder v. Bull*.[39] The Connecticut legislature had set aside a probate decree in Bull's favor and ordered a new trial. A unanimous Supreme Court rebuffed Bull's argument that this act violated the Ex Post Facto Clause of the Federal Constitution, which the Court said was limited to criminal legislation. In the course of his opinion, Justice Chase observed in dictum: "There are certain *vital* principles in our *free Republican governments*, which will determine and over-rule an *apparent and flagrant* abuse of *legislative* power. . . . An ACT of the Legislature (for I cannot call it a *law*) contrary to the *great first principles* of the *social compact*, cannot be considered a *rightful exercise* of *legislative* authority."[40]

Agreeing with Chase on the outcome of the case, Justice Iredell nevertheless repudiated his colleague's account of judicial authority. Some "speculative jurists" may have reasoned that "a legislative act against natural justice must, in itself, be void," Iredell conceded, but it did not follow that "any Court of Justice would possess a power to declare it so."[41] Because "[t]he ideas of natural justice are regulated by no fixed standard" and "the ablest and the purest men have differed upon the subject," judges could have no basis for preferring their understanding of its "abstract principles" to those of the Legislature. Judicial review was limited to written constitutions, which "define with precision the objects of the legislative power" and "restrain its exercise within marked and settled boundaries."[42]

Modern scholars have frequently wondered about Chase's seeming embrace of natural law as an independent ground for judicial invalidation of legislation, finding Iredell's text-bound positivism more familiar and comforting. Some simply refuse to believe that Chase departed from the modern tenet that constitutional principles must be derived, either directly or indirectly, exclusively from the text. John Hart Ely worked zealously to bring Chase into the fold, insisting that Chase recognized "no judicially enforceable notion of natural law other than what the terms of the Constitution provide"; Chase's reference to "great first principles," Ely concluded, meant no more than principles "embodied in our Constitution."[43] Other scholars think Ely's interpretation forced, unperturbed to find that Chase was measuring Connecticut's law against natural justice as well as the Constitution.[44]

As we saw in chapter 1, however, while few lawyers in the eighteenth century doubted either the existence of natural law or the importance of nature as a source of rights, these rights were rarely conceived as having positive authority independent of their incorporation into fundamental law.[45] Arguments based on natural law were part of a centuries-old constitutional tradition that presumed a concordance between principles of the customary constitution and those of natural law, enabling legal actors to draw interchangeably on both. The arguments thus remained grounded in a kind of positive law, albeit one based on custom, prescription, and implicit popular consent. This, in fact, was Chase's position, for he said, after elaborating with examples of laws contrary to "great first principles":

> It is against all reason and justice, for a people to entrust a Legislature with SUCH powers; and, therefore, it cannot be presumed that they have done it. The *genius*, the *nature*, and the *spirit*, of our State Governments, amount to a prohibition of *such acts of legislation*; and *the general principles of law and reason* forbid them. . . . To maintain that our Federal, or State, Legislature possesses *such powers*, if they had not been *expressly* restrained; would, in my opinion, be a *political heresy*, altogether inadmissible in our *free republican governments*.[46]

This distinction between fundamental and natural law may seem overly fine to modern sensibilities, particularly as contemporary actors felt so little compunction to emphasize it. The point, however, is not to apologize for eighteenth-century constitutionalism so much as to identify its features and show how these help us to understand better the basis of Chase's position. Chase's argument fit squarely within the customary constitutional tradition, and his opinion evidences its persistence after the Revolution and the adoption of written texts.

Iredell's response should similarly be understood through this lens. For Iredell does not deny that laws against "great first principles" are void; he denies only that such laws can be declared so by courts. The newfangled practice of judicial enforceability, in Iredell's view, is a product of (and so limited to) written constitutions—a point to which we will return later.

The decision to include the Ninth Amendment in the Bill of Rights can also be explained by the continued vitality of principles derived from the customary constitution. Modern commentators are often baffled by this amendment, which too many mistakenly conclude was meant to preserve some ill-defined body of natural rights.[47] Once again, however, natural law was a source of enforceable positive rights only in conjunction with and through incorporation into the customary constitution. Rights under this constitution were drawn from a variety of sources, moreover, of which natural law was only one, and not necessarily the most important one at that.[48] The most logical reading of the Ninth Amendment's reference to "other" rights "retained by the people," then, is to rights already or potentially secured within the customary constitutional tradition.[49]

Of greater interest than these legal arguments is the persistence of the customary constitution's methods of popular enforcement—evidence that constitutions continued to be seen in their traditional light, as a form of popular and not ordinary law. In his 1791 "Lectures on Law," for example, James Wilson described how the most powerful force in government, the legislative power, was controlled in the American system:

> The effects of its extravagancies may be prevented, sometimes by the executive, sometimes by the judicial authority of the governments; sometimes even by a private citizen, and, at all times, by the superintending power of the people at large. . . . [T]his general position may be hazarded—That whoever would be obliged to obey a constitutional law, is justified in refusing to obey an unconstitutional act of the legislature—and that, when a question, even of this delicate nature, occurs, every one who is called to act, has a right to judge: he must, it is true, abide by the consequences of a wrong judgment.[50]

Numerous instances of popular enforcement could be cited (for politics in the 1780s and 1790s was often an unruly affair),[51] but the point is sufficiently illustrated by an example involving the Virginia judiciary. In 1788 the state legislature enacted a law requiring judges of the court of appeals to sit on a newly created district court. The judges concluded that this amounted to a constitutionally prohibited diminution in their salary. They refused to appoint clerks (making it effectively impossible to transact business) and issued "The Respectful Remonstrance of the Court of Appeals," drafted by Chancellor Edmund Pendleton.[52] Formally addressed to the General Assembly, it was in reality written for the benefit of the public. The Remonstrance laid out the judges' concerns about the law and appealed to state legislators to rectify their error. Failing that, the judges concluded:

> They see no other alternative for a decision between the legislature and judiciary than an appeal to the people, whose servants both are, and for whose sakes both were created, and who may exercise their original and supreme power whensoever they think proper. To that tribunal, therefore, the court, in that case, commit themselves, conscious of perfect

integrity in their intentions, however they may have been mistaken in their judgment.[53]

The legislature responded by suspending the challenged act and passing a new court reorganization law designed to meet the judges' objections.[54]

The content of the Remonstrance (not to mention its mere existence) embodies and perfectly reflects the basic structure of popular constitutionalism described earlier—particularly the inversion of interpretive authority that distinguished constitutional law from ordinary law. The legislature and the judiciary are, the remonstrants say, the people's "servants." As such, acting with proper intentions and exercising their best judgment, they must try to comply with the constitution. If conflicts arise, however, it is "the people" who constitute the authoritative "tribunal" to whom such conflicts must be submitted. And make no mistake: this was neither empty rhetoric nor a veiled threat of revolution. It was the invocation of a very real, very available legal remedy, albeit one not to be called upon lightly.

This view of the people's role in constitutional law pervaded political and legal debate throughout the 1780s, and it remained the dominant understanding until well into the nineteenth century. It is this conception, for example, that lay behind Jefferson's proposal, in his 1783 draft of a constitution for Virginia, to permit the calling of a convention whenever "[a]ny two of the three branches of government concur[] in opinion . . . that a convention is necessary for altering this constitution, *or correcting breaches of it.*"[55] Jefferson hoped by this means to formalize the people's role in supervising constitutional law while at the same time bringing some regularity to the process.

Madison went out of his way to criticize his friend's proposal in *Federalist* 49–50, and we should take a moment to examine Madison's argument, if for no other reason than it was among the most elaborate statements on popular constitutionalism of the Founding era.[56] In these oft-quoted essays, Madison surprisingly argued against popular participation in interpreting and enforcing a constitution: a position that resonates with scholars today, who tend to be skeptical of robust democratic participation, especially when it comes to matters of fundamental law. Yet it would be wrong to read Madison as repudiating or disavowing popular constitutionalism. Quite the contrary, as a careful reading makes clear, Madison—like Jefferson, like everyone else at the time—took the principle for granted. His quarrel was not with the idea of popular constitutionalism, but with how best to make it operational.

Consistent with views expressed throughout his lifetime, Jefferson wanted popular politics to be the first and major line of defense in securing constitutional limits. Madison disagreed, and he offered three pragmatic objections by way of explanation. First, as we saw in chapter 1, he worried that a too-frequent appeal to the people would "deprive the government of that veneration, which time bestows on every thing, and without which perhaps the wisest and freest government would not possess the requisite stability." Second, he said, "[t]he danger of disturbing the public tranquility by interesting too strongly the public passions, is a still more serious objection against a frequent reference of constitutional questions, to the decision of the whole society." But "the greatest objection of all," according to Madison, was that the people could not be trusted because they would invariably side with the legislature in any conflict:

> The members of the legislative department ... are numerous. They are distributed and dwell among the people at large. Their connections of blood, of friendship and of acquaintance, embrace a great proportion of the most influential part of the society. The nature of their public trust implies a personal influence among the people, and that they are more immediately the confidential guardians of the rights and liberties of the people. With these advantages, it can hardly be supposed that the adverse party would have an equal chance for a favorable issue.[57]

It is worth noting that these arguments were penned in February of 1788, when Madison's anxiety about popular politics and elected legislatures was at its peak. Having recently completed three frustrating years in the Virginia assembly, Madison was thoroughly disgusted with politics as it was then being practiced in his state.[58] His correspondence from these years bristles with contempt for legislators who lack "liberality or light" and barely suppressed fury at "those who mask a secret aversion to any reform under a zeal for such a one as they know will be rejected."[59] It was at this moment, still angry and bruised by his lack of success as a state legislator, that Madison led the movement to adopt a national constitution. The point deserves mention because scholars have too seldom appreciated that Madison's feelings about republican politics in the years immediately following this unhappy experience were uncharacteristically pessimistic. Madison never wholly abandoned his fear of unbridled populism or legislative aggrandizement, but his alarm diminished in intensity over time—especially after he saw what someone like Alexander Hamilton could do with executive power if left unchecked by the people.[60]

Yet even in 1788, when the perilousness of popular politics loomed largest in Madison's eyes, he recognized that constitutional disputes could not ultimately be resolved "without an appeal to the people themselves, who, as grantors of the commission, can alone declare its true meaning and enforce its observance."[61] This was not inconsistent with Madison's simultaneous rejection of Jefferson's proposal, which Madison regarded as unworkable. He felt that Jefferson failed adequately to appreciate just how ticklish constant unmediated appeals to the people could become. The trick, as Madison saw it, was to devise a system that would reduce the need for such appeals—a problem he thought could be solved at the national level (he went on to explain in *Federalist 51*) by institutional design, that is, "by so contriving the interior structure of the government, as that its several constituent parts may, by their mutual relations, be the means of keeping each other in their proper places."[62] This meant, in particular, such things as extensive size, bicameralism, an executive veto, and federalism.[63] Through such means, Madison reasoned, ambition could be made to counteract ambition, most constitutional usurpations could be checked at their inception, and resort to the people would be necessary only on "certain great and extraordinary occasions."[64]

Madison was typical of Federalist leaders in this respect. The men who led the campaign for a new Constitution were not fans of the people out-of-doors; they preferred a more sedate style of politics, safely controlled by gentlemen like themselves.[65] Signs of popular unrest, of which Shays's Rebellion was only the most famous example, made them nervous. Their hope, and the impetus behind their reform effort, was to devise institutional solutions that could discourage these frequent popular interventions by "refining" them or otherwise rendering them unnecessary.

Yet that is a far cry from being anti-democratic. "A dependence on the people is no doubt the primary controul on the government," Madison wrote in *Federalist 51*.[66] Structural innovations were just "auxiliary precautions," contingent devices to forestall conflict, not an abandonment of the more basic commitment to popular constitutionalism. Certainly the Father of the Constitution never wavered in his belief that final authority to resolve disagreements over its meaning must always rest exclusively with the people. As he reiterated in 1789, during the debate over the President's removal power:

> There is not one government on the face of the earth, so far as I recollect, there is not one in the United States, in which provision is made for a particular authority to determine the limits of the constitutional division of power between the branches of the government. In all systems there are points which must be adjusted by the departments themselves, to which no one of them is competent. If it cannot be

determined in this way, there is no resource left but the will of the community, to be collected in some mode to be provided by the constitution, or one dictated by the necessity of the case.[67]

Christopher Wolfe observes, rightly it seems, that Madison meant the amendment process when he referred to a "mode . . . provided by the constitution," and elections, impeachments, and other forms of political action when he referred to a mode "dictated by the necessity of the case."[68]

Recall, too, that Madison was not wholly allergic to popular appeals even in 1788. *Federalist 49–50* dealt only with "keeping the several departments of power within their constitutional limits"[69]—that is, with separation of powers within the federal government. As we have seen, Madison worried that appealing to the people in this context would fail because the community would too often back the legislature, encouraging it to draw ever more power into its "impetuous vortex."[70] In sharp contrast, Madison embraced the potential for appealing to the people when it came to keeping the new federal government from swallowing the states. In the context of federalism, Madison no longer feared that conventional forms of popular constitutionalism might work against the Constitution's design, because—as he explained in *Federalist 45–46*—"the first and most natural attachment of the people will be to the governments of their respective states," thus according states complete security from any risk of federal overreaching.[71]

Countless other examples can be cited similarly attesting to the persistence of popular constitutionalism in the early Republic. The people's interpretive authority—their active control over the meaning and enforcement of their constitutions—is what James Wilson had in mind in 1787, when he exulted that "the people possess, over our constitutions, control in *act*, as well as in right."[72] It is what John Randolph meant when he insisted, in 1802, that while the branches may try to check one another, the people control the constitution through elections, "the true check; every other check is at variance with the principle, that a free people are capable of self-government."[73] "[A]n appeal . . . through the elections," Randolph explained, ensured that constitutional limits on power were interpreted by "the nation, to whom alone, and not a few privileged individuals, it belongs to decide, in the last resort, on the Constitution."[74] It is what President James Madison was referring to in 1815, when he declined to veto the bill establishing a Second Bank of the United States on constitutional grounds, because—though his own views of its unconstitutionality remained unaltered—the matter was "precluded . . . by repeated recognitions under varied circumstances of the validity of such an institution in the acts of the legislative, executive, and judicial branches of the Government, accompanied by indications . . . of a concurrence of the general will of the nation."[75] And it is why, in 1819, Thomas Jefferson could, without being the least bit ironic, describe his own election two decades earlier as "the revolution of 1800."[76] The great controversies of the 1790s had been *constitutional* controversies: the power to incorporate a bank or encourage manufactures, the question of neutrality, the proper handling of the Whiskey Rebellion, the Jay Treaty, the Alien and Sedition Acts, the election deadlock—these all raised or were entangled in constitutional questions. The issues before the country in these years were *constitutional* issues: strict versus broad construction, federal versus state power, the existence or not of federal common law, the meaning of freedom of the press. The escalating party struggles of the 1790s were, in Jefferson's eyes, an extended national referendum on whose views of the Constitution were correct, a referendum that reached its climax in the fiercely contested election of 1800. The people's unequivocal choice in that election had been for Republican principles and the Republican Constitution. Jefferson was thus being both literal and sincere in calling the rejection of Federalism:

> [A]s real a revolution in the principles of our government as that of 1776 was in its form; not effected indeed by the sword, as that, but by the rational and peaceable instrument of reform, the suffrage of the people. The nation declared its will by dismissing functionaries of one principle, and electing those of another, in the two branches, executive and legislative, submitted to their election.[77]

Popular Constitutionalism, circa 1786

The continued vitality of these traditional constitutional understandings and practices—particularly the understanding of constitutions as popular rather than ordinary law—is hardly surprising. Firmly rooted beliefs and deep-seated background assumptions seldom change quickly. Certainly they never do so unless something specifically forces those who share them to undertake a reexamination. If anything, however, the opposite was true of the American Revolution: its whole point had been, in a sense, to affirm the principles of popular sovereignty and the customary constitution. Nevertheless, the practicalities of reestablishing government after independence inevitably produced changes and exerted pressure on existing understandings and practices of fundamental law. Four factors, in particular, were significant in this respect, and from these emerged the first concept of something recognizable as true judicial review.

First, with independence came responsibility to govern. Suddenly, and for the first time, Americans had to handle for themselves all those matters that were formerly dealt with by Great Britain. This was obvious at the national level, where inexperienced officers of a new and uncertain federal government had to manage and finance a war, deal with foreign affairs and interstate disputes, and find solutions to a variety of other thorny problems.[78] But it was equally true in the states, which similarly found themselves forced to address numerous matters that had formerly been handled by imperial authorities. Plus, the Revolution changed the demands that were made of government, as modern conceptions of public power replaced older notions of monarchical government. Gordon Wood explains:

> From the outset the new republican states thus tended to view with suspicion the traditional monarchical practice of enlisting private wealth and energy for public purposes by issuing corporate privileges and licenses to private persons. . . . Consequently, the republican state governments sought to assert their newly enhanced public power in direct and unprecedented ways—doing for themselves what they had earlier commissioned private persons to do. They carved out exclusively public spheres of action and responsibility where none had existed before. They now drew up plans for replacing everything from trade and commerce to roads and waterworks and helped to create a science of political economy for Americans. And they formed their own public organizations with paid professional staffs supported by tax money, not private labor.[79]

It was precisely this rage for reform that Madison lamented in his memo on the *Vices of the Political System of the United States*, complaining of a "luxuriancy of legislation" that had, in a few short years, "filled as many pages as the century which preceded it."[80] Madison's explanation for the phenomenon—that state legislatures were too responsive to the whims of majorities—simply underscores the point: with independence, and for better or worse, America's legislatures found themselves doing far more than ever before.

Second, the new constitutions were written. Contrary to a common misperception among present-day constitutional lawyers, putting a constitution into writing was not thought to alter its fundamental character.[81] As we have already seen, customary constitutional law regularly drew on written sources, while lawyers and statesmen continued to rely on customary sources even after formal texts had been drafted.[82] The chief effect of writing constitutional principles down, as the Founding generation saw it, was to give these principles a degree of explicitness and clarity that was new. Recall that, while there was consensus about many principles of the customary constitution, it necessarily suffered the debility of uncertainty that inheres in all forms of customary law. "But, with us," boasted St. George Tucker in *Kamper v. Hawkins*, "the constitution is not an 'ideal thing,' but a real existence: it can be 'produced in a visible form:' its principles can be ascertained from the living letter, not from obscure reasonings or deductions only."[83] William Paterson made the same point in his charge to the jury in *Vanhorne's Lessee v. Dorrance*:

> It is difficult to say what the Constitution of *England* is; because, not being reduced to written certainty and precision, it lies entirely at the mercy of the Parliament: It bends to every governmental exigency; it varies and is blown about by every breeze of legislative humor or political caprice. . . . Besides, in *England* there is no written constitution, no fundamental law, nothing visible, nothing real, nothing certain, by which a statute can be tested. In *America* the case is widely different: Every State in the Union has its constitution reduced to written exactitude and precision.[84]

Paterson was, of course, exaggerating in both directions. The customary constitution was unambiguous in many respects, while two centuries of wrestling with written texts has made their imprecision abundantly clear. There was, nevertheless, a difference in degree that mattered, and by reducing their constitutions to writing, Americans made that much more immediately, easily useable.

One by-product of the new explicitness and clarity associated with written constitutions was the decision to create formal provisions for amending them.[85] A distinction between "making" and "interpreting" fundamental law already existed under the customary constitution, part of an intellectual tradition stretching back to the ancients that had been carried forward in the work of such figures as Machiavelli, Locke, Montesquieu, and Rousseau.[86] Yet the distinction had little practical significance. The foundational principles of the Ancient Constitution were thought to be immutable; improvements and alterations were possible only in their instantiation and application. Correction along these lines, in the meantime, occurred mainly through prescription and the accretion of precedent—a process of gradual evolution that was seen more as adaptation to changing circumstances than the making of new law. Abrupt revisions were unusual, happening mostly during violent upheavals like the Glorious Revolution, and even these were justified on grounds of protecting or restoring ancient liberties. In short, circumstances and fortuity had deflected the need to worry much about any conceptual distinction between interpreting existing law and making new law.

Reducing constitutions to writing put new pressure on the distinction by making the terms of fundamental law specific and more easily demonstrable, and thus narrowing the space for "improvements" that were not undeniably alterations.[87] The difficulty, moreover, was not just that written constitutions were more certain and precise, but also that the new American constitutions hazarded numerous innovations. This made it virtually certain, as Elbridge Gerry was to note during the debates over framing a new Federal Constitution, that "periodical revision" would be necessary because of "[t]he novelty & difficulty of the experiment."[88]

One could have left such problems to be handled by the people at large, as they always had been; Charles Pinckney said during the same debate as Gerry that he "doubted the propriety or necessity" of a formal amendment mechanism.[89] But most Americans associated precipitous changes in fundamental law with violence and revolution, and many immediately perceived the benefits of creating a regular process to alter established law peacefully— a process that, as the townsfolk of Lexington put it in objecting to its absence from an early draft of the Massachusetts constitution, "might give Satisfaction to the People; and be an happy Means, under Providence, of preventing popular Commotions, Mobs, Bloodshed and Civil War."[90] George Mason made the case succinctly in supporting an amendment provision at the Federal Convention: "The plan now to be formed will certainly be defective, as the Confederation has been found on trial to be. Amendments therefore will be necessary, and it will be better to provide for them, in an easy, regular, and Constitutional way than to trust to chance and violence."[91]

Lawyers and scholars today generally misunderstand the part these amendment provisions originally played in a constitutional scheme. We imagine "the people" only as lawmakers—constitutional legislators for a day, as it were—but nothing more. Ratification makes a constitution "law," but also turns the constitution over to government agents (mainly judges) who assume responsibility for its interpretation and enforcement. The people retain authority to correct mistakes or change courses, but only by again exercising their original power to make law. That power might exist even without a formal mechanism for amendment, though such provisions are useful in a constitution because they make the people's authority explicit and establish known procedures for its exercise. Either way, this revisionary, lawmaking power is seen as the sole means of direct popular control of constitutional law.

Eighteenth-century Americans had a less cramped image of popular constitutionalism. They took for granted the people's responsibility not only for making, but also for interpreting and enforcing their constitutions—a background norm so widely shared and deeply ingrained that specific expression in the constitution was unnecessary. Constitutional provisions for amendment made sense within this framework to deal with a new problem created by having embarked on a course of constitutional experimentation in written form. Anticipating a need for frequent revision of clearly established constitutional rules, the drafters of the new constitutions deemed it expedient to provide an easier, more orderly mechanism for changing them. This was intended not to limit, but rather to respect and preserve popular authority over constitutions, while simultaneously reducing the prospect of political unrest.

Striking a proper balance among these various concerns was no simple task. Many participants worried that the amendment process could stir up more trouble than it prevented if it were made too easy. Gently chiding Jefferson for his harebrained proposal to have the laws and constitutions expire every nineteen years, Madison reiterated his arguments from *Federalist 49* while adding a warning about the danger of "engender[ing] pernicious factions that might not otherwise come into existence."[92] Different compromises with respect to the ease or difficulty of making amendments were reflected in the various approaches taken in different states and in the Federal Constitution.[93] But in every case, choices were imagined and ultimately made against a background of unmediated popular intervention, which provided the implicit baseline for measuring legitimacy.

By the same token, adopting formal procedures to change fundamental law in no way altered the people's role when it came to conventional problems of constitutional interpretation. As we have seen earlier (and will see again), if a constitution was unclear, government officials were expected to do their best to ascertain and follow its requirements, subject to popular oversight and review expressed by a range of "political-legal" means. A separate problem arose when a constitution was clear—either because its text was unmistakable or because an ambiguity had been resolved through a course of popular reactions—but what was once clearly mandated no longer seemed desirable. Relying on traditional popular means to overturn entrenched rules or reform established institutions was difficult at best, often inviting violence and civil unrest. So Americans chose instead to address this problem by creating, in Mason's words, "an easy, regular and Constitutional way" to make such changes. The amendment device could also be used to cure ambiguities, but this was neither its motivation nor its main purpose. The possibility of amendment was thus situated in a political and intellectual framework in which interpretive authority remained where it had always been, with the people at large.

The synergy between these first two changes—more active government, on the one hand, and more explicit constitutions, on the other—produced yet a third. There were now many more opportunities for constitutional conflict: more problems to address, more questions that might arise, more disputes likely to become manifest. A number of additional factors exacerbated this state of affairs. It was a revolutionary time whose radical overtones did not fade quickly; institutions throughout the society were being overturned, sharpening an incipient class conflict as well as the ordinary tussle of competing interests.[94] It was, moreover, a time of economic hardship and dislocation,[95] with the inevitable concomitant pressures to stretch the law to provide relief. Then there was the matter of loyalists and others who had backed the wrong side, as Americans proved no more capable than anyone else at keeping bitter memories and vindictive urges from overwhelming ordinary legal process, giving in to what Alexander Hamilton despairingly called a "popular phrenzy" of punitive legislation.[96] Lastly, as already noted, the new constitutions contained numerous innovations—institutions and ideas whose very novelty left their operation uncertain. In some instances, such as relations between the state and federal governments, Americans knew they were in uncharted waters. In others, such as separation of powers, they did not discover how little they understood until they attempted to implement what they had written.

The fourth and most important change produced by the Revolution was the new nation's explicit, emphatic embrace of popular sovereignty. This was not a new idea, for Americans believed it had always been a feature of their constitutions. But this belief was not put to the test until the Revolutionary crisis of 1763–1776, from which popular sovereignty emerged more clearly defined as the central principle of American constitutionalism—producing that initial rage for republicanism documented by Gordon Wood in *The*

Creation of the American Republic.[97] The concept of popular sovereignty pre-dated 1776 by more than a century, but in American hands, and through the crucible of the American Revolution, it acquired a concreteness and impor-tance that was wholly new and wholly different. Gerald Stourzh elaborates:

> The rise of the constitution as the *paramount law*, reigning supreme and therefore invalidating, if procedurally possible, any law of a lower level in the hierarchy of legal norms, including "ordinary" legisla-tor-made law, is *the* great innovation and achievement of American eighteenth-century constitutionalism. Awareness of *this* innovation, not of constitutions reduced to written documents, was what evoked the proud commentary of eighteenth-century Americans such as Tom Paine, James Iredell, and James Madison.[98]

As it emerged, moreover, the principle of popular sovereignty was subtly transformed. Its movement from wings to center stage gave the principle an immediate serviceableness that it had not previously possessed. No longer just a background norm or explanation of original authority, the idea of popular sovereignty was right there on the surface, an immanent, impendent force to be dealt with.

While Stourzh is right, moreover, that putting constitutions into writing was not seen as a profound innovation, the process of doing so nevertheless gave a powerful boost to the new awareness of popular sovereignty. Reducing constitutions to writing may have begun as a matter of practical necessity, but it did not end that way. The work itself infused "the people" with an immediacy and tangibleness that penetrated beyond the conscious, beyond the intellectual, to invigorate the affective side of the Revolution. "You and I, my dear friend, have been sent into life at a time when the greatest lawgivers of antiquity would have wished to live," marveled John Adams:

> How few of the human race have ever enjoyed an opportunity of mak-ing an election of government, more than of air, soil, or climate, for themselves or their children! When, before the present epocha, had three millions of people full power and a fair opportunity to form and establish the wisest and happiest government that human wisdom can contrive?[99]

Similar expressions of euphoria and awe were ubiquitous as men threw themselves into the work of writing new constitutions.[100]

This heightened awareness of popular sovereignty—the sense of "the people" as a palpable, active entity making conscious choices—transformed certain implicit understandings about the nature of a constitution. The customary constitution was popular law, but of a fundamentally conservative cast. Its defining tropes were all about antiquity, settled practice, and custom established since "time out of mind." It changed constantly, but changes were seen (and more importantly, were felt) primarily in terms of preservation: responses to events undertaken in order to maintain an ancient, unchanging balance between liberty and power. Infused with Revolutionary fervor, the new American understanding of constitutionalism was active, reformist, optimistic, and progressive. In short, the customary constitution metamorphosed into something that could, for the first time, truly be called a popular constitution.

The new provisions for amendment were perhaps the clearest and most obvious manifestation of the new attitude.[101] Haunted by the specter of "corruption" of the British constitution, Whig writers in the colonial period had directed all their energies toward preservation—toward restoring (as Jefferson once described it) "that happy system of our ancestors, the wisest and most perfect ever yet devised by the wit of man, as it stood before the 8th century."[102] Now, Americans looked eagerly forward, toward the future, instead of backward—trusting in their abilities to adjust and adapt and improve. One function of amendment remained to protect the purity of the constitution, and no one doubted that a "frequent recurrence to fundamental principles" was "absolutely necessary to preserve the blessings of liberty."[103] But the old preservationist mood was rapidly supplanted by a buoyant new willingness to experiment, of which the ease of making amendments was an integral part. Fear not the possibility of mistakes, urged the drafters of Massachusetts's 1780 constitution, for we can make repairs at a later date in whatever manner "Experience, that best Instructor, shall then point out to be expedient or necessary."[104]

The new possibility of amendment was just one reflection of the changing temper of the time. A sense of popular empowerment was pervasive, as Americans confidently decided that they could fashion their own constitution and government and control their own destinies.[105] Madison hit this note perfectly in rebuking opponents of the Federal Constitution for dreading its novelty:

> But why is the experiment of an extended republic to be rejected merely because it may comprise what is new? Is it not the glory of the

people of America, that whilst they have paid a decent regard to the opinions of former times and other nations, they have not suffered a blind veneration for antiquity, for custom, or for names, to overrule the suggestions of their own good sense, the knowledge of their own situation, and the lessons of their own experience? ... Happily for America, happily we trust for the whole human race, [the Revolutionary generation] pursued a new and more noble course. They accomplished a revolution which has no parallel in the annals of human society: They reared the fabrics of governments which have no model on the face of the globe. They formed the design of a great confederacy, which it is incumbent on their successors to improve and perpetuate.[106]

With so much in flux, complications were inevitable. Constrained as they were by the exigencies of war with England, and lacking useful precedents other than the problematic example of 1688, it took Americans a few years to work out a theory of the proper way to ratify a constitution and make it supreme, paramount law.[107] In most states, new constitutions were adopted by ordinary legislative means, without either direct submission to the people or a special convention called solely for the purpose of creating fundamental law.[108] The actual status of some of these first state constitutions thus remained ambiguous, with authorities as esteemed as John Adams and Thomas Jefferson suggesting that theirs could be altered by ordinary legislation.[109] More commonly, factors like those discussed above—revenge against loyalists, economic hardship, and the like—induced state legislators to ignore clear commands of their constitutions without bothering to make any fancy claims of authority to do so. Either way, blatantly unconstitutional laws became a too-common feature of politics in the 1780s. James Madison placed the "numerous" state violations of the Articles of Confederation at the top of his list of "Vices," and he complained to Jefferson of "[r]epeated" transgressions of bills of rights committed "by overbearing majorities in every State."[110] Alarm at just this sort of development provided one of the chief motivations for Federalist leaders in 1787.[111]

"Being Judges for the Benefit of the Whole People"

This combination of factors—more active government, more explicit constitutions, more constitutional conflict and arguably unconstitutional laws, and, above all, a heightened sense of popular sovereignty—could be interpreted in different ways, and it pulled people in different directions as they confronted the new experience of managing a constitutional republic. The resulting tensions shaped the first concept of judicial review.

To many, respect for popular sovereignty demanded that judges enforce duly enacted laws and leave constitutional questions to be settled elsewhere. No one doubted that a properly ratified constitution was, as Edmund Pendleton observed, "a rule obligatory upon every department, not to be departed from on any occasion."[112] It did not follow, however, that the judiciary could therefore invoke the constitution's authority against another department. No one of the branches was meant to be superior to any other, unless it were the legislature, and when it came to constitutional law, all were meant to be subordinate to the people. Just as it is not your place to punish me for violating ordinary law, so too in a regime of popular constitutionalism it was not the judiciary's responsibility to enforce the constitution against the legislature. It was the people's responsibility: a responsibility they discharged mainly through elections, but also, if necessary, by other, extralegal means. For courts to interfere, to presume to judge the actions of a coordinate branch, was to meddle in affairs that were none of their business. Worse, it was to imply, as Judge William Nelson characterized the argument in *Kamper v. Hawkins*, "that the judiciary . . . claims a superiority over the legislature" on matters peculiarly within the legislative arena, which encompassed decisions respecting the constitutionality of legislation as well as its necessity.[113] This is what was meant when people said, as St. George Tucker put it in the same case, that "the constitution of a state is a rule to the *legislature only*."[114]

We need to be clear on this argument, which is critical if we are to understand the setting in which judicial review eventually emerged. In suggesting that the constitutionality of legislation was not a matter for judicial cognizance, no one was saying that the authoritative interpreter of the constitution was the legislature rather than the judiciary. That would have been inconsistent with the whole framework of popular constitutionalism because it would have assumed that final interpretive authority rested with one or another of these public agencies. In fact, neither branch was authoritative because interpretive authority remained with the people. Of course, public officials still had to interpret the constitution in going about their business, since they were the regulated entities (again, just as we must interpret ordinary law in going about our business). But underlying the argument described by Nelson and Tucker was an assumption that the people's restrictions on which laws could be enacted were directed to the lawmaking branch, and not to the other branches. It was the legislature's delegated responsibility to decide whether a proposed law was constitutionally authorized, subject to oversight by the people. Courts simply had nothing to do with it, and they were acting as interlopers if they tried to second-guess the legislature's decision. It would be as if the people had hired two agents to perform distinct tasks and one agent kept interfering with the other agent's job, insisting that it knew better.

Judging by the public response to early decisions exploring judicial review, this was the position of most Americans prior to the 1790s.[115] Their reactions are hardly surprising given the premises of popular constitutionalism and the lack of any previous experience with, or practice of, judicial monitoring of fundamental law. To be sure, some of those who rejected judicial review were uncomfortable having to rely so heavily on traditional "political-legal" means of enforcing constitutional limits. These might have worked during the colonial era, when issues of fundamental law arose only rarely, and they remained essential for combating profound, pervasive usurpations, like those that led to the Revolutions of 1688 and 1776. But could these traditional devices control the numerous smaller unconstitutional measures that seemed daily to issue from state legislatures? Could they be relied upon to prevent laws that were supported by a majority of the community, such as paper-money laws or legislation confiscating the property of loyalists? Richard Dobbs Spaight fervidly rejected judicial nullification as "absurd, and contrary to the practice of all the world," but he acknowledged that some kind of better check might be "absolutely necessary to our well-being."[116] He just could not think of one; "the only one that I know of," he confessed, "is the annual election."[117]

Others were more imaginative. Many of the structural changes adopted by state constitution writers were at least partly about constitutional control—not just annual elections, but also rotation in office, the right to instruct, bicameralism, and the like. Still other innovations were developed specifically and exclusively with the problem of preventing unconstitutional action in mind. We have already considered Jefferson's proposal to "correct breaches" of the constitution by allowing any two branches to call a convention of the people. The anonymous author of *Four Letters on Interesting Subjects* thought that "preserving a Constitution" could easily be accomplished by electing at some fixed interval "a *Provincial Jury* . . . to enquire if any inroads have been made in the Constitution [with] power to remove them"[118]—a proposal adopted in slightly modified form by Pennsylvania and Vermont, both of which provided for a "council of censors" to review the state of the constitution every seven years and recommend changes to the people.[119] The drafters of the New York constitution came up with the idea of a delaying veto, a sort of preemptive strike on potentially unconstitutional laws. New bills were submitted to a "council to revise" that consisted of the governor, chancellor, and high court judges and was empowered to investigate proposed legislation for its constitutionality; the council's veto could be overridden only by a two-thirds majority in both houses of the legislature.[120] Madison heartily approved this measure, which he urged at one time or another (though never successfully) on Kentucky,[121] Virginia,[122] and the Federal Convention.[123] He later devised the most imaginative solution of the period, deciding that still more and better protection could be provided simply by enlarging the sphere of the republic. The legislature of an extensive territory, Madison reasoned (though, once again, he failed to persuade others), would be less likely to enact unconstitutional laws and could be entrusted with a veto over the laws of the states.[124]

Not everyone agreed that judicial enforcement of a constitution was improper, however. Interpreting the same events and circumstances differently, a few people reasoned that respect for popular sovereignty actually *required* judicial review. If the constitution was supreme, fundamental law, then legislative acts contravening its terms were ultra vires and void: not law at all. Judges before whom such acts were brought could not just ignore this fact. The principle of popular sovereignty demanded that they treat such laws as the nullities they were. Here was a truly novel idea, albeit one with trace roots in existing practices of enforcing superior laws over inferior ones. For unlike the Americans' other innovations, which they had expressly incorporated in the texts of their constitutions and which had long been part of Whig political tradition, no one before had proposed relying on courts for general constitutional enforcement.

The most thoughtful presentation of this new principle, which began making sporadic appearances in the early 1780s,[125] was penned by future Supreme Court Justice James Iredell in 1786. Iredell was, at the time, representing a client whose property had been confiscated without a jury in a case still pending before the North Carolina courts. Writing pseudonymously as "An Elector," Iredell published a newspaper essay in which he argued in favor of judicial authority to declare an unconstitutional law void; the court was evidently persuaded, for it ruled in his favor when it heard the case a year later.[126]

Iredell began his argument with a proposition that even he conceded no one was denying: that the state's constitution was "the *fundamental* law, and unalterable by the legislature, which derives all its power from it."[127] Writing for rhetorical effect, he reminded readers of "the extreme anxiety in which all of us were agitated in forming the constitution," having been "sickened and disgusted for years with the high and almost impious language from Great Britain" respecting Parliament's supreme authority over the people. But things were otherwise in North Carolina, where the legislature could act only as permitted by the constitution, "for we have as much agreed to be governed by the Turkish Divan as by our own General Assembly, otherwise than on the express terms prescribed."[128] That established, Iredell moved on to what he called "[t]he great argument":

> [T]hat though the Assembly have not a *right* to violate the constitution, yet if they *in fact* do so, the only remedy is, either by a humble petition that the law may be repealed, or a universal resistance of the people. But that in the mean time, their act, whatever it is, is to be obeyed as a law [by the judges]; for the judicial power is not to presume to question the power of an act of Assembly.[129]

Iredell "not unconfidently" rejected these remedies as insufficient.[130] The "remedy by petition" presupposed "that the electors hold their rights by the *favor of their representatives,*" a claim so insulting the "mere stating of this is surely sufficient to excite any man's indignation." Popular resistance, on the other hand, was a proper remedy, but undesirable and deficient as an exclusive one. "We well know how difficult it is to excite the resistance of a whole people," which is why resort to such measures must be considered a "dreadful expedient" and a "calamitous contingency." Besides, since widespread popular resistance could be expected only where there was "*universal oppression,*" many unconstitutional acts would go unredressed. "A thousand injuries may be suffered, and many hundreds ruined, before this can be brought about." In the meantime, individuals and minorities would suffer, and the only safe citizens would be those who managed always to stay in the majority, whom Iredell contemptuously dismissed as "sycophants that will for ever sacrifice reason, conscience, and duty, to the preservation of a temporary popular favor."

Having proved the inadequacy of these conventional remedies, Iredell argued that judicial review followed naturally from the supposition that the constitution expressed the sovereignty of the people:

> For that reason, an act of Assembly, inconsistent with the constitution, is *void*, and cannot be obeyed, without disobeying the superior law to

which we were previously and irrevocably bound. The judges, therefore, must take care at their peril, that every act of Assembly they presume to enforce is warranted by the constitution, since if it is not, they act without lawful authority. This is not a usurped or a discretionary power, but one inevitably resulting from the constitution of their office, they being judges *for the benefit of the whole people,* not *mere servants of the Assembly.*[131]

A number of observations are appropriate at this point. First, a word of caution: the whole idea of judicial review was new, and however obvious it may seem to us, only a small number encountered and understood the arguments purporting to justify it. No more than a handful of cases arose prior to 1787 in which a question of judicial power to declare legislation unconstitutional was clearly presented, and courts ducked the issue in most of these.[132] Regularly published reports did not yet exist,[133] and what was known about the cases came mostly from sketchy newspaper accounts or from letters and pamphlets written by lawyers who had sought judicial protection for their clients. The handful of men who were pondering judicial review had not yet worked out the theory's kinks, as they themselves well knew. This was part of the reason Edmund Pendleton chose not to address the matter in *Commonwealth v. Caton,* explaining that "how far this court . . . shall have power to declare the nullity of a law passed in its forms by the legislative power . . . is indeed a deep, important, and I will add, a tremendous question, the decision of which might involve consequences to which gentlemen may not have extended their ideas."[134]

This uncertainty about the precise terms of judicial review is found not only in the 1780s, but for a number of additional decades to come. Judicial review was a moving target, one small piece in a much larger transformation of the role of the judiciary in American life.[135] There was, at every moment, a range of views both as to its propriety and its justifications. Movement was in the direction of increasing acceptance, fairly rapidly so after 1790, but accurately describing just *what* was being accepted is complicated by the diversity of ideas about fundamentals.

That said, Iredell's 1786 essay is useful because it was the clearest and best-reasoned presentation of the initial justification for judicial review and because, in most respects, it reflected basic assumptions that were shared by most proponents. Chief among these were the assumptions of popular constitutionalism: the same assumptions made by those who rejected judicial review. The constitution was fundamental law (that is, law made by the people to regulate their rulers) and so not like ordinary law at all. Iredell never suggested, or even hinted, that courts should exercise judicial review because they possessed some special competence for the task or because interpreting and enforcing laws is what courts do. Rather, he argued that courts *must* exercise judicial review because they are the people's agents *too*. To ignore the unconstitutionality of a law presented in the course of litigation would be to violate their agency. Hence, they must "take care at their peril" to enforce only constitutional laws or they themselves would be lawbreakers, acting "without lawful authority." Rather than overstepping its bounds or intruding on legislative turf, a court that refused to enforce an unconstitutional law was following the people's command—acting within the scope of responsibilities delegated by the people to the judiciary, which encompassed adjudication.

Nor was this all, for judicial review offered significant pragmatic benefits as well. By exercising review, judges could act on behalf of the people, supplying a peaceful remedy that substituted for the "dreadful expedient" of popular resistance and offered relief in circumstances where it might not otherwise be available.[136] James Varnum likewise emphasized this last point in his argument to the court in *Trevett v. Weeden*:

> But as the Legislative is the supreme power in government, who is to judge whether they have violated the constitutional rights of the people?—I answer . . . the people themselves will judge, as the only resort in the last stages of oppression. But when [legislators] proceed no further than merely to enact what they may call laws, and refer those to the Judiciary Courts for determination, then, (in discharge of the great trust reposed in them, and to prevent the horrors of a civil war, as in the present case) the Judges can, and we trust your Honours will, decide upon them.[137]

Judicial review, in other words, was not an act of ordinary legal interpretation. It was a political—perhaps we should say a "political-legal"—act of resistance. Gordon Wood rightly describes it as "akin perhaps to the interposition of the states that Jefferson and Madison suggested in the Kentucky and Virginia Resolutions of 1798."[138] Even closer to the point is the resistance to the Stamp Act sought by rebel leaders in 1765, when they urged courts to remain open and carry on business without stamped paper.[139] In refusing to enforce unconstitutional laws, judges were exercising the people's authority to resist, providing a supplemental remedy for ultra vires legislative acts that averted the need to mobilize popular opposition.

Early proponents of judicial review were quite self-conscious in recognizing the awful nature of what they were doing: "awful" in the eighteeth-century sense of something full of awe. Edmund Randolph initially rejected judicial review when he considered the issue for the first time while preparing to argue for the state in *Commonwealth v. Caton*. Randolph changed his mind as he worked through the issues,[140] but recognizing the extraordinary nature of what he was proposing, stepped out of his role as state attorney general and ascribed the position favoring judicial review to himself alone.[141] He said:

> Do I tremble at the decision of my own mind, that a law against the constitution may be declared void? or do I dread the resentment of the court, when I bear testimony against their competency to pronounce the invalidity of the law?
>
> No! The revolution has given me a coat of mail for my defense, while I adhere to its principles. That bench too is reared on the revolution, and will arrogate no undue power.
>
> I hold then, that every law against the constitution may be declared void.[142]

George Wythe, who sat as a judge in the same case, was still more candid, melodramatically proclaiming that, if ever a branch of the legislature should overstep its constitutional boundaries:

> I shall not hesitate, sitting in this place, to say, to the general court, *Fiat justitia, ruat coelum*; and, to the usurping branch of the legislature, you attempt worse than a vain thing; for, although, you cannot succeed, you set an example, which may convulse society to its centre. Nay more, if the whole legislature, an event to be deprecated, should attempt to overleap the bounds, prescribed to them by the people, I, in administering the public justice of the country, will meet the united powers, at my seat in this tribunal; and, pointing to the constitution, will say, to them, here is the limit of your authority; and, hither, shall you go, but no further.[143]

The clash between these opposing views of judicial review shaped the doctrine as it emerged. Those who rejected judicial nullification were plainly in the ascendant, as their position more closely conformed to conventional wisdom and expectations. Judicial review was, in the context of the times, such a radical departure from experience that even proponents regarded its possibility with what Gordon Wood describes as "a sense of awe and wonder."[144] "Most Americans," he says, "even those deeply concerned with the legislative abuses of the 1780s, were too fully aware of the modern positivist conception of law (made famous by Blackstone in his *Commentaries of the Laws of England*), too deeply committed to consent as the basis of law, and from their colonial experience too apprehensive of the possible arbitrariness and uncertainties of judicial discretion to permit judges to set aside laws made by the elected representatives of the people."[145] Hence, James Monroe can be found informing Madison as late as 1788 that the Virginia legislature avoided discussing the issue "as calculated to create heats & animosities that will produce harm."[146]

Advocates of judicial power were thus cautious in formulating the limits of the principle. "In all doubtful cases . . . the Act ought to be supported," James Iredell conceded in a letter justifying his position to an incensed Richard Dobbs Spaight, "it should be unconstitutional beyond dispute before it is pronounced such."[147] This limiting principle instantly became an article of faith among the supporters of judicial review, accompanying virtually every statement of the doctrine. We should understand it, moreover, as grounded in something other than simple defensiveness. The principle that laws should be declared void only if "unconstitutional beyond dispute" was a logical corollary given the rationale for judicial action. Judges might be justified in acting as the people's proxy, to avert reliance on dangerous and undependable forms of popular resistance. But they remained mere agents, acting in a manner they presumed their principal had commanded. Such presumptuousness could not be indulged lightly, but should await conditions of near certainty because the principal was capable of acting on its own and retained primary responsibility for doing so.

"Such Power in Courts would be Destructive of Liberty"

Even thus confined, early efforts to exercise judicial review drew stinging rebukes. *Rutgers v. Waddington* involved a statute that precluded defendants in trespass actions from pleading in justification that their use of plaintiff's property was authorized by military order of the occupying British forces. Representing the defendant, Alexander Hamilton urged first that the statute was inconsistent with the law of nations, which he maintained was incorporated into the New York constitution; and second that it violated the Treaty of Paris, which Hamilton said was binding national law. Following a suggestion in Hamilton's brief,[148] the court sidestepped the problem, finding it unnecessary to rule on the validity of the Trespass Act because the statute did not explicitly say that it revoked the law of nations or should apply if inconsistent with the treaty. James Duane's rambling opinion for the court is pure Blackstone, the heart of his analysis lifted straight from the great British jurist's *Commentaries*:

> The supremacy of the Legislature need not be called into question; if they think fit *positively* to enact a law, there is no power which can controul them. When the main object of such a law is clearly expressed, and the intention manifest, the Judges are not at liberty, altho' it appears to them to be *unreasonable*, to reject it: for this were to set the *judicial* above the legislative, which would be subversive of all government.
>
> But when a law is expressed in *general words*, and some *collateral matter*, which happens to arise from these words is *unreasonable*, there the Judges are in decency to conclude that the consequences were not foreseen by the Legislature; and therefore they are at liberty to expound the statute by *equity*, and only *quoud hoc* to disregard it.
>
> When the judicial make these distinctions, they do not controul the Legislature; they endeavor to give their *intention* it's proper effect. [149]

Notwithstanding Duane's jurisprudential conservatism, merely exercising this aggressive form of statutory interpretation elicited outrage. The state legislature adopted a resolution denouncing the opinion as "in its tendency subversive of all law and good order, and lead[ing] directly to anarchy and confusion,"[150] which was apparently just enough to blunt a subsequent effort to impeach the judges as well. Shortly thereafter, *The New York Packet and the American Advertiser* printed an open letter from a committee of nine prominent citizens. Occupying nearly four full columns, the letter accused the court of exercising "a power to set aside an act of the state," and warned:

> That there should be a power vested in courts of judicature whereby they might controul the supreme Legislative power we think is absurd in itself. Such power in courts would be destructive of liberty, and remove all security of property. The design of courts of justice in our

government, from the very nature of their institutions, is to declare laws, not to alter them.

Whenever they depart from this design of their institution, they confound legislative and judicial powers.[151]

The same reactions followed the refusal of the New Hampshire courts in several cases to enforce a law eliminating trial by jury in cases for sums of less than ten pounds:[152] local newspapers published editorials condemning the decisions, and the legislature received petitions demanding that the judges be impeached. A motion to impeach was entertained but narrowly defeated. Instead, state legislators adopted a resolution affirming the law's constitutionality (by a vote of 44 to 14).[153] Six months later, and in the face of continuing pressure, the legislature entertained a motion to impeach that was narrowly defeated, after which they decided to repeal the troublesome law.[154] This initiated a tug of war between the branches in which the legislature continued to insist on its prerogatives despite the judiciary's protests; it took nearly thirty-five years, until 1818–19, before judicial review was firmly established in New Hampshire.[155]

The case that lay behind James Iredell's essay, *Bayard v. Singleton*,[156] provoked a similar outcry in North Carolina. In May 1786, Bayard brought an action to recover property confiscated by state authorities in 1777. A year before Bayard's suit had been commenced, the North Carolina legislature enacted a provision requiring the state's courts to dismiss actions by loyalists seeking to recover property taken during the war. When judges hearing Bayard's case failed promptly to grant the defendant's motion to dismiss under this law, they were ordered to appear before the legislature. A committee that included two future delegates to the Federal Convention (William Davie, who was representing Bayard, and Richard Dobbs Spaight) found the judges guilty of the facts charged against them, though they did not recommend any formal sanction.[157]

Expecting this none-too-subtle legislative message to produce a more agreeable outcome the second time around, the defendant renewed his motion to dismiss. The judges struggled to avoid ruling, trying by various means to persuade the parties to settle.[158] Their efforts failed, and in May 1787, "after every reasonable endeavour had been used in vain for avoiding a disagreeable difference between the Legislature, and the judicial powers"—and just as the Federal Convention was getting under way—the court "with much apparent reluctance, but with great deliberation and firmness" denied the defendant's motion on constitutional grounds.[159] Its action incited violent protest throughout the state and provoked the legislature to deny the judges a pay increase, though the controversy died down after a sympathetic jury promptly returned a verdict for the defendant.[160]

And then there was *Trevett v. Weeden*. James Varnum argued to the court that Rhode Island's law requiring merchants to accept paper money at face value was unconstitutional because it could be enforced in civil trials without a jury; the court appeared to avoid the issue by dismissing for lack of jurisdiction instead.[161] Although the judges had neither declared the law unconstitutional nor even stated forthrightly that they had the power to do so, the governor convened a special session of the legislature, which summoned the court to explain its actions. At first, the judges refused to answer, boldly asserting that they were "accountable only to God and [their] own consciences."[162] After further prodding, they tried to placate the irate legislators by explaining how they had not actually declared the law unconstitutional. The assembly nevertheless formally recorded its dissatisfaction and entertained a motion to dismiss the entire bench. The judges petitioned for an additional hearing, accompanied by a written memorial "disclaim[ing] and totally disavow[ing] any the least power or authority, or the appearance thereof, to contravene or controul the constitutional laws of the State."[163] This ambiguous declaration appeased the assembly just long enough for the judges to keep their seats until the next election, at which time all but one were turned out of office.[164]

Similar reactions were recorded throughout the 1780s whenever and wherever a court considered exercising review, with the possible exception of Virginia.[165] The issue arose early in that state, in the 1782 case of *Commonwealth v. Caton*.[166] Three prisoners condemned to death for treason petitioned the House of Delegates for a pardon. The House granted their petition, but the Senate demurred. Under the Treason Act, both houses had to approve a pardon, whereas the state constitution appeared to vest this power in either the governor or the House of Delegates. Lawyers for the defendants asked the court to declare the statute void and grant their pardon under the House resolution. The case achieved a degree of notoriety in the state, with letters and newspaper accounts anticipating and debating what was soon being referred to as "[t]he great constitutional question."[167] Ultimately, the Virginia court, too, avoided having to decide by interpreting the state constitution to permit the act. A number of the court's members nevertheless opined on their power to set aside unconstitutional legislation, with one (Peter Lyons) firmly opposed, two (George Wythe and James Mercer) just as firmly in favor, and five others undecided or unwilling to address a question that was not necessary to decide the merits.[168]

Unlike in other states, no public outcry followed. William Treanor reports that "[t]here is no record of popular criticism of the two judges who asserted that the judiciary had the power to invalidate statues. There was no move in the Senate against them. Moreover, the Senate joined the House in providing the three prisoners the relief they had sought from the outset."[169] Treanor attributes this to the unique structure of Virginia politics, whose controlling elite looked more favorably on lawyers and lawyering than in other states. But while this may have been sufficient to dampen public displays of opposition, it did not mean there was none—as indicated by Monroe's report to Madison that state legislators avoided discussing the issue because it made people too angry.[170] In any event, the Virginia experience was unique, and, elsewhere, talk of judicial review predictably embroiled courts in controversy.

The status of judicial review on the eve of the Federal Convention was thus uncertain at best. It was not even clear just what the argument was. There had been few cases, and no court had yet published an opinion affirmatively explaining, much less defending, judicial authority to nullify legislation. Although one or two courts had actually refused to enforce a law on constitutional grounds, most had avoided the issue. The extra-judicial literature was barely more informative. There was James Iredell's written justification, which made arguments similar to those advanced by James Varnum in *Trevett v. Weeden*. Both men's views had been published, but neither publication circulated widely. Certainly there is nothing to suggest that theirs was a dominant view, even among those who might have looked favorably on judicial intervention.

A number of scholars have suggested that the doctrine of judicial review that emerged in the 1780s was limited to laws regulating courts and judicial process.[171] They rely mainly on the fact that four of the six well-known Revolutionary era cases involved the right to trial by jury,[172] while one other (*Rutgers v. Waddington*) technically concerned a pleading rule. Certain statements made at the time appear to support this narrow understanding of the doctrine. Elbridge Gerry observed at the Federal Convention that judges had "a sufficient check agst. encroachments on their own department by their exposition of the laws which involved a power of deciding on their Constitutionality,"[173] while James Wilson wanted a Council of Revision because, even assuming judicial review, "[t]he Judiciary ought to have an opportunity of remonstrating agst projected encroachments on the people as well as on themselves."[174] Against the background of the actual decisions, such statements make it seem plausible to assume the existence of a "middle" position confining review to laws directly regulating courts.[175]

Yet on closer inspection, it seems unlikely that anyone at the time was thinking in these terms. Most of the cases may have involved questions that would today be classified under the rubric of adjudicatory process, but not all of them. *Commonwealth v. Caton* concerned the right to a pardon, which is a nonjudicial right, and the defendant's actual challenge in *Rutgers v. Waddington* was to the legislature's power to eliminate a substantive justification for his conduct. Given the small number of cases involved, these are telling exceptions.

Even the jury cases provide little support for the notion that judicial review was restricted to laws regulating courts. Today, we think of the jury mainly as a procedural device, but the eighteenth-century view was more complex. Juries existed first and foremost to protect the people from the government, *including* courts. Laws restricting the right to a jury were seen not as legislative encroachments on judicial power, but rather as governmental efforts to "destroy the Power of the People."[176] One might just as well deprive citizens of the right to vote as deprive them of trial by jury, John Adams explained, for both rights equally prevented "Arbitrary Government" by requiring "the Concurrence of the Voice of the People."[177] Where the franchise constituted "the Part which the People are by the Constitution appointed to take, in the passing and Execution of Laws," juries played a homologous role in the administration of justice: "As the Constitution requires, that, the popular Branch of the Legislature, should have an absolute Check so as to put a peremptory Negative upon every Act of the Government, it requires that the common People should have as compleat a Controul, as decisive a Negative, in every Judgment of a Court of Judicature."[178] All of which is not to deny that juries were part of the judicial process. But because juries were so much more, one cannot infer anything about the scope of judicial review from the fact that many of the early cases were concerned with them.

Read in context, even the remarks quoted above from Elbridge Gerry and James Wilson do not support a view of judicial review as limited to laws regulating courts and process. Consider Wilson's discussion of the Council of Revision. The first thing one notices is that others in the same discussion described judicial review in broader terms, yet did not seem to understand themselves (and were not understood by others) to be making a different point.[179] The same is true of statements Wilson himself made after the Convention, which likewise refer to judicial review with no hint that it is limited to laws regulating judicial process.[180] It is possible, of course, that Wilson changed his mind during the course of the discussions in Philadelphia and that he was persuaded to embrace a broader understanding of judicial review. It seems more likely, however, that he was saying the same thing both times. To describe judicial review in terms of departmental self-defense was an eighteenth-century phrasing that meant nothing more or different than judicial power to consider the constitutionality of laws generally.

Recall that the dispute over judicial review revolved mainly around questions of agency and delegated authority. Those who opposed the practice believed that constitutional limits were a direction from the people to the legislature alone; if the legislature overstepped its bounds, that was a matter for the people themselves to address. By investigating the constitutionality of a statute, courts were meddling in legislative affairs. On the other side, some sophisticated legal thinkers had concluded that constitutional limits *became* a judicial matter whenever a potentially unconstitutional law was relied on in litigation. They pointed out that the constitution delegated responsibility for adjudication to the judiciary, which was acting within its proper arena when enforcing constitutional limits in the context of adjudication—which was, indeed, required to enforce constitutional limits in that context. For the legislature to expect, much less to require, a court to ignore constitutional limits was tantamount to forcing judges to act illegally, thereby corrupting the process of adjudication. This is what Wilson and Gerry meant when referring to judicial review in terms of encroachments on the judiciary: protecting adjudication from legislative corruption through the medium of unconstitutional laws. But their concern encompassed any unconstitutional law, without regard for its subject matter—which is why no court at any time ever drew the suggested distinction or implied that judicial review was applicable to less than the full panoply of constitutional measures.

In saying all this, we must be careful not to lose sight of how seldom the issue came up in the years before the Federal Convention. Obsessive attention to the minutiae of judicial review in the early 1780s can easily mislead. An argument to assign courts a role in enforcing the constitution may have been in the air, but it was hardly one that had achieved widespread notice or approbation so far as the general public was concerned or that could be called established. Our intensive focus on the question is an artifact of what judicial review subsequently became and of our natural curiosity, as a result, to understand its origins. In trying to get a sense of the historical context, however, it is important not to exaggerate the significance of what was, in fact, insignificant to the vast majority of Americans. For most, including most politicians and public leaders, the focus remained on traditional popular means of enforcing the constitution, the major change being a new emphasis on elections. Judicial review was either something they had never heard of or thought about, or, at most, a barely audible note in the background that had not, as yet, attracted their attention in a serious way.

3

The Power under the Constitution Will Always Be in the People

THE MAKING OF THE CONSTITUTION

"The Supreme Law of the Respective States"

The delegates to the Federal Convention brought this whole range of attitudes and ideas with them to Philadelphia. During the course of the deliberations, a number of delegates assumed or openly supported a power of judicial review.[1] A few just as openly opposed it—the most forthright statement to this effect coming from John Francis Mercer, whose brother James had been one of the judges to affirm the power in *Caton*.[2] Still others admitted to being uncertain,[3] while most of the delegates had probably not given the matter much thought. Of course, only a minority of the delegates, no more than ten out of fifty-five, are recorded as having expressed any sentiments at all. Further complicating matters, there was no comprehensive or direct discussion of judicial review at any point in the proceedings, only a series of comments made during debates on other topics. Nevertheless, the record we have does support a few conclusions.

First, the Framers clearly opted for judicial review as a device to control state law. Preventing "[e]ncroachments of the States on the [federal] authority"[4] was a matter of paramount importance to constitutional reformers in the 1780s. "Examples of this are numerous," Madison recorded in his *Vices* memorandum, "and repetitions may be foreseen in almost every case where

73

any favorite object of a State shall present a temptation."[5] Madison wanted to handle the problem by giving Congress a negative over state laws "in all cases whatsoever"[6]—an overambitious solution that the other Virginia delegates were willing to incorporate into their initial proposal to the Convention only in the watered-down form of a negative over "all laws passed by the several states, contravening in the opinion of the National Legislature the articles of Union."[7]

Even this, as it turned out, was too much for the Convention's small-state delegates, who countered in the New Jersey Plan with a proposal to make the laws and treaties of the United States "the supreme law of the respective States" and to provide that "the Judiciary of the several States shall be bound thereby in their decisions, any thing in the respective laws of the Individual States to the contrary notwithstanding."[8] Here, as Jack Rakove has convincingly argued, lie the seeds of judicial review as a formal element of the Federal Constitution.[9] For the Convention eventually compromised by spurning New Jersey's weak scheme in favor of the nationalist Virginia Plan, but with a strengthened supremacy clause that replaced Madison's legislative negative and that could be enforced by state and national courts.[10]

The critical discussion took place on July 17, the day after Madison's and the other nationalists' bitter defeat on the issue of proportional representation in the Senate (the so-called Great Compromise). The proposal for a negative on state laws had previously been considered on June 8, with a slew of delegates offering reasons why it was a bad idea.[11] This time, too, the debate began with a number of speeches opposing a legislative veto—including one by Roger Sherman, who for the first time suggested that it was "unnecessary, as the Courts of the States would not consider as valid any law contravening the Authority of the Union."[12] Madison countered that reliance could not be placed on the judiciary. Any check that operated only after laws were enacted would come too late because these laws could "accomplish their injurious objects before they can be repealed by the Genl Legislre. or be set aside by the National Tribunals" and because "Confidence can <not> be put in the State Tribunals as guardians of the National authority and interests."[13] At that point, Gouverneur Morris—usually one of Madison's staunch allies, but fiercely opposed to the negative—reentered the debate. Although he had spoken against a congressional veto just moments before,[14] he had not thought to make this point about judicial review. Morris jumped at Sherman's argument, stating that he was "more & more opposed to the negative" and that "[a] law that ought to be negatived will be set aside in the Judiciary departmt."[15] After some further discussion, the negative was voted down 7–3. Immediately thereafter, Luther Martin moved to incorporate into the Constitution the proposed supremacy clause from the defeated New Jersey Plan, and this was agreed to unanimously without further discussion.

Martin's decision to move this amendment after the negative had already been defeated is exceedingly curious. If, as Sherman and Morris had suggested, a legislative veto was unnecessary because judicial review was already implicit, why move after the negative had been voted down to add a provision explicitly ordering state judges to treat federal law as supreme? And why do so if you are Luther Martin and interested mostly in keeping any limits on state power as weak as possible?

Two reasons seem likely, both related to Martin's desire to ensure that the legislative veto was dead once and for all. First, some delegates were presumably willing to vote against Madison's negative only if they had assurances of an alternative check, even one generally regarded as weaker than the negative.[16] Some of these delegates, moreover, surely shared Madison's concern that state courts would not be eager to uphold national authority against the authority of their own legislatures; hence, the proposed clause "bound" state judges to give federal law priority. Second, adding the Supremacy Clause made explicit the authority to do something that might or might not have been implicit without it. Sherman, Morris, and a few others may have been confident that courts would exercise judicial review, but not everyone was so certain—and with good reason, given the novelty of the idea and the spotty record in the states. By adding the Supremacy Clause, Martin removed all doubts, again allaying the fears of others who wanted guarantees of an effective alternative. An express command for judges to prefer federal to state law answered the leading objection to judicial review, which was that judges had not been authorized by the people to make such decisions. From this point on, then, the delegates assumed the existence of judicial review over state laws in their deliberations.[17]

No similar decision was made to endorse judicial review of federal legislation. For some participants, it may have been the case that no decision was necessary. As we have seen, a few of the delegates believed that courts should exercise review, presumably for reasons like those offered by Iredell,[18] and they could also have assumed that courts would in fact do so. Yet whatever one's views on the former point, even the most sanguine proponent of a judicial check presumably would have recognized the uncertain status of the practice. This is why it made sense to include the Supremacy Clause as a way to ensure judicial review of state laws. No similar proposal was made, or even suggested, when it came to review of federal legislation, a failure made all the more striking by the fact that the Supremacy Clause had been added.

While this silence may seem puzzling at first, the Convention's inaction is intelligible in context. The device offered in the Virginia Plan to address concerns about federal legislation was a Council of Revision, which would have joined federal judges with the executive to review and possibly veto proposed laws (subject to being overridden by a supermajority in Congress).[19] The idea ran into trouble from the start, chiefly in the form of objections that it "involved an improper mixture of powers,"[20] and that judges would be biased in applying a law if they had "participated in its formation."[21] Elbridge Gerry suggested giving the revisionary power instead to the national executive alone, and it was in this connection that he made his comment about courts having "a sufficient check agst. encroachments on their own department by the exposition of the laws, which involved a power of deciding on their Constitutionality."[22] Despite protests from the likes of Wilson and Madison, who worried that the executive would be too weak to wield an effective veto without additional support, a purely executive check was approved by a substantial margin.[23]

The question of judicial involvement in the veto process was raised again on July 21, as the Convention was completing its formulation of general principles. James Wilson moved to reconsider the decision to limit the veto to the executive. Conceding that the proposition "had been made before, and failed," Wilson explained that he was nevertheless "so confirmed by reflection in the opinion of its utility, that he thought it incumbent on him to make another effort." A Council of Revision was needed, according to Wilson, because:

> [t]he Judiciary ought to have an opportunity of remonstrating agst projected encroachments on the people as well as on themselves. It had been said that the Judges, as expositors of the Laws would have an opportunity of defending their constitutional rights. There was weight in this observation; but this power of the Judges did not go far enough. Laws may be unjust, may be unwise, may be dangerous, may be destructive; and yet not be so unconstitutional as to justify the Judges in refusing to give them effect. Let them have a share in the Revisionary power, and they will have an opportunity of taking notice of these characters of a law, and of counteracting, by the weight of their opinions the improper views of the Legislature.[24]

The proposed Council was again defeated, this time after a somewhat fuller exchange in which a variety of arguments were offered for and against the idea.[25] During the course of the discussion, two other delegates came back to Wilson's point about judicial review. Opposing the Council, Luther Martin reiterated the objection that, because "the Constitutionality of laws . . . will come before the Judges in their proper official character," putting them on a Council of Revision would give them "a double negative."[26] Responding to Martin, George Mason repeated Wilson's rejoinder that, in their official character: "[The judges] could impede in one case only, the operation of laws. They could declare an unconstitutional law void. But with regard to every law however unjust oppressive or pernicious, which did not come plainly under this description, they would be under the necessity as Judges to give it a free course."[27] No one else is recorded as speaking to the issue, which was dropped without resolution. And since Wilson's motion was rejected, while no other motion was made pertaining to the role of judges, we are left uncertain what role, if any, judicial review was expected to play when it came to federal legislation.

On further reflection, this silence is less inexplicable than it may seem at first. Judicial review was not the question before the Convention. The question was how best to prevent the enactment of unwise and unconstitutional federal legislative measures. The answer was an executive veto. (And not just a veto, either. Additional checks on the risk of bad legislation included federalism, bicameralism, and the likelihood that "the best men in the Community would be comprised in the two branches of [Congress].")[28] Some delegates were afraid that the executive might be too weak, but a solid majority felt otherwise and were concerned not to involve judges in the lawmaking process. That settled, there was simply no need to say or do anything more.

In the course of discussing the veto, a few of the delegates had expressed the belief or hope that courts would also exercise judicial review. But unlike the question of federal supremacy over state laws, there was no need to decide what role the judiciary should play when it came to federal legislation. Some delegates might have favored judicial review, others might have opposed it, but most were now satisfied that they had already done what was needed to make the Constitution work.[29] Disagreements about the desirability or not of an additional judicial check were irrelevant and moot.

One might well ask why none of the proponents of judicial review thought to make a motion to add this power as well. Since no one did, we can only guess as to their reasons. One thing is certain, though: it was not because everyone, or even a majority, agreed that the power was necessarily implicit and so nothing needed to be said. An assumption that judicial review is somehow natural or that it automatically inheres in the judicial power would not be made until the nation had considerably more experience with the practice than was true in 1787. As with other checks, judicial review of federal legislation would have been separately discussed and expressly incorporated into the text had the delegates contemplated using it to enforce the Constitution—as they had done, for example, with respect to federal supremacy over state law. Why did no one seek something similar when it came to the constitutionality of federal legislation? It could be that even those who recognized the possibility of judicial review were not yet imagining a substantial or powerful enough check to make this worthwhile. Or they might have believed that any effort to add such a provision would fail, presumably defeated by a combination of delegates opposed to judicial review and delegates who did not want to invite needless controversy in getting the new Constitution ratified. Whatever the explanation, the power of courts to review federal legislation was left unaddressed.[30]

The Dog That Didn't Bark—and the One That Did

Thoughts expressed by the Framers behind closed doors in Philadelphia are ultimately of less interest than the public debate that took place over ratification. After all, this is what elevated the Constitution to the status of law of the land. "As the instrument came from [the Convention]," Madison was to observe a decade later, "it was nothing more than the draught of a plan, nothing but a dead letter, until life and validity were breathed into it by the voice of the people, speaking through the several State Conventions."[31] Understandings expressed during the discussions about whether to ratify, gathered from what was published in newspapers and pamphlets as well as from what was said in the state conventions, are what matter most.[32] Not surprisingly, the evidence from this quarter suggests that Americans did not suddenly discover the miracle that is judicial review.

In fact, the substance of the ratification debate was precisely what the experience of the 1780s should have led one to expect. A handful of participants saw a role for judicial review, though few of them imagined it as a powerful or important device and none seemed anxious to emphasize it. Others were opposed to the notion of judicial review, citing its possibility as one of the proposed Constitution's liabilities. The vast majority of participants were

still thinking in terms of popular constitutionalism and so focused on traditional popular and political means of enforcing the new charter. The notion
of judicial review seems never to have crossed their minds.

It is striking, for example, that only a single exchange on judicial review
can be described as anything other than cursory, that between Brutus and
Publius in the New York press. The Anti-Federalist Brutus sparked the
dispute by devoting three essays in the *New York Journal* to showing how
"nothing could have been better conceived to facilitate the abolition of the
state governments than the constitution of the judicial."[33] Blending the fal-
lacious with the prophetic, Brutus charged that, by conferring jurisdiction
on the Supreme Court to decide cases in "equity" as well as law, the Framers
had authorized the Justices to expound the Constitution "not only according
to the natural and ob[vious] meaning of the words, but also according to the
spirit and intention of it."[34] Add to that the Court's independent status and
the finality of its judgments, which meant that "[t]he power of this court is
in many cases superior to that of the legislature," together with the bias a
national body must be expected to hold in favor of the federal government,
and one could reliably predict that the Supreme Court would "extend the
limits of the general government gradually, and by insensible degrees."[35]

Alexander Hamilton answered for Publius in the now-famous *Federalist 78*.[36] Hamilton's essay is usually presented as staking out a thoroughly
modern position on judicial review. In fact, Hamilton was refuting Brutus's
suggestion that the Constitution conferred sweeping power on the courts by
instead defending the more limited power that had begun to find acceptance
in a few corners during the 1780s. Hamilton's argument thus followed (and
in most respects parroted) that of Iredell point for point. The chief difference, as Sylvia Snowiss has noted, was "in tone and emphasis," as Hamilton
"dropped Iredell's argumentativeness."[37]

Although Hamilton portrayed the case for judicial review as obvious and
uncontroversial, he also presented it in uncommonly strong language for the
time. He said at one point, for example, that constitutional limits could "be
preserved in practice *no other way* than through the medium of the courts
of justice"; and he dismissed a suggestion that Congress could be the constitutional judge of its own power by urging that "[i]t is far more rational to
suppose that the courts were *designed* to be an intermediate body between
the people and the legislature, in order, among other things, to keep the latter within the limits assigned to their authority."[38] Yet while comments such
as these appear to assign courts an important role, nothing Hamilton said
was incompatible with the accepted premises of popular constitutionalism,

which, as Iredell and others had already argued, made room for courts to act as the people's agent in checking legislative mistakes or abuses.

Hamilton appears to have edged closer toward sounding a modern note of judicial preeminence in observing that the "independence of the judges is equally requisite to guard the constitution and the rights of individuals from the effects of those ill humours which the arts of designing men . . . sometimes disseminate among the people themselves."[39] That the people could alter or abolish their fundamental charter, Hamilton explained, in no way supported allowing their representatives to violate it "whenever a momentary inclination happens to lay hold of a majority of their constituents incompatible with the provisions in the existing constitution." Unless and until properly amended, a constitution is "binding upon [the people] collectively, as well as individually; and no presumption, or even knowledge of their sentiments can warrant their representatives in a departure from it prior to such an act."[40] Judges had a duty to resist invasions of the constitution, in other words, even if these had been "instigated by the major voice of the community."

Once again Hamilton's reasoning was consistent with the theory and practice of popular constitutionalism. Everyone agreed that a constitution was binding, just as everyone agreed that legislators could not ignore or depart from one. Most people (meaning not just Federalists but also a great many Anti-Federalists) had learned from experience to fear what elected legislatures might do when overcome by "momentary inclinations" of the sort Hamilton mentioned. But rather than abandon republicanism or qualify popular constitutionalism, their solution was to slow politics down, to force greater deliberation by complicating the lawmaking process with a system of checks and balances along the lines sketched out by Madison in *Federalist 51*. The whole point was to preserve popular control of constitutional government by finding (in Madison's words) "a Republican remedy for the diseases most incident to Republican Government."[41]

Federalist 78 attempts to integrate courts into this process—a position that would emerge more clearly and find widespread support in the 1790s as "departmentalism." Judicial review was yet one more device with which to force popular reconsideration of possibly unconstitutional measures. It could be called into play in the relatively rare instances in which such measures got past both Houses of Congress and the Executive, but judicial interpretations were no more final and binding on the people than those of these other branches. Final interpretive authority always and necessarily remained in the community. Hence, Hamilton emphasized how the "dangerous innovations" that might be produced by transient majorities and that could be checked by judicial review "speedily give place to better information and more deliberate reflection."[42]

Could Hamilton have been staking out a still more extreme position, defending an idea of judicial supremacy that assigned courts the final word on constitutional interpretation while confining "the people's" role to amendment? Anything is possible, though this would have been an exceedingly impolitic position for the politically savvy and strategically-minded Publius to have taken. The most conservative wing of the Federalist party would eventually find its way to this position, but it would take until at least the mid-1790s and require additional provocation from the French Revolution and the rise of an opposition party in the United States. Perhaps Hamilton was out ahead of everyone else in this respect. Certainly it would not have been the first time (or the last). If so, however, Hamilton was indeed all alone, for no one else defended judicial review with an argument along these lines.

Whatever Hamilton's position, we can be fairly confident that it had no influence on ratification. This is because hardly anybody saw either *Federalist 78* or Brutus's essays during the campaign. Brutus was well regarded among a small circle of the most intellectual participants in ratification, but he was not widely circulated or read. Of Brutus's three essays on judicial review, two were not reprinted anywhere—not even in New York—while the third was reprinted only twice.[43] Publius's audience was hardly larger, the canonical status of *The Federalist* most definitely being a post-ratification phenomenon.[44] This is particularly true of *Federalist 78*, which was not included in the original newspaper series and first saw the light of day only upon publication of the second volume of *The Federalist* at the end of May 1788—too late to influence any ratifying convention except (possibly) that of New York, where the question of judicial review never came up.[45]

No one else discussed the nature, importance, or role of judicial review in anywhere near the same depth as Brutus and Hamilton. Indeed, only a handful of other Federalists mentioned the power at all.[46] In most instances, their references were too fleeting or obscure to attract attention. Fabius, for example, sought to quell fears of federal overreaching by showing that the Framers took "the strongest cautions against excesses":

In the *senate* the *sovereignties* of the several states will be *equally* represented; in *the house of representatives*, the *people* of the whole union will be *equally represented*; and in the *president*, and the federal independent *judges*, so much concerned in the execution of the laws, and in the determination of their constitutionality, the *sovereignties* of the several states and *the people* of the whole union, will be *conjointly* represented.[47]

In one or two instances, the reference to judicial review was more pointed and substantive, though in no case was it developed at length or presented as anything more than one among numerous safeguards. The most elaborate presentation of this sort came from James Wilson in one of his less celebrated speeches at the Pennsylvania Ratifying Convention. Wilson responded to Anti-Federal charges that the federal government would swallow the states by citing the protections afforded by separation of powers, bicameralism, the structure of the Senate, and the power of election. In the midst of this rebuttal, he added:

I say, under this Constitution, the legislature may be restrained, and kept within its prescribed bounds, by the interposition of the judicial department. This I hope, sir, to explain clearly and satisfactorily. I had occasion, on a former day, to state that the power of the Constitution was paramount to the power of the legislature, acting under that Constitution. For it is possible that the legislature, when acting in that capacity, may transgress the bounds assigned to it, and an act may pass, in the usual *mode*, notwithstanding that transgression; but when it comes to be discussed before the judges—when they consider its principles and find it to be incompatible with the superior power of the Constitution, it is their duty to pronounce it void.[48]

A few other speakers made the same claim, albeit less emphatically than Wilson. Rapidly ticking off responses to the many objections raised against the Constitution by Patrick Henry at the Virginia Ratifying Convention, John Marshall came to what he characterized as Henry's claim that "the Government of the United States [has] power to make laws on every subject." Not so, retorted Marshall, for federal lawmakers cannot go beyond their delegated powers. "If they were to make a law not warranted by any of the powers enumerated," Marshall continued, "it would be considered by the Judges as an infringement of the Constitution which they are to guard:—They would not consider such a law as coming under their jurisdiction.—They would declare it void."[49] Statements to the same effect were made by John Stevens, writing as "Americanus"; by Oliver Ellsworth in the Connecticut Ratifying Convention; and by Samuel Adams at the Massachusetts Convention.[50] In addition,

William Davie argued to the North Carolina Convention that federal courts would be able to prevent states from violating the specific prohibitions of Article I, section 10.[51]

We thus find a smattering of references to judicial review from some fifteen or so speakers (of whom one-third were Virginians, where judicial review had achieved the greatest acceptance). This, in itself, is not surprising. Given the national scope of the debate, it would have been unnatural had there not been at least a few references to the developing principle of review. What is extraordinary—particularly given the weight so many modern champions of judicial review place on the so-called original meaning—is that this paltry collection of citations exhausts the discussion.

Few issues in American history have engrossed public attention like the debate about whether to adopt the Constitution. For more than nine months, from the middle of September, 1787, until at least the following July, the public was "wholly employed in considering and animadverting upon the form of Government proposed by the late convention."[52] Writing to a friend overseas, one observer described how the Convention's handiwork "has put us all in an uproar:—Our public papers are full of attacks and justifications of the new system: And if you go into private companies, you hear scarcely anything else."[53] Yet in all the flood of pamphlets and essays and editorials that streamed from the presses, and in all the voluminous records of debate in the state ratifying conventions, there is no more than this handful of references to judicial review.

It is not as if the question of enforcing constitutional limits was not discussed. On the contrary, Anti-Federalists were convinced that the Constitution's restrictions would be porous and ephemeral, an indictment they pressed throughout the campaign. And because virtually every Anti-Federalist offered this threat as one of the best reasons to reject the Constitution (the absence of a Bill of Rights being the other), practically every Federalist was forced to refute the claim by showing how the Constitution would be enforced.

But how did Federalists think this would happen, if not by judicial review? By now, the answer should be obvious: politics, the kind of politics that we have seen defined popular constitutionalism throughout the seventeenth and eighteenth centuries. When Anti-Federalists insisted that Congress would disregard its limits, Federalists invariably responded that any effort to do so would run smack into opposition from the people. Let Congress try to misuse its powers, they said time and again, and federal lawmakers would find themselves facing formidable popular resistance—via elections, juries, popular outcries, or, in the unlikely event that all these failed, by more violent forms of opposition.

Arguments along this line dominated all others in both pervasiveness and emphasis.[54] Scarcely any Federalist responding to charges of federal over-reaching failed to make a point about popular control, and other arguments (such as references to the Constitution's structure) were offered as subsidiary elements of this more fundamental reply. Even those sympathetic to judicial review emphasized politics as the primary, essential, and indispensable safeguard. Drawing on his experience in state government, Edmund Pendleton acknowledged to the Virginia Ratifying Convention that some constitutional violations had occurred in the state, adding:

> An instance has been mentioned already, where [constitutional rules] have not been attended to. . . . My brethren in that department (*the judicial*) felt great uneasiness in their minds, to violate the Constitution by such a law. They have prevented the operation of some unconstitutional acts. Notwithstanding those violations, I rely upon the principles of the Government—that it will produce its own reform, by the responsibility resulting from frequent elections.—We are finally safe while we preserve the representative character.[55]

John Steele of North Carolina likewise mentioned judicial review in conjunction with, and as a subordinate adjunct, to the more basic and fundamental popular check:

> If the Congress make laws inconsistent with the Constitution, independent judges will not uphold them, nor will the people obey them. A universal resistance will ensue. In some countries, the arbitrary disposition of rulers may enable them to overturn the liberties of the people; but in a country like this, where every man is his own master, and where almost every man is a freeholder, and has the right of election, the violation of a constitution will not be passively permitted.[56]

The vast majority of speakers relied on the same logic without tying their arguments to or even mentioning courts. The national government will not violate the Constitution, a New Jersey correspondent wrote, because "[e]very two years the people may change their Representatives if they please; and they certainly would please to change those who would act with so much baseness and treachery."[57] An exasperated George Washington complained to his nephew Bushrod (a future Justice of the Supreme Court) about the stubborn unwillingness of Anti-Federalists to face this axiomatic point:

> The power under the Constitution will always be in the People. It is entrusted for certain defined purposes, and for a certain limited period, to representatives of their own chusing; and whenever it is executed contrary to their Interest, or not agreeable to their wishes, their Servants can, and undoubtedly will be, recalled.—It is agreed on all hands that no government can be well administered without powers—yet the instant these are delegated, altho' those who are entrusted with the administration are no more than the creatures of the people, act as it were but for a day, and are amenable for every false step they take, they are, from the moment they receive it, set down as tyrants—their natures, one would conceive from this, immediately changed—and that they have no other disposition but to oppress.[58]

Particularly with a proper scheme of separation of powers in place, the basic republican nature of American society would provide its own security from abuse. "[I]f we cannot entrust [the necessary powers of government] in the hands of our own citizens," wrote Publicola, "persons of our own choice, and whom we may remove at stated, and short periods, we must be contented to live without any effective government."[59] Comments along these lines were legion.[60]

By way of illustration, we may consider the debate over federalism, or, as it was framed at the time, over "consolidation," viz, whether the Constitution was calculated to annihilate state sovereignty and "ultimately to make the states one consolidated government."[61] The issue is worth special consideration not only because of its present-day importance but also because it was "the main substantive issue" for both sides at the time, a question raised and argued at every turn and in every forum.[62]

As with every other issue, the debate about federalism focused almost exclusively on popular and political checks. Quite a few Federalists emphasized the politics built into constitutional structure, arguing that state sovereignty was safe because "the general government depends on the state legislatures for its very existence"[63]—an argument familiar to lawyers today from Herbert Wechsler's famous essay on "the political safeguards of federalism."[64] In contrast to his perfunctory treatment of judicial review, James Wilson developed this argument at length in the Pennsylvania Ratifying Convention.[65] The inference that state governments are threatened was "rather unnatural," Wilson noted dryly, inasmuch as no government would endanger that "upon the very existence of which its own existence depends." Pointing to the House of Representatives, Wilson argued that the Framers had taken care to ensure that "even the popular branch of the general government cannot exist unless the governments of the states continue in existence" by leaving control over "the important subject of giving suffrage" in the hands of state legislators. As for the Senate, Wilson remarked sardonically, "[i]n the system before you, . . . those tyrants that are to devour the legislatures of the states, are to be chosen by the state legislatures themselves. Need anything more be said on this subject?" The Electoral College was similarly arranged to protect states, by requiring that the President be chosen "by electors appointed in the different states, in such manner as the [state] legislature shall direct."

Wilson's long speech is but one example among many, as speaker after speaker made the same points in response to Anti-Federal charges that state sovereignty was threatened—all without mentioning courts or judges or judicial review.[66] Note, too, that while many Federalists followed Wilson in describing an array of devices that guaranteed states a voice in the national government, most appreciated that the Senate had been particularly designed with this concern in mind. A considerable number thus singled out the upper chamber to highlight its role in safeguarding the interests of state governments.[67]

Yet here, too, the reliance on structure turns out on closer inspection to be nothing more than an application of a less formal but more basic popular check.[68] With respect to federalism, moreover, the argument from popular enforcement was further refined in recognition of the special role state politicians could play by drawing on their inherent political strength to rouse public support against unconstitutional federal measures. As Edmund Randolph explained to the Virginia Ratifying Convention, if Congress "attempt . . . an usurpation, the influence of the State Governments, will stop it in the bud of hope. I know this Government will be cautiously watched. The smallest assumption of power will be sounded in alarm to the people, and followed by bold and active opposition."[69]

Publius developed this line of reasoning at length. Using *The Federalist* to gauge the perceptions of other participants in the Founding can be problematic, and it is often misleading to rely too heavily on this one source. On almost every issue, Publius's reasoning was more complex, his logic more novel and striking, than that of anyone else. In some instances, Madison's and Hamilton's arguments were simply over the heads of other Federalists.[70]

But not when it came to federalism. On this issue, what Publius had to say was no different from what every other Federalist was saying; it was simply more cogently articulated.

References to federalism are pervasive in *The Federalist*, but Publius's principal discussion of the topic is in a series of eight essays, numbers 39–46, all written by Madison.[71] Madison began his investigation by showing in *Federalist 39* how the design of the new system was neither "national" nor "federal" (in the eighteenth-century sense, which today we would call confederal), but was rather "a composition of both."[72] Five essays followed in which Madison recounted the reasons for bestowing each of the powers conferred on the national government. Finally, in *Federalist 45*, Madison reached the critical question: whether, assuming "no one of the powers transferred to the federal Government is unnecessary or improper, . . . the whole mass of them will be dangerous to the portion of authority left in the several states."[73] Madison's answer, in this essay and the next one, epitomizes basic Federalist convictions and illuminates how the Founders imagined this new system of federalism would work.[74]

The main reason states were safe in the new system, Madison conjectured, was simple. They would always have the political wherewithal easily to defeat the national government in any test of wills:

> The State Governments will have the advantage of the federal Government, whether we compare them in respect to the immediate dependence of the one or the other; to the weight of personal influence which each side will possess; to the powers respectively vested in them; to the predilection and probable support of the people; to the disposition and faculty of resisting and frustrating the measures of each other.[75]

In *Federalist 46*, Madison made explicit what is here only implicit—that because efforts by either side to extend its reach would depend on the ability of officials at each level to gain popular support, the Constitution's allocation of authority was controlled by the people themselves:

> Notwithstanding the different modes in which [the state and federal governments] are appointed, we must consider both of them, as substantially dependent on the great body of the citizens of the United States. . . . The Foederal and State Governments are in fact but different agents and trustees of the people, instituted with different powers, and designated for different purposes. The adversaries of the Constitu-

tion seem to have lost sight of the people altogether in their reasonings on this subject; and to have viewed these different establishments, not only as mutual rivals and enemies, but as uncontrouled by any common superior in their efforts to usurp the authorities of each other. These gentlemen must here be reminded of their error. They must be told that the ultimate authority, wherever the derivative may be found, resides in the people alone; and that it will not depend merely on the comparative ambition or address of the different governments, whether either, or which of them, will be able to enlarge its sphere of jurisdiction at the expence of the other. Truth no less than decency requires, that the event in every case, should be supposed to depend on the sentiments and sanction of their common constituents.[76]

With this fundamental postulate established, Madison dedicated the remainder of the two essays to demonstrating the states' greater capacity to protect themselves through appeals to the "common superior." No mention was made of courts or judicial review, and only a single paragraph was spent describing the states' role in the composition of the federal government.[77] Instead, Madison devoted almost the entirety of both essays to cataloguing the states' political advantages "with regard to the predilection and support of the people."[78]

These advantages are, he said, considerable. To begin with, the states will employ many more officials than the federal government, and the relationships these state officials form with their constituents will give them substantial influence in the event of a contest with the federal government.[79] Adding to this influence is the different nature of the powers exercised by the respective governments. It was in this connection that Madison made his oft-quoted remark about how "[t]he powers delegated by the proposed Constitution to the Federal Government, are few and defined" while those that remain to the states "are numerous and indefinite."[80] His point was less to appease anxieties about whether the federal government was already too powerful than it was to establish the basis for his claim that "the first and most natural attachment of the people will be to the governments of their respective States."[81] Because the limited powers delegated to the national government would "be exercised principally on external objects" and were likely to be important only "in times of war and danger," the operations of the federal government would rarely touch the lives of most citizens.[82] "The powers reserved to the several States," in contrast, "will extend to all the objects, which, in the ordinary course of affairs, concern the lives, liberties and properties of the people; and the internal order, improvement, and prosperity of the State."[83] And because state officials would thus be responsible for "all the more domestic, and personal interests of the people,"[84] it would be

> [w]ith the affairs of [the state governments that] the people will be more familiarly and minutely conversant. And with the members of these, will a greater proportion of the people have ties of personal acquaintence and friendship, and of family and party attachments; on the side of these therefore the popular bias, may well be expected most strongly to incline.[85]

Given these advantages, it was fatuous to say that the states had anything to fear from Congress. But suppose that Congress were to overreach, Madison queried, suppose it were to stretch its powers "beyond the due limits."[86] The states "would still have the advantage in the means of defeating such encroachments."[87] The greater sympathy of the people for their state governments, in conjunction with the superior capacity of state officials to rally support, would ensure that Congress failed:

> [S]hould an unwarranted measure of the Foederal Government be unpopular in particular States, which would seldom fail to be the case, or even a warrantable measure be so, which may sometimes be the case, the means of opposition to it are powerful and at hand. The disquietude of the people, their repugnance and perhaps refusal to co-operate with the officers of the Union, the frowns of the executive magistracy of the State, the embarrassments created by legislative devices, which would often be added on such occasions, would oppose in any State difficulties not to be despised; would form in a large State very serious impediments, and where the sentiments of several adjoining States happened to be in unison, would present obstructions which the Foederal Government would hardly be willing to encounter.[88]

Nor did measures such as these exhaust the states' political resources in combating federal usurpation, for state officials could coordinate their efforts to force Congress to repeal the offending legislation:

> But ambitious encroachments of the Foederal Government . . . would not excite the opposition of a single State or of a few States only. They would be signals of a general alarm. Every Government would espouse

the common cause. A correspondence would be opened. Plans of resistance would be concerted. One spirit would animate and conduct the whole. The same combination in short would result from an apprehension of the foederal, as was produced by the dread of a foreign yoke; and unless the projected innovations should be voluntarily renounced, the same appeal to a trial of force would be made in the one case, as was made in the other.[89]

In truth, Madison was quick to add, matters never would reach the extreme of armed conflict because, unlike in the showdown with Britain, the two contending sides were controlled by the same master: the people of the United States. The suggestion of military confrontation was a "visionary supposition," not to be taken seriously. "[W]hat would be the contest in the case we are supposing?" Madison wondered, "Who would be the parties? A few representatives of the people, would be opposed to the people themselves; or rather one set of representatives would be contending against thirteen sets of representatives, with the whole body of their common constituents on the side of the latter."[90]

Of course, the results of such a clash, should it somehow occur, could never be in doubt. As "[t]hose who are best acquainted with the late successful resistance of this country against the British arms" would attest, the states and their multitudinous militia would easily prevail.[91] But fretting about this sort of nonsense was pointless, a waste of time. The states had nothing to fear because the regulation and control of political power at both levels of government is in the people's hands. The point was decisive:

> Either the mode in which the Foederal Government is to be constructed will render it sufficiently dependent on the people, or it will not. On the first supposition, it will be restrained by that dependence from forming schemes obnoxious to their constituents. On the other supposition it will not possess the confidence of the people, and its schemes of usurpation will be easily defeated by the State Governments; who will be supported by the people.[92]

Closely tracking the argument of his co-author Madison, Alexander Hamilton likewise reminded the New York Ratifying Convention why "the natural strength and resources of state governments . . . will ever give them an important superiority over the general government":

If we compare the nature of their different powers, or the means of popular influence which each possesses, we shall find the advantage entirely on the side of the states. This consideration, important as it is, seems to have been little attended to. . . . Whenever, therefore, Congress shall mediate any infringement of the state constitutions, the great body of the people will naturally take part with their domestic representatives. Can the general government withstand such a united opposition? Will the people suffer themselves to be stripped of their privileges? Will they suffer their legislatures to be reduced to a shadow and a name? The idea is shocking to common sense.[93]

The result, Hamilton said, and many, many Federalists reiterated, was "a complicated, irresistible check, which must ever support the existence and importance of the state governments."[94]

That the Founders expected constitutional limits to be enforced through politics and by the people rather than in courts is hardly surprising. Their history, their political theory, and their actual experience all taught that popular pressure was the only sure way to bring an unruly authority to heel. We should not forget that the Founding took place against the background of the Glorious Revolution and the American Revolution, not the civil rights movement. The colonial experience resisting king and Parliament served as the model from which the Founders constructed their theories, and the Revolution itself, beginning with the Stamp Act protests, provided their blueprint for opposing a government that exceeded its constitutional authority. This is why courts and judicial review were so rarely featured during ratification: members of the Founding generation had a different paradigm in mind. The idea of depending on judges to stop a legislature that abused its power never even occurred to the vast majority of participants in the debates.

* * *

Given that most of the Framers and Founders were not thinking about judicial review, it may not be clear at the end of the day just what the few who had thought about it expected to happen. We should keep in mind, however, that even those who wanted or expected courts to review legislation were thinking about the courts' role in a world of popular constitutionalism. If judicial enforcement was implicit in the Constitution, it was not because the Constitution was the kind of law that courts were normally responsible for overseeing or because it was a kind of law that judges were uniquely qualified to interpret and enforce. The Constitution was still fundamental law, made by the people to govern the governors. If judicial review was to occur, it would be on the terms described by men like Iredell and Varnum: as a "political-legal" act, a substitute for popular resistance, required by the people's command to ignore laws that were ultra vires—though only when the unconstitutionality of a law was clear beyond dispute.

4

Courts, as Well as Other Departments, Are Bound by That Instrument

ACCEPTING JUDICIAL REVIEW

The United States experienced a run of dizzying economic growth in the 1790s. Propelled by war in Europe, demand for American produce and raw materials skyrocketed.[1] Profiting as well from Alexander Hamilton's brilliant stewardship of the Treasury Department, not to mention the advantage accruing to the United States as possessor of the world's largest neutral fleet, the value of domestic exports more than tripled, while the value of re-exports increased by fiftyfold and earnings from the carrier trades quadrupled. New wealth seeped into every sector of the economy and every region of the country as demand for skilled and unskilled labor mushroomed and wages soared.[2]

All the more remarkable in the face of this unparalleled good fortune, the 1790s were also a time of "vicious party warfare" and "almost hysterical fear."[3] Federalists delivered precisely the kind of good government they had promised during the ratification campaign, yet domestic political conflict achieved a level of ferocity exceeded only by the Civil War in its paranoid and frenzied overtones. Reassessing these years in 1813, Thomas Jefferson and John Adams disagreed about which side bore the greater blame, but concurred that "terror" and "terrorism" were apt descriptions of what had transpired.[4]

The source of all this turmoil lay in an escalating series of political and constitutional crises, as men who had collaborated for nearly two decades to create a stable Union suddenly discovered they had profoundly different ideas about what to do with it. Along the way, the Federalists of the late 1780s saw all their careful plans for bringing politics under their control fail and learned that almost everything they had thought about how the new government would function was wrong. Enlarging the sphere of the Republic did not produce a filtration of talent, did not "extract from the mass of Society the purest and noblest characters" to serve in government.[5] Nor did it frustrate the operation of factions, as political parties of a kind the Founding generation never imagined (and still did not want) rapidly began to form.[6] An important impetus for this development was the unexpectedly dominant role assumed by the Chief Magistrate, whose cabinet also upended assumptions about separation of powers by using "the art and address of ministerial management" to control Congress's agenda.[7] Federalism, too, failed to work as expected. Rather than suspiciously eyeing each other from opposite sides of a natural divide of ambition and institutional interest, state and federal officials were absorbed into the emerging parties and worked together or in opposition based on party rather than institutional affiliation.[8] The nation survived, barely, due in no small part to the pragmatism and flexibility of its Founding Fathers, who proved to be better politicians than political philosophers and who found ways to make the Constitution work even amidst their bitter conflicts and despite their earlier miscalculations. (A fact that ought to make one wonder why any sensible person, even a lawyer, would privilege the speculative writings of the 1780s over the hard-earned experience of subsequent decades.)

The controversies of these years are familiar, having been recounted in detail by many fine historians.[9] Each new crisis raised or was entwined with constitutional questions. All were fought with the tools of popular constitutionalism, though these were modified some as the decade proceeded and traditional forms of politics were absorbed by the developing parties. None of the major constitutional issues made its way into court.[10] In a decade noteworthy for its many constitutional crises, the validity of a federal tax on carriages was, literally, the most momentous constitutional question to be faced by the Supreme Court.[11] A handful of other constitutional issues made their way to the High Court during these years, of which the most significant was the Justices' decision to uphold jurisdiction in an action by a private party against the state of Georgia.[12] The stir this created led to the adoption of the Eleventh Amendment a few years later. The question of federal common law was also controversial in the 1790s, though the controversy as it emerged partly involved fears that, if the common law was available as a source of federal law, then Congress could alter it (as federal legislators attempted to do in the Sedition Act). Hence, the focus of political concern centered as much on the behavior of Congress as that of courts—though courts too became a sore point for Republicans. In any event, the role of judges remained a peripheral matter until the end of the decade, when certain federal (and Federalist) judges made the mistake of too eagerly promoting prosecutions under the Sedition Act. It was a mistake for which the Republicans would make them pay after Jefferson's election.

"A Matter of High Gratification to Every Republican and Friend of Liberty"

Though federal courts remained mostly on the sidelines during the major battles of the Federalist era, it was not as if nothing happened to them. But where the 1790s were a time of tremendous revision and reformation for other organs of the federal government, they were mainly years of consolidation for the judiciary—at least with respect to judicial review, as the controversial new practice began to find more widespread acceptance. In contrast to the handful of cases in the first decade after independence, the second decade produced some twenty cases in the state courts in which at least one judge asserted the courts' power to invalidate a statute. There were also a dozen or so cases in the new federal circuit courts, plus perhaps another half dozen or more in the Supreme Court.[13]

Some of these cases provoked criticism, but nothing compared to the 1780s. By way of illustration, consider the controversy surrounding *Hayburn's Case*, in which federal judges for the first time questioned the constitutionality of an act of Congress. Under the Invalid Pensions Act, adopted in March 1792, injured veterans could apply for benefits to their state's federal circuit court, which was comprised of a district court judge joined by two Supreme Court Justices "riding circuit." The circuit court was supposed to determine whether an applicant was eligible (that is, whether the alleged disability was due to injuries sustained in the war) and to submit its findings in writing to the Secretary of War. The Secretary was authorized to review the court's determination and to withhold payment if he had "cause to suspect imposition or mistake."[14]

Within just a few months, all three federal circuit courts—comprising every Supreme Court Justice—had questioned the Act's constitutionality on separation-of-powers grounds, objecting that non-judicial duties had been assigned to federal judges acting in their judicial capacity.[15] Significantly, and still more evidence of the persistence of popular constitutionalism, none of these courts exercised judicial review in the context of deciding a case or ruling on an application. Instead, all three chose to proceed as the Virginia Court of Appeals had done in its "Respectful Remonstrance" of 1788: by writing formal letters of protest addressed to the appropriate political official.[16] In this instance, that official was President Washington because, as the judges of the Middle Circuit explained, "[t]o you it officially belongs to 'take care that the laws' of the United States 'be faithfully executed.'"[17] A subsequent effort by Attorney General Edmund Randolph to force a decision from the Supreme Court was first rebuffed on procedural grounds and then delayed while Congress solved the problem with new legislation. There was, as a result, no formal decision from the Supreme Court declaring a federal statute unconstitutional. But the views expressed by the Justices in their letters—as well as the refusal of some to proceed under the Act[18]—were publicly known, and the matter attracted attention both inside and outside of Congress.[19]

Many disapproved, but their reactions were surprisingly mild. Fisher Ames reported that the judges' actions were "generally censured as indiscreet and erroneous."[20] William Vans Murray wrote that "without entering on th[e] great question" whether a court should ever refuse to enforce a properly enacted law, "[i]t seems pretty generally admitted that the Judges chose rather a singular occasion—as it is merely a personal duty which they avoid by the exercise of the right."[21]

Newspaper opinion was divided. The pro-Administration *Gazette of the United States* adopted a neutral stance, observing only that "[i]t might be arrogant to express a doubt whether the opinion [the judges] have expressed be sound," while plaintively "hop[ing] that the invalids will not be neglected."[22] The opposition *National Gazette*, in the meantime, had nothing but praise for the judges, calling their actions a "matter of high gratification to every republican and friend of liberty."[23] The *General Advertiser* recorded only that "the novelty of the case produced a variety of opinions."[24] But no one was heard shrieking about a usurpation of power, and there were no calls for anyone's impeachment, at least none that were taken seriously. One irritated supporter of the judges, who complained in the *General Advertiser* about "high-fliers, in and out of Congress" who "talk of nothing but impeachment! impeachment! impeachment!" was answered the very next day by "Camden," who insisted this was "not true" while also wondering why anyone would assume that three circuit judges were more capable than Congress at interpreting the Constitution.[25]

More indicative of the new mood was the reaction to the 1792 decision in *Champion & Dickason v. Casey*,[26] in which a federal circuit court for the first time invalidated a state law on Contract Clause grounds—in this instance, a Rhode Island law retroactively extending the time to pay a debt. In sharp contrast to *Trevett v. Weeden*, not only was there no public outcry, but the Rhode Island legislature resolved that "[i]n conformity to [the] decision of the Circuit Court," in the future it "would not grant to any individual an exemption from arrests and attachments for his private debts, for any term of time."[27] Similarly, when a federal circuit court in Connecticut struck down a state statute depriving British creditors of interest accrued during the war, its actions were praised as giving "general satisfaction,"[28] and one newspaper hoped that the law struck down "might never rise again in this world to our shame, or the world to come to our confusion."[29] One should not exaggerate the degree of change: very few laws were actually struck down.[30] But attitudes were definitely changing.

Particularly telling in this regard were the deliberations in Congress, which attest to the widening acceptance of the possibility and rightness of judicial review as an element of the constitutional system.[31] A lengthy debate in the House of Representatives over the President's removal power in June 1789 generated considerable discussion of the courts' role. There was a great deal of ambiguity and confusion about the scope of judicial review—with a broad range of theories and understandings represented—but most speakers accepted or assumed its existence.[32] This was true throughout the decade. In his first long speech explaining the reasoning behind a Bill of Rights, James Madison picked up on a remark made to him in a letter from Jefferson and argued that, if certain rights were incorporated into the Constitution, "independent tribunals of justice will consider themselves in a peculiar manner the guardians of those rights."[33] And in protesting the willingness of some members of the House of Representatives to take up a Quaker petition on slavery, Georgia Representative Abraham Baldwin declared himself without fear that the House could interfere with the South's peculiar institution because, even if such a bill got past the Senate and the President, it would still need "the approbation of the Supreme Court of the United States . . . probably one of the most respectable Courts on earth."[34] During the famous debate over Hamilton's Bank Bill, a number of speakers on both sides of the question referred to the judiciary's power to review the constitutionality of the law.[35] Similar remarks were made during debates on a variety of other matters as well, including the Post Office Bill, the Carriage Tax Bill, the Foreign Intercourse Bill, and the Sedition Act.[36]

As political divisions sharpened and grew bitter, first one side then the other might opportunistically invoke or oppose the authority of the Supreme Court to invalidate particular legislation. But acceptance of the Court's general power to examine the constitutionality of laws was at all times, if not uncontroversial, at least acknowledged. It was only at the close of the decade, after Republicans learned what a determined Federalist bench could do with the Sedition Act, that some of Jefferson's supporters began to rethink the practice more globally, though even then seldom to the point of denying the propriety of review altogether. A few of the most radical Republicans questioned the legitimacy of judicial review in any form during the debate over repeal of the Judiciary Act of 1801,[37] but most were content to assert the inferiority and subordination of any judicial check to politics, leaving courts free to dare to exercise review with a threat of impeachment hanging over their heads.[38] As one Representative put it, "although [refusing to enforce unconstitutional laws] is a right of which every officer of the United States, as such, is constitutionally possessed, for the due exercise of this, as also of all other such rights, he is responsible. He is not vested with a right to do wrong."[39]

"Do Actually Decide on Behalf of the People"

Modern commentators often seem surprised at the volume of evidence supporting judicial review before *Marbury*, as well as baffled by the apparent absence of significant controversy.[40] They should not be. For what achieved acceptance in these years was not new; nor was it what we think of today as judicial review. What achieved acceptance in the 1790s was the theory of review formulated by men like James Iredell in the 1780s. Representatives in Congress might prattle on about the power of courts to do this or that, thinking only of the bill in front of them and whether they liked it or not. But judges tended to be more circumspect in explaining and acting on their newfound authority, and the practice as it actually emerged in the courts closely tracked the model articulated in the years leading up to the adoption of the Federal Constitution—a model whose defining characteristics were thoroughly grounded in popular constitutionalism. Courts exercising judicial review in the 1790s made no claims of special or exclusive responsibility for interpreting the Constitution. They justified their refusal to enforce laws as a "political-legal" act on behalf of the people, a responsibility required by their position as the people's faithful agents. Judicial review was a substitute for popular action, a device to maintain popular sovereignty without the need for civil unrest. It was, moreover, a power to be employed cautiously, only where the unconstitutionality of a law was clear beyond doubt—though in making these determinations judges did not confine themselves strictly to the text but drew on well-established principles of the customary constitution as well.

James Wilson's "Lectures on Law" of 1791, among the decade's most significant scholarly treatments of judicial review, illustrate this conception. Given in honor of his appointment as a law professor at the College of Pennsylvania, Justice Wilson had grand ambitions for these inaugural lectures, which were delivered to an audience of notables that included both the President and Vice President of the United States. Wilson wanted nothing less than to produce a complete philosophy of American law, grounded in psychology and theology as well as jurisprudence.[41] The resulting lectures, which were published only posthumously, did not live up to these high aspirations. There are moments of real brilliance, but Wilson's analysis is uneven in quality, often pedantic, and occasionally quite strange.

Wilson drifted into a discussion of judicial review near the end of a lecture comparing the constitutions of the United States and Great Britain. Despite his stature as a Justice on the first Supreme Court, not to mention his important role in framing and ratifying the Constitution, Wilson's argument for judicial review has attracted far less attention than Hamilton's better known *Federalist 78* or even Iredell's newspaper essay. This is probably due partly to the failure of Wilson's lectures generally and partly to posterity's inexplicable neglect of this crucially important Founder. But the explanation could also be that Wilson mainly regurgitated Hamilton's and Iredell's arguments, adding little or nothing that was new.

For Wilson, as for these earlier writers, judicial review was not a consciously crafted feature of the Constitution so much as an accidental, if fortunate, by-product of its status as supreme law. Courts were not specially charged with interpreting or enforcing the Constitution, but neither could they ignore it. "The business and the design of the judicial power is, to administer justice according to the law of the land," and the law of the land necessarily included the Constitution: "that supreme law" to which "every other power must be inferiour and subordinate."[42] Courts became involved in constitutional interpretation and enforcement not because the Constitution was ordinary law within their special province, but because judges were no less obligated to respect the Constitution's commands than any other institution or citizen.

Like Hamilton, Wilson made his point by analogy to a conflict of laws, though where Hamilton posited a choice between an earlier and a later law, Wilson used two contradictory laws. "According to two contradictory rules," he observed, "justice, in the nature of things, cannot possibly be administered."[43] It followed that if both rules were to "come regularly before the court, for its decision on their operation and validity," one of them "must, of necessity, give place to the other."[44] And if the two rules were the Constitution and a statute "manifestly repugnant to some part of [it]," it was obvious which rule this had to be:

> The supreme power of the United States has given one rule: a subordinate power in the United States has given a contradictory rule: the former is the law of the land: as a necessary consequence the latter is void, and has no operation. In this manner it is the right and it is the duty of a court of justice, under the constitution of the United States, to decide.[45]

Like Iredell, Wilson emphasized that judges could not do otherwise without acting illegally themselves. "If that constitution be infringed by one [department]," he urged, "it is no reason that the infringement should be abetted, though it is strong reason that it should be discountenanced and declared void by the other."[46] Reflecting the same pragmatism as Iredell, Wilson celebrated "[t]he effects of this salutory regulation," a fortuitous means to secure the "bounds of the legislative power" by rendering congressional transgressions "vain and fruitless."

Wilson's is one of a handful of extrajudicial treatments of judicial review in the 1790s. Yet if scholarly analysis was rare, a surprising number of judges (surprising, at least, by comparison to the 1780s) chose to address judicial review in written opinions. Of these, the opinions in *Kamper v. Hawkins* were by far the best known and most influential in the years before *Marbury v. Madison.*[47] *Kamper* was part of a prolonged farce over court reform that played itself out in Virginia during the 1780s and 1790s. Having botched its response to the judges' "Respectful Remonstrance" of 1788, the Virginia legislature kept searching for cheap ways to staff and run a new district court. In 1789, as part of a comprehensive package of reforms, it enacted legislation giving district court judges "the same power of granting injunctions . . . as is now had and exercised by the judge of the high court of chancery."[48] The validity of this grant of power came before the General Court in 1793, which ruled unanimously that the legislature had acted improperly. In a sign of the changing times, on this iteration the court expressed its views in the context of a case—through judicial review—rather than seeking relief by appealing directly to the public, as it had done five years earlier.

Writing seriatim, four of the five judges rested their decisions on constitutional grounds, holding that the legislature could not assign the same person functions of more than one judicial office.[49] Different opinions highlighted different themes developed by writers in the 1780s. St. George Tucker emphasized the binding effect of a constitution on every agent of the people. The constitution is, he said, "the voice of the people themselves, proclaiming to the world their resolution . . . to institute such a government, as, in their own opinion, was most likely to produce peace, happiness, and safety to the individual, as well as to the community."[50] It is "the first law of the land" and "a rule to all the departments of the government, to the judiciary *as well as to the legislature.*"[51] As the first law of the land, moreover, "whatsoever is contradictory thereto, is *not* the law of the land."[52] It is void, not law at all—a fact every department is duty-bound to acknowledge in the course of doing business, judges no less than anyone else: "Now since it is the province of the legislature to make, and of the executive to enforce obedience to the laws, the duty of expounding must be exclusively vested in the judiciary. But how can any just exposition be made, *if that which is the supreme law of the land be withheld from their view?*"[53]

Spencer Roane's opinion laid out the pragmatic basis for acting, namely, to provide a peaceful means of securing the supreme authority of the people. Roane agreed with Tucker that it was illogical to say that judges must blind themselves to constitutional considerations. "In expounding laws," he observed, "the judiciary considers *every* law which relates to the subject: would you have them to shut their eyes against that law which is of the highest authority of any, or against a part of that law, which either by its words or by its spirit, denies to any but the people the power to change it?"[54] More than just illogical, the proposition was foolish, for it would remove the institution most capable of supplying an orderly resolution to conflicts between the people and their governors. Reiterating an argument made by the North Carolina court in *Bayard v. Singleton*, Roane insisted that the judges are "not only the proper, but a perfectly disinterested tribunal" who "do actually decide on behalf of the people" in resolving what "is in fact a controversy between the legislature and the people."[55]

John Tyler was of a like mind, though he emphasized the need for judicial review if judges were not to act illegally themselves. The constitution is "the great contract of the people," and it binds all three branches equally to ensure that it is "faithfully and rightly executed."[56] The legislature acts illegally when it enacts laws that violate the constitution, and judges who enforce such laws become party to the same illegal act: "To be made an agent, therefore, for the purpose of violating the constitution, I cannot consent to.—As a citizen I should complain of it; as a public servant, filling an office in one of the great departments, I should be a traitor to my country to do it."[57] Tyler returned to the point in the conclusion of his opinion, this time setting it on more personal grounds as the act not of a judge, but of a citizen who believed in the importance of the constitution: "To conclude, I do declare that I will not hold an office, which I believe to be unconstitutional; that I will not be made a fit agent, to assist the legislature in a violation of this sacred letter; that I form this opinion from the conviction I feel that I am free to think, speak, and act, as other men do upon so great a question."[58] At the same time, Tyler cautioned, judges must be careful in taking it upon themselves to disparage what the legislature had done. "[T]he violation must be plain and clear, or there might be danger of the judiciary preventing the operation of laws which might be productive of much public good."[59]

Kamper provided the single most elaborate discussion of judicial review in the 1790s, but the opinions of other courts were similar in both tone and reasoning. If there was any respect in which *Kamper* was unrepresentative, it was that other judges took even greater pains to emphasize the importance of limiting judicial intervention to laws whose unconstitutionality was clear (an argument made in *Kamper* only by Judge Tyler).[60] The federal courts were particularly insistent on this point, though state courts routinely noted it as well.[61] James Iredell recorded Justice Wilson and Judge Peters agreeing on circuit in *United States v. Ravara* that "tho an Act of Congress plainly contrary to the Constitution was void, yet no such construction should be given in a doubtful case."[62] Justice Chase similarly announced in *Calder v. Bull* that "if I ever exercise the jurisdiction [to review legislation,] I will not decide *any law to be void, but in a very clear case,*"[63] reiterating a point he had made previously in *Hylton v. United States.*[64] Bushrod Washington said much the same thing in *Cooper v. Telfair*, noting that "[t]he presumption, indeed, must always be in favour of the validity of laws, if the contrary is not clearly demonstrated."[65] William Paterson concurred, observing that "to authorise this Court to pronounce any law void, it must be a clear and unequivocal breach of the constitution, not a doubtful and argumentative application."[66] The Supreme Court was as good as its word, too, reaching to uphold a federal tax law in *Hylton v. United States*[67] and generally showing great reluctance to find even state laws unconstitutional.[68]

Hylton is particularly interesting in this respect, inasmuch as the Washington Administration trumped up the case for the sole purpose of obtaining a judicial decree that a federal statute was constitutional.[69] Worried about growing opposition to a tax on carriages, federal officials contrived with Daniel Hylton to create a litigation vehicle for the Supreme Court to express its opinion—hoping that word from the Court might dampen a spreading popular movement to refuse payment on constitutional grounds. "I consider the question as the greatest one that ever came before [the Supreme] Court," Attorney General William Bradford wrote in urging recently retired Treasury Secretary Alexander Hamilton to argue the case for the government. "[I]t is of the last importance not only that the act should be supported, but supported by the unanimous opinion of the Judges and on grounds that will bear the public inspection."[70] The obliging Justices overlooked an astonishing number of procedural obstacles[71] and dutifully issued opinions supporting the government's authority—stretching as necessary to uphold the law by emphasizing policy over constitutional text and structure.[72] Contrary to the usual practice, which called for a Justice who decided a case on circuit to sit out, even Justice Wilson joined the effort, adding a brief statement to let everyone know that his "sentiments, in favor of the constitutionality of the tax in question, ha[d] not been changed."[73]

The "doubtful case" rule also explains why judges invariably illustrated their understanding of judicial review with blatantly unconstitutional laws, the most common example being a law denying the right to trial by jury altogether.[74] The point was not rhetorical. These were, literally, the only kinds of laws they could imagine declaring void. Recall that legislation contradicting explicit constitutional provisions had been a significant problem in the 1780s, so this apparently limited power of review would not have seemed insignificant or unimportant to judges of the period.

Apart from failing to emphasize the need for a law to be clearly unconstitutional, the opinions in *Kamper* accurately reflected the theory of judicial review that gained acceptance in the 1790s. Rather than claiming to exercise review because constitutional interpretation is a uniquely judicial task, courts emphasized the fact that unconstitutional laws were void and insisted that courts were no less obligated than anyone else to attend to this fact. The Constitution applied to the judiciary "as well as" to the other branches, and judges could not permit themselves to be made "fit agents" in abetting legislative illegality, but should instead uphold constitutional values "on behalf of the people." In charging a Georgia grand jury, now-Justice James Iredell affirmed his earlier essay, explaining that when laws violated the Constitution, "the courts of justice, in any such instance coming under their cognizance, are bound to resist them, they having no authority to carry into execution any acts but such as the constitution warrants."[75] Justice Paterson stressed the same theme in his charge to the grand jury in *Vanhorne's Lessee v. Dorrance*:

> I take it to be a clear position; that if a legislative act oppugns a constitutional principle, the former must give way, and be rejected on the score of repugnance. I hold it to be a position equally clear and sound, that, in such case, it will be the duty of the Court to adhere to the Constitution, and to declare the act null and void. The Constitution is the basis of legislative authority; it lies at the foundation of all law, and is a rule and commission by which both Legislators and Judges are to proceed. It is an important principle, which, in the discussion of questions of the present kind, ought never to be lost sight of, that the Judiciary in this country is not a subordinate, but co-ordinate, branch of the government.[76]

Note the structure of Paterson's argument. A law that "oppugns" the Constitution must give way and be rejected. By whom? The statement precedes and is independent of any reference to courts or judges because such laws (which are not laws) should be rejected by everyone.[77] But everyone includes courts and judges. Hence, it is "equally clear and sound" that judges have a duty to declare such laws void. Paterson's chief concern was to establish that courts *too* could engage in constitutional enforcement, that the judiciary was a coordinate and not a subordinate branch. It would take a few years more before any judge would go farther than this and claim that the legal nature of the Constitution made courts uniquely responsible for interpreting and enforcing it. Bear in mind, too, as the actions of the Justices in *Hayburn's Case* illustrate, that judicial review had not yet fully displaced extrajudicial forms of protest even among judges, much less among the people at large.

Remember that any statement describing what judicial review "was" should be treated with caution because a range of views existed as to both its propriety and its nature. Very conservative Federalists had already begun to articulate a theory recognizable today as judicial supremacy,[78] while there were still people—including some more moderate Federalists—who rejected judicial review altogether. "[T]ho very popular and very prevalent," wrote Connecticut's Zephaniah Swift in 1795, the idea of judicial review "requires some consideration."[79] It was indeed likely, he conceded, that a legislature would sometimes pass laws that violated the Constitution, but "it is as probable that the judiciary will declare laws unconstitutional which are not, as it is, that the legislature will exceed their constitutional authority." The people being ultimate judge in all events, there was no warrant for courts to pass on the constitutionality of laws:

> The legislature are not under the controul or superintendence of the judiciary—if they pass laws which are unconstitutional, they are responsible to the people—who may in the course of elections dismiss them from office, and appoint such persons as will repeal such unconstitutional acts. On this power of the people over the legislature, depends their security against all encroachments, and not on the vigilance of the judiciary department.[80]

That there was this range of views is not surprising.[81] As Swift notes, however, by the mid-1790s, acceptance of judicial review was becoming "very popular and very prevalent." And while beliefs about its specific content were not completely uniform, mainstream opinion embraced a modest doctrine in which, consistent with popular constitutionalism, courts acted as the people's agents to supplement and enhance popular control over the interpretation and implementation of constitutional law.

Popular Constitutionalism, circa 1800

The emergence of judicial review, even in this limited and restrained form, still needed to be fit into a theory of the Constitution. The argument for review was ultimately straightforward—to wit, that judges, no less than other citizens or government officials, were bound to take notice of the Constitution if and when it became relevant in the ordinary course of business. Yet however innocuous the proposition might sound stated abstractly, its application in practice raised an embarrassing theoretical problem. James Madison pointed to the difficulty in his 1788 observations on Jefferson's draft constitution for Virginia: "[A]s the Courts are generally the last in making their decisions," he explained, "it results to them by refusing or not refusing to execute a law, to stamp it with its final character. This makes the Judiciary Department paramount in fact to the Legislature, which was never intended and can never be proper."[82]

William Blackstone had addressed a similar dilemma in the portion of his *Commentaries* that tried to make sense of *Dr. Bonham's Case.* For even as a rule of statutory interpretation, Coke's opinion could be read to give courts a leeway over statutes inconsistent with Blackstone's principle claim of unconditional legislative supremacy. Constrained by this latter commitment, the only solution Blackstone could come up with was to restrict judicial authority, so he interpreted *Bonham's Case* to affirm only a limited equitable power in courts to disregard collateral consequences of a statute that were not clearly spelled out.[83]

Working within a system based on popular sovereignty created new theoretical possibilities for Americans, whose solution to their version of the dilemma is known today as the "departmental" or "concurrent" or "coordinate" theory.[84] Madison himself was among its earliest and strongest proponents. During the 1789 debate over the President's removal power, and notwithstanding the misgivings he had communicated to Jefferson the previous year, Madison conceded the basic argument for judicial review. "I acknowledge, in the ordinary course of government, that the exposition of the laws and constitution devolves upon the judicial," he said. It did not follow, however, that judicial decisions should therefore acquire any special stature or status:

> But, I beg to know, upon what principle it can be contended that any one department draws from the constitution greater powers than another, in marking out the limits of the powers of the several departments. The constitution is the charter of the people to the government; it specifies certain great powers as absolutely granted, and marks out the departments to exercise them. If the constitutional boundary of either be brought into question, I do not see that any one of these independent departments has more right than another to declare their sentiments on that point.[85]

Thomas Jefferson, who embraced this theory throughout his political life,[86] expressed the idea succinctly: "[E]ach of the three departments has equally the right to decide for itself what is its duty under the constitution, without regard to what the others may have decided for themselves under a similar question."[87]

Modern commentators find this theory puzzling, seeing in it a formula for chaos and anarchy. Many openly concede to finding the argument confusing, or confused. Others assume that proponents of the departmental theory must have recognized its incompleteness and continued to search for an alternative "effective method of resolving differences over constitutional interpretation."[88] One historian pejoratively labels the theory "arbitrary review" because, he says, it provides no "principled functional limits" for resolving constitutional conflicts.[89] Even modern scholars who purport to endorse departmentalism seem to find Madison's and Jefferson's version of it unintelligible. They typically propose to assign different branches different degrees of authority for different sorts of questions, though always and ultimately, it seems, subject to a judicial veto.[90]

This generic confusion is revealing of the extent to which we have lost touch with the idea of popular constitutionalism. For what underlies the commentators' uncertainty is the assumption not just that *someone* must have final authority to resolve routine constitutional conflicts, but that this someone must be a *governmental agency*. From such a perspective, any theory that purports to leave decision-making power equally in all three branches obviously appears nonsensical, an invitation to endless conflict.

The assumption that final interpretive authority must rest with some branch of the government belongs to the culture of ordinary law, not to the culture of popular constitutionalism. In a world of popular constitutionalism, government officials are the regulat*ed*, not the regulat*ors*, and final interpretive authority rests with the people themselves. Hence, Madison, Jefferson, and their supporters had no difficulty whatsoever explaining how constitutional conflicts would finally be resolved: they would be decided by the people. As Virginia Senator Stevens Thomas Mason explained:

> Though . . . each department ought to discharge its proper duties free from the fear of the others, yet I have never believed that they ought to be independent of the nation itself. . . . All the departments of a popular Government must depend, in some degree, on popular opinion. None can exist without the affections of the people, and if either be placed in such a situation as to be independent of the nation, it will soon lose that affection which is essential to its durable existence.[91]

Ideally, of course, disputing branches of government would achieve an accommodation on their own, though Jefferson once observed that "[w]e have . . . in more than one instance, seen the opinions of different departments in opposition to each other, & no ill ensue."[92] Accommodation among the branches, after all, was what all that checking and balancing in separation of powers theory was supposed to be about.[93] But if no compromise was forthcoming and a final resolution was needed, it was obvious who would decide. The issue would be answered, in Madison's words, by "the will of the community, to be collected in some mode to be provided by the constitution, or one dictated by the necessity of the case."[94] Jefferson, too, urged that "[w]hen the legislative or executive functionaries act unconstitutionally, they are responsible to the people in their elective capacity":

> The exemption of the judges from that is quite dangerous enough. I know of no safe depository of the ultimate powers of the society but the people themselves; and if we think them not enlightened enough to exercise their control with a wholesome discretion, the remedy is not to take it from them, but to inform their discretion by education. This is the true corrective of abuses of constitutional power.[95]

Senator John Breckinridge described how this departmental theory would work in practice. "Although . . . the courts may take upon them to give decisions which impeach the constitutionality of a law, and thereby, for a time, obstruct its operations," he explained:

> [Y]et I contend that such a law is not the less obligatory because the organ through which it is to be executed has refused its aid. A pertinacious adherence of both departments to their opinions, would soon bring the question to issue, in whom the sovereign power of legislation resided, and whose construction of the law-making power should prevail.[96]

By "bring the question to issue," Breckinridge meant, of course, that "pertinacious adherence" by different branches to conflicting views would force the public to decide.

Looking back on statements like these from a distance of two centuries, modern commentators sometimes read them as sounding in natural law and reserved for a dissolution of the Lockean contract.[97] From the perspective of the 1790s, however, an idea of "the people" as a collective body capable of acting independently from within the political system was more serviceable. Obviously it would be best to resolve disputes without popular intervention, just as we prefer seeing ordinary law disputes settled without litigation. But if a dispute could not be settled and needed authoritative resolution, politics was the proper forum, the people were the proper agent, and "political-legal" devices were the proper means.

The plausibility of this understanding was, if anything, enhanced by social and political developments in the 1790s, which vastly enlarged the role and importance of an emerging democratic public sphere.[98] As republican government steadied itself, the numbers of citizens engaged in politics swelled, as did their demands to control the course of government. This was reflected in much more than expanded suffrage and higher voter turnouts, though these were certainly important.[99] It appeared as well in the emergence of new organizations, new forms of communication and political expression, and new public rites and rituals.[100] Juries, mobs, and other traditional local institutions remained important, but now so too were the budding political parties, the Democratic-Republican societies, and the new partisan press. Americans organized and voiced opinions as never before. They mounted petition campaigns and called conventions; they paraded in the streets, planted liberty poles, and burned effigies; they held feasts and delivered public toasts. The popular voice changed and grew more insistent as these new institutions and practices became the means by which that voice was defined and refined.[101] Americans—including even women and free blacks—learned "to fight over the legacy of their national Revolution and to protest their exclusion from that Revolution's fruits."[102]

Anxious Federalists scrambled to squelch the rising populist tide, to preserve the patrician-led counterrevolution they thought they had won in 1788.[103] Instead they found themselves dragged, unwittingly and unwillingly, into the same public sphere, forced to imitate their opponents' practices and copy their opponents' organizational strategies.[104] And as this happened, "common folk affirmed that they were far more than simple subjects of power," demanding that political authority be "exercised in the negotiations between rulers and ruled that took place in public places and print as much as in congressional and state assembly chambers."[105]

Within this new political culture, the departmental theory made perfect sense. Each branch could express its views as issues came before it in the ordinary course of business: the legislature by enacting laws, the executive by vetoing them, the judiciary by reviewing them. But none of the branches' views were final or authoritative. They were the actions of regulated entities striving to follow the law that governed them, subject to ongoing supervision by their common superior, the people themselves. The achievement of judicial review in this early period was thus a successful bid by judges to an equal place in the scheme—to status as members of a coordinate branch, capable of making and acting upon independent judgments about the meaning of the Constitution.

The departmental theory was a self-conscious adjustment by the governing elite to new social, political, and cultural conditions: an adaptation that had appeal because it reflected and responded to how popular constitutionalism had changed since the Revolution, but did so in a way that maintained the theoretic preeminence of active popular control without at the same time inviting incoherence or anarchy. The biggest change, of course, was the repudiation of the monarchical political and social order, which generated new possibilities for conceptualizing the relationship of the people to their governors. Where eighteenth-century constitutionalism had imagined a wholly independent people checking the government from without, republicanism made it easier to think of the people acting in and through the government, with the different branches responding differently to popular pressure depending on their structure and their relationship to the polity.[106] Madison's and Jefferson's references to resolving conflicts by finding an accommodation among the branches, for example, rested crucially on this idea.

Emphasizing a republican people's ability to act through the government (rather than against it) put pressure on certain traditional forms of popular constitutionalism, particularly those associated with the use of extralegal violence. As early as 1784, we find Samuel Adams criticizing mob activity in western Massachusetts, what would subsequently become known as Shays's Rebellion. "County Conventions & popular Committees servd an excellent Purpose when they were first in Practice," Adams wrote to Noah Webster—hardly surprising given how Adams had used these very instruments in the 1760s and 1770s to torment poor Governor Thomas Hutchinson.[107] "No one therefore needs to regret the Share he may have had in them." But, Adams continued, "I candidly owe it is my Opinion . . . that as we now have constitutional & regular Governments and all our Men in Authority depend upon the annual & free Elections of the People, we are safe without them."

By no means did mobbing disappear. Even the Shaysites evoked mixed reactions.[108] There was, moreover, plenty of mob activity in the 1790s and beyond: from the Whiskey Rebellion to the continued activities of frontier "regulators" to Fries Rebellion and much of the opposition to the Jay Treaty and Alien and Sedition Acts to the Baltimore Riots of 1812.[109] But for many, including many Republicans, this sort of behavior had started to become less acceptable. Popular constitutionalism itself was unaffected, and it continued to be simply assumed by most people. But there was a marked shift (especially among elites) toward elections, petitions, and nonviolent forms of political protest as the proper means by which to express and measure public opinion.

One should not overstate the extent of the changes taking place. New and old attitudes about popular uprisings continued to coexist, and support for or condemnation of mob activity remained (as it had always been) partly a matter of whether one supported or opposed the mob's cause. But, increasingly, even those who shared the discontent of insurrectionists were troubled by their use of violent extralegal means. A dozen years after Shays's Rebellion, as Republican leaders conferred about tactics to use against the Alien and Sedition Acts, Jefferson responded to word of Fries Rebellion by counseling caution and patience. "[W]e fear that the ill designing may produce insurrection," he worried in a letter to Edmund Pendleton. "Nothing could be so fatal":

> Anything like force would check the progress of the public opinion & rally them round the government. This is not the kind of opposition the American people will permit. But keep away all show of force, and they will bear down the evil propensities of the government, by the constitutional means of election & petition.[110]

Jefferson's concerns about violent protest were echoed by others, both Federalist and Republican, elite and plebeian.[111] For present purposes, however, what matters is to note that this reflected a change in means, not ends. Preserving the people's active control of their government and their Constitution remained paramount. But new devices were emerging to secure that control without violence, particularly as political parties formed and introduced novel practices to make the people's voice effective. Jefferson's and Madison's departmental theory had considerable appeal in this context.

Popular constitutionalism was changing in more subtle ways as well. Before the Revolution, it had depended on a cluster of social practices that historians typically lump together under the broad label of "deference."[112] These practices served to mediate and guide popular action by enabling a "well born" elite to gauge when resistance was appropriate and, even if not always fully in control, to ensure that opposition to government did not go too far or grow too violent. By 1800 the emerging democratic culture had begun to change the way such political relations were conceived and practiced. The idea of deference did not wholly disappear—that process would take several more generations to complete. But relationships between ordinary citizens and their political leaders and social betters were nevertheless changing, a change manifested among political leaders attuned to the insistent democratic pressures in a newfound respect for "public opinion."

"Public opinion," wrote Madison in an essay of that title, which he published in December 1791, "sets bounds to every government, and is the real sovereign in every free one."[113] This was more than a paraphrase of Hume's point about ultimate authority resting with the people because "FORCE is always on the[ir] side."[114] It was a normative and not just descriptive claim. Public opinion should be sovereign because republicanism meant, first and foremost, that "after establishing a government [the people] should watch over it as well as obey it."[115]

In affirming the authority of public opinion, Madison was not preaching simple majoritarianism. The opinion that he believed should hold sway was more than the fleeting preferences of the moment, more than the unrefined passions of a majority of citizens. As Colleen Sheehan explains, those who championed popular supervision of government:

> did not simply equate public opinion with the will of the majority. Public opinion [was] not the sum of ephemeral passions and narrow interests; it [was] not an aggregate of uninformed minds and wills. Rather, public opinion require[d] the refinement and transformation of the views, sentiments, and interests of the citizens into a public mind guided by the precepts of reason, resulting in "the reason . . . of the public" or "the reason of the society."[116]

This was Jefferson's point when he urged in his first inaugural address that Americans "bear in mind this sacred principle, that though the will of the majority is in all cases to prevail, that will to be rightful must be reasonable."[117]

Ensuring that the will of the majority was reasonable was a responsibility of leadership. Those whose situation in life had afforded them the opportunity to elevate their minds had a concomitant obligation to elevate those of their fellow citizens, particularly on matters of politics and government. "The class of the literati," Madison wrote in notes to himself, "are the cultivators of the human mind—the manufacturers of useful knowledge—the agents of the commerce of ideas—the censors of public manners—the teachers of the arts of life and the means of happiness."[118] It was the task of this elite to educate and edify, to foster a process of deliberation that refined and enlightened public sentiment in a fashion sufficient for the demands of self-government. This responsibility lay particularly heavily on elected officials. Just as public opinion must be obeyed once it had settled, Madison observed, "where not . . . fixed, it may be influenced by the government."[119] Among the most important devices for securing the sovereignty of public opinion, he added further, matched only by "a *circulation of newspapers through the entire body of the people*," was "*Representatives going from, and returning among every part of them.*"

The political process imagined by such comments was different from the deferential politics of colonial America. "Symbolically," explains historian Christopher Grasso, "the 'public' came to be seen, not as a body ruled by a sovereign head, but as a mind that ruled itself."[120] This did not mean the flattening or elimination of all distinctions, but it did embody a profound, if subtle, shift in the nature of politics. At the risk of oversimplifying, one can describe the general direction of change as follows: where the earlier system emphasized the power and patronage of a wealthy gentry, the new theory of republican politics was better characterized as a conversation—a conversation in which the elite now led by persuasion an electorate actively engaged in making its own judgments and decisions. As described by one historian of this idea of public opinion:

> Representatives traveling to and from the nation's capital provide links of communication and act as agents for the exchange of political ideas among the citizenry. As elected officials whose task was to deliberate on issues of national import, they both attend to the views of their constituents and convey back to them the concerns and interests of the nation at large. . . . The process of forming and fixing public opinion over an extensive federal republic is a slow and gradual one. The sentiments and views of the people are acted on and modified by enlightened members of society, by national representatives, and by their own experiences in local self-government. This process of refining and enlightening the public's views results in a common and settled opinion among the national public. Once settled, public opinion is an authoritative source that influences government and presides over its decisions.[121]

Not everyone would have embraced this description of politics. Federalists were still holding out (with diminishing success) for an older idea of passive deference, while increasing numbers of ordinary citizens probably resented the emphasis on elite leaders enlightening the ignorant masses. Then, as now, politics was messier, more contested, than any single theory or theorist could capture. This was, nevertheless the dominant public ideology that emerged over the course of the 1790s, an ideology most Americans seem either to have embraced or grudgingly accepted.

Two critical features of this ideology need to be emphasized if we are to understand how popular constitutionalism had evolved and how its essence was preserved by the departmental theory. On the one hand, the citizenry had become "an operationally active" sovereign as well as an authoritative one.[122] It was the people themselves who decided, and only their opinion ultimately mattered. Madison stressed the need for an active citizenry in his essay on "Government":

> A republic involves the idea of popular rights. A representative repub-
> lic *chuses* the wisdom, of which hereditary aristocracy has the *chance*;
> whilst it excludes the oppression of that form. . . . To secure all the
> advantages of such a system, every good citizen will be at once a centi-
> nel over the rights of the people; over the authorities of the confederal
> government; and over both the rights and the authorities of the inter-
> mediate governments.[123]

On the other hand, public opinion would work to secure rather than undermine republican government only if and for so long as the public was guided by reason. Among the principle benefits of federalism and separation of powers (not to mention the extensive size of the Republic) were thought to be that these complicated and slowed politics long enough for reason to prevail. And though courts had not originally or conventionally been considered part of this process, by the 1790s judicial review was being included among these complicating devices—adding another voice capable of forcing further public deliberation when it came to constitutional matters. But judges were no more authoritative on these matters than any other public official, and their judgments about the meaning of the Constitution, like those of everyone else, were still subject to oversight and ultimate resolution by the people themselves.

Marbury v. Madison

This, in fact, is all that *Marbury v. Madison* actually says or does. It has recently become quite fashionable to dismiss *Marbury* as an altogether trivial case—a predictable reaction, perhaps, to the previous generation's hyperventilated celebration of it. Most of us were taught that *Marbury* was, as Robert McCloskey gushed, a "masterwork of indirection, a brilliant example of Marshall's capacity to sidestep danger while seeming to court it, to advance in one direction while his opponents are looking in another."[124] More fawning still is Alexander Bickel's breathless introduction in *The Least Dangerous Branch*:

> [T]he institution of the judiciary needed to be summoned up out of the constitutional vapors, shaped and maintained; and the Great Chief Justice, John Marshall,—not singlehanded, but first and foremost—was there to do it and did. If any social process can be said to have been "done" at a given time and by a given act, it is Marshall's achievement. The time was 1803; the act the decision in the case of *Marbury v. Madison*.[125]

Eventually, this sort of fulsome reverence was bound to incite rebellion, and *Marbury* revisionism is now all the rage.[126] Michael Klarman derides Marshall's ruling for having "offered no arguments that would have persuaded anyone who still questioned the legitimacy of [judicial review] in 1803," and doing "nothing to facilitate the Court's acquisition of the political stature necessary to make judicial review practically as well as theoretically significant."[127] James O'Fallon dismisses *Marbury* as already obsolete when it was decided, a testament to the way in which ideas can persist long after they have lost their utility.[128] Mark Graber jeers that *Marbury* "merely established the judicial power to utter such declaratory sentences as 'it is emphatically the province and duty of the judicial department to say what the law is,' a power possessed by anyone with a minimal knowledge of English."[129] The author of one of the leading constitutional law casebooks has disclosed in conversation that he even considered leaving *Marbury* out of the book altogether, as a signal to students of its true unimportance.

Yet care must be taken, lest the reaction against *Marbury* match its predecessor for excessiveness. To be sure, *Marbury* did not stake out new territory in the theory of judicial review. That most people thought the power existed, even as to federal laws, was already clear from the debates in Congress as well as from cases like *Hylton v. United States* and *Hayburn's Case*. Justice Chase could thus observe three years before *Marbury*, in *Cooper v. Telfair*, that "[i]t is, indeed, a general opinion, it is expressly admitted by all this bar, and some of the Justices have, individually, in the Circuits, decided, that the Supreme Court can declare an act of Congress to be unconstitutional, and, therefore, invalid."[130] But, he quickly added, "there is no adjudication of the Supreme Court itself upon the point."[131] *Marbury* was the first, and important for that alone. Yet there is more, for the circumstances in which *Marbury* was decided add to the significance of the case and make its reputation, if not quite up to hero worship of the past, at least more deserved than is currently fashionable in revisionist circles.

The case of *Marbury v. Madison* played a supporting role in a bigger drama about the place of the judiciary in American government, and while only a minor player, its part turned out to be important in unexpected ways. The stage was set by the election of 1800, in which Jefferson and the Republicans trounced the divided and demoralized Federalists. Jefferson's and Burr's margin over Adams in the Electoral College was only 73–65, but peculiarities in the way electors were chosen obscure from us (though not from contemporaries) the actual strength of the Republican showing.[132] The elections for Congress more clearly evinced just how sweeping a victory Jefferson's party had won. Going into the election, Federalists held sixty-three seats in the House of Representatives to the Republicans' forty-three. The vote in 1800 more than reversed these numbers, leaving the Republicans with a 65–41 edge and a clear mandate to change the government's direction.[133]

Faced with the loss of the executive and legislative branches, the lame duck Federalist Congress acted quickly to secure its adherents a sanctuary in the judiciary. Federalists had talked about court reform for years: Attorney General Edmund Randolph had recommended steps as early as 1790; the Supreme Court had repeatedly petitioned for relief; and President Adams had urged Congress to take some sort of action as recently as December 1799.[134] But nothing came of these efforts until the embarrassment of Jefferson's election finally spurred the Federalists to act.[135] Gouverneur Morris justified their doing so in a letter to Robert Livingston: "[T]he leaders of the federal party . . . are about to experience a heavy gale of adverse wind; can they be blamed for casting many anchors to hold their ship through the storm?"[136]

These anchors were to consist chiefly of new judgeships in a substantially restructured third branch. The main feature of the Judiciary Act of 1801 was thus to relieve the Supreme Court Justices of circuit-riding duties by creating six new circuit courts staffed by sixteen new judges; the Supreme Court was at the same time reduced in size from six to five, said reduction to take effect when the next vacancy occurred.[137] By this none-too-subtle means, the Federalists rewarded themselves with numerous appointments to the inferior courts—not just the judges, but also marshals, clerks, federal attorneys, and all the other supporting personnel attached to a court—while simultaneously requiring the incoming Republican Administration to wait for two vacancies on the Supreme Court before it could make its first appointment there.

But time was short. The Judiciary Act became law on February 13, 1801. The new Administration was scheduled to take over at 12:01 a.m. on March 4. This meant the outgoing Federalists had less than three weeks to • select, nominate, and confirm all the new judges and support staff.[138] Nor was the bonanza of last-minute appointments limited to circuit courts created in the Judiciary Act. For on February 27, just four days before Jefferson's inauguration, Congress rushed through yet another law creating yet another circuit court, this one for the District of Columbia; the President was authorized to nominate three more judges and also to appoint "such number of discreet persons to be justices of the peace, as the President of the United States shall from time to time think expedient, to continue in office five years."[139] President Adams immediately nominated the allotted circuit judges, and the Senate hurriedly confirmed his choices. In addition, Adams selected forty-two justices of the peace, most stout Federalists. The outgoing President thus spent his last days in office signing commissions prepared for him by his overworked Secretary of State, John Marshall, who was also already serving as Chief Justice of the Supreme Court.

Once the commissions were signed, it was Marshall's responsibility to make them official by affixing the seal of the United States and arranging to have them delivered. Commissions for the circuit judges went out before Adams's term expired, but some justices of the peace were still waiting when time ran out—including one William Marbury. Legend has it that Marshall was frantically scribbling away in his office when Jefferson's Attorney General Levi Lincoln flung open the door and interrupted him carrying a watch whose hands showed midnight, March 3, 1801.[140]

Republicans were plenty angry about the federal courts even before these last-minute shenanigans. They had not forgiven the exuberance with which Federalist judges tried to muzzle Republicans under the Sedition Act; nor had they forgotten the judges' frequently outrageous conduct of the trials and aggressive use of the bench to campaign for Federalist candidates and policies.[141] There were other issues, too, like the claim that common law was available to federal courts, which Jefferson called an "audacious, barefaced, and sweeping pretension" in comparison to which other Federalist doctrines were "unconsequential, timid things."[142]

Yet despite all this, Jefferson and most Republicans were prepared to live and let live. Jefferson was furious at Adams for his last-minute appointments—he later singled them out as the only "personally unkind" act Adams had ever committed against him[143]—but Jefferson was also willing to forgo a purge if the newly appointed officeholders would act honorably and responsibly. The new President went out of his way to be conciliatory in his inaugural address, and he pursued (at some considerable political cost) a restrained policy with respect to patronage. For example, Jefferson reduced the number of justices of the peace in the District of Columbia from forty-two to thirty, but he included twenty-five of Adams's original appointees in this group.[144]

Jefferson's correspondence in the months between March and December 1801, when the new Congress finally convened, indicates that he continued to brood about the judiciary.[145] Yet Jefferson barely alluded to the matter in his December 8 opening address to Congress, and he recommended no specific action. "The Judiciary system of the United States, and especially that portion of it recently erected will, of course, present itself to the contemplation of Congress," was all that he said, adding a hint in the guise of some hastily compiled (and not very accurate) caseload statistics.[146] While a number of historians interpret this as evidence that Jefferson was already intent on repealing the Judiciary Act of 1801,[147] most now believe he had not yet committed to such a policy.[148] Strong elements within Jefferson's party were pushing for action—infuriated by, among other things, continued diatribes in the Federalist press and the audacity of Federalist judges in the new D.C. circuit who, despite the election results, instituted a common law libel prosecution against the editor of the Republican *National Intelligencer*.[149] But moderates in the party had doubts about the propriety of repeal and were not anxious to begin their turn at the helm by plunging into what promised to be a bitter partisan affair, and Jefferson probably felt the same way. So he equivocated, neither advocating nor ignoring the possibility of repeal.

Then, on December 16, Secretary of State James Madison was served with notice that a motion would be made in the Supreme Court the following day asking Madison to show cause why a writ of mandamus should not be issued directing him to deliver commissions as justices of the peace to William Marbury, Dennis Ramsay, Robert R. Hooe, and William Harper.[150] Madison ignored the summons and Chief Justice Marshall granted the motion to show cause; argument about whether the petitioners were entitled to a writ was scheduled for the beginning of the next term. Richard Ellis hypothesizes that Federalists deliberately chose this moment to challenge Jefferson, believing "a show of determination would deter the Republicans on the court issue before they could unite themselves."[151] If so, the strategy backfired, for filing *Marbury v. Madison* turned out to be the crucial act that united Republicans behind the repeal effort.[152] Interpreting the Court's show cause order as confirmation of Federalist plans to use the judiciary to obstruct Jefferson's Administration, angry Republicans—including now, most importantly, the

President himself[153]—decided to strike first. "The conduct of the Judges on this occasion," Virginia Senator Stevens Thomas Mason told Madison, "has excited a very general indignation and will secure the repeal of the Judiciary Law of the last session, about the propriety of which some of our Republican friends were hesitating."[154]

The repeal debate proved to be every bit as ugly and contentious as moderate Republicans had feared. Overwrought Federalists ranted about the demise of an independent judiciary and hysterically charged Republicans with bringing the nation to "the brink of that revolutionary torrent, which deluged in blood one of the fairest countries in Europe."[155] Republicans shrieked back that repeal was justified to counter a Federalist abuse of power and preserve a proper constitutional balance as well as to protect the public fisc. The pending *Marbury* case was referred to by both sides—Republicans offering it as evidence of judicial overreaching, Federalists citing it as an example of why an independent judiciary was necessary.[156] Numerous arguments both for and against judicial review were heard, including some Republican denunciations of the practice in any and all forms.[157] In the end, which came on March 3, 1802, the Act was of course repealed.[158]

A small coterie of ultra-Federalists would not accept defeat and embarked on a campaign to sabotage the Republicans' victory. They asked the Supreme Court Justices to refuse to resume circuit-riding duties on constitutional grounds, but were rebuffed; Justice Chase was prepared to confront the President by this means, but he acquiesced in the unanimous views of his brethren to hold the circuit courts as scheduled.[159] Unwilling to let matters rest, the same group of Federalists—Jefferson called them "the bitterest cup of the remains of Federalism rendered desperate and furious by despair"[160]—formulated a new, three-pronged attack. First, they sought to drum up public support by circulating a pamphlet entitled *The Solemn Protest of the Honorable Judge Bassett*. Written by the father-in-law of Federalist stalwart James Bayard (who tried to talk him out of it), Judge Bassett claimed to speak for all the removed judges in rehashing the arguments made against repeal and calling upon the Supreme Court to declare the Repeal Act unconstitutional. Second, eleven of the removed circuit judges petitioned Congress for a redress of grievances, hoping in this way to revive divisions in the Republicans' ranks.[161] Finally, a number of test cases were brought challenging the Repeal Act in the restored federal circuit courts.

Nothing came of these efforts. The public relations campaign failed, due partly to the ham-fisted and insulting manner in which the Federalists presented their case, but even more because repeal was genuinely popular.[162] The results in Congress were still more disheartening. Republicans in the House of Representatives turned down the judges' request without dissension on the very day it was filed; the Senate took somewhat longer but reached the same result on a party-line vote. Adding injury to insult, Congress also voted to deny a petition by Marbury and friends for a transcript showing the exact dates of their nominations and confirmations (necessary because the hapless petitioners were finding it difficult to prove that they had actually been appointed).[163]

But the most crushing blow came when the Federalists' various court actions challenging repeal were summarily rejected in the circuit courts. Anticipating the possibility of such challenges, the Republican Congress had already passed legislation designed to put off a ruling from the Supreme Court. This was accomplished by legislation adopted in early April that abolished the Supreme Court's June and December terms, thus delaying the Court's next sitting until February 1803, by which time Jefferson hoped that tempers in the capital would have cooled.[164] An incidental effect of this legislation was to put off the hearing in *Marbury v. Madison*, which otherwise would have been heard in June.

Undeterred, some of the removed Federalist judges challenged the constitutionality of repeal in four lower court cases. They argued, first, that Congress had no power to order the transfer of actions already pending in courts established under the Judiciary Act of 1801. Second, they said it was unconstitutional for Supreme Court Justices also to sit as judges in the circuit courts. But mainly they argued that Congress had no power to remove judges who were guilty of no malfeasance or dereliction in office. In three of these challenges—presided over by Justices Washington and Cushing and by Chief Justice Marshall—their arguments were rejected on the spot.[165] In the fourth, heard by Justice Paterson, the proceedings were adjourned overnight, leaving time for conversations that led a "very much mortified" Theophilus Parsons to withdraw his plea the next morning.[166]

Incredibly, though four of six Supreme Court Justices had now indicated their unwillingness to rule against the Administration, the pigheaded Federalists pressed on by appealing Chief Justice Marshall's ruling to the full Court. The argument and decision in the case, captioned *Stuart v. Laird*, trailed those in *Marbury* by a few days each. Predictably, given what they had already said and done, the Justices affirmed the lower court. Justice Paterson's opinion for a unanimous Supreme Court was brief, though not fully to the point. It was clear that Congress could abolish the inferior courts set up in the Judiciary Act of 1801 and transfer their cases to a different

tribunal, the Court said, there being "no words in the constitution to prohibit or restrain" Congress's authority to "establish from time to time such
inferior tribunals as they think proper."[167] As for the objection that Supreme
Court Justices could not sit on circuit courts, "it is sufficient to observe, that
practice and acquiescence under it for a period of several years, commencing
with the organization of the judicial system, affords an irresistible answer,
and has indeed fixed the construction. . . . [T]he question is at rest, and
ought not to be disturbed."[168] Remarkably, Paterson and the Court ignored
the appellant's most fundamental objection, which was that Congress could
not remove Article III judges by any means other than impeachment or
for any reasons other than misbehavior in office. But that argument was no
longer essential to the case once the Court had concluded that Congress
could transfer pending actions from one court to another, and the Justices
chose in *Stuart* to say no more than was absolutely necessary to decide the
case before them.

We are now, finally, in a position to understand the many-sided calculation that lay behind Chief Justice Marshall's enigmatic opinion in *Marbury*.
Like every Federalist, Marshall worried about how far Republicans would
go to vitiate the political order established under the leadership of Washington and Hamilton. Bear in mind that disagreements between the parties
were not confined to questions of policy, but reflected profoundly different
social philosophies.[169] A major organizing principle of Federalism was fear
of populism and demagoguery. In its most extreme manifestations, Federalism exhibited open contempt for ordinary citizens and a sure conviction that
republicanism would fail unless those citizens left problems of governing to
their social and intellectual betters. Gouverneur Morris perfectly expressed
this tenet during the debate over repeal: "Look into the records of time, see
what has been the ruin of every Republic. The vile love of popularity. Why
are we here? To save the people from their most dangerous enemy; to save
them from themselves."[170] A week later, Morris took umbrage at the suggestion that he had sought popular approval by one of his arguments. "[S]ure I
am that I uttered nothing in the style of an *appeal to the people*," he sneered. "I
hope no member of this House has so poor a sense of its dignity as to make
such an appeal."[171] Marshall himself seldom spoke this bluntly, and he was
generally moderate when it came to particular policies. But he shared with all
Federalists these core convictions as well as the belief that Jefferson and the
Republicans pandered too much to popular opinion.

Marshall was, at the same time, reasonably certain that any attempt by
the Court to stand in Jefferson's way would be crushed. What doubts he may

have harbored in this respect, moreover, were presumably laid to rest when, just before the Court reconvened in February, Jefferson asked the House of Representatives to look into whether New Hampshire District Judge John Pickering's erratic behavior warranted impeachment.[172] There was, as a result, a new "overhanging threat" to unsettle the Justices as they sat down to decide *Stuart* and *Marbury*.[173]

Of the two cases, *Stuart v. Laird* represented the greater dilemma and more intractable problem, for the Repeal Act challenged more fundamental constitutional values and reflected a much greater threat to judicial independence than the Administration's failure to deliver some commissions in the circumstances of Marbury's case. Plus, Federalists and Republicans alike cared far more about the fate of Jefferson's repeal than they did about Marbury, and they were watching closely to see what the Supreme Court would do—which is why there was never really any question that the Court would do nothing. As Dean Alfange explains:

> *Stuart v. Laird* was manifestly not an example of nonpartisan fairness, but of craven unwillingness on the part of the Court even to admit the existence of the principal constitutional issue presented by the case. The Court refused to consider the constitutional question even though the author of its opinion had earlier categorically written that he believed the law to be invalid for precisely the reasons that he here chose not even to mention. The Court acted out of a fully justified fear of the political consequences of doing otherwise, not out of an overriding compulsion to reach the correct legal result at whatever sacrifice of their own political preferences.[174]

As much as the Court may have wanted to say something that signaled its opposition to what the Republicans had done and were doing, it was abundantly clear that anything less than total submission to the Repeal Act would be suicidal.

Effectively silenced in *Stuart*, *Marbury* became the Court's only outlet for making a statement. Yet the prospects for getting away with something here were scarcely more promising than in *Stuart*. Secretary of State Madison had simply ignored the initial motion to show cause, and he displayed equal disregard for the Court's proceedings on whether to grant the petitioners' request—not bothering to appear or even to offer an argument. It was abundantly clear that an order directing Madison to deliver the commissions would likewise be ignored. Unwilling to say that Jefferson was right, but also not wanting to have its impotence openly put on display, the Court decided instead to dismiss for lack of jurisdiction.

Yet Marshall could not bring himself simply to rule that Marbury and his co-petitioners were entitled to no relief. This would have meant letting Jefferson completely off the hook in both cases, and that was to concede too much to the Republicans. Marshall deemed it imperative to make some kind of statement: to send a message that the Court had views and might step in at some point. Marshall therefore prefaced his jurisdictional ruling with a lengthy dissertation explaining why the Administration had acted unlawfully by withholding the petitioners' commissions. By coupling this essay with a dismissal for want of jurisdiction, Marshall was, in effect, leaving open the question whether the Court would stand up to the Executive. He was also, as one biographer has put it, "throwing a sop to the High Federalists," offering something to take the edge off their disappointment.[175]

It was a risky strategy. Marshall's lecture infuriated Jefferson, who perceived it as a politically motivated attack on his presidency.[176] And not just because, having already decided that the Court lacked jurisdiction, Marshall's discussion was gratuitous and wholly improper (which it was) but also because, in Jefferson's eyes, Marshall was so obviously wrong on the merits (which he was).[177] Marshall nevertheless decided to gamble. Richard Ellis explains: "[T]he Chief Justice was an experienced politician, and he probably realized that Jefferson, preoccupied as he was with the diplomatic intricacies of the Louisiana Purchase and with the clashing interests within the Republican Party, was not likely to get into a fight over a lecture that had no practical meaning."[178] Marshall's gamble paid off, and he succeeded in rebuking Jefferson without triggering a Republican backlash or even strong criticism in the press.[179]

And what about judicial review? Marshall definitely went out of his way (quite a bit out of his way, in fact) to address the issue. It would have been perfectly easy to have reached the same result in the case—that the Supreme Court lacked original jurisdiction to entertain Marbury's petition—without striking anything down. Section 13 of the Judiciary Act of 1789 did not read like a grant of jurisdiction, and the better interpretation was that it authorized writs of mandamus only in cases where the Court otherwise had jurisdiction.[180] Indeed, this would have been a stronger legal position than the one Marshall actually took, for (as countless scholars have argued) Marshall's conclusion that Article III prohibited Congress from enlarging the Supreme

Court's original jurisdiction was anything but obvious.[181] As it was, Marshall had to stretch very far to reach the result he did through an exercise of judicial review.

Why did he do it? Why force a potentially controversial question that no one had raised or even hinted at, particularly one wholly unnecessary to accomplish the Court's main objective? And why do so at this highly charged moment, when the Court's position was so precarious? The answer may be that the very precariousness of the Court's position is what led Marshall to conclude that he needed to do something about judicial review. The federal courts had been under attack for five years, beginning with Republican denunciations of their role in enforcing the Sedition Act. This assault had become a full-fledged siege after Republicans took office and assumed the offensive by repealing the Judiciary Act of 1801. In the course of debating repeal, the Supreme Court's authority had been questioned and condemned, and the concept of judicial review had come under challenges of a type and temper not heard since before the Constitution was adopted.[182] Suddenly, a practice that had seemed so uncontroversial throughout the 1790s no longer seemed immune to attack.

At the same time, outright rejection of judicial review was not yet a position embraced officially by Republicans, most of whom shared Jefferson's more moderate departmental theory and were willing to live with review on his theory's limited terms. This was the moment to make a statement, Marshall apparently decided, before more extreme sentiments against judicial review spread or grew into something more threatening. Yet such a statement would be effective only if the Court could make it in a way that dampened rather than inflamed further hostility. Marshall's goal was, in effect, to get judicial review into the record—not to establish its existence, but to deflect an incipient movement to delegitimate it. Dean Alfange captured the likely drift of Marshall's thinking thus:

> [I]t was important to invoke the power of judicial review in order to establish a precedent for its later use and to include in the Reports of the Supreme Court a statement of the reasoning by which the power could be shown to be absolutely necessary. Thus, since judicial review could not safely have been used to invalidate a law that the Republicans cared about, it was necessary to find a law that the Republicans did not care about. And what more perfect law could have been found for this purpose than § 13 of the Judiciary Act of 1789?[183]

Robert McCloskey, it turns out, may have been right after all in praising *Marbury* as an example of Marshall's "brilliant" capacity to sidestep danger.[184]

It is tempting, and perhaps too easy, to assume that since Marshall was daring in finding a way to introduce judicial review into the case, he must have been equally bold and imaginative in developing the doctrine. If anything, the opposite was true. The circumstances of *Marbury* led Marshall to write cautiously and to formulate the Court's authority to nullify legislation conservatively.

Many Federalists had, by the time of *Marbury*, begun to espouse a theory of judicial review broader and more ambitious than anything we have seen so far—a theory recognizable today as judicial supremacy, or the notion that judges have the last word when it comes to constitutional interpretation and that their decisions determine the meaning of the Constitution for everyone.[185] A few had pushed this theory aggressively during the debates over the Repeal Act,[186] in turn prompting the most forceful Republican denunciations of judicial review. But judges were generally more circumspect than politicians in declaring the scope of their authority, and Marshall was doubly inclined to be cautious in *Marbury*. His opinion thus carefully and self-consciously avoided the language and arguments of his Federalist allies. Instead, it offered a straightforward application of principles that were widely accepted by most Republicans (including, significantly, President Jefferson), and fully consistent with the premises of popular constitutionalism. Marshall himself acknowledged as much, for he was being neither ironic nor misleading when he introduced the topic by observing that it was "not of an intricacy proportioned to its interest" and could be decided by "certain principles, supposed to have been long and well established."[187]

Like every other writer of the period, Marshall began with the principle that the Constitution is "a superior, paramount law," and that, therefore, "an act of the legislature, repugnant to the constitution, is void."[188] He then asked, again like every other writer of the period, "does [such a law], notwithstanding its invalidity, bind the courts, and oblige them to give it effect?"[189] Though this would seem, "at first view, an absurdity too gross to be insisted on,"[190] Marshall proposed nevertheless to say more and explain why. Then, the famous line: "It is emphatically the province and duty of the judicial department to say what the law is."[191]

Read in context, this sentence did not say what, to modern eyes, it seems to say when read in isolation. That is, it did not say "it is the job of courts, alone, to say what the Constitution means." Nor did it say, "it is the job of courts, more so than others, to say what the Constitution means." What it said was "courts, too, can say what the Constitution means." Marshall thus followed his celebrated sentence with exactly the same point as that made by Tucker and Roane in *Kamper*: "Those who apply the rule to particular cases, must of necessity expound and interpret that rule. . . . Those then who controvert the principle that the constitution is to be considered, in court, as a paramount law, are reduced to the necessity of maintaining that courts must close their eyes on the constitution, and see only the law."[192]

Marshall added a textual argument. Federal judicial power extends to cases "arising under" the Constitution.[193] "Could it be," he asked incredulously, "[t]hat a case arising under the constitution should be decided without examining the instrument under which it arises?"[194] To anyone still unpersuaded of the "extravagan[ce]" of such a supposition, Marshall offered a list of blatantly unconstitutional laws that would have to be enforced by courts if they ignored questions of constitutionality.[195] "From these, and many other selections which might be made," he concluded, "it is apparent, that the framers of the constitution contemplated that instrument, as a rule for the government of courts, *as well as of the legislature*."[196] Piling on with the point that the judges' oath of office—which required administering justice "agreeably to *the constitution*"—would be "worse than solemn mockery" and "a crime" were judges required to ignore the Constitution, Marshall closed: a law repugnant to the Constitution is void, and "courts, *as well as other departments*, are bound by that instrument."[197]

The consistency between Marshall's reasoning and that of every other judge and commentator we have studied is apparent and requires no elaboration. There are some differences: Marshall's emphasis on text was unique—as it was unique to his constitutional jurisprudence generally.[198] More interesting, while Marshall referred to the superior authority of the people and to the Court's role acting on their behalf, the point was made *sotto voce*—though he did acknowledge (along the lines first articulated by James Iredell back in 1786) that the people "can seldom act" because an exercise of their "original right" requires "a very great exertion."[199] Whether Marshall was intentionally downplaying this argument because, in the depths of his heart, he was already secretly plotting to eliminate the people's role cannot be known for sure, though this seems unlikely. Marshall was a Federalist and so not much interested in celebrating the people's active role in constitutional politics—particularly not in 1803, with his party and his institution reeling from the anticourt, pro-populist Republican onslaught. In any event, to readers of the time, unaware of what judicial review would become a century or more later, such an omission would not have been visible because the point would have been implicit in the opinion's whole structure and analysis. To contemporary readers, Marshall was simply insisting—like practically every other judge and writer of the era—that courts had the same duty and the same obligation to enforce the Constitution as everyone else, both in and out of government.

* * *

Did Marshall achieve his various objectives in *Marbury*? He managed to reprimand Jefferson for what amounted to dereliction of duty without bringing the wrath of Republicans down on the Court, thus weaving his way through the most politically treacherous territory. The Court may not have blocked the Administration's measures, but neither did it prostrate itself. With respect to judicial review, judgment is more complicated. Conventional wisdom long held that Marshall succeeded magnificently, almost single-handedly creating judicial review "out of the constitutional vapors."[200] More recent commentators have disparaged this sort of remark as nonsense. Not only did Marshall not invent judicial review, they say, but *Marbury* had little or nothing to do with its subsequent emergence as a formidable constitutional weapon, which happened decades later.

In fact, neither position seems quite right. *Marbury* was an important statement at the time and under the circumstances in which it was made. Whether or how judicial review would have developed without it is a question we will never be able to answer. Maybe Marshall's fears were overstated. Maybe judicial review would have continued to evolve as it did without a push from the Court. At the very least, however, asserting and exercising the power of judicial review at just this moment and in just this way helped to preserve a practice that might otherwise have been forced down a dead end road.

5

What Every True Republican
Ought to Depend On

REJECTING JUDICIAL SUPREMACY

With the benefit of hindsight, we can find seeds of a more ambitious theory
of judicial power as early as the late 1780s, an argument that would before
long blossom into the modern idea of judicial supremacy.[1] Federalism was
from the first a reaction to the popularizing, equalizing social and political
effects of the Revolution: a rejection of the volatile style of politics that Revolutionary leaders had practiced against England in the 1760s and an effort to
preserve the tradition of deference and the social order it implied.[2] Somewhat
muted in the 1780s, this conservatism became increasingly pronounced as
time passed. Federalists were never really monarchists, as Jefferson charged,
but the "democracy" they believed in was "a patrician-led classical democracy
in which 'virtue exemplified in government will diffuse its salutary influence
through[out] the society.'"[3] Federalists witnessed the effects of the Revolution, observed their leadership being challenged by farmers, mechanics, and
shopkeepers, and did not like what they saw. As ordinary men began asserting an equal right to govern, suddenly all that petitioning and mobbing and
rousing of public opinion started to look scary. It threatened too easily to spin
out of control. During his brief period of High Federalism, Benjamin Rush
complained: "It is often said that 'the sovereign and all other power is seated
in the people.' This idea is unhappily expressed. It should be—'all power is
derived *from* the people.' They possess it only on the days of their elections.

After this, it is the property of their rulers, nor can they exercise it or resume it, unless it is abused."[4]

Rush's reference to political authority as a property right was not accidental. Federalists viewed political leadership as an entitlement as well as a responsibility: the natural right of a natural aristocracy distinguished by its wealth and breeding, its gentility, and its education and "character."[5] Federalists recognized that they needed permission to rule—permission sought in rowdy, carnivalesque elections that called upon gentlemen to spend a few days "familiariz[ing]" themselves by "personal solicitation" or by "tak[ing] a chearful cup" with ordinary folk.[6] But, as Rush protested, once permission had been granted, ordinary citizens were supposed to lose their political agency. "[T]he *sovereignty of the people* is delegated to those whom they have *freely appointed* to administer [the] constitution, and by them alone can be rightly exercised, save at the stated period of election, when the sovereignty is again at the disposal of the *whole people*."[7] Between elections, the people needed only to listen and to obey. Unity, "respectability," order, and, above all, reverence for "constituted authorities" were the hallmarks Federalists looked for in a well-functioning political system.[8]

This is why Federalists so resented the "Democratic-Republican Societies" of the mid-1790s, which sought self-consciously "to act as intermediaries between [the] political elite and a larger local citizenry," and why they were so discomfited by the new forms of electioneering and politicking that emerged over the course of the decade.[9] Having to worry about "collecting the will of the community" between or even during elections made Federalists nervous. It felt disorderly, and Federalists hated disorder. When Republicans mounted a petition campaign against the Jay Treaty, the Federalists responded with one of their own; they had no choice. But they detested doing it. "The appeal to the people by the disorganizers the last summer," whined Federalist propagandist John Fenno, was "a gross violation offered to Freedom of Deliberation, in the constituted authorities."[10] The matching appeal made by "the friends of the Constitution" might be pardoned, because it was in support of the administration, but having to make such appeals was a bad business all around—a practice liable to be "misused and perverted to dangerous purposes."[11]

In the Federalist worldview, ordinary citizens had no business trying to influence the direction of government outside of election day, unless through respectful petitions "humbly" beseeching duly constituted authorities for relief.[12] Individuals might offer a "decent manly statement of opinion,"[13] yet free speech did not go so far as to include the right to publish something whose "professed design is the superintendence of [the] government" or whose "evident tendency, by obtaining an influence, is to lessen the power of officers of government, and to lead, or rather to drive, the legislature, where ever they please."[14] Such speech must be stopped, Samuel Kendal warned, lest it "prove destructive to 'liberty and order.'"[15] Oliver Wolcott went so far as to say it was "unlawful" for any group or organization to assemble "for the avowed purpose of a general influence and control upon the measures of government."[16]

Particularly after 1793, as news spread of the Terror in France, this anxiety to contain popular politics veered toward hysteria. Federalists grew obsessed with the need to make citizens show "respect" and "deference" and "obedience" to constituted authorities. Nathaniel Emmons preached a sermon in 1799 whose talk about what "subjects" owe their "rulers" makes Republican suspicions about the Federalists' monarchical aims appear almost reasonable:

> The duty of submission naturally results from the relations, which subjects bear to their rulers. There would be no propriety in calling the body of the people subjects, unless they were under obligation to obey those in the administration of government. Every people, either directly or indirectly promise submission to their rulers. Those, who choose their civil magistrates, do voluntarily pledge their obedience, whether they take the oath of allegiance or not. By putting power into the hands of their rulers, they put it out of their own; by choosing and authorizing them to govern, they practically declare, that they are willing to be governed; and by declaring their willingness to be governed, they equally declare their intention and readiness to obey.[17]

"The Proper and Intended Guardians of Our Limited Constitutions"

With a philosophy built around curbing the people's active part in politics, in a world in which those very people were increasingly successful in demanding such a part, is it any wonder that some Federalists soon found themselves championing a new and radical role for courts? The argument appeared as early as 1789, during the debate over the President's removal power. As we saw in chapter 4, almost everyone who spoke to judicial review in this debate accepted the practice. Most seemed implicitly to assume some version of the same departmental theory as Madison, though few explained it as clearly as he did. A few even recognized, without sharing Madison's concern, that courts might gain primacy over the Constitution as a practical matter, simply by virtue of coming last in order.[18]

William Loughton Smith of South Carolina advanced a more extreme position. Noting that "[a] great deal of mischief has arisen in the several states, by the legislature undertaking to decide constitutional questions," he contended that Congress had no business interpreting the Constitution at all: "Sir, it is the duty of the legislature to make laws, your judges are to expound them."[19] Smith found no support for his radical claim that Congress could not even consider the Constitution, if for no other reason than "without such a power, [Congress] could pass no law whatever."[20] In time, however, an increasing number of Federalists came to embrace the deeper assumption implicit in Smith's argument—that because the Constitution is "law," the power to interpret it with authority belonged exclusively to the judiciary.

In 1794 James Kent was 31 years old, a first-year law teacher at Columbia, and a dedicated Federalist.[21] He prepared a series of introductory lectures in which he explained why it was important for lawyers to study the Constitution (a still novel idea). Though Kent flopped as a teacher—his course was apparently so dull that no one attended[22]—Kent's materials are nevertheless worth careful consideration. Alongside James Wilson's lectures, they are among the few extended extrajudicial treatments of judicial review of the 1790s. Even were this not so, the mere fact that these were James Kent's lectures might be thought sufficient to warrant our attention; many would join two of Kent's admiring editors in viewing him as "one of the half-dozen jurists who have put the deepest imprint on American jurisprudence."[23] Yet Kent's analysis of judicial review is of interest mainly because it was unoriginal. For Kent was no Hamilton. He was not gifted or innovative; he was not even particularly interesting. Kent was a plodder, a follower and regurgitator of other people's ideas, especially in his youth.[24] At compilation and synthesis, however, Kent quite excelled—making his lectures useful to us precisely because they so cleanly set forth what by the mid-1790s was starting to emerge as the orthodox position of High Federalism.

Kent's discussion of judicial review differs from the others we have looked at in a number of respects. Mainly, Kent placed greater emphasis than prior writers on the need for "the firmness and moderation of the Judicial department" to protect "the equal rights of a minor faction" from "the passions of a fierce and vindictive majority."[25] Fear of tyrannical majorities was pervasive among Federalists, a critical element of their philosophy (though modern readers would do well to remember that the "minority" they worried about protecting were the wealthy). Yet this fear had not previously been emphasized in connection with judicial review. Some earlier writers had referred in passing to problems of faction while discussing the courts' role in enforcing the Constitution. But these references were brief because earlier backers of judicial review were thinking mostly about legislative mistakes or efforts by legislators to aggrandize their own power at the people's expense.[26] That this should have been so is unsurprising given judicial review's original basis in eighteenth-century forms of popular constitutionalism and resistance. Recall in this regard, for example, Spencer Roane's argument in *Kamper* that the judiciary was resolving a dispute between the legislature and the people of the state.

Kent, in contrast, made majority tyranny the heart of his argument for judicial review; and unlike the prior writers we have studied, he offered it as the best reason to prefer judges to legislators when it came to interpreting the Constitution. More even than this, Kent turned the fear of faction into an argument also against relying on "the force of public opinion":

> [S]ad experience has sufficiently taught mankind, that opinion is not
> an infallible standard of safety. When powerful rivalries prevail in the
> Community, and Parties become highly disciplined and hostile, every
> measure of the major part of the Legislature is sure to receive the sanc
> tion of that Party among their Constituents to which they belong.
> Every Step of the minor Party, it is equally certain will be approved by
> their immediate adherents, as well as indiscriminately misrepresented
> or condemned by the prevailing voice.[27]

This was different from, and more radical than, what courts and judges at the time were saying. Judicial review in Kent's hands was not a substitute for popular resistance that would be difficult to organize, nor was it a peaceful means of rendering such resistance unnecessary. It was a check on the whims and caprice of an easily led mob.

The polemical drift in Federalist thinking reflected in Kent's argument—a shift from seeing judicial review mainly as a device to protect the people from their governors, to viewing it first and foremost as a means of guarding the Constitution from the people—might have been inevitable, just a matter of time given the Federalists' general predilections and prejudices. A need for judicial review to serve as a check on faction, a need seen only hazily at first, could eventually have come into sharper focus no matter what. But political developments in the 1790s intervened to give this line of reasoning a powerful boost, generating (or perhaps merely accelerating) a heightened appreciation among Federalists of the potential usefulness of courts in securing constitutional limits from the threat posed by a partisan majority.

After adoption of the Constitution, most Federalists had expected to amicably govern a quiescent population content to follow their wise leadership. Instead, they were shocked to find themselves wrestling with an unruly, rambunctious democracy-in-the-making.[28] Between the burgeoning newspapers, raucous parades, partisan holiday celebrations, and disrespectful debating societies, the people out-of-doors seemed literally to be taking leave of their senses. Suddenly everyone apparently felt entitled to express an opinion—more, felt that "constituted authorities" should be listening to their views. Sharp fault lines opened as people divided on incendiary issues like Hamilton's financial program or whether to side with England or France in the European wars. Federalist leaders were caught flat-footed, unsure how to cope with this confusing new world in which, as Kent put it, "powerful rivalries prevail in the Community; and Parties become highly disciplined and hostile."

Alarmed Federalists watched in dismay as the opposition threat grew with each passing year. Jefferson's supporters seemed to capture state after state, also taking possession of the House of Representatives and threatening, eventually, to control the Senate as well. So far as the Federalists were concerned, the Republicans' leaders were all demagogues and agitators, their party the very avatar of a factional majority. Recklessly kowtowing to fickle public opinion and heedless of consequences, the Republicans seemed willing, almost eager, to overthrow the Constitution's careful balancing act.

No one had expected this. Certainly not at the federal level, where size and complexity were supposed to ensure harmonious rule by (in the words of turncoat James Madison) "representatives whose enlightened views and virtuous sentiments render them superior to local prejudices and to schemes of injustice."[29] As these naive expectations collapsed amidst growing partisan acrimony, an enhanced role for courts protecting the Constitution from the corrosive effects of faction must have seemed obvious, almost natural—as if the federal judiciary had been deliberately constructed with precisely this purpose in mind. Courts, Kent concluded, because they are "organized with peculiar advantages to exempt them from the baneful influence of Faction," were "the most proper power in the Government to . . . maintain the Authority of the Constitution."[30]

This was so, Kent continued, for a second reason as well: separation of powers. The three departments of government, he observed, are kept "as far as possible separate and distinct" in order to prevent the introduction of "Tyranny into the Administration." It followed that interpretive authority should be vested exclusively in courts of law:

> [T]he interpretation or construction of the Constitution is as much a JUDICIAL act, and requires the exercise of the same LEGAL DISCRETION, as the interpretation or construction of a Law. The Courts are indeed bound to regard the Constitution [as] what it truly is, a Law of the highest nature, to which every inferior derivative regulation must conform.[31]

Here was another newfound claim: a constitution is ordinary law. And because its interpretation is an ordinary judicial and legal act, it is not an act to be performed by legislative or executive officials. Judges, Kent repeated, are "the proper and intended Guardians of our limited Constitutions."[32]

By the late 1790s, ideas such as these were no longer being expressed only by pamphleteers and politicians. Capitalizing on public outrage at France in the wake of the XYZ affair, Federalists waged what one commentator has aptly called a "cultural offensive" against the democratic discourse that had flourished within Republican circles.[33] The Alien and Sedition Acts embodied the formal and legal manifestation of this campaign, but they were accompanied by a relentless stream of propaganda calling upon Americans to reject the French-influenced, popular politics of Jefferson and return to a virtuously passive and deferential concept of democratic citizenship.

As part of this broader effort, some Federalist judges—with enthusiastic plaudits from their party's newspapers[34]—began voicing the new constitutional theory from the bench. Presiding over the seditious libel prosecution of Matthew Lyon, Justice William Paterson instructed the jury that it could not pass on the constitutionality of the Sedition Act. Jurors must treat the law as valid, Paterson insisted, unless and until it was "declared null and void by a tribunal competent for the purpose."[35] Samuel Chase preached an even stronger line in charging a Pennsylvania Grand Jury. "The Judicial Power," he said:

> is *co-existent*, *co-extensive*, and *co-ordinate* with, and *altogether independent* of, the *Legislature* & the *Executive*; and the Judges of the Supreme, and District Courts are bound by their *Oath of Office*, to regulate their Decisions *agreeably to the Constitution*. The Judicial power, therefore, are the only *proper* and *competent* authority to decide whether any Law

made by Congress; or any of the State Legislatures is contrary to or in Violation of the *federal* Constitution.[36]

Chase, too, was as good as his word when presiding at trial—lecturing John Fries that questions of constitutionality were the sole province of the judiciary as he sentenced him to death for leading a mob protest against federal taxes,[37] and refusing to permit Thomas Callendar's defense attorney to argue to the jury the unconstitutionality of the Sedition Act.[38] (John Adams, who recognized the ludicrousness of treating Fries's actions as treasonous, subsequently gave him a full pardon; Chase's conduct of Callendar's trial, in the meantime, several years later earned him an impeachment citation from the House of Representatives.)

We should be careful not to overstate the extent to which judges pushed their authority as constitutional interpreters. These precocious judicial gestures toward the courts' supremacy were sporadic, highly localized, and obviously wrapped up in Federalist anxieties over America's quasi-war with France. Fear that the French Revolution was about to reach American shores unbalanced many normally sensible politicians in the late 1790s, and it was apparently enough also to induce some otherwise cautious judges to espouse what at the time was an extreme position. Efforts made to take constitutional questions from the jury at this particular moment, in other words, reflected Federalist skittishness as much as some sort of determined judicial commitment—which is why they occurred only in cases involving the Sedition Act or other war-related matters, and why even judges who took this position did not adhere to it consistently. In less politically charged cases, some of the same judges continued to recognize the jury's traditional discretion respecting constitutional decision making. Just three days before instructing Lyons's jury, for example, Justice Paterson charged the jury in another case—this one challenging a statutory land confiscation—that "if legislatures assumed to themselves the power to enact unconstitutional laws they ought not to be binding upon juries; and . . . courts and juries were the proper bodies to decide on the constitutionality of laws."[39] But whether or not judges continued to speak more cautiously than politicians, by the late 1790s an argument that courts were peculiarly responsible for constitutional interpretation, that their word ought indeed to be final, had become part of the Federalist canon.

Republicans obviously disagreed. They were willing to acknowledge that courts might take notice of the Constitution in the ordinary course of business, but only within the terms of their departmental theory. Judicial interpretations, on this view, had no more intrinsic weight than those of Congress or the executive, and all were subordinate to the "will of the community," which retained final interpretive authority.

This split in views was nowhere more apparent than in the Republican response to the Alien and Sedition Acts. Worried, with good reason, that the real purpose behind the legislation was to crush the Republican opposition,[40] Jefferson and Madison secretly authored a series of resolutions promulgated by the Kentucky and Virginia legislatures.[41] These were, in context, a good deal less radical than legal scholars today assume. A custom of turning to state legislatures to rally opposition to an overreaching central government was well established, with a long pedigree in colonial practice. This was how Americans had protested the Stamp Act and other imperial measures, and it was the device most frequently proffered by Federalists in 1788 to rebut Anti-Federal charges that states would not survive under the new Constitution.[42] State legislatures had issued similar resolves questioning the constitutionality of previous federal legislation, such as Pennsylvania's proclamations challenging the 1791 excise and Virginia's earlier protests against assumption and the Jay Treaty.[43] Nor did these new resolves go even as far as Madison had condoned in *Federalist 46*. For after explaining why they believed both laws to be unconstitutional, the Kentucky and Virginia legislatures resolved merely to transmit their objections to the states' representatives in Congress and to the other states, so that all could jointly urge federal lawmakers to repeal the offending legislation.[44]

But Federalism had become less tolerant and more paranoid by 1798, and what might once have seemed legitimate now smacked of treason and disunion.[45] Ten states, all with solid Federalist majorities, answered Virginia and Kentucky, and, not surprisingly, all ten censured their sister states.[46] Responses varied from Delaware's curt dismissal of the resolves as "not fit subject for . . . further consideration" to Connecticut's equally compact praise of the Alien and Sedition Acts as "merit[ing] the [state's] entire approbation" and Massachusetts's lengthy disquisition defending the laws.[47] A number of states took the southerners to task for even raising a question of constitutionality, accusing them of meddling in judicial matters that were none of their business. "[S]tate legislatures are not the proper tribunals to determine the constitutionality of the laws of the general government," admonished representatives from New Hampshire, "the duty of such decision [being] properly and exclusively confided to the judicial department."[48] Federalist Rhode Island agreed, insisting that the Constitution "vests in the federal courts, exclusively, and in the Supreme Court of the United States, ultimately, the authority of deciding on the constitutionality of any act or law of the Congress of the United States."[49] Vermont, too, reproached Virginia and Kentucky for encroaching on a power "exclusively vested in the judiciary courts of the Union."[50]

Madison offered the Republican reply in his famous Report of 1800 for the legislature of Virginia. Adhering to views he had expressed since the early 1780s, Madison denied "that the judicial authority is to be regarded as the sole expositor of the constitution."[51] Even apart from the fact that many constitutional questions would never get to court (a concern of greater significance in 1800, when standards of justiciability were more exacting than today), Madison warned that because "the Judicial Department also may exercise or sanction dangerous powers beyond the grant of the constitution," the right of the people "to judge whether the compact has been dangerously violated, must extend to violations . . . by the judiciary, as well as by the executive, or the legislature."[52] Reiterating the assumptions of popular constitutionalism, Madison reasoned:

> However true therefore it may be that the Judicial Department is, in all questions submitted to it by the forms of the constitution, to decide in the last resort, this resort must necessarily be deemed last in relation to the authorities of the other departments of the government; not in relation to the rights of the parties to the constitutional compact, from which the judicial as well as the other departments hold their delegated trusts. On any other hypothesis, the delegation of judicial power, would annul the authority delegating it; and the concurrence of this department with the others in usurped powers, might subvert forever, and beyond the possible reach of rightful remedy, the very constitution, which all were instituted to preserve.[53]

Madison trusted that the "temperate consideration and candid judgment of the American public" would vindicate Virginia's efforts. Recalling the Revolution as precedent, he reminded readers that "[t]he authority of constitutions over governments, and of the sovereignty of the people over constitutions, are truths which are at all times necessary to be kept in mind."[54]

With lines thus clearly drawn between a Republican Constitution and a Federalist one, the two parties squared off in the election of 1800. This pivotal contest exhibited something rarely seen in national elections in the United States: a choice between well-defined alternatives, both clear and clearly understood. Like the question of a national bank in 1832 or the New Deal in 1936, Republicans and Federalists in 1800 offered the public sharply drawn, alternative visions of the Constitution. And the Federalists were decisively, indeed, overwhelmingly, repudiated. The American public, or at least that portion of it permitted to vote, opted for Republican principles and the Republican understanding of constitutionalism. So complete was the rout that Jefferson's party would dominate American politics for the next generation.

"To Defend Them from Their Worst Enemies, Themselves"

The Federalists made one last stab at selling their vision of judicial power to the American people, during the fight over repeal of the Judiciary Act of 1801. This closely watched contest reprised and elaborated many of the arguments made in the late 1790s, and it serves as a fitting epilogue to this part of our story. Both sides detailed their positions in greater depth than before, exposing how far apart their respective positions had become. It was, as it turned out, the last gasp of what we might call the first Federalism movement, at least as an intellectual force.[55] The Federalist party would hang on for a few more years, with pockets of strength in New England. It would even experience a small rally or two, but what remained was a pale shadow of the confident fellowship that gave shape to the Republic in 1788.[56]

Treating repeal as a thinly veiled effort to destroy judicial independence, Federalist speakers urged the necessity of an effective judicial check on Congress and on politics generally. Predictably, their first concern was for preserving order. Judicial supremacy was imperative, they said, because the alternative was violence and bloodshed. "What security is there to an individual, if the Legislature of the Union or any particular State, should pass [an unconstitutional] law?" asked Uriah Tracy in the Senate. "None in the world but by an appeal to the Judiciary of the United States, where he will obtain a decision that the law itself is unconstitutional and void, or by a resort to revolutionary principles, and exciting a civil war."[57] Samuel Dana grimly evoked "scenes of the Revolutionary war" and foretold strife among friends and neighbors "far more violent than is known in any contest against a foreign Power."[58] Roger Griswold made the same argument while avoiding histrionics. Everyone on both sides conceded that some kind of check on Congress was needed, he observed, and "[i]f this power of checking the unconstitutional acts of the Legislature is necessary, where can it reside with so much propriety as in your courts?"[59]

With the people themselves, answered Republicans—a reply that seemed to infuriate Federalists. "Not so, sir, is the case with us," John Rutledge, Jr., snarled: "[W]e do not wish to guard the Constitution by appeals to the people; we will do nothing calculated to produce insurrection; we do not want to protect the great charter of our rights by the bayonet. No, sir, we rely on honest and legitimate means of defence; we wish to check these gentlemen only with Constitutional checks."[60]

Gouverneur Morris was even more disturbed. Adopt the Republicans' argument, he thundered, and "there is an end to all constitutions." Take this check from the judiciary and nothing will prevent Congress "from committing the greatest follies and absurdities." Take Republican ideas about the Constitution seriously and "here is an inestimable treasure put into the hands of drunkards, madmen, and fools."[61] This was not a style of argument calculated to win great public affection; but, then, Federalists were deeply conflicted when it came to public affection. Morris had been among the first to assert in this debate that the people were their own worst enemy.[62] First but not last, as Federalist after Federalist reiterated this basic principle of their creed—all to the great delight of Republicans, who mockingly threw the language back in their faces on every possible occasion.

It was Morris, too, who offered the most strongly worded defense of judicial supremacy. A number of Republicans had suggested that judicial review lacked any constitutional basis. "If it is derived from the Constitution," said John Breckinridge, "I ask gentlemen to point out the clause which grants it. I can find no such grant."[63] Most Federalists responded by citing precedent or by pointing to the Supremacy Clause or to the clause that grants jurisdiction over cases "arising under" the Constitution.[64] But not Morris. Perhaps he understood that these sources might support only judicial review and not the more ambitious project of judicial supremacy; or perhaps by this point in the debate he was simply too angry to quibble about technicalities. Whatever the reason, Morris turned the full force of his ire on the Senator from Kentucky:

And he asks where judges got their pretended power of deciding on the constitutionality of laws? If it be in the Constitution (says he) let it be pointed out. I answer, they derived that power from authority higher than this Constitution. They derive it from the constitution of man, from the nature of things, from the necessary progress of human affairs. When you have enacted a law, when process thereon has been issued, and suit brought, it becomes eventually necessary that the judges decide on the case before them, and declare what the law is. They must, of course, determine whether that which is produced and relied on, has indeed the binding force of law. The decision of the Supreme Court is, and, of necessity, must be final. This, Sir, is the principle, and the source of the right for which we contend.[65]

Of course, most Federalists—including Morris in his calmer moments—defended judicial review without invoking "the constitution of man," by repeating the same argument made since the 1780s: that courts had a duty to "pronounce on the validity of acts of Congress" because the Constitution is "paramount, and limits as well the power of the Legislature as the power of the court."[66]

What these Federalists now added to this familiar argument, reflecting concerns like those that had motivated James Kent, was an insistence that "the Judiciary decide at last, and their decision [be] final,"[67] together with an emphasis on faction and majority tyranny by way of justification. "Legislatures will, in violent times, enact laws manifestly unjust, oppressive, and unconstitutional," explained Calvin Goddard, "and that, too, under the specious pretext of relieving the burdens of the people. Such laws, it is the business of the judges, elevated above the influence of party, to control."[68] John Stanley threw in a dig at the Republicans: "Popular assemblies are as much under the dominance of passion as individuals; they feel as sensibly and resent as malignantly. He who has not made this observation is a stranger to what has passed in all popular governments; and I am sorry to add, a stranger to what has so lately passed in this country."[69]

For just this reason, Federalists argued, in 1788 the people of America "had vested in the judges a check—a check of the first necessity, to prevent an invasion of the Constitution by unconstitutional laws—a check which might prevent any faction from intimidating or annihilating the tribunals themselves."[70] John Rutledge, Jr., said much the same, insisting that the federal judiciary had been specifically and self-consciously "designed" to control what the legislature and executive might do to the Constitution.[71] This was pure revisionism, of course; we have already seen how little attention or emphasis was given to judicial review when the Constitution was written and ratified. But things looked different now. Speaking for his party, Rutledge waxed poetic in limning the new Federalist consensus on the centrality of courts in the scheme of the Constitution:

We say it is the sheet-anchor which will enable us to ride out the tornado and the tempest, and that if we part from it there is no safety left; that it is the only thing which can preserve us from the perilous lee-shore, the rocks and the quicksands, where all other Republics have perished. The Judiciary is the ballast of the national ship; throw it overboard and she must upset.[72]

Republicans answered these arguments, of course, but often they simply permitted their opponents to rail against them without bothering to reply. This was especially noticeable in the House of Representatives, where Jefferson's party had a huge advantage in numbers yet more Federalists spoke and at greater length. Already confident of public support, Republican leaders seemed content to give the Federalists additional rope with which to hang themselves.

Not that the Republicans sat idly and let their adversaries lecture them about constitutional interpretation and enforcement. They may not have responded to every angry denunciation, but they did lay out their own, alternative vision of the Constitution. Where Federalists began with a concern for order, Republicans started with the authority of "the people themselves." Senator James Jackson of Georgia explained:

My principle is, that the creator is the people themselves; that very people of the United States whom the gentleman from New York had declared ourselves to be the guardians of, to save the people themselves from their greatest enemies; and to save whom from destroying themselves he had invoked this House. Good God! is it possible that I have heard such a sentiment in this body? Rather should I have expected to have heard it sounded from the despots of Turkey, or the deserts of Siberia, than to have heard it uttered by an enlightened legislator of a free country, and on this floor.[73]

Similarly avouching his belief that "the people . . . are able to take care of themselves, without the aid or protection of any set of men paid by them to defend them from their worst enemies, themselves,"[74] Speaker of the House Nathanial Macon belittled Federalist declamations about how popular constitutionalism must lead to revolution and civil war. Pointing to the Republicans' own resistance to Federalist depredations in the 1790s, Macon elaborated:

Whenever we supposed the Constitution violated, did we talk of civil war? No, sir; we depended on elections as the main corner-stone of our safety; and supposed, whatever injury the State machine might receive from a violation of the Constitution, that at the next election the people would elect those that would repair the injury and set it right again; and this in my opinion ought to be the doctrine of us all; and when we differ about Constitutional points, and the question shall be decided against us, we ought to consider it a temporary evil, remembering that the people possess the means of rectifying any error that may be committed by us.[75]

The problem with the other side, Macon implied, was that it was too cynical and suspicious, too quick to attribute to others its own angry fears:

Power, says the gentleman, in whatever hands it may fall, will be abused. I hope that he is mistaken, and that time will convince him of his error; but if it should be so, no one in this country will hold power long, because there is a peaceable corrective in the nation, the application of which is perfectly well understood, and is, in my opinion, a sovereign antidote to prevent the abuse. I mean a remedy to which I have often already referred the gentleman; it is an answer to almost everything that has been said—I mean elections. These gentlemen seem to depend on threats and bayonets. We always had a better dependence; it was elections and the good sense of the people; and these, it seems to me, is what every true republican ought to depend on, in a country where the people would as soon change a President as a constable for doing wrong.[76]

Republicans were particularly unforgiving about Federalist allegations that only judges could be trusted faithfully to preserve constitutional values. "We have been told that the nation is to look up to these immaculate judges to protect their liberties; to protect the people against themselves," inveighed William Cocke of Tennessee. "This was novel, and what result did it lead to? He shuddered to think of it. Were there none of these judges ready to plunge their swords in the American heart?"[77] James Jackson made explicit the real-life example that every Republican understood lay behind Cocke's words: "Have we not seen sedition laws? Have we not heard judges crying out through the land, sedition! and asking those whose duties it was to inquire, is there no sedition here?"[78]

John Randolph was especially cutting on this point. The question before the House, he said, was whether "a corrupt decision" on a constitutional question was more likely to issue from "men immediately responsible to the people" or from "those who are irresponsible."[79] Federalists offered "an extreme case" in arguing for the former: "a bill of attainder is passed; are the judges to support the Constitution or the law? Shall they obey God or Mammon?" "Yet you cannot argue from such cases," Randolph insisted, because the example already presupposed what would be in dispute, which was whether the Constitution in fact permitted something. Once the problem had been reframed to take this into account, reliance on Congress no longer seemed so farfetched: "[S]ir, are we not as deeply interested in the true exposition of the Constitution as the judges can be? With all the deference to their talents, is not Congress as capable of forming a correct opinion as they are? Are not its members acting under a responsibility to public opinion, which can and will check their aberrations from duty?"[80] It irked Randolph to listen to Federalists harangue the House with a hypothetical parade of horribles given the Republicans' own, very real experience:

> Let a case, not an imaginary one, be stated: Congress violate the Constitution by fettering the press; the judicial corrective is applied to; far from protecting the liberties of the citizen, or the letter of the Constitution, you find them outdoing the Legislature in zeal; pressing the common law of England to their service where the sedition law did not apply. Suppose your reliance had been altogether on this broken staff, and not on the elective principle? Your press might have been enchained till doomsday, your citizens incarcerated for life, and where is your remedy? But if the construction of the Constitution is left with us [say the Federalists], there are no longer limits to our power, and this would be true if an appeal did not lie to the nation to whom alone, and not a few privileged individuals, it belongs to decide, in the last resort, on the Constitution.[81]

Republicans did not reject judicial review altogether. A small number may have taken this position,[82] but most did not. What all Republicans rejected, however, was judicial finality, judicial supremacy. Judges "may, to be sure, for a while impede the passage of a law, by a decision against its constitutionality," explained Philip Thompson, "yet, notwithstanding the law is in force, is not nullified, and will be acted upon whenever there is a change of opinion."[83] As a group, Republicans adhered to the same departmental theory as that articulated by their party's leaders, Madison and Jefferson. In one of the more thoughtful speeches made on either side, John Bacon, Republican of Massachusetts, explained:

> The Judiciary are so far independent of the Legislative and Executive departments of the Government, that these, neither jointly or separately, have a right to prescribe, direct, or control its decisions. It must judge for itself, otherwise the decisions made in that department would not be the decisions of that, but of some other department or body of men. The Constitution, and the laws made pursuant thereto, are the only rule by which the Judiciary, in their official capacity, are to regulate their conduct. The same is the case with other departments. The Judiciary have no more right to prescribe, direct or control the acts of the other departments of the Government, than the other departments of the Government have to prescribe or direct those of the Judiciary.[84]

In the end, of course, the Republicans prevailed easily. The vote was close in the Senate, but this reflected electoral lag due to its staggered terms rather than real political strength.[85] More indicative of public sentiment was the vote in the House, where the measure carried by almost 2–1.[86] More indicative still was the public's utter indifference to Federalist efforts to arouse indignation over the repeal or to make it an issue in the 1802 midterm elections. Rather than being discredited, Republicans gained ground everywhere in the country except for a single district in Delaware.[87] This being so, one might have supposed that the idea of judicial supremacy would pass away with the Federalist party, which limped along for a few more years before finally expiring for good after the War of 1812. Yet, rather than perish, the principle of judicial supremacy went into hibernation, all but disappearing from respectable public debate until it emerged with restored vigor several decades later.

6

Notwithstanding This Abstract View

THE CHANGING CONTEXT

OF CONSTITUTIONAL LAW

Let us jump ahead for a moment, to the year 1834. Settled for many years in peaceful retirement at his family's gracious estate in Montpelier, James Madison—"the last of the fathers"[1]—wrote the following remarkable letter:

Dear Sir,—Having alluded to the Supreme Court of the United States as a constitutional resort in deciding questions of jurisdiction between the United States and the individual States, a few remarks may be proper, showing the sense and degree in which that character is more particularly ascribed to that department of the Government.

As the Legislative, Executive, and Judicial departments of the United States are co-ordinate, and each equally bound to support the Constitution, it follows that each must, in the exercise of its functions, be guided by the text of the Constitution according to its own interpretation of it; and, consequently, that in the event of irreconcilable interpretations, the prevalence of the one or the other department must depend on the nature of the case, as receiving its final decision from the one or the other, and passing from that decision into effect, without involving the functions of any other.

It is certainly due from the functionaries of the several departments to pay as much respect to the opinions of each other; and, as far as official independence and obligation will permit, to consult the means of adjusting differences and avoiding practical embarrassments growing out of them, as must be done in like cases between the different co-ordinate branches of the Legislative department.

But notwithstanding this abstract view of the co-ordinate and independent right of the three departments to expound the Constitution, the Judicial department most familiarizes itself to the public attention as the expositor, by the *order* of its functions in relation to the other departments; and attracts most of the public confidence by the composition of the tribunal.

It is the Judicial department in which questions of constitutionality, as well as of legality, generally find their ultimate discussion and operative decision: and the public deference to and confidence in the judgment of the body are peculiarly inspired by the qualities implied in its members; by the gravity and deliberations of their proceedings; and by the advantage their plurality gives them over the unity of the Executive department, and their fewness over the multitudinous composition of the Legislative department.

Without losing sight, therefore, of the co-ordinate relations of the three departments to each other, it may always be expected that the judicial bench, when happily filled, will, for the reasons suggested, most engage the respect and reliance of the public as the surest expositor of the Constitution, as well in questions within its cognizance concerning the boundaries between the several departments of the Government as in those between the Union and its members.[2]

It seems scarcely possible that this letter was written by the same hand that, in 1785, omitted judicial review entirely while giving advice about how to preserve constitutional limits;[3] the same hand that, in 1788, acknowledged the courts' place as last in order, but condemned any apparent superiority this implied for judges as something that "was never intended and can never be proper";[4] the same hand that, in 1789, "beg[ged] to know" how any one department could claim "greater powers . . . in marking out the limits" of the Constitution,[5] and in 1800 denied "that the judicial authority is to be regarded as the sole expositor of the constitution."[6]

Of course, even in 1834 Madison was not saying that the Constitution formally delegated more authority over constitutional interpretation to judges. He remained committed to departmentalism as a theoretical matter, continuing to profess that each branch of government "must, in the exercise of its functions, be guided by the text of the Constitution according to its own interpretations of it." Madison's argument for judicial priority in constitutional interpretation came "notwithstanding this abstract view" and rested on pragmatic considerations. It was based not on the judges' greater authority to interpret, but on the greater confidence the judiciary might inspire by the frequency and order with which it addressed constitutional issues and by qualities inherent in the structure of the institution.

Still, the difference in tone from Madison's earlier position is unmistakable. The young Madison came grudgingly to concede to the Supreme Court a certain unavoidable role, which he then fought tenaciously to subordinate and confine. The elder Madison all but lionized the Court, offering both a prediction of and a testimonial to its place as *primus inter pares*.

There were others, too, willing to go farther and to propound a strong and unqualified assertion of the judiciary's formal supremacy in constitutional interpretation. Joseph Story published the first edition of his *Commentaries on the Constitution of the United States* in 1833, and he made a claim for judicial priority in much stronger language, with none of Madison's hesitancy. In a chapter entitled "Who is Final Judge or Interpreter in Constitutional Controversies," Story declared unequivocally that "there is a final and common arbiter provided by the constitution itself, to whose decisions all others are subordinate; and that arbiter is the supreme judicial authority of the courts of the Union."[7] Pointing in particular to the "arising under" clause of Article III, Story reasoned:

> [I]t is the proper function of the judicial department to interpret laws, and by the very terms of the constitution to interpret the supreme law. Its interpretation, then, becomes obligatory and conclusive upon all the departments of the federal government, and upon the whole people, so far as their rights and duties are derived from, or affected by, that constitution.[8]

By now, this should seem an astounding statement, particularly coming from a judge. One problem is that Story's argument is so completely and obviously question begging. Of course the arising under clause can be read to support judicial authority to interpret the Constitution; Chief Justice Marshall had said as much in *Marbury*. But nothing in the language of Article III (or Article VI, for that matter) supports Story's further claim that judicial interpretations are "obligatory and conclusive"—and not only on the other departments of government, but on "the whole people" of the United States.

Certainly *Marbury* asserted nothing of the kind. Story's claim is, indeed, doubly surprising given how cautious and restrained we have seen courts were in the 1780s and 1790s, when they were scrambling for permission to take cognizance of the Constitution at all, not to mention how decisively earlier efforts to establish judicial supremacy had been repudiated. Where, then, did this renewed idea of judicial supremacy come from? And what changed to make it seem plausible even to so committed a former skeptic as James Madison?

"Never Forget That It Is a Constitution *We Are Expounding"*

A number of circumstances contributed to resurrecting the argument for judicial supremacy. One is suggested in Madison's letter, when he notes that "[i]t is the Judicial department in which questions of constitutionality . . . generally find their ultimate discussion and operative decision." This was an overstatement, to be sure. More so in Madison's era even than today, the vast majority of constitutional problems never found their way into court.[9] But Madison's assertion reflected a perception formed by the greatly enlarged number of constitutional issues that did come before judges, as well as the approbation and acceptance of judicial review this gradually fostered. Judicial decisions on constitutional matters grew exponentially after 1800. William Nelson reports that:

> [B]y 1820 . . . eleven of the original thirteen states were publishing reports of their cases, and the courts of ten of them had either invalidated acts of their legislatures or unequivocally asserted their right to do so. Moreover, all five of the states admitted to the Union between 1790 and 1815 had accepted judicial review by 1820, while the four states admitted between 1815 and 1819 all accepted the doctrine in cases published in the first two volumes of their reports. By 1820, in short, the principle of judicial review was "well established by the great mass of opinion, at the bar, on the bench, and in the legislative assemblies of the *United States*."[10]

At first, of course, the "principle of judicial review" that took root during these years was nothing more or different than the principle developed in the 1780s and 1790s. This is why courts seldom found it necessary to offer lengthy explanations of what they were doing, and why Pennsylvania's Justice

John Gibson was exaggerating only slightly when (disowning judicial review in a dissenting opinion) he claimed that "no judge has ventured to discuss it, except Chief Justice Marshall" in *Marbury*.[11] Many courts did offer at least brief justifications of the practice, typically copying from or paraphrasing earlier cases.[12] Judges in the first decades of the nineteenth century thus emphasized that sovereignty lay with the people, that legislators and judges were the people's servants, and that a constitution was "the commission whence [government agents] . . . derive[d] their power."[13] Laws that violated the constitution, they said, "must be void, because the legislature, when they step beyond the bounds assigned them, act without authority, and their doings are no more than the doings of any other private man."[14] Courts were obligated to treat such laws as nullities because judges were equally and independently bound to respect the constitution and would themselves be doing wrong if they failed to take cognizance of it.[15]

Gradually, imperceptibly, the meaning of statements like these began to change. The words were no different, but certain implicit assumptions that lay behind them were. In particular, the original sense of a constitution as popular law for the people themselves to interpret and enforce began to lose some of its vitality and immediacy. Judges did not set out deliberately to produce this change, did not self-consciously seek to transform the Constitution into a kind of law routinely associated with litigation. But, as suggested by Madison's reflexive assumption that the judiciary would normally resolve constitutional disputes, the mere fact that courts were working with constitutions so much, doing to their language and principles the sorts of things that lawyers and judges do, tended inevitably to foster this sense.

Picking up on a suggestion first made in *Federalist 78*, for example, Chief Justice Marshall applied ordinary rules of statutory construction to the text of the Constitution.[16] This was not something that Marshall explained or justified, and certainly not something he strategically plotted. He just did it, in case after case, because that was how judges thought about texts—until this legalistic way of talking about a constitution came to seem so natural and normal that no one thought twice about it. We saw Marshall apply conventional legal reasoning of this sort to Article III in *Marbury*, and it quickly became a staple of his, and so (almost by default) of the Court's, jurisprudence. "[A]lthough the spirit of an instrument, especially of a constitution, is to be respected not less than its letter," Marshall wrote in *Sturges v. Crowninsheild*, "yet the spirit is to be collected chiefly from its words."[17] The words, in turn, were to be interpreted according to their "use, in the common affairs of the world" and given "their full and obvious meaning"—unless this produced a result "so pernicious in its operation that we shall be compelled to discard it."[18] The meaning of one word could be derived by comparing other words associated with it, or by examining the same word in other contexts.[19] And so on.

Nor was Marshall alone in treating the Constitution to a dose of conventional legal analysis or in formulating distinctly legal principles by which to interpret it. Lawlike rules and common law reasoning, the very stuff of ordinary legal interpretation, began appearing routinely in judicial opinions, as judges and lawyers in both state and federal courts grappled with constitutional questions using the sorts of tools with which they were familiar. What unfolded was, in the words of historian G. Edward White, "a fusion in early-nineteenth-century American jurisprudence of a methodology by which common law rules were promulgated by courts and a methodology by which the text of the Constitution was interpreted."[20] Courts began handling constitutional and nonconstitutional cases similarly, White continues, "as if the same interpretive methodology were appropriate to both areas."[21] And as the body of cases treating the Constitution just like ordinary law grew—as lawyers and judges began, for the first time, to speak of a new genre of "constitutional law"[22]—the critical linguistic distinction between it and ordinary law blurred, until the Constitution at last came to seem like ordinary law.

This transformation was, to some extent, facilitated by the very modesty enjoined by the original understanding of judicial review, which enabled courts to build the practice and make it seem commonplace while drawing a minimum of political fire. Judges did not typically intervene unless the unconstitutionality of a law was clear beyond doubt, which as a practical matter left questions of policy and expediency to politics.[23] They also shied away from divisive social conflicts—at least in their constitutional jurisprudence, and in sharp contrast to their handling of private law[24]—striking laws down only in the situations where judicial intervention was least likely to be controversial.[25] Courts were generally respectful of political outcomes, acting in a manner that remained consistent with long-standing practices of popular constitutionalism. According to William Nelson's study of judicial review in the early nineteenth century, "[o]nce a legislature had resolved a conflict in a manner having widespread public support, judges would in practice view the resolution as that of the people at large . . . at least so long as a finding of inconsistency with the constitution was not plain and unavoidable."[26] At the federal level, the Supreme Court systematically deferred to Congress, acting aggressively only in reviewing state legislation—an area clearly designated for judicial scrutiny given the Supremacy Clause, and one in which the Court could speak as a national authority against one or a small number of particular communities.[27]

One should not paint too rosy a picture. Judicial review continued to spread and find acceptance, but its growth was not without controversy, and different views persisted about the practice's meaning and legitimacy. Most constitutional theorists today are familiar with Justice Gibson's dissent in *Eakin v. Raub*, in which the Pennsylvania jurist adroitly dissected Chief Justice Marshall's arguments in *Marbury* while insisting that "it rests with the people, in whom full and absolute sovereign power resides, to correct abuses in legislation, by instructing their representatives to repeal the obnoxious act."[28] But historians have treated Gibson's apostasy as more exceptional and lonesome than was in fact the case, for his was not the only voice raised against judicial review in the early decades of the nineteenth century.

In 1807 the Ohio Supreme Court struck down legislation expanding the small claims jurisdiction of justices of the peace, triggering a confrontation that dominated state politics for the next five years.[29] Ohio legislators responded to the court's decision by impeaching the judges in the majority for "wilfully, wickedly, and maliciously" seeking "to introduce anarchy and confusion in the government of the state of Ohio."[30] The impeachment failed by a single vote, but matters remained volatile enough that a nervous state bar association pledged in a circular letter to ignore the state supreme court and treat the legislation as if it were constitutional—hoping in this way to forestall further attacks on the judiciary.[31] Instead, opponents of judicial review found another way to punish the offending judges by shortening their terms. Angry and frustrated, the judges threatened to continue sitting anyway, and for a brief moment, it looked as if Ohio might experience a judicial schism. But the court's supporters persuaded them to accede to their removal and seek repeal of the legislation redefining judicial terms. By the time this effort succeeded in 1812, it was too late to help the beleaguered judges whose original terms had expired.

The schism that had merely been threatened in Ohio actually occurred in Kentucky a decade later.[32] After the state high court struck down popular debtor relief legislation,[33] outraged opponents swept the next election, winning the office of the governor together with substantial majorities in both houses of the state legislature. Still a few votes shy of the two-thirds necessary to impeach or "address" the judges, the anti-review majority simply abolished the existing court and replaced it with a new one—identical except for the identities of its members and a requirement that the court be unanimous before it could declare legislation void.[34] This time, the judges who had been removed decided to fight; they ignored the statute purporting to do away with their seats and continued to hear appeals. For two years, two high courts sat in Kentucky. Supporters of each court empaneled grand juries and swore out indictments against the other, while lawyers and lower court judges hedged their bets by certifying appeals to both courts. Defenders of the "old" court won the next round of elections, only to watch the incumbent governor veto their bill dissolving the new court. It took yet a third election before the supporters of repeal could resolve the schism by restoring the old court.

One should not make too much of these controversies. In most states, as William Nelson observed, judicial review achieved acceptance without serious travail. Still, the fact that these conflicts occurred—and were significant enough to dominate state politics for several years each—suggests that matters were not quite so settled. A range of views about judicial review continued to persist. In both Ohio and Kentucky, the antagonists proffered visions of the courts' role that ran a gamut from complete rejection of judicial review to full-blooded judicial supremacy. Significantly, the denouement in both states was a decisive rejection of these extremes in favor of the more modest departmental theory, which continued to reflect the mainstream American understanding.[35]

Nothing quite so dramatic occurred at the federal level, at least not as regards judicial review. A number of the Court's opinions reviewing state laws encountered resistance, in challenges that occurred on average once a year and inspired frequent legislative overtures to alter or weaken the Supreme Court.[36] Some twenty-six such proposals were made between 1810 and 1835—seeking everything from withdrawal of the Supreme Court's authority to review state courts to a supermajority requirement for the Court to invalidate state actions to modified rules for removing federal judges to limiting the judges' terms, providing for appeals from the Supreme Court to the Senate, increasing the number of Justices, and requiring seriatim opinions.[37] Eighteen of these proposals received at least cursory consideration in Congress, a few considerably more than that. But none was enacted into law, and state resistance to the Supreme Court's decisions was largely unsuccessful everywhere except in Georgia and Kentucky.

We will come back to these controversies in chapter 7, because they were ultimately important in persuading some observers to reconsider the attractions of judicial supremacy. For now—the present point being simply to mark how routinizing judicial review helped foster a new understanding of constitutions as a species of ordinary law—what matters is to note that these challenges were not attacks on judicial review. They were attacks on the propriety of allowing the U.S. Supreme Court to review decisions by state authorities: a question of jurisdiction and federalism rather than separation of powers. Put another way, what was at issue was not the general propriety of review, but rather a specific question of substantive constitutional law, to wit, who should decide clashes between state and federal authorities.[38] Governor George Troup of Georgia made this clear in a letter to his state's congressmen in which he anticipated the Supreme Court's subsequent efforts to protect the Cherokee Nation from state lawmakers:

> I consider all questions of mere sovereignty as matter for negotiation between the States and the United States until the competent tribunal shall be assigned by the Constitution itself for the adjustment of them. . . . According to my limited conception, the Supreme Court is not made by the Constitution of the United States the arbiter in controversies involving rights of sovereignty between the States and the United States. . . . The States cannot consent to refer to the Supreme Court, as of right and obligation, questions of sovereignty between them and the United States, because that Court, being of exclusive appointment by the Government of the United States, will make the United States the judge in their own cause.[39]

To say that the issue in these controversies was federalism and not separation of powers is not to say that judicial review was never mentioned. Arguments that could be seen as broader challenges to the Supreme Court's general authority to review legislation did occasionally find their way into the mix. In context, however, these arguments clearly read as alternative, albeit clumsy, formulations of the same basic claim that a federal tribunal could not be trusted to determine the rights of a state. In *Tyranny Unmasked*, for example, peckish John Taylor of Caroline scoffed at the idea that "the Federal court is the guardian of the rights of both [state and federal] governments."[40] Urging that federal judges were given no such power by the Constitution, Taylor wrote:

> I have never heard before so novel a political doctrine, as that courts of justice are instituted to dispense political law to political departments. It is to be found in no writer; it has never been a component part of any government; and it is highly probable when the constitution was made, that not a single person in the United States contemplated the

idea, of its having empowered the Federal Supreme Court to divide political powers between the Federal and State governments, just as it does money between plaintiff and defendant.[41]

That judicial review generally was not under attack is clear from the fact that the practice went unchallenged in most states and was resolved in its favor in the few states where challenges arose. Even Justice Gibson abandoned his protest once it became clear that no one was paying attention.[42] John Marshall's most relentless and unforgiving adversary, Spencer Roane, had written an opinion defending judicial review in *Kamper v. Hawkins* and, indeed, never wavered in his support for the Virginia court's power to declare laws void. Some commentators treat this as evidence of inconsistency or hypocrisy on Roane's part,[43] but it was nothing of the sort. Roane's complaint, like that of the Court's other critics, was not directed at judicial review in some abstract or general sense. Roane simply did not believe that the U.S. Constitution meant for controversies between the state and federal governments to be resolved by a federal court—a position one could easily hold while still accepting judicial review in general and in other contexts.

Nor were serious questions raised respecting the Supreme Court's authority to review federal legislation. On the contrary, in the only case that presented this problem, *McCulloch v. Maryland*, the chief complaint of the Court's assailants was not that the Justices had dared to review federal legislation; it was that the Court had construed the Constitution too liberally and should have more narrowly circumscribed the power of Congress. Writing as "Hampden," Roane expressed his "regret" at the Court's statement that only Congress could decide whether the requisite degree of necessity existed for a measure. "And if congress should assume a power under a degree of necessity short of that contemplated by the constitution, ought not the court to interfere?" he asked, "Are congress, 'although there is a written constitution, to follow their own will and pleasure'?"[44]

Which brings us back to the main point: that in the first two decades of the nineteenth century a regular practice of judicial review matured and became routine at both the state and federal levels. The periodic squabbles provoked by the Marshall Court or in a few states in the West appear as brief outbursts against this background, and around and between these flare-ups judicial review came to seem natural and unremarkable.[45] And as this happened, the difference between constitutional controversy and ordinary adjudication lost some of its former salience. Indeed, by the time *M'Culloch* was decided, in 1819, this development had reached a point where Chief Justice

Marshall felt he needed to remind the public that the Constitution was *not* just like ordinary law, that "[w]e must never forget that it is *a constitution* we are expounding."[46]

Naturally, the assimilation of constitutional law into ordinary law—that is, a kind of law normally managed through litigation and judicial interpretation—did not instantly change the practice of judicial review. As with any legal, social, or political disposition, this unself-conscious shift in background assumptions opened up new possibilities and made it easier to put pressure on older ways of doing things. But it did not immediately or even necessarily affect what anyone actually did or thought they should do. Understanding the Constitution as ordinary law, in other words, may have helped to create conditions in which an argument for judicial supremacy could more easily make headway, but it did not itself constitute any inducement to make or accept such an argument. That would take time and, as discussed in the next chapter, a new awareness of possible need for a more-definite-someone's word to be final.

That the time was not yet ripe for broad engagement with the issue of judicial supremacy can be observed in the public indifference to this aspect of *M'Culloch*. For Marshall (unreconstructed Federalist that he was) began his opinion by noting the importance of the case and asserting that "by this tribunal alone can the decision be made. On the supreme court of the United States has the constitution of our country devolved this important duty."[47] That, of course, was going too far for the Richmond junto, which was willing to accept judicial review on a departmental theory but violently opposed this stronger claim. Having just finished urging the Supreme Court to check Congress, Roane thus immediately added: "I differ entirely from the supreme court when they say, that by *that tribunal*, alone, can the decision which they have made be made; and when they further say, that on the supreme court has the *constitution* devolved that important duty."[48] Marshall fought back, publishing his own series of essays under the pseudonym "A Friend of the Constitution" in which he reiterated the same arguments Federalists had made without success in 1802. "[W]here else could this important duty of deciding questions which grow out of the constitution . . . be safely or wisely placed?" he asked. "Would any sane mind prefer to the peaceful and quiet mode of carrying the laws of the union into execution by the judicial arm, that they should be trampled under foot, or enforced by the sword?"[49]

Marshall's opinion and exchange with Roane are of interest to lawyers and historians today because they come so early and because they show the issue of judicial supremacy beginning again to percolate. But we should not make too much of them, for no one at the time seems to have paid a great deal of attention.[50] Judicial supremacy was a small point even in the essays of Marshall and his adversaries, which focused mainly on the question of implied powers and the proper interpretation of the Necessary and Proper Clause. Public inattentiveness to the issue was mirrored as well in the new treatises on constitutional law that seemed suddenly to be pouring from the presses—almost all written by authors of avowedly Federalist sentiments yet paying scant attention to the question of judicial finality and often ignoring it altogether.[51] If the brief exchange on judicial supremacy provoked by *M'Culloch* reads to us like the beginning of something, it is only because we have the benefit of hindsight. At the time, and other than the immediate participants, no one took much notice.

"The Law, Gentlemen, Is a Science of Great Difficulty"

The conceptual absorption of the Constitution into ordinary law was unintentionally aided by two further developments of the early nineteenth century. One was that the ordinary law itself came to look more like ordinary law, or what we now regard as ordinary law. So far, we have focused on the evolution of constitutional law from the seventeenth to the nineteenth centuries, tracking its long existence as a special kind of "popular law," structurally and analytically distinct from what we normally think of as law. By the second or third decade of the nineteenth century this sense of the Constitution was beginning to change. But there was in the colonial and early national periods an equally robust popular aspect to ordinary law—something likewise transformed in the early nineteenth century.

The popular aspect of ordinary law in eighteenth-century America found expression in a variety of ways. The forms of popular enforcement discussed in chapter 1, for example, were never limited to fundamental law. Mobbing, in particular, could be triggered by all sorts of governmental action (or inaction), and it occurred in connection with workaday political matters as much as constitutional controversies. There were bread riots and land riots and riots provoked by labor disputes and by press-gangs, by monetary policy and by any number of other things.[52] This kind of activity dropped off in the later eighteenth century,[53] but popular enforcement never existed in perfect one-to-one correspondence with fundamental law. Nor did courts yet have a monopoly even on formal litigation, and legislatures continued to adjudicate certain kinds of disputes throughout the eighteenth and into the early nineteenth century.[54]

The principal device expressing popular control over ordinary law, however, was the jury. Not only did juries decide nearly every case, but, as William Nelson has documented, "they had vast power to find both the law and the facts in those cases"—power they used to retain command of law's substance.[55] According to Jack Rakove, "juries were the basic agents of decisionmaking in nearly every matter where the general authority of the state intersected with the private concerns and rights of citizens."[56] This is why Anti-Federalists in 1787 felt such intense anxiety over whether the proposed Constitution adequately protected the right to a jury trial, and why the possibility that it might not had provided one of their most effective arguments against ratification.[57] "To threaten the jury trial in any form was to place the entire structure of governance, as eighteenth-century Americans conceived it, in danger."[58]

Much more lay behind this emphasis on juries than merely giving jurors more power to decide individual cases than is typically true today. The eighteenth-century jury was situated within a procedural system and a legal culture whose every feature tended to underscore and reinforce the centrality of lay control. Start with personnel: the number of trained lawyers may have increased in the eighteenth century, so that "by the eve of the Revolution there existed a large number of lawyers and judges skilled in the intricacies of the common law,"[59] but untrained or poorly trained lawyers remained by and large the rule. Bar associations were virtually nonexistent outside New England, and even there the requirements for admission were minimal and haphazard.[60] Formal legal education was still in its infancy, with few law schools teaching few students and a stochastic system of apprenticeship providing what little legal training most lawyers received.[61]

Judges, too, were not generally trained in the law, and there was no telling what the "ministers, would-be theologians, physicians, shoemakers, tailors, and farmers [who] became judges" might tell a jury.[62] The low prestige of being a judge, combined with nettlesome circuit-riding duties and low salaries, were such that many of these lay judges ironically turned out to be better lawyers than the judges who had legal training. "What a court we have," sighed William Plumer, a leading New Hampshire lawyer (and future governor), in 1798:

> The Chief Justice is incapable of close reasoning. Farrar is a better judge, but is not a lawyer. Wingate, who has just been appointed, has

talents too; but a clergyman, put upon the bench at sixty, is too old to enter with success on a new career. These are your eight hundred dollar judges, worth no doubt what they cost; but is not the state entitled to better men; and can she have them while she refuses to pay for their services?[63]

Even apart from issues of personnel, the judiciary was ill-suited to exercise significant control over the law. Trials were presided over by multi-member panels, with each judge required to instruct the jury separately.[64] Their instructions were not binding, and the frequency with which members of the panel disagreed—an occurrence made likely by lack of professional training and a dearth of published precedent—weakened even the persuasive authority of the court's legal exegesis. "[T]here was often as much difference in the law, as expounded from the bench," wrote Plumer's son, "as there had been contradiction in the testimony on the stand."[65] Rules of evidence were more informal and less controlling than today, diminishing the judges' ability to shape what happened at trial, while the absence of special pleading (a legal device for winnowing down issues) left the court few opportunities to take a case from the jury.[66] Once a jury decided, of course, its judgment was almost always final, for there were as yet few grounds upon which to order a new trial and virtually none permitting the court to overturn a jury verdict.

Nor were judges in a position to develop the law even when appeals could be taken. Many courts had only a single term, which meant that legal issues had to be decided at the same time the judges were hearing trials, leaving them little time to consult or reflect. Worse, because rulings on questions of law had to be made while the judges were riding circuit, they were unable to do research unless they happened to be in a place where someone owned a legal library.[67] It goes without saying that such libraries were rare.[68]

Even had there been time to do research and a library to use, the judges would have found little to consult. Written opinions were practically nonexistent. Few judges published their decisions, and the only available sources of American case law consisted of handwritten manuscripts, which could be copied but were seldom widely available; partisan pamphlets; and unreliable newspaper accounts from a handful of notorious cases.[69] The first unofficial reporter did not appear until 1789, when Ephraim Kirby published a volume of decisions of the high court of Connecticut, followed the next year by Alexander Dallas in Pennsylvania.[70] As late as 1805, the appearance of the first volumes of official reports in Massachusetts and New York was considered so noteworthy an event that the leading New England journal published reviews written by the likes of rising star Daniel Webster and New Hampshire's Chief Justice Jeremiah Smith.[71] Nor were there, as yet, treatises or systematic digests of American law to which lawyers and judges could turn in lieu of official reports. There was only Blackstone, who became important almost by default. But even Blackstone was of limited utility given prevailing sentiments against English law and the widespread belief in American exceptionalism: what was right and good for England simply was not automatically right or good for America.[72]

Obviously, not every colony's or state's legal system shared all these traits. The structure of legal practice differed considerably from place to place, as did the pace of development. But the overall pattern was everywhere the same, and it made the jury powerful indeed. Making no effort to hide his disapproval, one mid-nineteenth-century commentator described how things looked at the turn of the century: "The justice of the case was held up as the law of the case; and the jury were to judge both of the law and the fact. Of course there could be no uniformity in the decisions. There were no fixed principles; but each case must have been decided according to the impulse of the jury, who could have no rule but their own fluctuating ideas of justice."[73]

From a modern perspective, as from the perspective of this 1845 commentator, such a system seems intolerably capricious, scarcely lawlike at all. But those who had been raised within it saw things differently. The rules of eighteenth-century litigation conformed to their expectations of how a proper legal system should operate—at least, a proper American and republican legal system—even as those expectations helped produce and perpetuate the very rules in question. It was a way of thinking about law that has been aptly labeled a "jurisprudence of common sense."[74] At its heart lay one very simple idea, well articulated in a widely circulated pamphlet of the early nineteenth century:

[A]ll those laws which relate to property, and the common intercourse among men, which are just and ought to be valid, are in every age and country, the simplest rules, and fitted to the plainest capacities, with few exceptions; insomuch that any and every ignorant man, who has barely a knowledge of the truth, and of right and wrong, can decide any question agreeable to law, although he never heard a law read during his life.[75]

It is hardly surprising, given this belief, that ordinary citizens mistrusted lawyers and often viewed the formalities and technicalities of the legal process as little more than an elite device to obfuscate and conceal the truth.[76] Common sense rather than knowledge of technical law, John Reid informs us, was the juridical attribute most often praised; lay judges frequently substituted the phrase for the word "law" and said they applied not law but common sense in their jobs.[77] "This is a short and simple case," wrote Chief Justice Savage of New York in typical fashion, "addressing itself to the common sense and common justice of the plainest man, and seems to require no legal training to decide it."[78]

The most famous proponent of this school of jurisprudence—largely by virtue of the publicity he received from detractors—was New Hampshire farmer-turned-judge John Dudley.[79] "It is our business to do justice between the parties," Justice Dudley would reportedly say, "not by any quirks of the law out of Coke or Blackstone, books I never read, and never will, but by common sense and common honesty between man and man."[80] Or again: "[Y]ou and I know but little law, that is, lawyers' law; but we know what is right, and we can do justice between man and man. If there is something more, in the present case, let the lawyers look to it. We need not trouble our heads with their nice distinctions."[81] Dudley is most famous for a particular jury charge, often cited as "the classic pronouncement of common-sense jurisprudence":[82]

You have read, gentlemen of the jury, what has been said in this case by the lawyers, the rascals! but no, I will not abuse them. It is their business to [make] a good case for their clients; they are paid for it; and they have done in this case well enough. But you and I, gentlemen, have something else to consider. They talk of law. Why, gentlemen, it is not law that we want, but justice. They would govern us by the common law of England. Trust me, gentlemen, common sense is a much safer guide for us, —the common sense of Raymond, Epping, Exeter and the other towns which have sent us here to try this case between two of our neighbors. A clear head and an honest heart are worth more than all the law of all the lawyers. There was one good thing said at the bar. It was from one Shakespeare, an English player, I believe. No matter. It is good enough almost to be in the Bible. It is this: "Be just and fear not." That, Gentlemen, is the law in this case, and law enough in any case.[83]

Pressure to reform this system had been building gradually throughout the eighteenth century, as the legal profession grew and expanded its influence.

This pressure slackened during the Revolution, which wreaked havoc on the established bar and fostered an anti-professional and anti-elitist spirit that, in turn, nurtured the populism of common-sense jurisprudence.[84] Demand for reform then reemerged after adoption of the Constitution, triggering a decades-long struggle to define the role of courts and lawyers in America.

Some of the impetus for change came from within the profession itself, as lawyers sought to establish the respectability of their craft and to secure their position as part of the intelligentsia.[85] But mainly, social and economic conditions evolved in ways that were no longer suited for a jurisprudence of common sense. The United States expanded rapidly in the early nineteenth century, both geographically and in population; and as population increased the nation grew more diverse and at the same time more economically inter-dependent. Economic development, in turn, fueled changes in the expected role of law and legal services. "Law now had to serve business interests, and no longer was mainly concerned with agistment of cows, fairness of con-tracts, or collection of debts. Agreements had to be enforced to carry out the wills of the parties, not the morality of the community."[86] Demand for legal rules that could reliably be known beforehand—something the eigh-teenth-century's jury-dominated system was manifestly incapable of provid-ing—grew increasingly insistent.[87]

The absence of published opinions was, of course, a major problem. "When I came to the Bench," recalled James Kent years later, "there were no reports or state precedents. The opinions were delivered *ore tenus* [orally]. We had no law of our own, and nobody knew what it was."[88] But the capriciousness of unregulated juries was of greater concern still. "Deci-sions formed at one term were not only no precedent for cases precisely similar at the next term," complained one Portsmouth correspondent, "but not even for those occurring the next day, nor perhaps even the next hour."[89] The problem was obvious to businessmen and politicians alike: "If similar questions are to be determined differently in different cases, then no counsel can advise his clients."[90]

Concerned lawyers began pressing for reform in some states as early as 1791, a movement that spread and escalated in urgency in the ensuing years.[91] But the reformers were hardly unopposed, and little they sought to accom-plish would come easily. The nation was, in fact, badly divided on the ques-tion of law reform. On one side were lawyers and businessmen who wanted to increase predictability in the law, especially in commercial law, by reducing popular control. They fought for greater professionalism on the bench and at the bar, as well as for an array of other changes designed to make the legal process more orderly. Opposing them were all those people who continued to view the legal system as serving "an essentially arbitral function" in which "[o]rdinary people, applying common sense notions of right and wrong, could resolve the disputes of life in localized and informal ways."[92]

Scholars have struggled to define these groups with greater precision. The battle was not drawn neatly along party lines, though Federalists were far more likely than Republicans to support measures that reduced the role of laymen.[93] John Reid suggests that attitudes toward the reception of English common law provide the best gauge for telling the antagonists apart.[94] Those with what Reid calls a "receptionist legal conviction" recognized the unsuitability of much English law for America; they were not advocates of importing wholesale the rules, doctrines, maxims, and precedents of English common law. Although they did look to England for guidance in commercial law, they were mainly interested in the procedures and the methodology of the common law—all those aspects of English practice, in other words, that located authority to articulate and develop law securely within a professional bench and bar. We could, with Reid, call men of this persuasion "receptionists," but they can just as easily (and more simply) be described as "professionals." Opposing them were theorists Reid describes as having "republicanist legal convictions": those who wanted law to be made by "the people themselves," in republican institutions, and who rejected the idea that better law could be "discovered" by lawyers and judges employing the artificial reasoning of the common law. Since not all Republicans fell into this group, for the sake of clarity we will call them "democrats."

The confrontation between these groups, the professionals and the democrats, took place on many fronts and over many years. In part, the battle was intellectual. Understanding "the laws and constitution of our own country," Blackstone had said, is a "science"[95]—a view that became increasingly fashionable among professionals in the early nineteenth century.[96] Law was more than a haphazard aggregation of holdings and statutes, they believed, more than just common sense and common justice. Law was a system of principles: an intelligible, predictable, harmonious ordering whose organic structure and dynamic rules could be understood and taught using the same methods practiced in other sciences.

For those who embraced it, this view of law as science had profound implications. It meant that legal outcomes were not things generated impulsively in and for each new case, but rather something that could be predicted based on knowledge of the appropriate principles—principles that could themselves be organized in a coherent, digestible fashion. Champions of this view set out to prove their claim, too, producing a steady stream of treatises, digests, and specialized texts covering nearly every aspect of American law.[97]

But the principles of the law were intricate and complex, not the sort of thing that could be grasped intuitively by the untrained. Special knowledge and long hours of study were required. Hence, professionals in the early nineteenth century worked hard to reform legal education: founding new law schools, changing the curriculum and style of teaching, and lobbying to make formal schooling prerequisite to joining the bar.[98] Their increasing emphasis on law's complexity, and on the resultant need for professionalization, can be spotted in an interesting feature of early treatise writing detected by G. Edward White. While the first American treatises presented law as something every responsible citizen could and should understand—White offers St. George Tucker's 1803 edition of Blackstone by way of illustration—scholars were soon writing exclusively for a professional audience of law students and practitioners.[99] And, of course, if law really was a complicated science that required intense study and special training, it could not be left to the common sense of laymen. Hence, the professionals sought to replace lay judges, to beef up requirements for admission to the bar, and to limit the authority and discretion of juries.[100]

The thrust of the professionals' critique is conveyed in an apocryphal story of an encounter between Pennsylvania Governor Thomas McKean (a Republican who sided with the professionals) and a delegation of democrats seeking his support for legislative measures designed to enhance lay control:

> [McKean] deliberately took out his watch and, handing it to the chairman, said, "Pray, Sir, look at my watch; she has been out of order for some time; will you be pleased to put her to rights." "Sir," replied the chairman with some surprise, "I am no watchmaker; I am a carpenter." ... "Well," said the Governor, "this is truly strange! Any watchmaker's apprentice can repair that watch; it is a simple piece of mechanism, and yet you can't do it! The law, gentlemen, is a science of great difficulty and endless complications; it requires a lifetime to understand it. I have bestowed a quarter of a century upon it; yet *you*, who can't mend this little watch, become *lawyers all at once*, and presume to instruct me in my duty!"[101]

Most of what the legal reform movement targeted for change were practical aspects of day-to-day administration.[102] The professionals sought to change—and the democrats to preserve or extend—virtually every feature of the system outlined above. There were fights over whether to allow a single judge to preside at trial or, barring that, to allow a single charge to the jury; whether to continue appointing lay judges or to appoint only lawyers to the bench; whether to make jury instructions binding and limit the jury's role to fact-finding; whether to institute a system of special pleading and incorporate other procedures enabling courts more easily to dispose of cases without submission to a jury; whether to abolish the common law writ system; whether to have a separate term for hearing appeals; whether to produce official reports or at least permit the publication of written opinions; and whether to hire court reporters.

In the end, the professionals triumphed, though their progress was slow and uneven and they suffered many setbacks along the way. Democrats won battles in some states in the South and West, for a time at least. By 1830, however, the process of professionalization was far advanced throughout the nation. The Jacksonians staged what amounted to a last ditch effort to stave off the triumph of the lawyers, but it was already too late. They had little choice but to concede control to the professionals, and they tried instead to make the professional bench and bar more accountable—mainly through a movement to codify law and by the enactment in many states of provisions for an elective judiciary. But their uphill struggle to recapture control of substantive law by codification never came close to displacing the common law.[103] Judicial elections, in the meantime, may have had both good and bad consequences—though nothing "so earthshaking . . . as proponents had hoped and opponents feared"[104]—but they did nothing to weaken the commitment to a professional bench or to shake the legal profession's monopoly on judicial posts.[105]

Which brings us back to the issue at hand: the slow, unconscious process by which constitutional law was recast as a kind of ordinary law. During the early decades of the nineteenth century, American legal culture manifested an extraordinary and pronounced tendency toward increasing judicial control of law in general. By the 1820s and 1830s, law and legality were firmly associated with lawyers and judges and viewed as a professional process inaccessible to laymen. Juries remained important, but their role was confined to fact-finding and much more closely regulated by the court. In such an atmosphere, the assimilation of fundamental law to ordinary law must have seemed just that much more natural and the potential appeal of an argument that constitutional law was for lawyers and judges to decide grew accordingly.

Earning "the Confidence of the People"

A third development, this one involving politics rather than law, also merits brief discussion in connection with changing conceptions of the Constitution and of law in the early decades of the nineteenth century: the absorption of popular politics by political parties. The emergence of parties was a surprise, something the Framers never imagined in 1787 and certainly would have abhorred. Yet parties turned out to be indispensable in making the Constitution work, and it is unlikely that the Republic could or would have survived without them (or something like them).[106]

Anti-Federalists in 1787 had worried that governing would be impossible in an extensive republic.[107] Representation could work only on a small scale, they said, though not for cryptic reasons like those offered by the oracular Montesquieu. Their argument was straightforward and intensely practical: there would be too many people with too many views on things and too few representatives to satisfy them. Constituents would scarcely know their own representatives in the huge districts required by the new national government, much less representatives from other states. As a consequence, voters would be unable to judge considerations that might have made a compromise seem reasonable in Congress or to appreciate whether congressmen from other states were even acting in good faith, and this, in turn, would make it difficult to measure the performance of Congress as a whole.[108] Size would also make it impossible for voters dissatisfied with the direction of national politics to coordinate their efforts to produce a change in membership sufficient to change policy.[109] The result would be a progressive loss of confidence and trust in government, leading to disunion and disaster.[110]

Federalists dismissed these fears as shallow and misinformed, assuring their opponents that all that was necessary to earn "the confidence of the people" was to govern well.[111] But they were wrong. Americans were not prepared to sit idly by and let their Federalist superiors rule, nor were they prepared to be told what constituted governing well. They had their own ideas about what to do and how to do it, ideas that differed not only from those of men in power but also from those of each other. Just as Anti-Federalists had predicted, inflammatory issues of national politics soon engaged the passions of previously unheard-of numbers of citizens, and within a few short years the country really did seem headed toward civil war.

But the Anti-Federalists had also miscalculated. They had assumed that the problem of size was insoluble, that the only option was not to have a national republic of any consequence. Instead, working both together and in opposition, former Federalists and Anti-Federalists faced the challenge of national politics and, very nearly in spite of themselves, found another way.

As political cleavages emerged in the 1790s, men in and out of office fumbled for appropriate responses, intuitively groping their way toward solutions to problems they had not properly anticipated. The initial impetus for party development came from the center. Treasury Secretary Hamilton began as early as 1790 to forge connections with members of Congress in order to obtain passage of his program for economic development; Madison and Jefferson countered by mimicking Hamilton's efforts in order to defeat his plans.[112] As competition grew more heated, both sides found it necessary to reach out to the countryside for support.[113] Given the lingering eighteenth-century political hierarchy and the still primitive state of the media, this naturally meant appealing to state and local political leaders to build a stable following.[114] None of this was done with the idea of establishing political parties, but with each successive controversy, these tentative contacts grew firmer and eventually a stable ideology and internal identity evolved.[115] Particularly after the election of 1796, fledgling party managers looked for ways to organize and coordinate campaigns: writing the first party tickets and party platforms, imposing the first weak forms of party discipline, and making the first uses of patronage. The result was a loosely integrated network of state and local alliances that linked politicians at these levels to politicians in the federal government working to advance a shared agenda.[116]

The genius of the parties that had emerged by 1800 was their capacity to solve the dilemma of size. Parties changed the nature of running for office and, with that, the expectations of both officials and constituents. Affiliation with a party became the crucial thing, as candidates began to run campaigns based on their attachment to the party's philosophy or platform.[117] The parties became a locus for formulating a nationally shared public agenda and a means of coordinating electoral campaigns in a way that linked the decisions of voters throughout the nation with a sense of shared purpose. The parties also assumed responsibility for organizing the government internally so that the prevailing party's general policies, if not its entire program, might stand a chance of being enacted. The standing committee system, congressional caucuses, and general practice of interbranch coordination are all partly products of the development of parties.

Even as they aggravated popular discontent, then, the emerging parties simultaneously became a device for channeling that energy back into the system. By replacing traditional forms of politics with the new rituals of partisan elections, parties provided the institutional infrastructure necessary to stabilize popular politics.[118] They did so by offering a platform through which to voice effective opposition and from which to compete for control, while at the same time making it possible for winners and losers to survey public sentiment nationwide. Party politics provided a measuring stick with which to assess what elections meant and to gauge how well the government performed.

It is when we focus on these concrete manifestations of party politics that we see the irrelevance of the endless debate among historians and political scientists about whether these first parties really were "parties" or really were a "party system."[119] It is undoubtedly true, as Joanne Freeman has convincingly demonstrated, that the bonds that connected men in these early political struggles were radically different from those that connect politicians today—bonds of honor and friendship more than membership in an organization.[120] It is equally undeniable that the first generations of American leaders were dreadfully uncomfortable with the idea of political parties and that they remained so throughout their lives. And it is just as surely the case that they never saw themselves building permanent institutions, but rather looked forward to the day when parties would no longer be necessary and could be eliminated.

None of this matters. However much they hated what they were doing, they did it. However much they longed to undo it, they failed. It may have taken until the 1840s or 1850s for modern attitudes about parties to develop. But the crucial practices of party politics—the use of stable institutionalized means to recruit candidates, organize campaigns, and arrange the government within to implement policy—were all in place by 1800. And it is these practices, however grudgingly followed, that mattered. Parties provided a way to make politics meaningfully accessible to an enlarged polity, while at the same time keeping the ensuing tensions manageable within a republican framework.

The first parties were not long-lived. The Federalists never recovered from their defeat in 1800. Unable to remove the stain of treason associated with the Hartford Convention, the Federalist party disintegrated after 1814 and disappeared from the national stage entirely after 1817. Republicans, in the meantime, lacking effective competition and handicapped by James Monroe's misguided quest for party reconciliation, degenerated into squabbling factions and ceased to function as an effective national organization a few years later. Within a decade, however, a second party system—this one considerably more structured and durable than the first—had begun to emerge, reassuming the functions of its predecessor as a device for organizing American politics.[121]

As the new politics settled and became normalized in the 1830s, the role of "the people" in it changed. By serving as formally structured mediating institutions between governed and governors, parties obscured the formerly sharp theoretical distinction that had existed between them. Party organizations now became the primary means by which preferences were transmitted, favors sought, problems communicated, and grievances addressed. Traditional forms of political expression did not disappear: they were co-opted and monopolized by the parties. This process had begun as early as the 1790s, when Federalists and Republicans sought to control and take advantage of the period's locally inspired and sometimes spontaneous parades and festivals.[122] But parties in the second party system were more determined and effective in controlling popular politics, and to a much greater extent popular meetings became party meetings—organized by party officials, for party ends. So, too, with most other traditional tools of popular politics. Petition campaigns were still mounted, but as often as not these were organized by and for a party. Mobbing alone was an exception to this pattern of party monopolization. Mob activity began falling out of favor in the 1790s, and there was relatively little of it during the first third of the nineteenth century; the mobbing that resumed in the 1830s and 1840s had evolved into a virulent expression of racial, religious, and class-based resentments, which further delegitimated rioting as a method of "normal" political expression.[123]

Popular politics was, in effect, swallowed up by party politics: and because party politics was all about winning office, popular politics started to lose its salience as a check operating from outside to control political institutions. The "voice of the people," as such, was now expressed mainly by elected representatives responding to political signals and popular movements as refracted through the parties.[124] Politics began to acquire its modern complexion, in which it is hardly comprehensible to speak of "the people" as a corporate entity, capable of independent action. In short, politics moved indoors.

* * *

The assimilation of constitutional law into ordinary law, on the one hand, and the domestication of popular politics, on the other, were both crucial in preparing the ground for renewed controversy over the role of the judiciary in constitutional law. But these complementary developments were still just background phenomena: changes that occurred slowly, without self-conscious engineering, and that did not themselves prompt anyone to rethink the Court's role in constitutional interpretation and enforcement. Certainly no one was moved to argue for an expanded judicial role *because* a rhetorical shift took place in understanding the Constitution as law, or *because* the people out-of-doors started speaking mainly through political parties. Something else happened to induce concerned citizens—including many who saw themselves as Jefferson's intellectual heirs—to look for a new and better way to settle constitutional conflicts. Once their search began, however, these changed background understandings would become part of what shaped people's response to a judicial solution.

7

To Preserve the Constitution, as a Perpetual Bond of Union

THE LESSONS OF EXPERIENCE

The idea of judicial supremacy, as we have already seen, never disappeared entirely. Federalists and former Federalists did not all change their minds simply because they lost the election of 1800 and suffered the repeal of the Judiciary Act of 1801. Some did, perhaps, but more than a few diehards clung to views about the judiciary formed in the 1790s, including the belief that federal courts were principally, and finally, responsible for the law of the Constitution. They even picked up an occasional convert along the way, like Joseph Story—an ostensible Republican, appointed to the Supreme Court by Madison and branded an "insidious democrat" by the high priest of High Federalism, Timothy Pickering.[1] Once on the bench, Story became John Marshall's most trusted lieutenant, someone who (again in Pickering's words) "never appeared more happy than when in the Society of respectable federalists."[2]

Story wrote Marshall in 1821 that he could hardly bear to read the arguments of those who, like Jefferson and Spencer Roane, challenged the Court's authority because they "make me too angry."[3] Jefferson's position on the judiciary, he confided, "appears to me so fundamentally erroneous, not to say absurd, that I have a good deal of difficulty in reading with patience the elaborate attempts of [Virginia's] political leaders to mislead and deceive us." Commenting on a letter denying judicial supremacy that had been written by Jefferson and posted in a local bookshop, Story said, "[t]here never was a period in my life when these opinions would not have shocked me . . . & in these critical times they fill me alternately with indignation and melancholy."

Such views were seldom aired publicly before the 1830s, however, and when on display they attracted little notice. Squelched in 1802, the issue of judicial supremacy receded into the background, due partly to Republican dominance of the political scene and partly to the general caution and modesty of courts, especially at the state level, when it came to constitutional interpretation. Outside a small circle of men who cared passionately about the Supreme Court, no one else seemed to give the matter much thought. Arguments for supremacy did crop up in the disputes over judicial review in Ohio and Kentucky, but they were widely and unequivocally rejected. For the moment, the Jeffersonian orthodoxy of departmentalism still reigned, albeit possibly as a handed-down interpretation only.

Consider, for example, the letter by Jefferson that prompted Story's bitter missive to John Marshall. William Jarvis, a Massachusetts Republican, had written a book on American government entitled *The Republican*, and he sent Jefferson a copy.[4] In acknowledging the gift, the retired President praised Jarvis's work, writing "I see much in it to approve, and shall be glad if it shall lead our youth to the practice of thinking on such subjects and for themselves."[5] (It was this, presumably, that prompted Story's local bookseller to post Jefferson's reply, a positive review from the "sage of Monticello" being undoubtedly good for sales.) Precisely because the book might be influential, however, Jefferson said he felt "an urgency to note what I deem an error in it": "You seem, in pages 84 and 148, to consider the judges as the ultimate arbiters of all constitutional questions; a very dangerous doctrine indeed, and one which would place us under the despotism of an oligarchy."[6] Jefferson then went on to relate, for the umpteenth time, his well-known views on the independence and equality of the three branches when it came to constitutional interpretation. Such views may have "shocked" Story, but Jarvis's faintly unctuous reply probably reflected the more common view:

I acknowledge that there is too much ground for the inference you have drawn in regard to those parts of the book; but I have satisfaction in saying that I have exposed myself to your judicious criticism much more from an unguarded mode of expression than from any difference of opinion between us, in relation to the subject upon which you have remarked.

I have never thought that the judicial power had any superiority or pre-eminence over any branches of the Legislature, or the supreme executive; nor have I considered that power as competent in all cases to control the doings of the legislative or executive departments of government. My idea simply is, that the judicial authority tends to keep the administration of government true to its fundamental principles by *refusing* to give effect to unconstitutional laws, when the rights of citizens litigating depend upon laws the constitutionality of which is questioned. . . . I have much satisfaction in saying to you that if I could recall the present edition, I should make such an alteration in pages 84 and 148 as would exclude the inference which now presents itself to the reader.[7]

Any conclusion about how much of the public shared Jarvis's view is, of course, pure guesswork—precisely because there was so little talk about judicial supremacy except among the small circle of concerned insiders. Perhaps the most we can say is that the question of judicial supremacy remained latent, with the Republican orthodoxy of 1800 as conventional wisdom among the general public if only because nothing had yet occurred to displace it.[8]

By the early 1830s, this had started to change. A series of constitutional altercations—conflicts that seemed to be escalating—had made the problem of settling constitutional differences into a major public headache. And with the issue now being openly debated and on practically everyone's mind, a larger circle came round to thinking that the judiciary might, after all, be the right place to turn for finality. What ultimately moved a greater number of Americans to embrace the idea that judges should have the preeminent word on constitutional meaning, in other words, was experience, which seemed to teach that popular constitutionalism in its traditional form might not work in a society as diverse and dynamic as the United States. Someone more definite and distinct than "the people" was needed to resolve constitutional disputes, which if left unsettled threatened to break apart the Union. Given the changes described above in the background understandings of both politics and the nature of the Constitution as law, that this someone should be judges presumably seemed natural.

Yet increasing conflict and controversy did not automatically point toward courts or judicial supremacy by way of solution, and other responses were also available. For those committed to the ideals of popular constitutionalism, judicial supremacy continued to seem *un*natural, not to mention anti-republican. Escalating discord was, in their view, a problem best addressed through

reform of political institutions, and their eventual solution—a new and radically different kind of political party—offered a very different response to the
same experience.

"The End of This Is War—Civil War"

To understand what elicited these varied reactions, it is useful once again to
begin with the Republican opposition of the 1790s, which had been based
throughout on the optimistic assumption that "the main body of our citizens . . . remain true to their republican principles."[9] It was only a matter of
time, Republican leaders assured one another, until the nation righted itself
and cast the Federalists out of office.[10] "[T]he superiority of numbers is so
great [on the Republican side]," wrote Madison in 1792, "their sentiments
are so decided, and the practice of making a common cause . . . is so well
understood, that no temperate observer of human affairs will be surprised if
the issue in the present instance should be reversed, and the government be
administered in the spirit and form approved by the great body of the people."[11] As it turned out, this took a few years longer than Madison and Jefferson had expected, but overwhelming victory in the election of 1800 seemed
to vindicate the Republicans' faith. Federalism was dead, they thought, and
with it the turmoil of the previous decade.

They were mistaken. The Federalist party might have been dead, or dying,
but the underlying divisions that had made politics so ferocious were not.
Rather than hand the triumphant Republicans a stable constitutional settlement (like the one Americans believed had been reached in England after
the Glorious Revolution), the "Revolution of 1800" turned out to be no more
than a lull in hostilities. Jefferson's first term in office was thus relatively
peaceful—at least, by comparison to John Adams's, and apart from the battle
over the judiciary, which ended inconclusively after Justice Chase escaped
conviction on impeachment charges.[12] But his second term did not go as
smoothly.

Most portentous was the resistance Jefferson encountered when he tried
to avoid war with England by imposing an embargo. Halting American trade
to intimidate Great Britain was a mistake: the embargo did very little to
pressure England (whose merchant fleet, in fact, profited handsomely from
the shipping business thus made available), but it did impose severe economic hardship on Americans, especially in the Northeast.[13] Facing disaster,
American carriers tried to break the embargo, which forced Jefferson to

adopt restrictive enforcement measures, which in turn triggered still greater resistance.[14] Opponents quickly adopted the Republicans' own strategy from 1798: organizing their opposition at the state level and insisting that states had equal authority to say what was or was not constitutional. Resistance became violent in some places, there was talk of secession and civil war in others, and the legislatures of Massachusetts, Delaware, Rhode Island, and Connecticut adopted formal resolutions challenging the embargo's constitutionality.[15] Connecticut went so far as to forbid state officeholders to aid in the enforcement of federal law.[16]

Resistance to the embargo was just the beginning, moreover, of what soon became a regular practice of state resistance to federal authorities on constitutional grounds.[17] Many of the most notorious challenges were provoked by decisions of the U.S. Supreme Court. Pennsylvania called upon its militia to resist the Justices' effort in *United States v. Peters* to resolve a dispute over prize money.[18] Virginia twice raised a ruckus over Supreme Court review of the state's courts under section 25 of the Judiciary Act—first in *Martin v. Hunter's Lessee*,[19] then later in *Cohens v. Virginia*.[20] Kentucky ignored the Court's mandate in *Green v. Biddle*,[21] while Ohio battled the Court in *M'Culloch v. Maryland*[22] in dramatic fashion, leading to a subsequent decision in *Osborn v. Bank of the United States*.[23]

At least as many constitutional challenges during these years did not involve courts. Madison faced persistent opposition from states during the War of 1812. Some Federalist governors in the North refused to send troops, arguing that only they—not Congress or the President—could decide whether a state of emergency existed sufficient to warrant calling out the state militia.[24] In 1814 Madison faced a threat of secession from New England states meeting at the ill-fated Hartford Convention.[25] Guided by some more moderate Federalists in attendance, the convention adopted a wait-and-see strategy and resolved in the meantime to send commissioners to Washington with a list of grievances. As luck would have it, just as the convention was breaking up, American negotiators were signing a treaty of peace and Andrew Jackson was winning his famous victory in New Orleans. Hartford thus became a huge embarrassment for states' rights advocates—though, as subsequent events would prove, no more than a temporary setback to their cause.

With the end of the war in 1815, a wave of nationalism swept the country, generating a program of federal legislation unlike anything seen since Hamilton's days at the Treasury.[26] Adopted under the leadership of House Speaker Henry Clay, this program—subsequently dubbed "the American

System"—included a second national bank, a system of protective tariffs, and a program of internal improvements.[27] Unfortunately for Clay and his supporters, the enthusiasm that made it possible to enact these ambitious laws just barely outlived their creation, and within a short time bitter disputes had broken out over the constitutionality of every aspect of Clay's program.

Still more ominous was the emergence of open conflict on the issue of slavery. Madison had worried about this from the beginning, observing as far back as the Federal Convention in 1787 that "the great division of interest" among the states was over slavery, and that this, more than anything else, would strain the bonds of Union over time.[28] If anyone doubted the truth of his premonition, the Missouri crisis of 1819–1821 exposed the underlying rancor of sectionalism and brought the government to a standstill until an expedient compromise could be cobbled together.[29] This settlement notwithstanding, the upshot of the Missouri controversy was to awaken Southern paranoia respecting the section's peculiar institution. "It has been said that the Missouri Compromise put the question of slavery to sleep for many years," observed a leading historian of the period. "But this is not true. It never slept again."[30]

Things were, nonetheless, at least somewhat quieter for a few years in the mid-to-late 1820s. A number of factors may have accounted for this. Spencer Roane died in 1822, silencing one of the most intelligent and articulate, not to mention persistent, voices for states' rights. Also important were the activities of the Marshall Court itself, which had been the target of much of the states' enmity. Numerous commentators have observed that the Supreme Court moderated its positions in the mid-to-late 1820s, yielding on a range of issues to the inexorable pressures it faced.[31] Other commentators disagree, claiming the Court never swerved from its nationalist course.[32] Be that as it may, the Justices were widely *perceived* to have curbed their aggression, which was all it took to ease the hostilities.[33] Another source of the let-up was the fickleness of state politicians. Indeed, the consistency with which states acted *in*consistently when it came to the supposed "principle" of states' rights is quite remarkable. Virginia protested decisions like *Martin v. Hunter's Lessee* and *Cohens v. Virginia*, but declined to support Kentucky's opposition to *Green v. Biddle* because the particular ruling in the case favored some Virginia landowners. Pennsylvania and Kentucky both defied federal authority and sought constitutional amendments at different points in time, but neither ever supported the other (or Virginia, for that matter). Kentucky, in particular, showed how its assertions of constitutional principle were contrived by becoming a great advocate for federal authority once the Supreme Court had yielded to its particular complaint by limiting the holding in *Green.*[34] This sort of incongruity was common throughout the period.

But just when it seemed as if the storm may have passed, it started up again. The early 1830s brought a spate of new problems, one atop the other in quick succession. In terms of both rhetoric and tactics, moreover, the new cycle was surlier and more venomous than what had come before.

The tone of the decade was set at the very outset, in January of 1830, when Robert Hayne and Daniel Webster stumbled into one of the great political debates in American history. It began innocuously enough. Calling attention to the fact that seventy-two million acres of western land had been surveyed but remained unsold, Samuel Foot of Connecticut introduced a resolution requesting a study to determine whether Congress should suspend further surveys and abolish the office of the Surveyor General.[35] Thomas Hart Benton of Missouri charged Foot, and "the East" generally, of conspiring to "pauperize" the West and to frustrate westward expansion through tightfisted land policy. He called for support from Southern senators.[36]

This was a calculated move on Benton's part, an effort to shift sectional alliances in the Senate to reflect the popular alignment that had recently elected Andrew Jackson.[37] Eagerly accepting Benton's invitation, South Carolina's Robert Hayne launched an attack in which he coupled federal land policy with tariffs and the American System as examples of Eastern exploitation of the South. Daniel Webster rose on the spur of the moment to defend his beleaguered section, and the debate took off from there—consuming five full days during which essentially no one but these two men spoke, drifting in their subject-matter from land policy to internal improvements to tariffs to slavery and, ultimately, to the nature of the Union itself. Consideration of Foot's resolution dragged on intermittently for another five months, giving several more Senators a chance to respond to either Webster or Hayne.

Few speeches in American history—only Lincoln's Gettysburg Address, his Second Inaugural, and perhaps Washington's Farewell—have been as widely circulated and read in their time as those of Webster and Hayne, particularly Webster's dazzling second reply.[38] While many issues were discussed, moreover, considerable attention was paid to the role of the judiciary in settling constitutional disputes, and in particular to the question of its finality. It is especially interesting to contrast what these men were saying in 1830 with the debates of 1802 over repeal of the Judiciary Act.

There were no longer any Federalists, of course, and with them had gone most of their arguments for judicial supremacy. No one in 1830 talked about saving the people from themselves or argued that judicial review was needed to combat faction. On the contrary, Daniel Webster—a former Federalist who used this opportunity, among other things, to remove the stain of Hartford[39]—invoked "the people" in ways that would have made even Jefferson blush:

> It is, sir, the People's Constitution, the People's Government; made for the People; made by the People; and answerable to the People. . . . We are all agents of the same power, the People. . . . I hold it to be a popular Government, erected by the People; those who administer it responsible to the People; and itself capable of being amended and modified, just as the People may choose it should be. It is as popular, just as truly emanating from the People, as the State Governments.[40]

Webster's oration is drenched in this sort of rhetoric, including even his argument for judicial supremacy:

> The People, then, sir, erected this Government. They gave it a Constitution, and in that Constitution they have enumerated the powers which they bestow upon it. They have made it a limited Government. They have defined its authority. . . . But, sir, they have not stopped here. If they had, they would have accomplished but half their work. No definition can be so clear, as to avoid possibility of doubt; no limitation so precise, as to exclude all uncertainty. Who, then, shall construe this grant of the People? . . . This, sir, the Constitution itself decides, also by declaring, *"that the Judicial power shall extend to all cases arising under the Constitution and Laws of the United States."* [That clause together with the Supremacy Clause], sir, cover the whole ground. They are, in truth, the keystone of the arch. With these, it is a Constitution; without them, it is a Confederacy.[41]

One can detect implicit in Webster's address some of the changes we have been discussing: both the normalization of judicial review as an act of ordinary legal interpretation and the loss of a strong sense that "the people" can express their views on the meaning of the Constitution on an ongoing basis through popular politics. Hence, unlike James Kent in the 1790s, Webster did not need to argue that judicial review was an ordinary legal act; he could simply assume it, along with his audience. And unlike Gouverneur Morris in 1802, it would not have occurred to Webster to suggest that the people could not interpret their own will: he assumed that too, but without any sense of active, ongoing involvement on their part. "The people" in Webster's universe had already been relocated to that abstract plane where most theorists still strand them: theoretically capable of exercising "their known and admitted power, to alter or amend the Constitution, peaceably and quietly, whenever experience shall have pointed out defects or imperfections,"[42] but otherwise unable to act and having delegated all their authority to the government itself. "Who shall interpret [the People's] will, where it may be supposed they have left it doubtful?" Webster queried in the midst of his reverie on popular sovereignty. "With whom do they repose this ultimate right of deciding on the powers of the Government?"[43] In 1800 triumphant Republicans led by Jefferson and Madison had declared that this "right" remained with "the people themselves." But Webster had a different answer in mind: "Sir, they have settled all this in the fullest manner. They have left it, with the Government itself, in its appropriate branches."[44] By "appropriate branches," Webster went on to explain, he meant ultimately the federal judiciary.

Context is everything, of course, and we cannot properly understand Webster's argument without appreciating its immediate context, which was nullification. Though Americans everywhere had supported Clay's federal program in the immediate wake of the War of 1812, that support waned rapidly in the South over the next decade as economic depression and worries about slavery took their toll. By the mid-1820s, sectionalism was on the rise all across Dixie—as was the belief that Southern weakness was being exploited in Washington to serve Northern economic interests, particularly through the expanding system of protective tariffs.[45] Northerners remained unaware of the depth of Southern discomfort until July 2, 1827, when Thomas Cooper of South Carolina suggested in a widely publicized speech that a time was fast approaching when the South would "be compelled to calculate the value of our union; and to inquire of what use to us is this most unequal alliance."[46] Over the next several years, as anti-tariff protesters centered in South Carolina grew increasingly agitated, economic interests in the North and West kept pressing for more and higher tariffs, finally succeeding all too well in 1828.[47]

The fire-eaters of South Carolina responded to what they called "the tariff of abominations" with the doctrine of state nullification. The Union, they said, was a league of independent sovereign states united for certain limited purposes only, and the Constitution was nothing more or fancier than a treaty or contract among these states. As with any such compact, moreover, each sovereign was fully entitled to interpret the terms of the agreement and act accordingly, which included a state's power to prevent the execution within its territory of any federal law the state deemed beyond Congress's power to enact.[48]

The theory of state nullification touched on the judiciary only secondarily. Advocates of nullification sought to establish the authority of states as against the national government; they were concerned with courts only insofar as their opponents insisted that the federal judiciary was the appropriate body to settle conflicts between the respective governments. Hence, the nullifiers did not argue that judicial review or judicial supremacy was inconsistent with the people's authority over their Constitution, as Republicans had done thirty years earlier. They made narrower, more technical arguments directed specifically at the jurisdiction of federal courts in a particular class of cases: arguments that sounded in treaty and international law rather than republicanism. "No independent state ever yet submitted to a Judge on the bench the true construction of a compact between itself and another sovereign," Hayne insisted, a point he deemed fully sufficient to refute claims made on behalf of the Supreme Court: "[A]s with regard to [international] treaties, the Supreme Court has never assumed jurisdiction over questions arising between the sovereigns who are parties to it; so under the Constitution, they cannot assume jurisdiction over questions arising between the individual States and the United States."[49]

Hayne acknowledged that parties to a treaty did sometimes incorporate into their agreement provisions for a special body to resolve conflicts, but, he said, "there can be no pretence that the Supreme Court have been specially constituted umpires" for this purpose.[50] Not only were "the Judiciary . . . from their character and the peculiar scope of their duties, unfit for the high office of deciding questions of sovereignty," but the federal judiciary was still "more strongly . . . disqualified from assuming the umpirage between the States and the United States, because it is created by, and is indeed merely one of the departments of the Federal Government."[51]

These points were, for the most part, merely a more extreme version of arguments states' rights advocates had been making for at least a decade. Like their predecessors, the nullifiers maintained only that federal jurisdiction was limited in a special subset of cases that directly affected state sovereignty. They never made clear just how this obviously important subset was to be defined, but they meant for their theory to implicate a limited class of problems only, with no necessary broader implications. One could thus accept or reject their reasoning without taking a position on the subject of judicial review or judicial supremacy in general. This is why proponents of nullification had nothing to say about the scope of judicial review in the states and why their arguments had no consequences one way or the other for the authority of federal courts in cases that did not involve state sovereignty.

Some of Hayne's supporters nevertheless did offer views on the courts' broader role in enforcing the Constitution. While defending interposition, for example, John Rowan of Kentucky observed that judicial review "is incidental to the exercise of the mere judicial power" and therefore "[t]he validity of a law involved by a case, may be incidentally decided, in deciding the law and justice of *the case*."[52] Thus confined, Rowan said, courts would not be exercising jurisdiction to regulate state sovereignty—a puzzling claim that he failed to clarify—but would "command the respect and confidence of the People, as a judicial tribunal."[53] This statement might be read to indicate Rowan's acceptance of judicial finality in appropriate circumstances but for earlier comments he had made espousing the classic Jeffersonian position:

> The independence of the Judiciary has, in my opinion, been greatly misconceived. Sir, the true independence of the Judges, consists in their *dependence* upon, and responsibility to the people. The surest exemption from dependence upon *any*, is dependence upon *all*. In free Governments we have nothing more *stable* than the will of the people. To be independent of that, is to rebel against the principle of free government. It is a dependence upon, and a conscious responsibility to, the will of the people, that will best secure the Judge from local, partial, and personal influences.[54]

Hayne's junior colleague, William Smith, offered similar sentiments in a less roundabout manner. "For the Judges of the United States," he said, "I entertain the highest respect, both in their judicial character, as well as in their individual character."[55] But "[i]f the opinions of the Judges are to be considered the Constitution; or if the Judges are clothed with this tremendous power [of settling constitutional disputes finally and for everyone] . . . is it not time to enquire, whether it be not fit to place it in some more responsible repository?"[56]

Opponents of nullification, in contrast, spoke strongly in favor of judicial supremacy. Technically, because they were responding only to the nullifiers' jurisdictional arguments, they were endorsing judicial authority only over states and state legislatures. But it seems clear that most were committed to judicial finality in a broader sense, for their argument was ultimately grounded in the need for a process by which constitutional conflicts of any sort "might be peaceably, but authoritatively, solved."[57] To say that every state

could interpret the Constitution and stand on its interpretation until a formal amendment had been procured must, Webster warned, "lead directly to
disunion and civil commotion."[58] "The end of this," John Clayton agreed, "is
war—civil war."[59]

Federalists had made similar arguments in 1802. But thirty years of experience had cast these claims in a sharper light, making such conjectures seem
less hysterical and more plausible. "It comes at last to this," Clayton said:

[T]hat we have no other direct resource, in the cases we have been
considering, to save us from the horrors of anarchy, than the Supreme
Court of the United States. That tribunal has decided a hundred such
cases, and many under the most menacing circumstances. Several states
have occasionally made great opposition to it. Indeed, it would seem
that in their turn most of the Sisters of this great family have fretted for
a time, sometimes threatening to break the connection and form others—but in the end nearly all have been restored, by the dignified and
impartial conduct of our common umpire, to perfect good humour.[60]

The general verdict, both then and now, was that Webster (and Union)
had defeated Hayne (and Nullification). At the very least, Webster's insinua-
tions of revolution and treason were thought to have isolated South Carolina
and blocked an alliance between West and South.[61] But radicals in the Pal-
metto State pressed on anyway, goaded by a failed compromise tariff in 1832
and encouraged by public endorsement of their position from Vice President
Calhoun.[62] In the fall of 1832, South Carolina's legislature called a special
convention, which swiftly adopted an ordinance of nullification proclaiming
the tariffs of 1828 and 1832 "null, void, and no law" and instructing the state's
legislature to "pass such acts as may be necessary . . . to prevent the enforcement and arrest the operation of the said acts of the Congress of the United
States, within the limits of this State."[63] President Jackson responded with a
Proclamation of his own, declaring nullification "*incompatible with the existence of the Union, contradicted expressly by the letter of the Constitution, unauthorized by its spirit, inconsistent with every principle on which it was founded,
and destructive of the great object for which it was formed.*"[64] A month later,
Jackson followed up with a request to Congress for authorization to deal with
South Carolina that anticipated the possible use of military force.[65]

By this time, no one was happy.[66] Criticism of South Carolina poured
into the state from around the country. Nullification was endorsed by no
one—not even any of the other Southern states. But Southerners were also

upset with Jackson for overreacting, and they adamantly opposed any use of force. The governor of Virginia confided to his diary that were Jackson to send troops into South Carolina, "I will oppose him with a military force. I nor my country [meaning state], will not be enslaved without a struggle."[67] Many in the North, including some of Jackson's closest allies, were similarly made uneasy by his belligerence, and Congress delayed acting on Jackson's request for what had come to be called the Force Act. At that point, both sides essentially blinked, and Henry Clay stepped in to broker a compromise. In February 1833 Congress passed Jackson's Force Act together with a new tariff that gradually reduced duties to a revenue standard. South Carolina then reassembled its convention and rescinded the nullification ordinance (though in an effort to preserve the principle of nullification and also to have the last word, the convention simultaneously adopted a superfluous ordinance nullifying the never-to-be-enforced Force Act).

Nullification may have been the most disturbing political confrontation of the early 1830s, but it was hardly the only one. Even as the drama in South Carolina unfolded, New York was busy denying the Supreme Court's jurisdiction in a boundary dispute with New Jersey, and New York's Governor Enos Throop was informing his state legislature that he would ignore any ruling against the state. Obviously reluctant to wade into yet another unmanageable interstate dispute, the Marshall Court postponed argument, giving New York and New Jersey time to settle out of Court, which they did in early 1833.[68]

Part of the Marshall Court's reluctance to face the dispute between New York and New Jersey may have derived from diffidence over whether any judgment it rendered would be enforced—uncertainty caused by President Jackson's support of Georgia's open defiance of the Court's efforts to protect Native Americans. In a series of cases decided between 1830 and 1832, Georgia's courts and elected officials battled the Supreme Court on the issue of state versus tribal sovereignty.[69] State executive officials ignored a writ of error issued by the Marshall Court to George Tassels, a Cherokee sentenced to death under Georgia law for the alleged murder of another Indian, and executed Tassels before argument could be heard.[70] The state also declined even to appear in two subsequent cases brought by or on behalf of the Cherokee Nation in the U.S. Supreme Court. The Alabama state supreme court responded to hints that favored Indian sovereignty in the first of these cases by issuing its own opinion strongly denying the Indians' claim,[71] and—with public support from President Jackson—Georgia officials ignored the Marshall Court's explicit recognition of tribal sovereignty in the second case, *Worcester v. Georgia*.[72] Governor Wilson Lumpkin subsequently pardoned the *Worcester* defendants as a favor to Jackson, who did not want events in Georgia to undermine his Administration's recently announced policy on nullification. But Georgia continued to ignore the Supreme Court's subsequent efforts to protect the rights of Indians in the state,[73] and other Southern states supported Georgia's position.[74]

Not every conflict of the early 1830s involved resistance from states. There was also renewed controversy over the bank, an issue that simply refused to go away and that in this iteration raised a question of separation of powers. The Second Bank's charter was due to run until 1836, but supporters in Congress (led by Daniel Webster) gambled and sought an early recharter in 1832—leading to Jackson's famous veto, in which he declared the bank unconstitutional and reasserted Jefferson's departmental theory.[75] It was irrelevant to Jackson that the Supreme Court had upheld the bank's constitutionality:

The opinion of the judges has no more authority over Congress than the opinion of Congress has over the judges, and on that point the President is independent of both. The authority of the Supreme Court must not, therefore, be permitted to control the Congress or the Executive when acting in their legislative capacities, but to have only such influence as the force of their reasoning may deserve.[76]

Which, in Jackson's opinion, was not much.

Jackson's veto caused an uproar, both for its economic policy and for its constitutional stance. Webster deplored Jackson's disrespect for the Supreme Court, while Henry Clay drew the comparison to South Carolina and labeled Jackson's doctrine "universal nullification."[77] But the public strongly backed Jackson, who made this veto the centerpiece of his reelection campaign and crushed Clay in the election of 1832.[78] Jackson followed up in 1833 by taking the unprecedented step of unilaterally removing the deposits of the United States from the bank—an action that required him to fire his Secretary of the Treasury, who refused to comply or resign, and that triggered an economic panic.[79] In early 1834, after three months of non-stop debate, the Senate voted to censure Jackson—in the words of one leading commentator, "a legislative act as extraordinary as the executive act which occasioned it."[80] Jackson responded by declaring war on the Senate and asserting the primacy of the President over Congress as the direct representative of the American people.[81] Jackson's supporters in the Senate set about working tirelessly to have the censure expunged, an act they finally succeeded in accomplishing three years later.[82]

"A Supreme Arbiter or Authority of Construing"

This discussion of conflicts in the early nineteenth century, though brief, should suffice to capture a sense of the volume and sheer relentlessness of the problem. Nor is the foregoing account by any means complete, and many other conflicts—some small, a few (like internal improvements) large—have been omitted.[83] Bear in mind, too, that the actual incidents would have seemed longer and loomed larger to men and women of the time than these abbreviated descriptions convey.

It is thus no coincidence that Madison and Story can both be found writing about the supremacy of the Supreme Court in the early 1830s, shortly after the Nullification Crisis and at the height of the Bank War. By then the Union seemed to be unraveling in the face of endless and escalating constitutional strife. What was needed, many apparently concluded, was a device to settle problems before they could escalate—a single authoritative voice to replace the cacophony of voices heard in the rapidly expanding and diversifying United States.

For Justice Story, who, though technically not a Federalist, may be taken as representative of a traditionally Federalist viewpoint, this had been obvious all along. Events only strengthened his conviction and slightly reshaped the argument. Rather than discuss faction, as Federalists had done in the 1790s, Story focused on nullification and the claim that every state could interpret the Constitution for itself.[84] But this was, for him, merely illustrative of why the Constitution needed a single interpreter capable of speaking with finality:

> There would be neither wisdom nor policy in [the departmental theory]; and it would deliver over the constitution to interminable doubts, founded upon the fluctuating opinions and characters of those, who should, from time to time, be called upon to administer it. Such a constitution could, in no sense, be deemed a law, much less a supreme or fundamental law. It would have none of the certainty or universality, which are the proper attributes of such a sovereign rule. It would entail

upon us all the miserable servitude, which has been deprecated, as the result of vague and uncertain jurisprudence. . . . It would subject us to constant dissensions, and perhaps to civil broils, from the perpetually recurring conflicts upon constitutional questions. . . . We find the power to construe the constitution expressly confided to the judicial department, without any limitation or qualification, as to its conclusiveness. . . . We find that, to produce uniformity of interpretation, and to preserve the constitution, as a perpetual bond of union, a supreme arbiter or authority of construing is, if not absolutely indispensable, at least, of the highest possible practical utility and importance.[85]

Story was, of course, fully aware that judicial review in any form had been controversial. Yet he presented this strong version of judicial supremacy as the only plausible way to think about the Constitution, emphasizing the need to bring conflicts to closure. Note, moreover, that in addition to pragmatic concerns, Story's argument was driven partly by the assumption that the Constitution is ordinary law and that its critical attributes must therefore be those we look for in ordinary law: certainty, predictability, uniformity, and the like. In fact, these had never been viewed as critical attributes of fundamental law, though the fact that putting fundamental law into writing created greater certainty had been deemed a great benefit.[86] Story's argument thus illustrates how the assimilation of constitutional law into ordinary law could, in the circumstances of politics in the 1820s and 1830s, make an argument for judicial supremacy more plausible than it might otherwise have been.

A longer and more complicated path was required before someone like James Madison—who may be taken as representative of the more common Republican viewpoint—could reach a like conclusion.[87] Madison's commitment to popular constitutionalism was sincere and long-standing, and his endorsement of judicial authority came slowly and in stages. As late as May 1821, Madison responded to the question "what is to controul Congress" when it exceeds its constitutional authority: "Nothing within the pale of the Constitution but sound argument & conciliatory expostulations addressed both to Congress & to their Constituents."[88] Two months later, he repeated this sentiment while reassuring Spencer Roane not to worry so about the Marshall Court's exercise of jurisdiction over state courts. "Is it not a reasonable calculation also that the room for jarring opinions between the National & State tribunals will be narrowed by successive decisions sanctioned by the Public concurrence?"—particularly since, as state courts improved, their decisions "at once indicating & influencing the sense of their Constituents

... could scarcely fail to frustrate an assumption of unconstitutional power by the federal tribunals."[89]

By 1823, the endless bickering between state and federal governments had led Madison to argue privately to Jefferson that such disputes should be decided finally by the Supreme Court. "To refer every point of disagreement to the people in Conventions" he wrote, referring to the solution Jefferson had proposed forty years earlier in his draft constitution for Virginia, "would be a process too tardy, too troublesome, & too expensive" not to mention something that "lessen[ed] a salutary veneration" for the Constitution.[90] Assigning the states final authority could never work because this "would soon make the Constitution & laws different in different States, and thus destroy that equality & uniformity of rights & duties which form the very essence of the Compact."[91] Conflicts could not be left to the parties to settle, since in the end this meant "a trial of strength between the Posse headed by the Marshal and the Posse headed by the Sheriff."[92] Nor, finally, could the respective governments be counted on to sort matters out, since this would produce "a question between Independent Nations, with no other *dernier* resort than physical force."[93]

That left only "the Judicial Authority of the U.S."—an option Madison now said he believed reflected "the prevailing view of the subject when the Constitution was adopted & put into execution."[94] Madison referred Jefferson to *Federalist 39*, saying he believed he had "never yielded my original opinion indicated" in that essay. There, Madison wrote:

[I]n controversies relating to the boundary between [the state and national governments], the tribunal which is ultimately to decide, is to be established under the general Government. . . . Some such tribunal is clearly essential to prevent an appeal to the sword, and a dissolution of the compact, and . . . it ought to be established under the general rather than under the local Governments.[95]

Madison's letter to Jefferson demonstrated a certain selective amnesia with respect to his writings as Publius. Certainly Madison was not defending a notion of judicial supremacy in 1787, and he followed this brief statement with two long essays (*Federalist 45–46*) explaining how the people would ultimately safeguard states from federal overreaching. In 1787, in other words, Madison had been prepared to assign the Supreme Court a role consistent with his departmentalist theory, subject to active supervision by the people.

By the 1820s, Madison's position had shifted and he was emphasizing courts more and the people less.

By 1830, moreover, the antics of the nullifiers persuaded Madison to take this position public, though he still held to the departmental theory for conflicts within the federal government. Disputes of this latter sort, Madison explained in a letter to Edward Everett that was published in the *North American Review* and the *Niles Weekly Register,* are naturally resolved through negotiation and do not require judicial supervision. Copying generously from his correspondence with Jefferson, Madison observed that, in conflicts among the branches of a single government, no one branch is "able to consummate its will, nor the Gov. to proceed without a concurrence of the parts." Consequently, "necessity brings about an accommodation."[96]

When it came to conflicts between the independent governments of a federation, however, "the case is practically as well as theoretically different," because "each party possess[ed] all the Departments of an organized Govt." and each had "a physical force to support its pretensions."[97] Accommodation in such circumstances no longer seemed credible. "Although the issue of negociation might sometimes avoid th[e] extremity [of force], how often would it happen among so many States, that an unaccommodating spirit in some would render that resource unavailable?"[98] Knowledge of "human nature" and "our own political history" suggested that the answer was too often—which is why, Madison said, the Constitution had "expressly declared" that such questions should be settled by federal courts, with the states' only political recourse being through elections and impeachments.[99]

None of this was technically inconsistent with Madison's position in 1800, inasmuch as even then he had sought to use the authority of state legislatures only to pressure Congress for a repeal or, in the alternative, to rally voters behind casting Federalist representatives out of office. Nevertheless, in both rhetoric and emphasis, Madison had elevated the courts' role considerably above what he had been prepared to concede in 1800. By 1830 Madison's chief concern was to see that conflicts were settled promptly and peaceably within the government itself. He adhered to departmentalism at the national level because he felt it could still plausibly work at that level. In conflicts between the state and national governments, in contrast, Madison's fears for the Union had overcome even his convictions respecting the people's right to judge independently whether their Constitution had been violated—leading him to support the propriety of judicial resolution in a way he never would have conceded to the Ellsworth Court of the 1790s. Talk of "the authority of constitutions over governments, and of the sovereignty of the people over constitutions"[100] was now replaced by a concern for "the utter inefficiency of a supremacy in the law of the land, without a supremacy in the exposition & execution of the law."[101] The people were still present, but rather than the front and center position they had occupied in 1800, they were now shoved into the background, a force to be summoned only "in the event of a failure of every constitutional resort, and an accumulation of usurpations & abuses, rendering passive obedience & non-resistance a greater evil, than resistance & revolution."[102] Popular opposition to governmental action had become "the last [resort] of all, an appeal from the cancelled obligations of the con-stitutional compact, to original rights & the law of self-preservation."[103] Self-conscious or not, the drift in Madison's thinking is unmistakable.

This change of heart is, perhaps, understandable given the country's change of circumstances. By 1834, moreover, Madison was prepared to extend judicial primacy even further, to conflicts "between the several departments of the Government as [well as] those between the Union and its members."[104] We do not know for sure what led him to take this final step, though watch-ing Andrew Jackson's catfight with Congress over the Second Bank prob-ably had much to do with it. At that moment, certainly, departmentalism hardly looked better or more stable than compact theory as a way to resolve constitutional controversies. And so Madison—and presumably others like him—came both to favor a pragmatic deference to a single authoritative interpreter and to support the Supreme Court in this role.

A turn to judicial supremacy was not the only available response to the alarming rise in constitutional conflict; other answers were found in the form of new political institutions designed to reinvigorate and preserve the people's active sovereignty over their Constitution and government. Before turning to these, however, we should pause to note something interesting about the character of the argument for judicial supremacy that was made in the 1830s. Modern champions of the Court's constitutional authority tend to offer two sorts of justifications. The first (and primary) position looks to judges to be a check on popular majorities, which are portrayed as unstable, shortsighted, incapable of acting on principle, and quick to inflict injustice on otherwise defenseless minorities and individuals.[105] A second, less empha-sized argument points to the so-called settlement function of law and argues for judicial supremacy as the best means to avoid interpretive anarchy and provide political stability.[106] The former argument hearkens back to claims made by the Federalists in the 1790s: claims that were overwhelmingly dis-credited in the early years of the nineteenth century and that seem to have played no role when the idea of judicial supremacy was resurrected in the 1830s. Instead, it was the latter argument—that there would be no end of controversy unless judges had the final say—that was now offered to justify the Court's supremacy. Yet even this argument, as it turned out, failed to achieve broad political acceptance before reaching its disastrous apotheosis in *Dred Scott v. Sanford.*

"We Are Ready to be Advised and Instructed by the Party—the People Themselves"

G. Edward White claims that the Marshall Court "had by the 1830s cemented its place as the final interpreter of the Constitution."[107] "By that achievement," White asserts, "the meaning of the supreme source of American law would be given by a federal court." Yet while there certainly were those in the 1830s who would have endorsed this proposition, White's claim is much too broad. For others were moving in a different direction, and their ranks included the popular and politically adept President, Andrew Jackson. Indeed, at the very moment when people like Story started for the first time publicly counseling judicial supremacy, Jackson reasserted the departmental theory, declaring in the message accompanying his famed Bank veto that "[t]he opinion of the judges has no more authority over Congress than the opinion of Congress has over the judges, and on that point the President is independent of both."[108]

Jackson was explicit, moreover, in grounding his argument in a Jeffersonian understanding of popular constitutionalism, according to which the validity of any department's position depended ultimately on popular acceptance. "Mere precedent is a dangerous source of authority," Jackson said, while rejecting an argument that the bank's constitutionality had already been settled by the Supreme Court in *M'Culloch.* It "should not be regarded as deciding questions of constitutional power except where the acquiescence of the people and the States can be considered as well settled."[109]

Jackson's position in this respect was supported by the press—the Democratic press, at least—which wondered how the President's critics could call him a tyrant when he was accountable to voters, while favoring deference to judges, "no one of whom is, or can be, brought to the judgment of the ballot-box."[110] Broader public support for Jackson's stance is suggested by the results of the 1832 election, which Jackson turned into a referendum on the Bank and then won by a landslide.[111] Such evidence is, of course, ambiguous.

Voters may have supported Jackson because they admired and trusted him personally, as opposed to agreeing with him about the Bank, and even those who concurred with Jackson's position on banking may have focused more on economic policy and political economy than separation of powers. In the absence of polling data or other means of obtaining a more refined picture of public opinion, it is difficult to gauge with any precision public sentiments on a question like judicial supremacy.

What we can say for sure, however, is that there was widespread concern about preserving popular constitutionalism and a mass political movement—with Jackson at its head, though not necessarily leading—to reinvigorate popular control over the Constitution and constitutional law. Hence, where some reacted to the escalating constitutional conflict by looking to the judiciary for answers, others thought about revamping the nation's political institutions, which had been stretched beyond their limits by the country's increasing size and diversity.

The tremendous growth and change that took place in the United States during the first four decades of the nineteenth century are matters of common historical knowledge. Between 1800 and 1840, the country doubled in size and tripled in population, with a corresponding increase in population density.[112] Much of this growth took place in urban areas: there were twenty-one cities of more than 5,000 people in 1800, of which only six had populations greater than 10,000; by 1840 the number of cities had quadrupled, including thirty-seven that were larger than 10,000 and several with populations in the hundreds of thousands.[113]

America was not only larger, it was also more diverse, as immigration and migration splintered the homogeneous enclaves of the early Republic. The largest immigrant group came from Ireland, with nearly a million Irish Catholics arriving in the three decades after 1815 (stirring old Protestant fears and giving rise to an ugly nativism).[114] Americans were, moreover, a people on the move. Within less than a generation frontier states like Kentucky and Ohio had become crowded, and still the extraordinary surge westward continued—a voluntary migration without parallel in Western history.[115] This movement west had significant cultural and political consequences, straining traditional social bonds while encouraging a new attitude (famously celebrated by Frederick Jackson Turner) that emphasized independence, equality, and self-sufficiency.

Together with improvements in communication, transportation, and technology, the expanding population helped fuel an explosive growth in the size and complexity of the economy—accompanied by the predictable social dislocations.[116] In the decades following the War of 1812, economic growth doubled, doubled again, then doubled yet again. The new prosperity, in turn, encouraged an accelerated division of labor in an increasingly integrated market economy. According to Charles Sellers:

> Hinterlands specialized to comparative advantage in producing agricultural and extractive commodities for Boston, New York, Philadelphia, and Baltimore. In exchange, urban manufacturers multiplied production for the countryside by subdividing tasks and exploiting labor more totally through wages and closely supervised central workshops. As surging trade set off surging productivity, capital began shifting from commerce to more profitable wage exploitation.[117]

Within a short period, a national market had begun to emerge, giving birth to what Sellers describes as a "staggeringly productive industrial revolution."[118] This, in turn, produced additional economic and social changes: mass production, more and greater concentrations of wealth, the growth and radicalization of unions, and so on. Adding to the mix were the Second Great Awakening—whose competitive protestantism excited a divisive sectarianism—and an unparalleled growth in voluntary and private associations.[119] De Tocqueville marveled at the way "Americans of all ages, all stations in life, and all types of disposition are forever forming associations":

> There are not only commercial and industrial associations in which all take part, but others of a thousand different types—religious, moral, serious, futile, very general and very limited, immensely large and very minute. Americans combine to give fetes, found seminaries, build churches, distribute books, and send missionaries to the antipodes. Hospitals, prisons, and schools take shape in that way. Finally, if they want to proclaim a truth or propagate some feeling by the encouragement of a great example, they form an association.[120]

All these changes took place against a backdrop of increasing demands for democracy and equality. The demands were, to be sure, limited to white men: women, blacks, and Native Americans continued to face exclusion from the ballot box, even as new social pressures shut them out of the celebratory culture of parades and festivals in which they had participated in the 1790s.[121] But wealth restrictions on voting by white men were abandoned in many states even before the 1820s, and other majority-restrictive devices were similarly replaced during these years.[122] By the time of Andrew Jackson's first election in 1828, significant property or tax-paying requirements for voting existed in no more than two or three states, and only in South Carolina were presidential electors not popularly chosen.[123]

Even these developments, as dramatic as they were in context, were mere reflections of a larger cultural shift signified by the outspoken and insistent rejection of status based on anything other than accomplishment and by an open embrace of the value of democracy.[124] Equality and equal rights emerged as critical ideals, joining liberty in defining the essence of republicanism. Hence, the zealous hostility of Jacksonians to anything (like a centralized bank) that smacked of privilege or looked as if it were meant to create a privileged class. "[A]ll distinctions but those of merit are odious and offensive and to be discouraged by a people jealous of their liberties," resolved New York's Loco-Focos at their inaugural meeting in 1835. Laws inconsistent with "equal rights and privileges by the great body of the people," they added, were not only detestable, but also "unjust, and unconstitutional."[125]

More striking still was the celebration of democracy itself. No longer a dirty word, "democracy" was now heralded as the proudest achievement of the American Revolution. "It is well for us to understand this word, so much ridiculed by the international enemies of our beloved country," exhorted Elias Smith as early as 1809. "The word DEMOCRACY is formed of two Greek words, one signifies *the people*, and the other the *government*, which is in the people.... My Friends, let us never be ashamed of DEMOCRACY."[126] In a telling vocabulary shift, "the people" became "the democracy" in this remarkable new world.[127]

The effect of all these changes was to make political consensus and even common ground increasingly difficult to find. A sudden upsurge of mob violence was part of the fallout,[128] but so too were a breakdown in party organization and the rise of sectionalism. "[B]y multiplying the different interests and causes for disagreement within representative bodies," Mary P. Ryan writes, "the democracy of the heterogeneous city inevitably fractured civic unity and made it more difficult to act in the name of the people."[129] Though Ryan is speaking here only of urban political culture, she could just as easily have been describing the country as a whole.

There is a twist. Where today we are inclined, with Ryan, to explain increased political conflict as a product of deep social forces and historical trends, men of the early nineteenth century had a different view of causation: things did not just happen; they were "brought about, step by step, by will and intention,"[130] deliberate products of conscious effort by some individual or individuals.[131] Hence, one group of politicians—the so-called Albany Regency led by Martin Van Buren—had their own explanation for the political turmoil: it was a product of behind-the-scenes machinations by a group of men who hated republicanism and sought to concentrate power in their own privileged hands.

Reiterating an argument made by Madison back in 1792,[132] Van Buren insisted that the United States was, and always had been, divided into "two great parties." "[W]ith occasional changes in their names only," he wrote, these parties "have, for the principal part of a century, occupied antagonistic positions upon all important political questions."[133] Their differing philosophies could

> be ascribed to the struggle between the two opposing principles that have been in active operation in this country from the closing scenes of the revolutionary war to the present day—the one seeking to absorb, as far as practicable, all power from its legitimate sources, and to condense it in a single head. The other, an antagonist principle, laboring as assiduously to resist the encroachments and limit the extent of executive authority. . . . The former is essentially the monarchical, the latter the democratical spirit, of society.[134]

Madison had said, and Van Buren agreed, that the "true policy" of the anti-republican party would always be "to weaken their opponents by . . . taking advantage of all prejudices local, political, and occupational, that may prevent or disturb a general coalition of sentiments."[135] It was these would-be aristocrats, Van Buren thought, who were responsible for the factiousness he witnessed all around him. Like any good Jeffersonian, Van Buren took it on faith that the great mass of Americans—"nineteen-twentieths" of the nation, they liked to say—actually shared a collective interest that could be identified and expressed through an uncorrupted majoritarian process. Conspiring against this mass, a small circle of well-born, high-toned men schemed to erect a system based on privilege and dependency. Small in numbers, these men could nevertheless be great in influence by virtue of their wealth, their power, their acknowledged talents, and their ruthless ability to act in concert. By keeping the people deluded and divided, the advocates of aristocracy connived to seize control of the national government in order to implement a vast, unconstitutional expansion of its power (and so of their own). "It is a striking fact in our political history," Van Buren wrote, "that the sagacious leaders of the Federal party, as well under that name as under others by which it has at different times been known, have always been desirous to bring every usage or plan designed to secure party unity into disrepute with the people, and in proportion to their success in that has been their success in the election."[136]

The necessary response to this ongoing threat was obvious to Van Buren and his allies: they must follow in the footsteps of their forebears, Jefferson and Madison, by using party organization to foil these latter-day Federalists and once again rescue the true Constitution. There was, however, a crucial difference between Van Buren's plans for the party and those of his role models. Jefferson and Madison had viewed the Republican party as a temporary expedient, a necessary evil to combat an insidious Federalist plot to turn America into a monarchy. Once the battle against aristocracy had been won, they believed, there would no longer be any need for party—a view shared by friend and fellow traveler James Monroe, who made the elimination of parties a primary goal of his administration.[137]

Van Buren and his followers saw things differently. As Gerald Leonard observes in his study of the origin of party politics, because a conflict among parties was the only politics they had ever known, these second-generation Republicans found it harder to imagine a world in which parties really could be dispensed with.[138] Their misgivings were confirmed, moreover, after observing the effects of Monroe's ill-advised program of party reconciliation, which "shattered [the Republican party] into fragments" and made possible the election of a Federalist-in-Republican-clothing, John Quincy Adams.[139] Where Jefferson and Madison had seen the "Revolution of 1800" as the climactic battle in a grand campaign to secure republicanism, Van Burenites saw it as "the origin of a permanent revolution, rewon in every quadrennial test of the American people's constitutionalism."[140] And this permanent revolution, they believed, required a permanently organized political party to ensure that the "democratical" spirit was never extinguished by the "monarchical" one.

Leonard makes two further points of significance respecting Van Buren's theory of parties. First, he convincingly refutes the conventional wisdom that Van Buren and the Democrats were thinking about party competition and policymaking in modern, pluralist terms. The antiparty tradition of the Founders was still regnant in the 1820s, and Democratic party organizers embraced it fully. The new partyists were concerned with the problem of sovereignty, which they understood to rest in a body that the Founding generation had referred to as "the people" and that they now relabeled "the democracy." Because this body could easily be led into divisions and factions—"party" in a narrow sense of the term—it was necessary to organize a single, grand party "of the democracy": an institution to ensure that the people's sovereignty became effective in practice as well as in theory (hence, the new party's name). "[I]t was only this identification of the party with the entire democracy—itself sovereign and free from party," Leonard explains, "that could reconcile party organization to a still dominant antiparty tradition."[141]

By organizing the entire democratic polity as a unit, Van Buren reasoned, the Democratic party could prevent slippage into the sort of narrow, interest-based parties that he and others still believed would be fatal to republicanism. Neither Van Buren nor his fellow Democrats imagined, much less embraced, the idea of a modern, competitive "party system" (though this is what they eventually got). The only competition they sought was from the minority of anti-democrats who were outside the democratic polity but whose continued opposition was useful "to keep alive the vigilance of the people and to compel their servants to act up to principle."[142] This, at least, seemed to be the lesson of Monroe's ill-fated effort at political reconciliation and his illusory "Era of Good Feelings": better a known and identifiable outside enemy than a fifth column corroding the democracy from within.

Second, Leonard demonstrates that Van Buren and his followers directed their labors toward restoring and preserving what we have been calling popular constitutionalism. The invention of parties thus turns out to be mainly a story about "the invention of party control of the Constitution."[143] "[P]arty organization, popular sovereignty, and the Constitution were inseparable" to the new partyists, whose "grand purpose ... was to preserve the sovereignty of the majoritarian democracy."[144] As Van Buren saw it, the Constitution "had to be the ward of a permanently and highly organized democratic party, by which every aspect of government would be made directly responsible to the majority will of the people."[145] Hence, while the battle over party emerged in the context of particular policy disputes, "its more proximate cause was a constitutional dispute: whatever the social issues of the day might be, how could the process of resolving them be reliably democratized?"[146] "The Democratic party of the reformers' vision," Leonard concludes, "was an essentially constitutional organization":

> The purpose of the new party was to replace lawmaking (and constitutional interpretation, for that matter) by a Madisonian deliberative Congress with lawmaking by expression of popular will through the party; to replace president-making by electoral college and House with president-making by popular will through party nomination; and to

replace constitutional interpretation by the consolidationist Supreme Court (and Congress, for that matter) with constitutional interpretation by a localist people through their party-disciplined representatives in the regular course of policymaking.[147]

The centrality of the Democrats' commitment to reinvigorating popular sovereignty casts new light on why party organizers were so concerned that the party's internal operations themselves be democratic: not just to avoid charges of hypocrisy but because the party was meant literally to be the democracy in action.[148] It also explains a feature of the original party that has long baffled commentators, namely, the apparent absence of a substantive political agenda. Michael Wallace, for example, was mystified to find that "[t]here were virtually no substantive planks in regency platforms—no programs of internal improvements, no plans for expansion of the franchise, virtually no demands at all."[149] This no longer seems odd, however, once we recognize that the motivating principle behind the Democratic party really was democracy itself. One could be a democrat only by placing the principle of popular sovereignty above any particular substantive policy.[150] "For ourselves we are ready to be advised and instructed by the party—the people themselves—we will always *obey the voice of the majority*," wrote a Democratic newspaper editor in Illinois. "But never will we admit the principle that a *few* individuals have a right to dictate to the people."[151] The sole exception to this rule was the party's commitment to states' rights, which in the context of Jacksonian America was seen by Democratic leaders as part and parcel of majority rule.[152] Centralization was the favored tactic of aristocrats and monarchists, and it was only by carefully limiting the authority of the central government that democratic rule could be preserved.

Popular Constitutionalism, circa 1840

Van Buren was unquestionably the preeminent party theorist of his day, if only for his critical role in converting Andrew Jackson and building the national party, but he was not the only one. Other Jeffersonian leaders and newspaper editors made similar pleas during Monroe's presidency to preserve the party.[153] These radical party men made little headway, however, until the election of 1824 shocked the complaisant into action and made reempowering the people a central concern of American politics.[154] The supposed "corrupt bargain" by which the House of Representatives made Adams president even though he trailed Jackson in the popular vote "was the great event that proved the elite's disregard of the popular will. It showed that the Constitution's mechanisms could be followed to the letter and yet leave the sovereign people without the power to choose their servants."[155] Even if the House proceedings did not demonstrate the existence of an actual conspiracy, as many believed they did, at the very least they showed that men in power were willing to ignore the popular voice. Adams's election thus gave real weight to the argument that ordinary citizens could secure their sovereignty over the government and over the Constitution only by organizing a party to coordinate and concentrate their voice.

But how to do this? Back in the 1790s, Federalists had ridiculed Republicans for opposing Administration measures in the name of the people. The opposition were nothing but a few malcontents, they said, meeting in clubs and issuing dire threats with no legitimate authority whatever. Republicans could not speak for the people without some plausible claim actually to represent the people. But how could any such claim supersede that of representatives actually chosen by the people in elections? "To avoid this difficulty," Fisher Ames jeered, "shall the whole people be classed into clubs? Shall every six miles square be formed into a club sovereignty?"[156]

Ames deemed his barb effective because organizing on such a scale seemed self-evidently preposterous. Yet this was, in effect, precisely what Van Buren and the Democrats set out to do. Various historians have traced the process by which a national Democratic party was formed, a feat of political entrepreneurship that was achieved rapidly in some parts of the country, slowly in others, and that took more than a decade to complete.[157] But by 1840 these party leaders had established the basic structures underlying the party's claim to constitutional sovereignty in nearly every state in the Union.[158]

Elections were the key. Elections had always been the key, of course, but the Jacksonians invested them with a role and a legitimacy that were new.[159] More than just a means and an opportunity for citizens periodically to replace officials whose performance was wanting, elections became critical moments for expressing the people's active, ongoing sovereignty. An attempt to draw or defend something like Bruce Ackerman's distinction between "normal" and "higher" politics would have struck a Jacksonian as bizarre and anti-republican: exactly the sort of ploy aristocrats were always inventing to divest the people themselves of authority.[160]

Consistent with the effort to make elections moments when "the democracy" spoke, campaigns acquired a more popular tone, replete with mass rallies, colorful processions, and other forms of pageantry marked by emotional appeals to party loyalty alongside suasion on issues.[161] Commentators inclined to think that democratic deliberation should be purged of emotion—a view, we should note in passing, that seems not just implausible but positively wrongheaded[162]—have sometimes dismissed these spectacles as forms of amusement used to divert and manipulate an unthinking crowd. But more was at stake in these boisterous events than entertainment, and the citizens who participated had a different view. Like the elections of which they were part, these partisan celebrations were "a direct exercise of political citizenship and brought into play the doctrine of popular sovereignty, a title to rights, and a token of power."[163]

Modern theorists who disparage Jacksonian politics may be missing the full context of its campaign rituals. Elections were critical, but democratic (and Democratic) politics consisted of more than "a single volley of voter acclaim on the eve of elections."[164] An election was but the final step in an extended and systematic process of convening the electorate. The process began with what contemporaries referred to as "primary assemblages of the people," which is to say local conventions held at the county, township, or ward level. These "primary assemblages" were held in advance and in anticipation of elections and formed the base of a pyramid by which the voice of the people was gathered, consolidated, and transmitted to higher authority: the Jacksonian realization in practice of Ames's sneering reference to "club sovereignty."

A primary assemblage was meant to bring together the democracy in a particular community, and Democrats worried when turnout was low.[165] The claims of representation made by these gatherings were apparent from their newspaper designations, such things as "The Great Meeting of the People—Triumphant Expression of Public Opinion" or "The Great Democratick Republican County Meeting." Mary P. Ryan quotes various contemporary sources describing a representative assemblage in New York City:

> First, "The people met together in open and democratic assemblies to select delegates to nominating committees to appoint persons to represent them in a state convention with direct reference to their known views on the presidential question." At each stage, representatives were reminded of their popular origins, that they were "chosen for their corresponding views, and thus when the body is assembled it truly represents the opinions of each of several counties in the state." Individual ward meetings always sent their nominations directly to the

local press and reported any evidence of chicanery in the process. In the spring election of 1835, for example, those attending the fourth ward meetings notified the *Evening Post* that the published account of their deliberations as transmitted by Tammany Hall had omitted certain critical resolutions, most notably attacks on monopoly in general and a privileged local ferry company in particular. This offense provoked the editor to deliver a soliloquy on the sacred principles of popular democracy. "If the whole democratic theory of Government is not a farce and a mockery, that resolution having been clearly and understandably adopted by the meeting" cannot be ignored by party officials. "When a public meeting is called, it is quite competent for that meeting to adopt the resolution which may have been prepared by those who called the meeting or to reject them or amend them or adopt part and reject part, or introduce new ones or take any word on the subject which may seem proper to a majority. The democratic theory is that the people's voice is the supreme law."[166]

As Ryan's description suggests, the critical innovation introduced by Democratic organizers was a shift from caucuses to conventions—the former having been discredited as a tool of aristocracy, the latter opening the way to "a system of politics . . . that will give the humblest citizen . . . a voice in selecting candidates."[167] The new system did not consist solely of local conventions, which were merely the bottom of a pyramid topped by the national convention and filled out by a mediating network of county, district, and state conventions.[168] Party theorists depicted this system of conventions as restoring popular sovereignty by closely tying decisions at each level to the popular will. That Van Buren's nomination for the presidency in 1836 reflected the true voice of the democracy, for example, was shown by the "fact, that the Democrats have had their township meetings, their county meetings, their State conventions, and finally their convention of delegates from each State at Baltimore, which nominated him."[169]

Hand in hand with the convention system went a new imperative of party discipline—a commitment that extended beyond the tactical to constitute a moral and ethical obligation.[170] "[W]e hold it a principle, that every man should sacrifice his own private opinions and feelings for the good of his party," intoned one newspaper editor, "and the man who will not do it is unworthy to be supported by a party, for any post of honor or profit."[171] The reason for the emphasis on party discipline was straightforward: majority rule would quickly unravel unless the minority at each stage not only acceded but affirmatively supported what a majority had decided; this was, after all, the whole point of the party.[172] Moreover, as Van Buren's ally William Marcy explained to his political lieutenant Azariah Flagg in 1825, "[t]he example of opposing a candidate nominated by political friends is bad not only as to its effect on the pending election but as to others that are to succeed it. An opposition upon the ground of principle will be used to authorize an opposition on the ground of caprice."[173]

This, then, was the Democratic party system for revitalizing popular sovereignty: the creation of grassroots popular conventions to select party-disciplined representatives in an upwardly sifting process of candidate nominations and political decision making. Naturally, given the party's democratic aims, independent courts were viewed as dangerous: an obvious tool of the aristocratic few. The basic Democratic creed in this respect was summarized by Van Buren in his *Inquiry into the Origin and Course of Political Parties in the United States*:

> Under no authority do [the anti-republicans] feel their interests to be safer than under that which is subject to the judicial power, and in no way could their policy be more effectually promoted than by taking power from those departments of the Government over which the people have full control, and accumulating it in that over which they may fairly be said to have none.[174]

Insistence on the supremacy of the people over courts was an important element of Jacksonian democracy, reflected in persistent efforts to make the bench more accountable—most notably by a movement to codify the law and by the enactment in many states of provisions for an elective judiciary.[175]

It went without saying (though many said it) that there was something deeply troubling about a doctrine as outrageously anti-republican as judicial supremacy. "It was upon [electorally accountable officials] that the entire political power of the Federal Government was intended to be conferred," Van Buren wrote, "and [it was] to the limited tenure by which they held their offices and to their direct responsibility to the people that the latter have always looked for the means to control their action. It is upon this swift and certain responsibility they have hitherto relied for their ability to bring the government back, without great delay, to the republican track designed for it by the Constitution, whenever it might be made to depart from it through the infidelity of their representatives."[176]

Van Buren and the Democrats were not opposed to judicial review. Rather, like Jefferson before them, it was judicial supremacy they opposed—believing instead in a departmental theory grounded in popular constitutionalism. Van Buren thus approvingly quoted Senator Hugh Lawson White, who in 1832 had offered the Administration's reply to Daniel Webster's attack on Jackson's Bank veto. In a "perspicuous and satisfactory speech," Van Buren urged, White had laid out the true "principles applicable to the question of the relative powers and duties of the several departments of the General Government."[177] As reported (accurately) by Van Buren, White said:

"The honorable Senator [Webster] argues that the Constitution has constituted the Supreme Court a tribunal to decide great constitutional questions . . . and that when they have done so, the question is put at rest, and every other department of the government must acquiesce. This doctrine I deny. . . . [A]s an authority, [the Supreme Court] does not bind either the Congress or the President of the United States. If either of these co-ordinate departments is afterwards called upon to perform an official act, and conscientiously believes the performance of that act will be a violation of the Constitution, they are not bound to perform it, but, on the contrary, are as much at liberty to decline acting as if no such decision had been made. . . . If different interpretations are put upon the Constitution by the different departments, the people is the tribunal to settle the dispute. Each of the departments is the agent of the people, doing their business according to the powers conferred; and where there is a disagreement as to the extent of these powers, the people themselves, through the ballot-boxes, must settle it."[178]

"This," Van Buren concluded, "is the true view of the Constitution"—taken not only by "those who framed and adopted it," but also, significantly, "by the founders of the Democratic party."[179] What was indeed remarkable, he added, was that "a doctrine [like judicial supremacy] so clearly anti-republican in its character and tendencies, should have been so long kept on foot under a system so truly republican as ours."[180] Remarkable, perhaps, but not surprising: "[M]ay we not trace its origin to the same inexhaustible fountain from whence have proceeded the most tenacious of our party divisions—an inextinguishable distrust on the part of numerous and powerful classes, of the capacities and dispositions of the great body of their fellow-citizens?"[181]

Although they dominated the political scene for a generation, the Democrats never did achieve their goal of a single party representing the whole democracy, and objectors and recusants of various ilks quickly formed an opposing Whig party.[182] As with the Democrats, the main impetus for party formation was not substantive policy, but popular sovereignty. An ideology emerged—it being necessary to advance some sort of platform or agenda in elections—but for both Democrats and Whigs, substantive political programs developed after the parties formed and were more the products of party formation than its source.[183] The initial impulse for party organization was fear for the Constitution and for the fate of republicanism, though Whigs of course saw the threat to popular sovereignty as emanating from different sources than did Democrats.

From the Whig perspective, it was in fact the Democratic party itself that threatened the Constitution. Drawing on traditional antiparty themes, Whig leaders condemned the Democrats' use of patronage and their emphasis on party discipline as vitiating majority rule and thwarting popular will. One Whig editor expressed amazement at the openness with which Democrats admitted their use of a "party test":

> [S]ome of the Van Buren members of Congress do not hesitate to say that there has existed a power in the government, unknown to the constitution and laws, which has been able to direct its policy, and heretofore, to compel the members of Congress, belonging to the party, to support it, whatever that policy might be. They instance as illustrations of this fact, the veto of the U. States Bank; the "pocketing" of Clay's Land bill; the removal of the deposites; the specie circular; the policy of all these measures having been opposed to the wishes of the people as expressed by their proper Representatives.[184]

According to the narrative constructed by Whigs, the Democrats' central objective was to concentrate power in the hands of the executive, displacing republicanism with a new American tyranny. A famous political cartoon, captioned "King Andrew the First," caricatured Jackson in crown and ermine robes, a scepter in one hand, Bank veto in the other. According to historian Michael Holt, "[n]o piece of propaganda summarized so forcefully the [Whigs'] conception of how the presidency had been perverted by Jackson."[185] Themes of executive usurpation and looming monarchy were pervasive in Whig literature, as the party self-consciously cast itself in the traditional Whig role of "country" opposition to a despotic "court" faction (hence the new party's name).[186] References to "corruption" and "dependency" by a new "dynasty" were common, as were arguments that the Democratic party was subverting the Constitution.[187] A typical meeting of Whigs in one Illinois county, for example, explained the decision to organize with the following resolutions:

> 2. *Resolved* ... that we firmly believe that [the Administration has] introduced new and dangerous principles—that the constitution has been grossly violated, and the known and oft expressed opinions of the majority of the people disregarded and contemned—the great agricultural, mercantile, and manufacturing interests of the country, trodden down—the currency and finances in a state of inextricable confusion and derangement, and the money of the people employed to reward unprincipled partizans ... from whom the only qualification sought or required, was servile submission to the dominant party.
>
> 3. *Resolved,* That the repeated and persevering efforts made by those now in power to unite the *purse* and the *sword*—to augment the executive power and patronage, and to reward or punish for "opinions sake," clearly demonstrates, that, in the hands of the present profligate and corrupt administration, our system of government is rapidly tending towards an elective monarchy.[188]

Most Whigs began their opposition with the idea that they could combat the Democrats without a formal party structure, or perhaps with a loose organization open to the possibility of continued dissent.[189] They very quickly discovered that such tactics made winning impossible, that Van Buren's insights were as true for them as for the Democrats. No-party parties were a thing of the past, and even antipartyism now required party organization. Within a short time, Whig leaders capitulated to political reality and adopted the same structures and procedures as their adversaries.[190] By 1840, American politics—including constitutional politics—was firmly controlled by a two-party "system," each party claiming to speak for "the people" and to be preserving popular sovereignty and the Constitution.

* * *

Some recent literature suggests that nineteenth-century reports by party editors and propagandists regarding the level and intensity of political involvement—reports all-too-often taken on faith by subsequent historians—may have been exaggerated. That voter turnout was high is, of course, undeniable. But reliance on numbers of voters as a measure of democratic participation can be misleading, for the relationship of ordinary citizens to political life is and was considerably more complicated. Glenn Altschuler and Stuart Blumin acknowledge that numerous Americans found their values reflected in the parties' ideas, symbols, and candidates. But, they say:

> [F]or many Americans the political party was not a "natural lens through which to view the world." Large numbers, we believe, embraced the institutions and rituals of self-rule hesitantly, limiting their political engagement to brief periods, distancing themselves from the wire-pullers and office seekers who ran the parties to their own advantage, and resisting the intrusion of politics into the more sacred precincts of family, church, and community. Nearly everyone affirmed democracy itself, and most Americans accepted voting as a civic responsibility, but a much smaller number of citizens found in the party and its politicians an entirely satisfactory embodiment of democratic ideals.[191]

John L. Brooke similarly suggests "[i]t can be argued that the parties of the Second Party system were designed to set limits on political discourse, to confine it to safe channels of debate. In an important sense, the parties, and the gate-keeping political editors, carried many of the exclusionary qualities of the classical public sphere into the nineteenth century."[192]

What to make of these facts, if true,[193] is a perplexing question. This early period is often viewed as a kind of golden age of political participation, with subsequent history treated as a long, slow decline into apathy and alienation. But what if democratic life in the nineteenth century really was not so very different after all? What if then, as now, most people felt disconnected and powerless, and rightly so? Doubtless there are theorists who will conclude (some reluctantly, others with glee) that it all just goes to show how we have never actually had a government that could accurately be characterized as successfully democratic.

Yet this seems like precisely the wrong response. If a gap has persisted between the theory of what it takes to make our politics properly democratic, on the one hand, and our actual practices, on the other, despite the best efforts of generations of Americans to close it, perhaps the problem lies with our theoretical demands. More so than most areas of philosophic inquiry, democratic politics is probably not a good place for ideal theory, and while high aspirations are important, so, too, is some perspective and a healthy dose of pragmatism. Referring to their findings, Altschuler and Blumin sensibly suggest that "[i]f we can agree that there was no golden age to envy, perhaps we can refrain from using the nineteenth century as a club with which to beat subsequent generations of declining voter turnout."[194] Their implicit point—that we should take each generation on its own terms—seems exactly right, especially if the goal is to understand and observe rather than to impose judgment.

To return to the question of popular constitutionalism, it may be that neither the Democrats nor the Whigs ever represented "the people" in quite the way they (and we) idealized. Nor did the Revolutionaries of 1776 or the Founders of 1789 or the Jeffersonians of 1800. (Nor, for that matter, has the Supreme Court ever lived up to the theories that supposedly justify its claim on judicial supremacy.) Yet like these earlier generations, Americans in the Age of Jackson seem to have done well enough—well enough, that is, to sustain what Edmund Morgan called "[t]he political world of make-believe" on which popular government necessarily rests.[195]

Morgan's point, which we have seen before,[196] is both simple and profound. Government is a messy, quarrelsome business. Some people get helped, others hurt. Decisions are made that imperil lifestyles, take money, make men and women fight wars; that tell them who they can and cannot marry, what they can and cannot eat or smoke, and where or with whom they can live. People need to justify this sort of control before they will willingly abide it. Telling themselves that the king is divine is one way to do this; telling themselves that "the people" have a voice and that it can be expressed by chosen representatives is another. Such beliefs are neither fact nor fiction. They are interpretations: strategies to explain the world; ways to make sense of our traditions and customs, our practices, and our day-to-day experience.[197] The success, or perhaps we should be more modest and say only the existence and persistence, of popular constitutionalism in the eighteenth century ultimately lay in its ability to make sense of the world as men and women of the time experienced it. In just the same way, the popular constitutionalism of mass parties fit the world of the 1840s. In its time, and in its context, the new democracy "worked."[198] Popular constitutionalism was rescued and revitalized as Democratic-dominated governments at both the state and national levels successfully marginalized the judiciary, repudiated the nationalist ethos of the Marshall Court, and reasserted popular control over constitutional development. Judicial supremacy did not die as an idea, but it remained tentative and marginal, held in abeyance by the Jacksonian-dominated Taney

Court. Preparing to retire in 1845, a despondent Joseph Story mourned that "the doctrines and opinions of the 'old court' were daily losing ground, and especially those on great constitutional questions. . . . [B]y remaining on the Bench I could accomplish no good, either for myself or my country."[199]

In this, at least, Story seems to have understood both his time and his place in it better than many of the historians who followed.

8

A Layman's Document, Not a Lawyer's Contract

THE CONTINUING STRUGGLE

FOR POPULAR CONSTITUTIONALISM

By the early 1840s, popular constitutionalism and judicial supremacy were sharing space in American political culture, coexisting in an uncertain and sometimes tense relationship. The very diffuseness and decentralization of popular constitutionalism, combined with uncertainty over the means through which it was expressed, helped make this possible by leaving room for advocates of judicial supremacy to continue nursing their claim. The resulting dialectical tug of war continues even today. Struggle has not been constant. It has consisted of periodic confrontations or blowups occurring after years or sometimes decades during which active backers of the two perspectives jostled for position while ordinary citizens remained largely indifferent or unconcerned.[1] Though we cannot know for sure, it is possible, and maybe even probable, that popular constitutionalism was the dominant public understanding during most of these latent periods, even as judicial supremacy was favored by and within the legal profession. What is certain is that popular constitutionalism was the clear victor each time matters came to a head. Yet the end of one cycle simply began another in which the Court and its supporters eventually renewed their efforts to establish judicial supremacy. Resurgent claims of judicial authority, in turn, gave rise to a new wave of criticism as opponents of the judiciary pushed back by advocating a revived or restored commitment to popular constitutionalism.

This claim runs counter to today's prevailing wisdom, which holds that "[f]or most of our history, most Americans have seen the Supreme Court as the ultimate interpreter of the Constitution, entitled (this side of an amendment) to impose its understanding of the Constitution on the states, the other branches of the federal government, and the people."[2] It seems quite likely, however, that this conventional wisdom is wrong. The Constitution was written against a background of popular constitutionalism, and while an argument for judicial supremacy had emerged by the end of the 1790s, it was decisively repudiated both then and later. The idea did not disappear: there were always those who favored giving courts final say over the Constitution "this side of an amendment." But they were a minority. Not surprisingly, this minority included prominent judges and members of the legal profession—men like Marshall, Webster, and Story—and we have tended (understandably perhaps, but without any real basis) to treat their views as authoritative, as reflecting an established practice and position. Yet the reality is that we have been privileging the views of men who suffered overwhelming political defeats each time they tried to establish their position. It was the views of Jefferson, Jackson, and Van Buren that carried the day and that reflected how most Americans apparently understood their Constitution.

Perhaps the point should not be stated so baldly, for we really have no way of knowing for sure who "most Americans" thought should have final authority to interpret the Constitution. A better inference to draw from the historical record might be that departmentalism and popular constitutionalism—which clearly were the rule in the beginning—probably continued to embody most people's intuitive sense of the matter. This conclusion rests partly on an assumption that prior beliefs normally persist unless and until something causes them to change. Change may occur either gradually or convulsively, but once realized it tends to be visible and easily spotted. Viewed in this light, it seems significant, as this chapter briefly recounts, that each time a controversy did arise—each time, that is, an event occurred affording us some opportunity to measure public sentiment—it resulted in a clear rejection of judicial supremacy and a reaffirmation of preexisting commitments to popular constitutionalism.

Bear in mind that popular constitutionalism never denied courts the power of judicial review: it denied only that judges had final say. During periods when no major controversies arose, most citizens (and most political leaders) were content to leave the Court's rulings unchallenged and to respect its status as, in Madison's words, "the surest expositor of the Constitution."[3] Even during these periods, there were groups and movements that called upon the tradition of popular constitutionalism to press their own visions of the Constitution.[4] Some of these movements sought and gained control of the political branches or the judiciary. Others had little immediate success but still helped to reshape American consciousness. Many simply petered out while a few suffered cataclysmic defeats. Yet what is most noteworthy is that whenever an issue or a leader managed to capture the general public's attention—whenever, in other words, circumstances impelled Americans to crystallize their latent beliefs and choose sides—they consistently chose popular constitutionalism over the view that the Constitution was subject to authoritative control by the judiciary.

"The Present Healthful and Beneficial Action of Public Opinion"

That popular constitutionalism remained ascendant in the antebellum era seems uncontroversial. One sees this reflected, for example, in the judiciary's general quiescence on constitutional matters for most of the period, which stood in sharp contrast to the openly instrumental jurisprudence courts employed when it came to private law.[5] There was, to be sure, a slight upsurge in state court constitutional activity in the 1840s and 1850s, facilitated by the fact that the state judiciaries had become electorally accountable, but this was still nothing compared to these courts' private law activities.[6] Equally noteworthy was the modesty of the claims made for the Court's authority by even its strongest advocates. Joseph Story divided the Constitution into "measures exclusively of a political, legislative or executive, character" and measures "capable of judicial inquiry and decision."[7] With respect to the latter, as we have seen, Story's position was that the Court's determinations are "obligatory and conclusive." With respect to the former, however, he wrote that "as the supreme authority, as to these questions belongs to the legislative and executive departments, they cannot be re-examined elsewhere."[8]

This, in itself, is unexceptional: even today's Supreme Court recognizes a "political question" doctrine. What stands out is the breadth of Story's political-question category, which included "the power to declare war, to levy taxes, to appropriate money, to regulate intercourse and commerce with foreign nations" as well as "the power to make treaties."[9] "[T]hese powers," Story said, "can never become the subject of reexamination in any other tribunal." Nor was Story saying merely that it is for Congress to decide whether to tax or appropriate money, subject to judicial review if it does so in an unconstitutional manner or for unconstitutional reasons. Rather, the supervision of these powers rested wholly beyond judicial scrutiny: "Yet cases may readily be imagined, in which a tax may be laid, or a treaty made, upon motives and grounds wholly beside the intention of the constitution. The remedy, however, in such cases is solely by an appeal to the people at the elections; or by the salutory power of amendment, provided by the constitution itself."[10]

As modest as Story's view of judicial authority seems by modern standards, at the time it was extreme, reflecting one end of the political spectrum. Most Jacksonians and even many Whigs would not have agreed with Story or gone as far as he did. Like Van Buren, they believed in a departmental theory and saw judicial supremacy as an unacceptable form of court-based oligarchy.

Once again, put so strongly this may overstate the matter. Because little happened to force the issue for a generation after John Marshall's death in 1835, the distinction between judicial review and judicial supremacy received little attention. Certainly this was true for ordinary citizens, but even politicians and party leaders had little reason to worry about the distinction in these years. Popular constitutionalism embodied their prior beliefs, and its preeminence could be taken for granted because it was reflected in everyday practice. The Justices did address some important questions, but not in ways that threatened prevailing Jacksonian orthodoxies or caused serious political friction.[11] The Supreme Court remained a presence on the constitutional scene, with a potential question respecting the nature of its authority lurking in the background.

The tensions implicit in this state of affairs were ultimately exposed by the problem of slavery in the territories—which brought the period of latency to an abrupt ending and produced yet another strong reaffirmation of popular constitutionalism with a matching repudiation of judicial supremacy. Whether and where to permit slavery in the territories dominated national politics for a decade and a half, from the moment in 1846 when David Wilmot introduced his famous proviso to prevent the introduction of slavery outside the old South, until the question was finally overtaken by secession in 1861. Framed on both sides as a constitutional problem, the issue was dealt with by the parties in politics as a matter for popular constitutionalism. The unhappy efforts of party leaders to find a solution were reflected in such brittle legislation as the Kansas–Nebraska Act and the Compromise of 1850. A small group lobbied to turn the dispute over to the Supreme Court, but their efforts to obtain legislation to this effect went nowhere as Whigs and Democrats alike questioned whether the Court was "a fit tribunal for the determination of a great political question like this."[12] And then the Justices rendered the issue of legislation moot by reaching out to address the slavery problem without it in *Dred Scott v. Sandford*,[13] perhaps the single most reviled decision in the canon of American constitutional law.

Dred Scott was, by almost any measure, a mistake. Mark Graber has recently produced some interesting data suggesting that Chief Justice Taney's opinion was initially received by many as a useful and moderate compromise, enabling Northern Democrats to make modest gains in state elections held soon after the decision.[14] If so, this acceptance was short lived, as opponents immediately set about discrediting the Court in the press. Their efforts soon bore fruit—unintentionally aided by Southern extremists, whose actions in Kansas destroyed any hopes for moderation or compromise. The wounds inflicted on the Supreme Court's reputation as a result of this assault took nearly a generation to heal.[15] Recoiling from what was perceived as Taney's high-handed assertion of judicial supremacy, Republicans and Northerners savagely denounced the Court for its "atrocious," "wicked," "abominable" decision and declared their support for the departmental theory.[16] The *New York Evening Post* charged the majority with "judicial impertinence" for presuming to "act as the interpreter of the Constitution for the other branches of the government";[17] while its competitor, the *New York Tribune*, commented that "[i]t has come to a pretty pass, indeed, if this Court, created by the people, is to be considered . . . as utterly irresponsible. If this were so, we might as well give up the executive and legislative branches of the Government at once."[18]

Southerners and some Northern Democrats continued to defend the Court and to insist on obeisance to its opinion, though the leading study of *Dred Scott* concluded that "the literature of defense was less impressive in both volume and quality."[19] Outside the South, the prevailing attitude became one of outrage at the majority, and especially at Chief Justice Taney. Old Democrats like Martin Van Buren and Thomas Hart Benton stirred themselves from retirement to write elaborate attacks, the first of a raft of books and articles critically examining the decision. Van Buren, who was willing to support the jurisdictional holding in *Dred Scott*, wrote his *Inquiry into the Origin and Course of Political Parties in the United States* largely to criticize the Court's assertion of supremacy respecting the Missouri Compromise and to urge Democrats not to enter "upon a path . . . which would in time substitute for the present healthful and beneficial action of public opinion the selfish and contracted rule of a judicial oligarchy."[20] Benton, in the meantime, rushed out a 130-page book in which he likewise attacked the Justices.[21] The chief effect of *Dred Scott* was thus to raise political consciousness in the North, rousing a considerable segment of the public to adopt views that were openly anti-Court and anti-judicial supremacy as well as anti-slave power.[22]

Abraham Lincoln, who had criticized *Dred Scott* on departmental grounds when he campaigned for the Senate against Stephen Douglas in 1858,[23] returned to the decision in his First Inaugural Address. Lincoln agreed that the Court's judgments should be enforced as to the parties immediately involved. "At the same time," he continued:

> [T]he candid citizen must confess that if the policy of the government upon vital questions, affecting the whole people, is to be irrevocably fixed by decisions of the Supreme Court, the instant they are made, in ordinary litigation between parties, in personal actions, the people will have ceased to be their own rulers, having to that extent practically resigned their government into the hands of that eminent tribunal.[24]

Lincoln's Administration acted consistently with these views, too, by ignoring the Court's opinion and recognizing black citizenship in a range of contexts, such as the regulation of coastal shipping and the issuance of passports and patents (not to mention by abolishing slavery in the territories and the District of Columbia).[25]

At the same time, Lincoln's critique of judicial supremacy was carefully phrased to reflect changes in the departmental position since Jefferson's and Jackson's time. In particular, Lincoln questioned only the finality of Supreme Court decisions dealing with "vital questions, affecting the whole people," and even with respect to these, he asked only whether they become binding "the instant they are made" when they had been rendered "in ordinary litigation" and "personal actions."[26] Apparently, Lincoln was prepared to concede the Court something more than were its opponents of fifty or even thirty years earlier.

We should be careful to read Lincoln in context, however. He spoke against a background in which the Court's actual role was still confined almost exclusively to enforcing constitutional limits against states, a role the new President seemed willing to accept. This was, of course, the easiest setting in which to justify aggressive judicial intervention, as it was expressly intended, arguably authorized by the text of the Constitution, well established as a matter of practice, and theoretically justified on the ground that the Court spoke as a national institution against a sub-national unit. That the contrary position was now closely associated with nullification and secession did not hurt either.

When it came to general federal legislation, in contrast, the judicial practice had been one of invariable and virtually complete deference. *Dred Scott* stuck out like a sore thumb partly because it was so unprecedented for the Supreme Court to assert its will over and against Congress. Having denounced the Court's pretensions in this respect, Lincoln had no particular interest in upsetting the preexisting balance or rejecting judicial authority across the board.

Modern commentators have tended mistakenly to view Lincoln's endorsement of departmentalism as something unusual and extraordinary, a departure from what they assume was a normal background rule of judicial supremacy. If anything, the opposite was true: rather than evoking a departure from "normal" practice, *Dred Scott* produced but the latest reaffirmation of what had always been the prevailing, if not always spoken, understanding. There were in the 1850s, as there had been in the 1790s and in the 1830s, people eager to promote judicial supremacy. So far, however, these advocates had failed to establish their position and had, in fact, been decisively repudiated each time they tried.

"The Masters and Not the Servants of Even the Highest Court in the Land"

The effects of *Dred Scott* were slow to expire. What Robert Jackson would later call "the struggle for judicial supremacy"[27] thus did not resume until the final decades of the nineteenth century, at which point the Justices tried once again to assert their authority in an aggressive manner. Though it took a good decade for the new jurisprudence to gather steam, a marked change overtook the Court between 1865 and 1905, the year of *Lochner v. New York*.[28] Having found only two federal laws unconstitutional during the entire antebellum period (in *Marbury* and *Dred Scott*), the Court struck down four federal statutes in the 1860s alone, followed by seven in the 1870s, four more in the 1880s, and five in the 1890s.[29] While these numbers seem small by comparison to today (the Court struck down thirty federal laws between 1990 and 2000, for example, the most in its history), the change was striking enough to convince some commentators that it was only in this period that judicial review "really" became established.[30]

A variety of factors contributed to the turnabout. The weight of *Dred Scott* gradually lifted as time passed and the Court's personnel changed. The political scene shifted as the nation grew weary of Reconstruction politics. The Republican party's ascendancy gave way after 1874 to several decades of divided government, which naturally gave the Justices more freedom to act.[31] Their desire to do so was very much influenced by politics, as the equal rights rhetoric of the Civil War era evolved among conservatives into a new anti-democratic, anti-redistributive orthodoxy.[32] Morally committed to a particular notion of property rights and fearful of the labor movement and other seemingly ominous signs of social unrest, the Court set about deliberately enlarging its role—seeking, as Robert Burt has convincingly demonstrated, "to transform all popular partisan disputes into questions for final determination by courts."[33] In a talk delivered in 1893, Justice Brewer spoke about "magnifying, like the apostle of old, my office" because "the salvation of the nation . . . rests upon the independence and vigor of the judiciary."[34] It was at this time, too, that we begin to hear again the old discredited Federalist arguments about how "what is now to be feared and guarded against is the despotism of the many—of the majority" and how through judicial review the "people had effectually protected themselves against themselves."[35]

Like most such developments, the Court's new activism was overdetermined, for change was facilitated as well by a significant jurisprudential shift when the pragmatic functionalism of the mid-nineteenth century gave way to formalism and what Duncan Kennedy has called "Classical Legal Thought."[36] Morton Horwitz succinctly described the central characteristics of this mode of legal reasoning as consisting of a sharp distinction between public and private spheres—and so between legitimate and illegitimate objects of government regulation—together with a pronounced tendency to emphasize broad, abstract legal categories, and a greater emphasis on deductive reasoning and bright-line classifications.[37]

Gradually, these developments altered the Court's constitutional jurisprudence. Because the change occurred slowly and (at least, initially) affected mainly laws that no longer had strong political support, it took a few years before the Court began to draw fire. By the early 1880s, however, legal commentators and political leaders had begun to take notice. A prolonged struggle began, eventually culminating in the New Deal crisis of the 1930s.[38]

There is no need to review that struggle here, for it has been extensively documented and analyzed by others.[39] Suffice it to say that the Justices continued and even accelerated their aggressive ways in the early decades of the twentieth century, subjecting more and more legislation to one test or another of judicial approval. Yet every step in this judicial campaign was contested, both on and off the Court. Indeed, if the years between Reconstruction and the New Deal were a period of judicial expansion, they were also a kind of golden age for popular constitutionalism: a time rife with popular movements mobilizing support for change by invoking constitutional arguments and traditions that neither depended upon nor recognized—and often denied—imperial judicial authority.[40] It was partly for this reason that politics in these years were so turbulent.

The organizing principle of Progressivism, for example, by far the most successful movement of the period, was explicitly to reinvigorate and restore popular control of government and the Constitution. Conventional accounts of the Progressives typically focus on their efforts to supplant the nineteenth-century "state of courts and parties" with a modern regulatory state dominated by the executive branch.[41] But Progressives also mounted a sustained effort to reconstruct the nation's constitutions, root and branch—not merely to legitimate the new administrative state, but even more to make lawmakers and policy makers accountable to the people.[42] To this end, they promoted a system of "direct democracy" through such measures as primary elections, popular selection of U.S. senators, lawmaking by initiative and referendum, provisions for recall, and a variety of other reforms designed to open up political parties and weaken the control of party bosses.[43] "We hold with Thomas Jefferson and Abraham Lincoln," declared the 1912 Progressive Party Platform, "that the people are the masters of their Constitution," and that "[i]n accordance with the needs of each generation the people must use their sovereign power to establish and maintain" the ends of republican government.[44]

Lawyers, judges, and legal scholars have too often assumed that the Court's supremacy somehow passed without challenge in this period—a historical blind spot that seems to come from ingenuously taking the rhetoric in judicial opinions at face value. There was, to be sure, strong conservative support for the Court's ambitious claims. But statements about the judiciary's place in the constitutional system, especially those of the Justices themselves, must be seen for what they were: partisan claims in contested territory. The Progressive era was a time of flux and uncertainty. The Court's role was hardly the central issue, for substantive matters of much greater immediate import were at stake. But courts made themselves a source of controversy by aggressively taking sides in the incipient class conflict, and the propriety of the role they sought to create became one of the questions up for grabs.[45]

It was in this spirit that Progressives demanded "such restriction of the courts as shall leave to the people the ultimate authority to determine fundamental questions of social welfare and public policy."[46] Not only must the state and federal constitutions be made readily amendable, urged Theodore Roosevelt in 1912, but the American people must be made "the masters and not the servants of even the highest court in the land" and "the final interpreters of the Constitution," for "if the people are not to be allowed finally to interpret the fundamental law, ours is not a popular government."[47] "I do not say that the people are infallible," Roosevelt declared:

> But I do say that our whole history shows that the American people are more often sound in their decisions than is the case with any of the governmental bodies to whom, for their convenience, they have delegated portions of their power. If this is not so, then there is no justification for the existence of our government; and if it is so, then there is no justification for refusing to give the people the real, and not merely the nominal, ultimate decision on questions of constitutional law.[48]

Various methods were proposed to reestablish this popular control over constitutional interpretation, including recall of judges and abolition of judicial review. Borrowing an idea from William Draper Lewis, then dean of the University of Pennsylvania Law School, Roosevelt offered what he viewed as a modest alternative designed to limit the necessity of resorting to judicial recall (which Roosevelt also supported)—namely, recall of state supreme court decisions.[49] "If any considerable number of people" in a state felt that a constitutional decision rendered by their state's highest court was erroneous, he explained, "they should be given the right by petition to bring [that decision] before the voters."[50] In this way, a progressive constitution would "permit the people themselves by popular vote, after due deliberation and discussion, but finally and without appeal, to settle what the proper construction of any constitutional point is."[51]

While many of the Progressives' democratic reforms were adopted, recall of judges or judicial decisions failed to attract broad public support. Apart from abolition of the short-lived and ill-conceived Commerce Court,[52] the judiciary survived the Progressive onslaught largely undamaged. Yet the battle hardly ceased.[53] Support for "the people" as the court of last resort in clashes between the judiciary and the legislature remained strong among liberal lawyers and intellectuals, and opposition to the judiciary continued to fester. For a variety of reasons, matters did not explode publicly until the 1930s, at which point the Supreme Court collided head-on with FDR's New Deal. The Court's role became a contested political issue for the general public, and the triumphant New Dealers reasserted the right of the people to decide the meaning of their Constitution.[54] As William Forbath has shown, Roosevelt made his case by appealing to "the legacy of popular constitutionalism, with its emphasis on the people's and popular leaders' interpretive authority."[55] "The Constitution of the United States," Roosevelt insisted, was "a layman's document, not a lawyer's contract":

> *That* cannot be stressed too often. . . . This great document was a charter of general principles. . . . But for one hundred and fifty years we have had an unending struggle between those who would preserve this original broad concept of the Constitution as a layman's instrument of government and those who would shrivel the Constitution into a lawyer's contract. . . .
>
> In this constant struggle the lawyers of no political party, mine or any other, have had a consistent or unblemished record. But the lay rank and file of political parties *has* had a consistent record.
>
> Unlike some lawyers, they have respected as sacred *all* branches of their government. They have seen nothing *more* sacred about one branch than about either of the others. They have considered as *most* sacred the concrete welfare of the generation of the day. And with laymen's common sense of what government is for, they have demanded that all three branches be efficient, that all three be interdependent as well as independent, and that all three work together to meet the living generation's expectations of government.
>
> That lay rank and file can take cheer from the historic fact that every effort to construe the Constitution as a lawyer's contract rather than a layman's charter has ultimately failed. Whenever legalistic interpretation has clashed with contemporary sense on great questions of broad national policy, ultimately the people and the Congress have had their way.[56]

No more than Lincoln did Roosevelt or his supporters mean entirely to reject judicial review. According to Forbath, however, like Lincoln, the New Dealers thought the Court's role should be limited. As Maryland Representative David J. Lewis explained to the House, because the Constitution was a "statesman's document," the "abstract phrases" by which it granted powers were best "interpreted in the legislative laboratory where and when the statute is being made."[57] Nor was there reason to fear that unless Congress were restrained by judges it would fail to respect constitutional limits on its power. Drawing on arguments made by proponents of popular constitutionalism from Jefferson's time onward, Lewis explained:

> The Constitution has made ample protective provision [for preventing unconstitutional laws]. A bill may be vetoed by a majority in the House or Senate, where it is first proposed; if not vetoed there, then by a majority in the other House; and if not vetoed by either House, then by the President. If vetoed by none of these, the people at the next election can elect a new Congress to repeal the act. Here are three successive occasions when responsible officials, sworn to uphold the Constitution, elected by and responsible to the people, may, as they often do, exercise a preventive veto. The unwise or unconstitutional bill is thus stopped before the obligations are fixed on the citizen. From 1789 to 1857—68 years—this kind of veto alone obtained. It surely sufficed the Republic through its period of greatest development, a chapter of changes and progress, I venture to affirm, without parallel in the history of nations.[58]

At the same time, Lewis continued, certain rights might most appropriately be safeguarded by an energetic judiciary: "Many of the prohibitions [in the Bill of Rights] concern concrete and specific subjects," he reasoned, and "[j]urisdiction might well be left in the courts to pass upon the validity of acts relating to such fully described subjects. In the case of such specific prohibitions the courts themselves can feel a real confidence in their opinions."[59]

Here, as early as 1935, Forbath observes, we find New Dealers in Congress and the liberal academy outlining the "preferred position" idea we associate with the jurisprudence of the post–New Deal Supreme Court.[60] But while this idea may have originated earlier and outside the Court, the Justices willingly adopted it in the years after 1937, albeit over strong opposition from a minority that insisted on an even more complete judicial withdrawal.[61] Hence, through a combination of changing votes and changing members, the Court repudiated key elements of its Progressive-era jurisprudence, and a new accommodation emerged defining more lasting boundaries for a chastened judicial supremacy and a resurgent popular constitutionalism.

"Ever Since Marbury"

The basic terms of this New Deal settlement are familiar, having been a centerpiece of constitutional law for more than three generations. Without getting sidetracked by the many doctrinal intricacies that emerged over the course of sixty years, the heart of the arrangement consisted of a sharp division between constitutional questions regarding the definition or scope of affirmative powers delegated by the Constitution to Congress and the Executive, and constitutional questions pertaining to a broad category of individual rights that limit the form or circumstances in which those powers can be exercised.

With respect to the former category—claims that a law is unconstitutional because not encompassed within an enumerated power—the determination of constitutionality was left for Congress and the Executive to make, subject only to a highly deferential "rational basis scrutiny" in the courts. The limits on judicial oversight built into this form of scrutiny consisted of two ingredients. First, Congress possessed nearly unreviewable discretion in its choice of whether and how to implement the Constitution's grants of power. In practice, this meant that courts would not second-guess congressional motives or means so long as a law could rationally be said to further a constitutional purpose. Second, courts were extremely respectful of legislative findings that some such purpose was served, which in practice meant deferring to Congress unless the legislature's factual conclusions were patently illogical or wholly unsupportable.

The critical thing to understand about rational basis scrutiny is that it was a rule of judicial restraint, not substantive constitutional law. It did not mean that laws were constitutional if they were rational. Rather, the decision whether a particular law was constitutional was made by the legislature, with the Court's power of review limited to questioning the legislature's determination only in the rare case where Congress could not be said to have had a "rational basis" for what it did. By using this device, the Court ceded a quite substantial area of constitutional authority to political officials.

In sharp contrast, the New Deal settlement preserved a more active role for courts in the second category of cases, which encompassed claims based on a range of individual rights, including those specified in or inferred from the Bill of Rights and Reconstruction Amendments; those pertaining to voting and the political process; and those necessary to protect racial, religious, or other "discrete and insular minorities."[62] Even within this category of rights, the Court reserved substantial room for the political branches to make constitutional judgments. It did so by limiting heightened judicial scrutiny over the most potentially capacious provisions—the Due Process and Equal Protection Clauses—to a subset of issues where judicial intervention was deemed most necessary, mainly those involving race and, later, privacy and gender. As to other issues, especially economic ones, the democratic pedigree and superior evaluative capacities of the political branches, and particularly of the legislature, were thought to warrant the use of minimal (i.e., rational basis) scrutiny.

On the surface of things, the New Deal settlement proved surprisingly durable. For nearly six decades, from the late 1930s to the mid-1990s, this basic allocation of constitutional responsibilities endured. The Warren and Burger Courts were definitely "activist," but their activism remained for the most part within the terms of the New Deal accommodation. While making their presence felt on questions of individual right, these Courts carefully respected the space carved out for popular constitutionalism at the time of the New Deal and left questions respecting the scope of national powers to the political process.[63]

The Justices of the Warren and Burger Courts nevertheless planted seeds, perhaps unwittingly, that set in motion a process of unraveling the constitutional settlement of 1937. For while these Courts may have confined their activism to the limited sphere marked out in the New Deal, within that sphere they effectuated tremendous change. When New Dealers advocated a two-tiered system of judicial review, they probably envisioned the courts' role protecting individual rights as a relatively small thing. This would have been a reasonable expectation given prior experience, and it was an accurate prediction, too—at first. But beginning with *Brown v. Board of Education*, the Supreme Court showed what a really ambitious judiciary was capable of accomplishing even within the previously limited domain of individual rights. To name only a few of the most well-known cases in addition to *Brown*, consider *Baker v. Carr* and reapportionment, *Roe v. Wade* and abortion, *Engle v. Vitale* and school prayer, *Craig v. Boren* and sex discrimination, *Brandenburg v. Ohio* and political speech, *Miranda v. Arizona* and police interrogation, and *Furman v. Georgia* and the death penalty. Constitutional settlement or not, decisions like these were not likely to pass unnoticed, and the Supreme Court was still frequently embroiled in controversy as different segments of society bridled at particular rulings.

Ultimately, to be sure, these challenges had only limited success. For while they may have played a role in getting the Court to pull back in some areas, they also induced it forcefully to reassert its supremacy: most famously in 1958, when all nine Justices signed an extraordinary opinion in *Cooper v. Aaron* insisting that *Marbury* had "declared the basic principle that the federal judiciary is supreme in the exposition of the law of the Constitution" and that this idea "has ever since been respected by this Court and the Country as a permanent and indispensable feature of our constitutional system."[64]

This was, of course, just bluster and puff. As we have seen, *Marbury* said no such thing, and judicial supremacy was not cheerfully embraced in the years after *Marbury* was decided. The Justices in *Cooper* were not reporting a fact so much as trying to manufacture one, and notwithstanding the Eisenhower Administration's reluctant decision to send troops to Little Rock to enforce the Court's judgment, the declaration of judicial interpretive supremacy evoked considerable skepticism at the time.[65]

But here is the striking thing: after *Cooper v. Aaron*, the idea of judicial supremacy seemed gradually, at long last, to find wide public acceptance. The Court's decisions were still often controversial. State legislatures sometimes enacted laws they knew the Court would strike down, and compliance with the Justices' most contentious rulings, like those on abortion and school prayer, was willfully slack in many places. But sometime in the 1960s, these incidents of noncompliance evolved into forms of protest rather than claims of interpretive superiority. Outright defiance, in the guise of denying that Supreme Court decisions define constitutional law, seemed largely to disappear.

Popular constitutionalism remained very much alive at first, as evidenced by the period's many protest movements, for example, or by Richard Nixon's law-and-order campaign in 1968. But by the 1980s, most protests that touched on constitutional matters were being directed *at* rather than against the Court, and acceptance of judicial supremacy seemed to become the norm.[66] Witness the conniptions evoked in 1986 when former Attorney General Edwin Meese dared to invoke the departmental theory and suggest that Supreme Court decisions might be binding only on the parties to a case.[67] Meese was accused of inviting anarchy and of "making a calculated assault on the idea of law in this country: on the role of judges as the balance wheel in the American system."[68] He quickly backed down, softening his criticism to concede that judicial decisions "are the law of the land" and "do indeed have general applicability."[69]

Explaining this rather extraordinary development is not easy. One factor in the background, certainly, was the general skepticism about popular government that came to characterize western intellectual thought after

World War II.[70] The seeming eagerness with which mass publics in Europe had embraced fascism and communism eroded intellectual faith in what political scientist Robert Dahl derisively referred to in the 1950s as "populist democracy." The new thinking, associated most closely with Dahl and with Joseph Schumpeter,[71] denigrated democratic politics as a site for developing substantive values and replaced it instead with a self-interested competition among interest groups. Viewing electoral politics in this unflattering light, in turn, made it easier to defend courts as a comparatively better setting in which to preserve constitutional commitments and carry on the moral deliberation that everyone agreed was a crucial aspect of democratic government. Thus was born the curious notion of the judiciary as a "forum of principle."

Closer to home in promoting acceptance of judicial supremacy was the still more curious fact of the Warren Court itself—a liberal activist Court that, for the first time in American history, gave progressives a reason to see the judiciary as a friend rather than a foe. This had never been a problem for conservatives. Going all the way back to the Federalist era, conservatives had always embraced an idea of broad judicial authority, including judicial supremacy, and they continued to do so after Chief Justice Warren took over. For them, the problem with the Warren Court was simply that its decisions were wrong. Their protests were directed at the substantive interpretations of the liberal Justices, whom they saw falsely using the Constitution as cover to deal with matters that constitutional law did not in fact address.

Beginning with Robert Bork's 1968 attack on the Court in *Fortune* magazine, many conservatives started to attack the Court using the traditionally liberal rhetoric of counter-majoritarianism.[72] In adopting this rhetoric, however, they were not embracing some abstract notion of judicial restraint unconnected to any substantive position, and they certainly were not adopting a principle of popular constitutionalism. They were arguing that one thing wrong with the Warren Court's unwarranted expansion of constitutional law was that it needlessly truncated ordinary politics. Few conservatives rejected judicial review, and almost all supported the idea of judicial supremacy over the Constitution as they understood and interpreted it.[73] Conservatives continued to insist, for example, that the New Deal Court had been wrong to abandon judicial enforcement of limits on federal power.

Liberals had a more difficult time deciding how to respond to the Warren Court. On the one hand, liberal intellectuals strongly supported what the Court was doing, believing deeply and without reservations in the substantive goodness and importance of the Court's reconstructive endeavors. On the other hand, their teachers and heroes had led the fight against *Lochner*, and many of them had devoted their professional lives to the idea that courts acted inappropriately when they interfered with the will of the people. An unspoken tension between this belief and the Supreme Court's "preferred position" jurisprudence was kept at bay during the 1940s and early 1950s by the Justices' general reluctance to act, evidenced most strikingly in the capitulation to McCarthyism. *Brown* and the other judicial innovations that soon followed were thus a wrenching test of the traditional liberal commitment to judicial restraint.

The tortured intellectual path required to reconcile these conflicting commitments has been insightfully documented by others, especially Edward Purcell, Morton Horwitz, Laura Kalman, and Barry Friedman.[74] For present purposes, we need simply note that as Warren Court activism crested in the mid-1960s, a new generation of liberal scholars discarded opposition to courts and turned the liberal tradition on its head by embracing a philosophy of broad judicial authority. Though familiar with the history of *Lochner*, these younger scholars had not lived through it. To them, the counter-majoritarian difficulty just did not seem so difficult, not when viewed through the lens of a Court obviously dedicated to helping (in Morton Horwitz's words) "those who are down and out—the people who received the raw deal, those who are the outsiders, the marginal, the stigmatized."[75]

Not every liberal made the change. A strand of the older concern for judicial restraint survived, reaching its apotheosis in the 1980 publication of John Hart Ely's much praised (though seldom followed) *Democracy and Distrust*.[76] But the main body of liberal intellectuals put aside misgivings about electoral accountability, frankly conceding that judicial review might be in tension with democracy while justifying any trade-off on the ground that courts could advance the more important cause of social justice.

The upshot was—again, for the first time in American history—that conservatives and liberals found themselves in agreement on the principle of judicial supremacy. They continued to disagree about its proper domain and even more about the appropriate techniques for judges to use in interpreting the text. But liberals and conservatives alike took for granted that it was judges who should do the interpreting and that the judges' interpretations should be final and binding. The idea of popular constitutionalism faded from view.

This is not to say that no one imagined a role for constitutional interpretation outside the courts. There was, for example, the political question doctrine—though the existence of this narrow principle, requiring special justifications like those offered in *Baker v. Carr*,[77] seems more like the proverbial exception that proves the rule. Still, other examples can be found of arguments that seemed to recognize a role for nonjudicial interpretation. Herbert Wechsler's famous essay on "the political safeguards of federalism" can be understood this way, though the better reading of Wechsler is that various constitutional structures work to make Article I limits on Congress self-enforcing.[78] The point, in any event, is that there are traces of popular constitutionalism in the debates, but these tend to be marginal and unfocused: fuzzy patches around the edges of a painting whose central details have absorbed all the attention.

As time passed, moreover, these traces grew fainter and less frequent. Once the Warren Court was in full swing, focus shifted almost entirely to the judiciary. Conservatives argued that the Court's decisions were wrong, while liberals defended its interpretive methods and outcomes. An idea of popular constitutionalism, of "the people" bridging the divide between law and politics by acting as authoritative interpreters of a constitutional text, was no longer a meaningful part of the intellectual universe.

As a descriptive matter, then, the principle of judicial supremacy came to monopolize constitutional theory and discourse.[79] What is more, the principle was no longer confined to a limited domain of individual rights—at least not according to the Court. As articulated by the Justices, the Court's supremacy in constitutional interpretation was unqualified: an aspect of the judicial power itself and equally applicable to every question of constitutional law. Yet the Court's actual behavior did not match this ambitious claim, for, as noted above, the Warren and Burger Courts continued to respect the New Deal settlement by leaving the political branches free generally to define the scope of their own constitutional authority.

The result was a ready-made disjunction between theory and practice—or, to be more precise, between a theory that assigned the Court responsibility for ascertaining the law of the Constitution generally, and a practice of leaving most questions respecting limits on federal power to be settled elsewhere. An immense body of scholarship soon emerged to rationalize and explain the post–New Deal structure of judicial review, but tension remained at a deep intellectual level. Most lawyers and judges were content with the resulting system and the explanations offered for it, but those who found its political consequences troubling latched on to the seeming disconnect between a Constitution that is ordinary law (and so subject to judicial oversight) and a practice of leaving certain questions respecting the Constitution's limits to be settled by political institutions. In recent years, this group has consisted chiefly of conservatives unhappy with what they viewed as an unwarranted expansion of federal authority. In time, men and women of this persuasion came increasingly to seek a solution in the form of more aggressive judicial enforcement of limits on Congress. By the late 1980s, five of them were on the Supreme Court.

The consequence has been a substantial change in Supreme Court practice, as the Rehnquist Court has carried the theory of judicial power developed by its predecessors to its logical conclusion. Treating claims of interpretive authority by nonjudicial officials as erroneous and illogical, the Court has moved to resolve the disjunction between theory and practice by changing the practice. Hence, while reaffirming its supremacy in the domain of individual rights, the present Court has gone beyond the activism of the Warren and Burger Courts by simultaneously discarding or constricting the doctrines and principles that served after 1937 to limit the Court's authority in other areas.

We need not rehearse the cases in detail or worry about parsing the Justices' handiwork, tasks that have been admirably performed by others.[80] What matters for our purpose is simply to recognize—and this much, at least, seems uncontroversial—that the Court's new jurisprudence rests explicitly on a claim that it is judges who are ultimately responsible for interpreting the Constitution and that this means the whole Constitution. "As we have repeatedly noted," Chief Justice Rehnquist wrote in *United States v. Morrison*:

[T]he Framers crafted the federal system of government so that the people's rights would be secured by the division of power. Departing from their parliamentary past, the Framers adopted a written Constitution that further divided authority at the federal level so that the Constitution's provisions would not be defined solely by the political branches nor the scope of legislative power limited only by public opinion and the legislature's self-restraint. It is thus a "'permanent and indispensable feature of our constitutional system'" that "'the federal judiciary is supreme in the exposition of the law of the Constitution.'"

No doubt the political branches have a role in interpreting and applying the Constitution, but ever since *Marbury* this Court has remained the ultimate expositor of the constitutional text.[81]

The Chief Justice's history is, as we have seen, deeply problematic. But that matters less than the neat way this passage encapsulates the overriding jurisprudence of the modern Supreme Court: a jurisprudence that treats constitutional limits as synonymous with judicial enforcement and that, as a result, calls for the Court to adopt an aggressive stance vis-à-vis the political branches.

9

As an American

POPULAR CONSTITUTIONALISM, CIRCA 2004

The present Court's activism is best understood as the latest instance of a recurring pattern in American politics. For more than two centuries, every reaffirmation of popular constitutionalism has predictably been followed by efforts to restore or enlarge judicial authority. In each instance, a supposedly tamed Court slowly extended its reach, usually starting with small steps, then quickening the pace as its confidence grew in response to public acceptance or indifference. In each instance, the Justices eventually went too far, seeking to control matters at the heart of contemporary politics and precipitating a confrontation with the political branches that called upon Americans to decide yet again whether judges should have so much say over their lives.

Americans in the past always came to the same conclusion: that it was their right, and their responsibility, as republican citizens to say finally what the Constitution means. The question is, would Americans today do the same? Are we still prepared to insist on our prerogative to control the meaning of our Constitution?

"Leaving the Care of Their Liberties to Their Wiser Rulers"

To listen to contemporary political debate, one has to think the answer must be no. Why else has the appointment process come to matter so much? Liberals fight hard to block conservative nominations because they believe and are ready to accept that once in office these Justices should have the power to decide matters once and for all. Nor do conservatives differ in this respect, as evidenced by their own passivity toward the Court's authority and their matching obsession on the subject of appointments.[1]

The acceptance of judicial authority is most apparent, however, in the all-but-complete disappearance of public challenges to the Justices' supremacy over constitutional law. Apart from a few academic dissidents, everyone nowadays seems willing to accept the Court's word as final—and to do so, moreover, regardless of the issue, regardless of what the Justices say, and regardless of the Court's political complexion. Opposition has become a matter of working to change either the Court's mind or its composition. No public official has questioned judicial supremacy since Edwin Meese received a drubbing for doing so in 1984. More common today is the attitude of Senator Patrick Leahy, a leading critic of the Rehnquist Court and among its most committed adversaries in Congress. Though often questioning the Justices' decisions, Senator Leahy takes great pains to purge his speeches of any hint that he means by this to challenge the Court's authority as final arbiter of constitutional law. "As a member of the bar of the Court, as a U.S. Senator, as an American," he says, "I, of course, respect the decisions of the Supreme Court as . . . the ultimate interpretation of our Constitution, whether I agree or disagree."[2] And in that "of course" lies the crux of today's reigning consciousness.

Whatever else one might think, this plainly represents a profound change from what we have seen was historically the case. Neither the Founding generation nor their children nor their children's children, right on down to our grandparents' generation, were so passive about their role as republican citizens. They would not have accepted—did not accept—being told that a lawyerly elite had charge of the Constitution, and they would have been incredulous if told (as we are often told today) that the main reason to worry about who becomes president is that the winner will control judicial appointments. Something would have gone terribly wrong, they believed, if an unelected judiciary were being given that kind of importance and deference. Perhaps such a country could still be called democratic, but it would no longer be the kind of democracy Americans had fought and died and struggled to create. Madison was being snide, after all, when he had Anti-republican say that the people "should think of nothing but obedience, leaving the care of their liberties to their wiser rulers."[3] What changed to make this deprecated sentiment not just real, not just respectable, but apparently prevalent?

Sometime in the past generation or so (it is impossible to pinpoint a moment in what was, after all, a gradual process), Americans came to believe that the meaning of their Constitution is something beyond their compass, something that should be left to others. Constitutional history was recast—turned on its head, really—as a story of judicial triumphalism. A judicial monopoly on constitutional interpretation is now depicted as inexorable and inevitable, as something that was meant to be and that saved us from ourselves. The historical voice of judicial authority is privileged while opposition to the Court's self-aggrandizing tendencies is ignored, muted, or discredited.

We see this in the excessive celebration of *Marbury v. Madison*, whose bloated significance seems immune to historical correction. We see it in the tendency to conflate constitutional history with the history of Supreme Court doctrine. We see it in chronicles that portray the Court as a major force advancing American liberty—as if most gains were not in fact made in spite of rather than because of the Justices. *Marbury* and *Brown* loom large in these histories. The judicially inspired prosecutions for sedition, *Dred Scott*, the dismantling of Reconstruction, the fifty years of opposition to social welfare legislation, *Korematsu*, complicity in the Red scares, and the current hobbling of federal power to remedy discrimination all somehow shrink into insignificance. We see it in histories that ignore resistance to the Court's view of the Constitution, unless it is to demonize and disparage the opposition as populist excess or political opportunism. We see it in the fiercely hostile reactions to evidence that the practical significance of even the Court's few genuine contributions (like *Brown*) may have been exaggerated. And we see it, above all, in the tendency to minimize moments of popular constitutional-ism, to portray opposition to the Court as something rare, exceptional, dan-gerous, and revolutionary: an act of civil disobedience to properly constituted authority.

It could be, of course, that what looks like widespread acceptance of judi-cial supremacy is nothing more than evidence that people are not unhappy with the Court in the way that provoked earlier controversies. Pressure for action against the Warren Court was building in the late 1960s, for example, until what might have become a dramatic confrontation was avoided by Richard Nixon's good fortune in being handed four quick appointments. The newly constituted Burger Court was still activist (to describe a court that fab-ricated the law of sex equality, invented a right to abortion, and struck down the death penalty in any other terms would be fatuous), but it somehow never seemed quite as revolutionary as its predecessor. The most far-reaching decisions, like *Roe v. Wade* and *Furman v. Georgia*, came early in Burger's tenure, and the Court quickly moderated its tone by backing away from their more radical implications. And, in the meantime, the Nixon appointees were generally successful in tempering or undoing much of what the Warren Court had attempted in the domain of criminal procedure, which had become the chief source of controversy by the end of Earl Warren's tenure.

A similar story can be told to explain the absence of popular resistance to the new activism of the Rehnquist Court. Since 1995, the year the Court's "federalism revolution" began in earnest, the Justices have struck down mainly minor provisions of statutes enacted prior to 1994, the year the Republicans regained control of Congress. As a consequence, not only have the laws held unconstitutional been insignificant—especially by comparison to such things as the Second Bank, the Missouri Compromise, or the New Deal—but by the time the Court acted, these laws also lacked strong political support from the electorate. The absence of a backlash thus indicates, at worst, public indifference to the Court's actions, and it could even reflect popular endorsement. Outside the liberal academy and the ever shrinking liberal wing of the Democratic party, in other words, it may simply be that no one thinks the Rehnquist Court is doing anything all that wrong.[4]

Even if accurate, as seems plausible, this account is missing something crucial. For implicit in stories of this nature is the assumption that a doctrine like judicial supremacy is irrelevant and epiphenomenal. All that matters is whether people agree or disagree with the Court's results. So long as they like the outcomes, or at least do not dislike them strongly enough to drain the Court's general reservoir of good will (what social scientists refer to as "diffuse support"),[5] the decisions stand. The Justices may, at some point, go too far too often on matters that people care about, and when that point is reached we will witness resistance. But this is entirely a matter of how the public and those who influence public opinion view the consequences of judicial activism.[6] There are, in other words, inherent limits on how far the Court can go in dictating to Americans what the Constitution means, but these are a straightforward product of substantive policy preferences.

What this way of thinking about the Court overlooks is that any inherent limits on judicial authority, whatever they may be, are not unconnected to or unaffected by beliefs about the formal status of the Court's rulings. Grant that the Justices will, at some point, inevitably reach the end of their ability to control constitutional law. The point at which this happens will nevertheless vary depending on how much authority ordinary citizens and political leaders believe that the Court ought to have.

The reason this is true, if not self-evident, is easily explained: whether we actively oppose a decision or course of decisions will depend on whether we think the decision or course of decisions is legitimate. But judgments about legitimacy turn not only on whether we agree or disagree with the Court's results, but also on whether we feel entitled to disagree and, more important still, to act on our disagreement. To draw an analogy to agency law, we will be quicker to second-guess and resist the decision of an inferior than that of a superior—and this even if it is the same substantive decision. The Court may, eventually, do things that would arouse active opposition even from people who generally endorse a philosophy of judicial supremacy. But it will take longer and require more extreme judicial misbehavior before such people resist than would be true if the same people rejected judicial supremacy for a more decentralized theory of interpretive authority. Put another way, a Court that embraces a philosophy of judicial supremacy and claims to be the Constitution's sole authoritative expositor will reach farther and do more than a Court that does not. By the same token, a people that accedes to the Court's pretensions in this respect will permit the Justices to go farther and do more than a people that does not.

Bush v. Gore is a telling example. One need not take sides on the merits of the case to see that public reactions to the Court's decision cannot be explained as a matter of widespread indifference, much less political consensus.[7] Nor is it anachronistic to observe that if the Supreme Court had stepped in this way when Hayes and Tilden deadlocked in 1876, the half of the country that supported the loser would not have stood passively by. They might have attempted to impeach the Justices or to impose new responsibilities designed to make their lives miserable (as Jefferson did). They might have sought to ignore or frustrate the Court's judgment (as Jackson and Lincoln did). They might have moved to slash the Court's budget or strip it of jurisdiction (as the Reconstruction Congress did), or tried to pack the Court with new members (as the Reconstruction Congress did and Roosevelt tried to do). They might have done any number of things. But they surely would have done something: something other than submissively yield while explaining that to challenge the Court would look unpatriotic. Which is why, of course, no one at the time of this earlier election—on or off the Court—ever dreamed of trying to resolve it in litigation.

The reaction to *Bush v. Gore* is merely suggestive, moreover, of a larger point. It could well be that a majority of the country presently supports what the Rehnquist Court is doing. That still does not explain why all those who disagree, and disagree strongly, nevertheless feel constrained passively to accept the Court's rulings while waiting for Justices to die or retire in the hope they can be replaced by judges whose views are more sympathetic. Nor does it explain why someone like Patrick Leahy thinks it his duty "as an American" to affirm that decisions of the Supreme Court are "the ultimate interpretation of our Constitution" no matter how wrong he thinks they are.

What presumably does explain facts like these is the broad change in public attitudes toward the Court that occurred in the latter half of the twentieth century. Where most people's unarticulated, intuitive sense in earlier generations presupposed the rightness and naturalness of popular constitutionalism, today that sense has switched to favor judicial supremacy—a turnabout in beliefs with effects across the whole political and ideological spectrum. In several recent surveys, more than 60 percent of respondents answered that the Supreme Court has the "last say" on constitutional questions, with another 11 percent responding that they did not know.[8] Equally interesting is that the surveys' authors thought it obvious that choosing the Court should be graded the "correct" answer.

These sorts of beliefs about the locus of constitutional authority are and always have been less a matter of active, self-conscious commitment on the part of ordinary citizens than an implicit background assumption of popular political culture. But background assumptions like these are crucial in framing how ordinary Americans understand their role as citizens and what they expect from their political leaders. And that, in turn, shapes what these leaders say and do. As products of the same political culture as their constituents, leaders like Senator Leahy and Vice President Gore may believe what they say about the Court's supremacy. But even were this not so, they are also astute politicians—astute enough to sense that trying to build opposition to the Court by decrying judicial supremacy will not go down well with most Americans. Not today, at any rate.

How and why this change in attitudes came about is a complicated story, though we have already alluded to some of the causes: heightened skepticism about popular democracy occasioned by twentieth-century totalitarianism; the historical anomaly of the liberal Warren Court; two generations of near consensus about judicial supremacy among intellectuals and opinion-makers on both the left and the right (not to mention among high school civics teachers).[9] But whatever the explanation, there can be little doubt either that a change occurred or that it has affected how the Supreme Court and its decisions are received by ordinary citizens as well as by public officials, and by opponents of the Court as well as by its supporters.

Furthermore, understanding this tells us something important about the nature of judicial supremacy itself. Supremacy is an ideological tenet whose whole purpose is to persuade ordinary citizens that, whatever they may think about the Justices' constitutional rulings, it is not their place to gainsay the Court. It is a device to deflect and dampen the energy of popular constitutionalism. That energy cannot ever be wholly contained, and history has repeatedly demonstrated how irresistible political pressures will be brought to bear against a Supreme Court that goes "too far." The object of judicial supremacy is to make this breaking point as distant as possible: to maximize the Court's authority by inculcating an attitude of deference and submission to its judgments. It is akin to telling jurors that they "must" follow the judges' trial instructions in order to mask and minimize the use of the jury's undoubted power of nullification.[10]

As with the jury, moreover, successfully persuading people to accept judicial authority does more than raise the barriers to rebellion. It affects how the whole system works. Public acceptance of judicial supremacy pervades constitutional law and politics. It changes how the Justices conceive their role, how they decide cases and write opinions. It changes how politicians, the press, and other affected actors internalize the Court's rulings—and in this way it changes the effects of those rulings beyond the particular case. It changes how Supreme Court decisions are "inscribed within the . . . institutional fabric of social relations" and so how citizens "reconstruct legal norms" in their own lives.[11] It changes everything, in other words, and in ways that are subtle and pervasive and not seen only (or even mainly) in big, explosive confrontations about whether to obey a particular decision.

"The Surest Expositor of the Constitution"

That being so, surely we should ask whether the principle of judicial supremacy makes sense. Not because the liberal Warren Court or the centrist Burger Court or the conservative Rehnquist Court should be judged good or bad or deserve our praise or condemnation, but because much bigger issues are at stake. Against the larger backdrop of American history, the acceptance of judicial supremacy in modern constitutional times is exceedingly anomalous. It is not too much to say that it has fundamentally altered the meaning of republican citizenship by, as a conceptual matter, taking ordinary people out of the process of shaping constitutional law. Except in the most abstract sense, "We the People" have—apparently of our own volition—handed control of our fundamental law over to what Martin Van Buren in an earlier era condemned as "the selfish and contracted rule of a judicial oligarchy."[12] Perhaps Van Buren was wrong, along with Jefferson, Jackson, Lincoln, Roosevelt, and all our other forebears who worked to contain judicial authority. Perhaps this really is the right thing to do. If so, however, there should be good reasons for it.

Most people who support the Court's supremacy in constitutional law today probably do so without thinking about it much, based either on an assumption that judicial supremacy follows naturally from the Constitution's status as law, or a belief that this supremacy was originally intended or established early on: both claims contradicted by the previous eight chapters. Academic defenders of the Court, however, have offered several additional reasons to justify giving it the last word on constitutional meaning, modern elaborations of arguments first developed in the eighteenth and nineteenth centuries. One frequently heard argument is that we need judicial supremacy to serve the so-called settlement function of law: absent firm judicial control, we are told, constitutional law would become unacceptably chaotic, unpredictable, and nonuniform.[13] The other still more common claim is that judges should have final say because the constitution entrenches particular rights and rules as precautions sensible democratic citizens take against their own future dangerousness, and courts are more trustworthy than electorally accountable bodies when it comes to respecting such commitments.

Much could undoubtedly be said both for and against these justifications. Much, indeed, has already been said, for the question of judicial supremacy has been at the heart of academic constitutional debate for more than two generations.[14] Thankfully, we need not rehearse the by-now elaborate arguments here, except to establish one crucial point—to wit, that both justifications turn out, after inspection, to rest on controversial empirical assumptions, assumptions about whose truth (if we are being honest) it is difficult to have too firm a conviction because they turn on "facts" that can never be tested or proved.

The claim that we need judicial supremacy to settle matters and bring an end to conflict is straightforwardly empirical: that this claim is anything but obvious is equally straightforward. To begin with, there is no such thing as perfect finality or "settlement" in law. Uncertainty and instability will exist even in a regime of total judicial supremacy, while we will find a considerable degree of finality and resolution even without it. The choice is not between order and chaos or stability and anarchy, but between different types of stability and different mechanisms for achieving it.[15] Whether there is a "settlement gap" between a world with judicial supremacy and a world without it, and if so, whether that gap is large or small, depends on how different institutions handle constitutional questions.[16] Proponents of judicial supremacy on settlement grounds have been notoriously inattentive to what we know about the way in which political institutions actually deal with the Constitution, content to argue from stereotypes and theoretic possibilities. Yet experience suggests that if there is a settlement gap, which is by no means clear, that gap is likely to be small.

This is so for a number of reasons. Nonjudicial actors also value stability and predictability and work hard to produce it.[17] The structure of American politics, in turn, reinforces these natural incentives by requiring large coalitions to bring about change.[18] For this reason, constitutional understandings determined in politics over the course of American history have been impressively stable, often lasting for decades and proving themselves at least as durable as judicial doctrine. For the same reason, moreover, it would never be the case that everything was up for grabs all the time. Issues might come and go; things that were once settled might again become controversial. But at any given time, the vast majority of constitutional law would be stable and settled.

Plus, Supreme Court decisions could still be expected to conclude most constitutional disputes even without a formal doctrine of judicial supremacy. Courts do come last, after all, if only as a matter of political consciousness and perception. This means that their rulings are going to be final as a practical matter except where opposition is strong enough to overcome the institutional hurdles our political system puts in the way of those seeking to upset an existing state of affairs. Once the Court has ruled, moreover, these hurdles consist of more than just getting a majority in the House, a filibuster-proof majority in the Senate, and the President to agree that a different decision would have been better. They now include getting agreement that the difference is important enough to challenge the Court, which can itself become a quite significant impediment. The Justices do not need a doctrine of judicial supremacy to earn respect and support from the public, including support for particular rulings that are unpopular. The Court can earn this support—can in effect make itself final—by handling its business intelligently and with political savvy.[19] This is what Madison meant back in 1834 when he remarked that, notwithstanding his and Jefferson's departmental theory of coordinate interpretation, "it may always be expected that the judicial bench, when happily filled, will . . . most engage the respect and reliance of the public as the surest expositor of the Constitution."[20] The difference, of course, is that the

Justices would have to earn their claim to have final say and (to paraphrase Justice Jackson)[21] would be neither final nor infallible beyond their ability to claim the confidence of a watchful public in going about their business. That the Court may successfully do this, however, is something historical experience makes abundantly clear.

None of this provides a clear answer to the settlement argument. It only muddies the waters while leaving some unanswerable questions. If the idea of judicial supremacy counts for anything, there probably is at least some difference in the amount of uncertainty and disagreement that exists with and without it. But how much? And does the difference pertain to issues or exist in forms that should bother us? And even assuming that there is a difference and that it should bother us, how much should it bother us? How important is an increase or decrease in settlement at the margins, which is the most we are talking about when all is said and done? Clarity and finality obviously matter, but they are not the only values or even the most important ones in a legal system, and no one thinks we should pursue them at all costs.

The second justification for judicial supremacy—that courts provide a more secure forum for the preservation or just determination of the Constitution's fundamental commitments—seems more plausible, though it, too, turns out to rest on uncertain empirical grounds. Here we begin with an inevitable fact of constitutional practice: the existence and persistence of pervasive disagreement. Jeremy Waldron explains:

> [I]n the constitutional case we are almost always dealing with a society whose members disagree in principle and in detail, even in their "calm" or "lucid" moments, about what rights they have, how those rights are to be conceived, and what weight they are to be given in relation to other values. They need not appeal to aberrations in rationality to explain or characterize these disagreements. . . . [D]isagreements about rights are sufficiently explained by the difficulty of the subject matter and by what Rawls refers to as "the burdens of judgment."[22]

As Waldron is at pains to emphasize, the intractability of disagreement is not a product of intellectual limitations or unwillingness to listen to reason or ignorance or prejudice or interest or anything like that.[23] These are simply hard questions, much too complicated ever to be solved or put to rest once and for all. This is so, moreover, even if one accepts the claims of moral realists that there are objectively "right" answers to questions about justice and rights. Whatever is objectively "out there," after all, is still accessible to us only insofar as our flawed, subjective capacities permit us to comprehend it, and on this level room for legitimate disagreement will always and necessarily remain.[24]

Advocates of judicial supremacy ask us nevertheless to turn our disagreements over to judges, arguing that certain characteristics of the judicial process make judges more likely to reach desirable outcomes than politicians or ordinary citizens. This assumes, of course, that while we might legitimately disagree about results and about justifications, we should nevertheless be prepared to agree that the particular characteristics attributed to courts and judges make them more likely to make decisions that are, in fact, right. But why should we do that? What is different about this question of process that makes anyone think we should be more prepared to agree on it than we are on results?

Consider, for example, the argument that judges can reason about questions of political morality "better" because institutional independence insulates them from the sort of grubby self-interest that distorts the thinking of ordinary citizens and politicians. Even granting the very questionable proposition that judges are meaningfully insulated from self-interest (as opposed to experiencing it in a different form), the argument that this is a good thing runs counter to other epistemic principles—for example, that hard choices are best made by those who have a sufficient stake in the matter to decide responsibly.[25] And how do we resolve that disagreement? Yet without concurrence on the necessary or proper circumstances for reaching morally correct results, any argument that judges are more likely to do so either lacks foundation or is question-begging.[26]

It does not follow that judicial supremacy must be rejected. Uncertainty about which answers or which processes are best does not automatically point us toward any other institution to resolve disagreements either. Perhaps backers of judicial supremacy should be less confident about their argument, but incertitude is not the same thing as incapacity. We still must decide who should decide, and one could still choose the judiciary because one believes (all things considered) that the judicial process offers the best solution. Ultimately, we cannot avoid making our best guess about which of our institutions is likely to do the best job in light of what we know about their relative capacities to act responsibly when it comes to the Constitution. It is, however, only a guess.

Most commentators seem to have little difficulty guessing that a political institution like Congress cannot be trusted to take constitutional questions seriously. Maybe it was different in the nineteenth century, they say, thinking of the erudite floor debates that fill the pages of the *Register of Debates* and *Congressional Globe*. But today? Except on rare occasions, congressional "debate" today consists of members making canned speeches to an empty house, hoping that what they say will be replayed for the folks at home on C-SPAN. This may have benefits politically, but who would seriously maintain that it is remotely as good as the deliberations of the Supreme Court?

Such comparisons are worth rethinking. Who said that the only or best place for serious congressional debate is on the floor in open session? This may have been how they did it in the nineteenth century, whereas today Congress limits serious floor debates to matters of great public import. Yet this is not because there is no serious discussion or deliberation. It is because, as with most public institutions, changes in the nature and amount of business to be transacted have forced Congress to bureaucratize. As a result, deliberations are now carried on mainly behind-the-scenes: in committees or caucuses, between individuals, by e-mail, through staff, and so on. But as anyone who has worked closely on legislation can attest, the process remains deliberative and, in fact, permits many more voices to be heard and much more information to be assimilated than would be possible if congressmen were wasting hours every day discussing matters on the floor. Indeed, the amount of discussion that takes place and information that is processed dwarfs what Congress did in the nineteenth century. It also dwarfs anything the Supreme Court can do—which is as it should be.

This is no less true when it comes to constitutional questions than anything else, and committees and staff devote hundreds of hours to understanding, debating, and resolving constitutional issues. Obvious examples include congressional discussions of war powers, line-item vetoes, interbranch relations, and federalism—all of which have received and continue to receive studious attention in Congress. Nor is the list of subjects limited to questions of constitutional structure. Keith Whittington observes:

> Continuing extrajudicial debates over affirmative action, euthanasia, the death penalty, pornography, school prayer, gay rights, Internet privacy, sexual harassment, and gun control reflect sustained concern with individual rights, constitutional values, and political principles. We may disagree with the conclusions that various extrajudicial bodies reach in these debates, as we may disagree with the conclusions of the courts. But it is difficult to maintain that such extrajudicial decisions are unconsidered or neglect considerations of justice and principle.[27]

If Congress does not do better, moreover, this may itself partly be a product of judicial supremacy—a possibility Mark Tushnet labels the "judicial over-hang."[28] "[I]f Congress does badly because the courts are on the scene," he points out, "[w]e really cannot know how Congress would perform if the courts exited."[29]

Standing behind the skepticism of Congress are certain stereotypes about legislators and the legislative process generally. In both scholarship and the press, legislators are dismissed as unthinking automatons, incapable of deliberating seriously. They are presented as either thoroughly unresponsive to those they represent and attentive only to private interests dangling campaign dollars before their eyes, or as thoroughly unprincipled and willing to act instantly on the most hateful urges of their constituents—who are themselves portrayed as creatures without reason, ever in thrall to irrational emotions.

Obviously such accounts are exaggerated and overdrawn. Scholars who study Congress generally agree that while legislators are naturally concerned with reelection, they have other things on their minds as well—not the least of which is making a difference and building a reputation by creating good public policy.[30] Which is not to say that members of Congress should be recast as ideal interpreters of a Constitution. To accomplish anything, legislators must work with interest groups. This has important benefits that legal commentators tend too easily to overlook, such as providing legislators with much needed information, helping them to understand and anticipate how legislation will affect relevant groups, reducing uncertainty about how different laws might be received by voters, and helping to communicate relevant information to the public.[31] But the process still inevitably requires making all sorts of compromises. Conscientious legislators must struggle against politics to find space for principled decision making, space that is rarely, if ever, unconstrained in the real world. Yet to say that legislators do not operate in some Habermasian ideal speech situation is not to say that the legislative process is therefore nondeliberative or devoid of principle. Congressional decisions still turn on whether appropriate justifications can be found for a vote: justifications that are persuasive, that a legislator believes he or she can publicly offer to constituents back home, and that are consistent with or reasonably distinguishable from other positions he or she has taken.[32] This is particularly true when it comes to high-profile constitutional issues that spark national controversy—meaning, at the very least, that Congress is a better institution than today's hyperbolic portrayals might lead one to believe.

Turning to the Supreme Court, we may want to question romanticized accounts of the Justices as lawyers-cum-philosophers/political scientists, studiously pondering weighty questions of principle before crafting careful explanations that reflect deeply on the theoretical dilemmas they have faced. After all, the Court has not been immune from the same pressures to bureaucratize that changed the rest of government, and like Congress, the Court now leaves most of its business to staff working behind closed doors. Indeed, if comparisons are wanted with the nineteenth century, consider the Court then and now. The Justices used to do all their own work. They used to hold oral arguments that lasted for days, laboring assiduously with counsel to understand a case and develop their ideas. They used to discuss each other's opinions in detail and at length. Today, most of the Justices rely on law clerks to prepare a case for them, seldom reading more than a "bench memo" or the parties' submissions. Oral argument is limited to one hour, which the Justices use essentially to get clear on the facts and to signal their thinking to one another. One reason they need to signal each other this way is that they spend so little time talking. Conferences are as short as possible, consisting mainly of terse declamations by each Justice explaining his or her vote, with little or no actual debate or discussion. The detailed legal analysis is done almost exclusively by the clerks, recent law school graduates with at most a year or two of experience. Opinions are drafted by a single chamber, with minimal input from other chambers (except via conversations among the clerks). The Justices almost never meet to discuss a drafted opinion and they never work out their reasoning as a group. The veneer of careful deliberation is generated almost entirely by the law clerks, who draft most of the long opinions that constitute the Court's only public statement. The Justices' role consists mainly of dictating the outcome, instructing the clerks on how an opinion should look, and editing. This does not mean that the Justices are not in control, but there is a considerable gap between this kind of control and the stories told to justify judicial supremacy.

To say these things is not to criticize. Supreme Court Justices work very hard and do a remarkable job considering the volume and difficulty of the work they face. If this description sounds harsh, it is only because we have stubbornly held onto a myth of the Court as some sort of institution that time forgot, the one public body that somehow managed to remain immune from pressures that remolded every other public institution. But, of course, the Court has not been immune, and these pressures have affected it as much as Congress. One can admire the Court for how it handles its responsibilities while still being realistic about who does what and under what circumstances.

None of this argues conclusively against the doctrine of judicial supremacy. It simply calls into question some assumptions that modern commentators have come to take for granted. Yet given our actual historical experience, not to mention the experience of other democracies that have flourished without judicial review, how confident should we be that it is necessary to assign the Court this high political authority? How significant is the difference, really, between the Court and Congress? Even assuming that the Court is less affected (or, more plausibly, differently affected) by short-term political pressures, what about the pressures that do distort its decision making—ideology, lack of information, ignorance of consequences, the confounding effects of law's technicality, and the like? And even if these distortions are for some reason less worrisome, how should we weigh any differences against the superior democratic pedigree attached to decisions made by other political institutions? Is it significant in this respect that the Court itself is invariably as divided as the rest of the country on controversial questions?

"A Matter of Sensibility"

"Once we reach this point in the argument," Mark Tushnet observes, "it is impossible to avoid personal judgments."[33] The question is, how do we make these judgments? Or, to pose the problem from a slightly more sociological perspective, what moves people to make the judgments they make? And, still more interesting, what makes them so certain? For while a small circle of scholars may be prepared to abandon judicial supremacy, most people not only favor ceding this power to courts, but think it obvious that our constitutional system would be significantly worse without it. Some go so far as to say, still without hesitating, that American constitutionalism might not survive if the judiciary did not have final say on constitutional questions. Given uncertainty about the empirical grounds, how do we explain such assurance?

The root of the matter, says Richard Parker, has nothing to do with logic or evidence or history or law. It is "a matter of sensibility."[34] And the dominant sensibility among lawyers, judges, scholars, and even politicians, Parker maintains, is "Anti-Populist"—by which he means of the view that "ordinary political energy . . . is problematic because of attributes that set it apart from, and identify it as qualitatively inferior to, more 'refined' sources of political participation."[35] All the anxiety about Congress is ultimately not so much about legislative institutions or legislators as it is anxiety about *us*, about what we will permit or encourage politically accountable actors to do. The modern Anti-Populist sensibility presumes that ordinary people are emotional, ignorant, fuzzy-headed, and simple-minded, in contrast to a thoughtful, informed, and clear-headed elite. Ordinary people tend to be foolish and irresponsible when it comes to politics: self-interested rather than public-spirited, arbitrary rather than principled, impulsive and close-minded rather than deliberate or logical. Ordinary people are like children, really. And being like children, ordinary people are insecure and easily manipulated. The result is that ordinary politics, or perhaps we should say the politics that ordinary people make, "is not just low in quality, but dangerous as well."[36]

It comes as no surprise that people who hold these sorts of beliefs about ordinary people would gravitate toward something like judicial supremacy. Seeing democratic politics as scary and threatening, they find it obvious that someone must be found to restrain its mercurial impulses, someone less susceptible to the demagoguery and short-sightedness that afflict common people. This is High Federalism redux. And like the High Federalists of the 1790s, modern commentators have come to see the whole point of the Constitution in exclusively counter-majoritarian terms—as if this were self-evident, as if a constitution could be nothing else.[37]

Other commentators have similarly noted the profoundly anti-democratic attitudes that underlie modern support for judicial supremacy: attitudes grounded less in empirical fact or logical argument than in intuition and supposition. Mark Tushnet points to a "deep-rooted fear of voting" among modern intellectuals and suggests they "are more enthusiastic about judicial review than recent experience justifies, because they are afraid of what the people will do."[38] Jack Balkin describes a dominant "progressivist sensibility," constituted by "elitism, paternalism, authoritarianism, naivete, excessive and misplaced respect for the 'best and brightest,' isolation from the concerns of ordinary people, an inflated sense of superiority over ordinary people, disdain for popular values, fear of popular rule, confusion of factual and moral expertise, and meritocratic hurbris."[39] In a particularly strong indictment, Roberto Unger identifies "discomfort with democracy" as one of the "dirty little secrets of contemporary jurisprudence."[40] This discomfort shows up, he says, in every area of contemporary legal culture:

> [I]n the ceaseless identification of restraints upon majority rule, rather than of restraints upon the power of dominant minorities, as the over-

riding responsibility of judges and jurists; in the consequent hypertrophy of countermajoritarian practices and arrangements; in the opposition to all institutional reforms, particularly those designed to heighten the level of popular political engagement, as threats to a regime of rights; in the equation of the rights of property with the rights of dissent; in the effort to obtain from judges, under the cover of improving interpretation, the advances popular politics fail to deliver; in the abandonment of institutional reconstruction to rare and magical moments of national refoundation; in the single-minded focus upon the higher judges and their selection as the most important part of democratic politics; in an ideal of deliberative democracy as most acceptable when closest in style to a polite conversation among gentlemen in an eighteenth-century drawing room; and, occasionally, in the explicit treatment of party government as a subsidiary last-ditch source of legal evolution, to be tolerated when none of the more refined modes of legal resolution applies. Fear and loathing of the people always threaten to become the ruling passions of this legal culture. Far from being confined to conservative variants of contemporary legal doctrine, these passions have left their mark upon centrist and progressive legal thought.[41]

Those who see themselves as targets of such critiques may bridle at the pejorative overtones, choosing to present what they think about ordinary people and politics using kinder, gentler adjectives. But they would not deny or repudiate the underlying core: that constitutional law is motivated by a conviction that popular politics is by nature dangerous and arbitrary; that "tyranny of the majority" is a pervasive threat; that a democratic constitutional order is therefore precarious and highly vulnerable; and that substantial checks on politics are necessary lest things fall apart. While perhaps wanting to say that Parker, Balkin, and Unger have used rhetoric to create a caricature, supporters of judicial supremacy would nevertheless insist on the fundamental correctness of the story that ordinary politics is too dangerous to permit without some independent body to control its excesses and injustices.

This sort of skepticism about people and about democracy is a pervasive feature of contemporary intellectual culture. We see it in persistent misreadings of the Founding that selectively focus on statements expressing fears of popular majorities, that do not even see the more important, more pervasive theme celebrating the rise of popular rule. We see it, too, in the rise of the "cult of the Court" and in the complacency accompanying even the most aggressive judicial interferences in politics, as if the judiciary were our parent or our teacher.[42] Consider in this respect that the *New York Times* summed up a recent Term of the Supreme Court as providing "a report card on the elected branches,"[43] and a leading public intellectual (and sitting federal judge) defended the Court's intervention in *Bush v. Gore* not because it was legally justified but on the ground that Congress was "not a competent forum" to decide matters of such importance.[44]

A profound mistrust of popular government and representative assemblies is, in fact, one of the few things (perhaps the only thing) that the right and the left today share in common.[45] From the right we have public choice, positive political theory, and law and economics: all centrally devoted to explaining why democratic institutions are irrational and inefficient. Better the invisible hand of a market—decentralized, unself-conscious, uncoordinated—than a body in which deliberate choices about how to govern are made. From the left, we get "deliberative democracy," a philosophical school that emphasizes preconditions for legitimate rule and that turns out to be mostly about deliberation and hardly at all about democracy. Popular rule is legitimate, we are told, only if certain stringent prerequisites are satisfied: prerequisites that it just so happens can be met only by small bodies far removed from direct popular control. And now we have the emerging discipline of behavioral economics, which at least some practitioners apparently find attractive because it helps them to "prove" by experiment and simulation how ordinary people cannot be expected to act rationally and need to defer more to experts and specialists.[46]

The point of all this is not to imply that modern scholars want to abolish democracy or are secretly hankering for some other form of government. Nor is it that they hate ordinary people. But Parker is right that most contemporary commentators share a sensibility that takes for granted various unflattering stereotypes respecting the irrationality and manipulability of ordinary people and their susceptibility to committing acts of injustice. To those who believe in the stereotypes, such weaknesses of mind and character are inevitable "facts" that must be confronted and dealt with by those who would preserve democracy. Accepting these facts, they say, is just being realistic. Those who would deny the stereotypes, who would defend the capacity of ordinary citizens to govern responsibly, are viewed as weak or naive or just catering to others who are weak or naive.

These deep-seated misgivings about ordinary citizens explain why modern intellectuals worry so about the risks associated with popular government and why these risks loom so large in their eyes. Their qualms consistently lead them to resolve disputes about the proper structure of democratic institutions in ways that favor minimizing or complicating popular participation. This is not a formal rule, of course. It is a matter of intuitive judgment: given plausible arguments for two versions of democracy or for two institutional arrangements, both of which can be abstractly justified under democratic theory, the one that complicates or qualifies popular participation or that places more or greater obstacles in its way invariably seems preferable. And it is this sensibility that explains why for so many of these scholars the question of judicial review is easy and obvious.

For those with a different sensibility, the opposite conclusion seems just as easy and just as obvious. Parker, for example, finds palpable "[t]he exaggeration on display" in conventional stories about majoritarian politics:

> Surely, the exertion of political energy is not—in and of itself—incipiently tyrannical. (Think of the Constitutional Convention of 1787.) Nor is the exertion of such energy by ordinary people. (Think of the Revolution or the Abolitionists or the Civil Rights Movement.) When we make sweeping claims about tendencies of majority opinion to intolerance, we display the same kind of exaggeration. . . . We frequently dismiss majority opinion as founded on nothing but prejudice—when it plainly is more complicated—simply in order to emphasize our disagreement with it.[47]

Balkin likewise questions whether depicting ordinary citizens as easily manipulated, unreasoning, unreasonable creatures reflects anything more than elite prejudice and distaste for popular culture. Ordinary people, he says, "are not mere passive receptors," and treating them as such is "just another way of denigrating [their] intelligence and abilities."[48] One may not agree with the conclusions they reach, but as Waldron urges, disagreement about hard and important questions is the very essence of democracy. Slogans like "the tyranny of the majority" are just that: slogans. Absent some reason to believe that other members of society are not approaching questions with the same good faith we attribute to ourselves—and the fact that they reach conclusions we disapprove is not itself such a reason—we have no basis to presuppose that "we" are right while "they" need discipline and control.[49]

Once again, one must be careful not to overdraw the argument. Just as supporters of judicial supremacy are not secretly itching for monarchy, its opponents are not dreaming of some pie-in-the-sky model of Athenian direct democracy. They recognize the need for representation, and do not object to institutional arrangements designed to slow politics down (i.e., to separation of powers). Still, there is a qualitative difference between political restraints like bicameralism or a veto and a system of judicial supremacy. It is the difference between checks that are directly responsive to political energy and those that are only indirectly responsive, between checks that explicitly operate from within ordinary politics and those that purport to operate outside and upon it.

Two conclusions follow. First, the difference between friends and foes of judicial authority is ultimately a matter of degree. One might wonder whether this difference is important enough to worry about, but most people clearly believe that it is—clearly believe, in other words, that the decision to have or not to have judicial supremacy matters. Second, the choice one makes in this regard does not turn on evidence or logic, much as intellectuals on both sides of the question might want to believe otherwise. It turns, as Parker says, on differing sensibilities about popular government and the political trustworthiness of ordinary people.

"A Proper Respect for the People"

This is, we can now see, a very old conflict: one that started the moment Americans set their sights on creating a republic and that has scarcely ever flagged since then. In the epigraph to this book, James Madison asks "Who Are the Best Keepers of the People's Liberties?" Madison's faux-debater Republican answers that "[t]he people themselves" are the safest repository—to which Madison has Anti-republican reply: "The people are stupid, suspicious, licentious" and "cannot safely trust themselves." "Wonderful as it may seem," Anti-republican continues, "the more you make government independent and hostile towards the people, the better security you provide for their rights and interests." Correcting for the peculiar phraseology of the period and for Madison's evident hostility to Anti-republican's side of the argument, is it not remarkable the extent to which this 1792 exchange prefigures the debate we are still having today?

Look ahead six decades, to Martin Van Buren's 1857 *Inquiry into the Origins and Course of Political Parties in the United States*, and one finds the same arguments being made. Following Madison, Van Buren says that American politics have always been defined by a struggle between two great principles, which Van Buren labels "democracy" and "aristocracy" and which he describes in terms of their appeal to those who have "a proper respect for the people" and those who have "an inexhaustible distrust . . . of the capacities and dispositions of the great body of their fellow-citizens."[50] Van Buren shares Madison's hostility to the aristocratic impulse, but he is neither wrong nor off base in identifying the persistence of these two views and in emphasizing their centrality in shaping politics.

Simply put, supporters of judicial supremacy are today's aristocrats. Once can say this without being disparaging, meaning only to connect modern apologists for judicial authority with that strand in American thought that has always been concerned first and foremost with "the excess of democracy." Today's aristocrats are presumably no more interested in establishing a hereditary order than were Alexander Hamilton, Gouverneur Morris, or Joseph Story. But like these intellectual forebears, they approach the problem of democratic governance from a position of deep ambivalence: committed to the idea of popular rule, yet pessimistic and fearful about what it might produce and so anxious to hedge their bets by building in extra safeguards.

Today's democrats, in the meantime, are no less concerned about individual rights than were their intellectual forebears: Jefferson, Madison, and Van Buren. But like these predecessors, those with a democratic sensibility have greater faith in the capacity of their fellow citizens to govern responsibly. They see risks, but are not persuaded that the risks justify circumscribing popular control by overtly undemocratic means. In earlier periods, aristocrats and democrats found themselves on opposite sides of such issues as executive power or federalism. Today, the point of conflict is judicial review, as it was for much of the twentieth century. Yet while the field of battle may have changed over time, it is still the same old war.

The question Americans must ask themselves is whether they are comfortable handing their Constitution over to the forces of aristocracy: whether they share this lack of faith in themselves and their fellow citizens, or whether they are prepared to assume once again the full responsibilities of self-government. And make no mistake: the choice is ours to make, necessarily and unavoidably. The Constitution does not make it for us. Neither does history or tradition or law. We may choose as a matter of what Sanford Levinson has called "constitutional faith" to surrender control to the Court, to make it our platonic guardian for defining constitutional values.[51] Or we may choose to keep this responsibility, even while leaving the Court as our agent to make decisions. Either way, we decide.

The point, finally, is this: to control the Supreme Court, we must first lay claim to the Constitution ourselves. That means publicly repudiating Justices who say that they, not we, possess ultimate authority to say what the Constitution means. It means publicly reprimanding politicians who insist that "as Americans" we should submissively yield to whatever the Supreme Court decides. It means refusing to be deflected by arguments that constitutional law is too complex or difficult for ordinary citizens. Constitutional law is indeed complex, for legitimating judicial authority has offered an excuse to emphasize technical requirements of precedent and legal argument that necessarily complicated matters. But this complexity was created by the Court for the Court and is itself a product of judicializing constitutional law. In reclaiming the Constitution, we reclaim the Constitution's legacy as, in Franklin D. Roosevelt words, "a layman's instrument of government" and not "a lawyer's contract."[52] Above all, it means insisting that the Supreme Court is our servant and not our master: a servant whose seriousness and knowledge deserves much deference, but who is ultimately supposed to yield to our judgments about what the Constitution means and not the reverse. The Supreme Court is not the highest authority in the land on constitutional law. We are.

Epilogue

JUDICIAL REVIEW

WITHOUT JUDICIAL SUPREMACY

An earlier, more tendentious article sketching out a preliminary version of the history in this book concluded with the following: "The Supreme Court has made its grab for power. The question is: will we let them get away with it?"[1] Surprisingly, these two short sentences elicited more responses than anything else in the article. "What does *that* mean?" numerous readers asked. "How are we supposed to stop them?"

That so many people had this reaction only proves how much things have changed, for these are not the sorts of questions that would have puzzled Americans in the past. And, indeed, to find answers one need only look to American history. What did earlier generations of Americans do? What did Jefferson, Jackson, Lincoln, the Reconstruction Congress, and Roosevelt do? The Constitution leaves room for countless political responses to an overly assertive Court: Justices can be impeached, the Court's budget can be slashed, the President can ignore its mandates, Congress can strip it of jurisdiction or shrink its size or pack it with new members or give it burdensome new responsibilities or revise its procedures. The means are available, and they have been used to great effect when necessary—used, we should note, not by disreputable or failed leaders, but by some of the most admired Presidents and Congresses in American history.

Just mentioning such devices sends a chill down the spines of most lawyers and legal scholars (not to mention judges). The same anxiety that leads them to favor judicial supremacy—that panicky feeling that popular politics is a wild animal to be kept at bay—makes the possibility of frontal attacks on the Court seem positively terrifying. That would be letting the animal out of its cage; worse, it would be letting the animal tear down its cage. Immediately we begin to hear how fragile and precarious judicial authority is, as if the Court would feebly collapse were it ever challenged in more than words. How ironic if the only way we can sustain this supposedly weakest branch is by making it the strongest one: letting it order the others about with impunity while forbidding them to resist and insisting that their only recourse is to wait for the Court's members to die or tire of the job.

The nations of modern Europe have found more sensible ways to handle this problem of control. Recognizing that constitutional enforcement is not and never could be like ordinary legal interpretation, the post–World War II constitutions of Europe established special courts, not part of the ordinary legal system, whose sole function is to review constitutional questions.[2] Given the high political station these courts occupy, additional safeguards were added to ensure an appropriate level of political accountability without needlessly compromising judicial independence. Appointment to the bench thus typically requires a supermajority in one or both houses of the legislature, guaranteeing that constitutional courts have a mainstream ideology, while judges serve terms that are limited and staggered to ensure a regular turnover.[3] In addition, the constitutions themselves are more easily amendable than ours. The combined effect of these innovations is to relieve the pressure a doctrine of supremacy creates by reducing the likelihood of serious breaches between the constitutional court and the other branches of government, and by making political correctives easier to implement when breaches occur. Partly as a result, constitutional courts in Europe have managed successfully to mimic American activism without the same controversy, though recent developments suggest that European judges, too, may be approaching the limits of their authority.[4]

No similar devices are found in the U.S. Constitution because when our Founding Fathers wrote no one had yet imagined anything even remotely like modern judicial supremacy. Judicial independence was thought of primarily in connection with the courts' ordinary law functions, and life tenure and salary protection were valued chiefly as devices to eliminate executive and legislative influence over ordinary litigation.[5] It was only as the judicial power expanded and its potential and political importance became clear that we discovered a need to compensate for this gap in our Constitution, so we scrambled to create a degree of control and accountability by turning to blunter political tools like those mentioned above and described in earlier chapters.

The resulting system has worked tolerably well over the course of American history, though its operations are hardly smooth and its costs can be high.[6] Given this experience, one might think it makes sense to amend the U.S. Constitution to incorporate some of these European improvements. The availability of a filibuster in the Senate already functions as a kind of supermajority requirement—though lack of constitutional formality, combined with lingering doubts about the filibuster's legitimacy, have hindered its use in the context of judicial appointments. But limited and staggered terms seem like obviously sensible reforms, and a strong case can be made for easing the difficulty of amendment as well.[7] Certainly any sensible constitution-maker today, if starting from scratch, would think seriously about incorporating such devices. Unfortunately, we are not starting from scratch. Realistically speaking, there is very little chance of revising the U.S. Constitution to incorporate European ideas given the cumbersomeness of our existing amendment process. We simply have to live with the jerry-built system of accountability that evolved for us in practice.

That system may be ill-defined and uncertain. It may be costly and clumsy. It is, however, all that we have. And one thing we can say about it with a fair degree of confidence is that there is little reason to fear that using it will destroy the Supreme Court's effectiveness. For experience shows the Court to be anything but fragile. As a historical matter, the Court has been able to get away with a great deal before being seriously attacked; it has also been capable of withstanding enormous pressure once its actions finally provoked an outcry. Except after *Dred Scott*, moreover, the Court recovered quickly from the few instances in which political weapons were finally brought to bear against it effectively. Not that one cannot imagine a scenario in which the political branches inflicted serious damage on the judiciary. But if history is any guide, this risk of wounding the Court is far smaller than the alternative danger—which is that we let excessive concern for injuring our supposedly fragile Court become an excuse for giving the Justices license to roam in deciding matters that could and should be left to constitutional politics.

Still, how do we explain the Court's apparent strength and durability? Certainly it cannot be attributed to judicial supremacy, which as we have seen was not the rule for most of American history. Rather, as social scientists have long understood, a reasonably prudent Court can establish and sustain a high degree of authority even without formal support from a doctrine of supremacy.[8] The reasons are mainly those identified by Madison back in 1834, which are worth quoting a second time. Even within a departmental framework, Madison speculated:

> [T]he Judicial department most familiarizes itself to the public attention as the expositor, by the *order* of its functions in relation to the other departments; and attracts most of the public confidence by the composition of the tribunal. . . . [T]he public deference to and confidence in the judgment of the body are peculiarly inspired by the qualities implied in its members; by the gravity and deliberation of their proceedings; and by the advantage their plurality gives them over the unity of the Executive department, and their fewness over the multitudinous composition of the Legislative department.[9]

What Madison does not say, but what is implicit in his argument, is that these sorts of factors carry weight because of certain expectations the public holds in respect to the Court and its role. The potential usefulness of the judiciary in a separation-of-powers scheme is not difficult to comprehend, and politicians and ordinary citizens alike can and do appreciate that there are advantages in giving the Court some leeway to act as a check on politics.[10] This includes understanding that many benefits of judicial involvement are long term and systemic and so may require accepting individual decisions with which one disagrees. It takes a lot to persuade a majority in this country that particular rulings are wrong enough to overcome this presumption.[11] To this, moreover, we must add the assorted obstacles our political system puts in the way of anyone seeking to change law (through bicameralism, the congressional committee system, filibusters, presidential vetoes, and the like), and the disproportionate power these obstacles give political minorities in blocking new measures. The upshot is that the Court's conduct must be quite provocative and very unpopular, usually over a sustained period, before it will produce actual legislative or executive countermeasures.[12]

It does not follow that nothing is at stake in the choice between a system of judicial supremacy and one based on departmental or coordinate construction. In the latter system, the authority of judicial decisions formally and explicitly depends on reactions from the other branches and, through them, from the public. This, in turn, can make an enormous difference in how the Justices behave. There may be political obstacles to punishing the Court that make it possible even without judicial supremacy for the Justices to have their way most of the time. But the obstacles are smaller: smaller by precisely the weight conferred on Supreme Court decisions by the doctrine of judicial supremacy, which, if that doctrine is widely accepted, can be considerable.

The result of removing this weight is not more conflict. Indeed, a great irony of making clear that we can and should punish an overreaching Court is that it will then almost never be necessary to do so. Rather than more or constant conflict, we will instead see a different equilibrium emerge, as a risk-averse and potentially vulnerable Court adjusts its behavior to greater sensitivity on the part of political leadership in the other branches.

Making this shift should not entail major changes in the day-to-day business of deciding cases. There would still be briefs and oral argument and precedents and opinions, and the job of being a Supreme Court Justice would look pretty much the same as before. What presumably would change is the Justices' attitudes and self-conception as they went about their routine. In effect—though the analogy is more suggestive than literal—Supreme Court Justices would come to see themselves in relation to the public somewhat as lower court judges now see themselves in relation to the Court: responsible for interpreting the Constitution according to their best judgment, but with an awareness that there is a higher authority out there with power to overturn their decisions—an actual authority, too, not some abstract "people" who spoke once, two hundred years ago, and then disappeared. The practical likelihood of being overturned by this authority may be small, but the sense of responsibility thus engendered, together with a natural desire to avoid controversy and protect the institution of the Court, would inevitably change the dynamics of decision making. It is this, in fact, that explains how the Supreme Court has historically husbanded its authority even without judicial supremacy, as well as why crises occurred only when an overconfident Court claiming to be supreme paid too little mind to the public's view of things.

Notes

INTRODUCTION

1. For full accounts of Henfield's case, see Stewart Jay, *Most Humble Servants: The Advisory Role of Early Judges* 127–28, 138–42 (1997); William R. Casto, *The Supreme Court in the Early Republic* 130–36 (1995); Stephen B. Presser, *The Original Misunderstanding* 68–76 (1991).

2. Petit Jury Charge, in *United States v. Henfield*, 11 F. Cas. 1099, 1119–20 (C.C.D. Pa. 1793) (No. 6360).

3. 2 John Marshall, *The Life of Washington* 273–74 (1807).

4. Republican Society of South Carolina, Toasts Drunk on a French Victory, Aug. 29, 1793, quoted in *The Democratic-Republican Societies, 1790–1800: A Documentary Sourcebook of Constitutions, Declarations, Addresses, Resolutions, and Toasts* 380 (Philip S. Foner, ed., 1976).

5. *National Gazette*, Aug. 3, 1793, quoted in Richard Buel, Jr., *Securing the Revolution: Ideology in American Politics, 1789–1815*, at 25 (1972).

6. For fuller accounts of this meeting, see Alfred F. Young, *The Democratic-Republicans of New York* 449–54 (1967); Joanne B. Freeman, *Affairs of Honor: National Politics in the New Republic* xiii–xv (2001).

7. *The Argus, or Greenleaf's New Daily Advertiser*, July 20, 1795.

8. Quoted in Freeman, supra note 6, at xiii, and John C. Miller, *Alexander Hamilton: Portrait in Paradox* 424 (1959).

9. Young, supra note 6, at 450.

NOTES TO PAGES 5–9

10. Speech of Edward Livingston to the House of Representatives, quoted in the *Washington Herald of Liberty*, Aug. 16, 1798.

11. Robert H. Churchill, "Popular Nullification, Fries' Rebellion, and the Waning of Radical Republicanism, 1798–1801," 67 *Penn. History* 105, 113 (2000).

12. Resolutions of the Seventh Regiment and Citizens of Madison County, Aurora, Jan. 4, 1799, quoted in id.

13. Quoted in id.

14. Gordon S. Wood, *The Creation of the American Republic, 1776–1787*, at 47 (1969); for a detailed treatment of how momentous Americans understood to be the change from monarchy to republic, see Richard L. Bushman, *King and People in Provincial Massachusetts* (1985).

15. 1 *The Records of the Federal Convention of 1787*, at 48 (comments of Elbridge Gerry) (Madison's notes, May 31, 1787) (Max Farrand, ed., rev. ed. 1937).

16. St. George Tucker, "On Sovereignty and Legislature," in *Blackstone's Commentaries*, app. A (Philadelphia, 1803), reprinted in St. George Tucker, *A View of the Constitution of the United States with Selected Writings* 19 (Liberty Fund ed. 1999).

17. Gerald Leonard, *The Invention of Party Politics* 15 (2002).

CHAPTER I

1. J. W. Gough identifies antecedents of fundamental law in the Middle Ages, but begins his account of fundamental law with Sir Edward Coke's failed efforts to challenge Crown authority and James I's claims respecting the royal prerogative. J. W. Gough, *Fundamental Law in English Constitutional History* 12–65 (1955). It was at approximately this time, moreover, that English-speaking people began using the word "constitution" to refer to their fundamental law and frame of government. Gerald Stourzh, "Constitution: Changing Meanings of the Term from the Early Seventeenth to the Late Eighteenth Century," in Terence Ball and J. G. A. Pocock, eds., *Conceptual Change and the Constitution* 35, 38 (1988). There was a still older history of constitutionalism, but it bore at most a tangential relationship to the tradition begun in late medieval Europe. See Giovanni Sartori, "Constitutionalism: A Preliminary Discussion," 56 *Am. Pol. Sci. Rev.* 853 (1962).

2. See J. G. A. Pocock, *The Ancient Constitution and the Feudal Law* 30–55 (1987); John Phillip Reid, "The Jurisprudence of Liberty: The Ancient Constitution in the Legal Historiography of the Seventeenth and Eighteenth Centuries," in Ellis Sandoz, ed., *The Roots of Liberty* 147, 169–76, 211–22 (1993) [hereinafter Reid, "Jurisprudence of Liberty"].

3. See Bernard Bailyn, *The Origins of American Politics* 52–54 (1968); Thomas C. Grey, "Origins of the Unwritten Constitution: Fundamental Law in American Revolutionary Thought," 30 *Stan. L. Rev.* 843, 849–50 (1978).

4. See 1 John Phillip Reid, *Constitutional History of the American Revolution: The Authority of Rights* 76 (1986) [hereinafter cited as Reid, *Authority of Rights*].

5. William Paley, *The Principles of Moral and Political Philosophy* (Phila. 1788), quoted in James Wilson, "Comparison of the Constitution of the United States with that of Great Britain," in 1 *The Works of James Wilson* 310 (Robert Green McCloskey, ed., 1967).

6. See Gough, supra note 1, at 2; Reid, *The Authority of Rights*, supra note 4, at 76.

7. See Charles Grove Haines, *The American Doctrine of Judicial Supremacy* 21 (1914).

8. 1 William Blackstone, *Commentaries on the Laws of England* *41 (1765).

9. See Gough, supra note 1, at 17–19.

10. *Sharington v. Strotten* (7 & 8 Elizabeth), 1 Plowden 298, 304.

11. Anon., *Touching the Fundamentall Laws, or Politique Constitution of this Kingdom* 3–4 (London, 1643), quoted in Gough, supra note 1, at 100.

12. See Thomas C. Grey, "The Original Understanding and the Unwritten Constitution," in *Toward a More Perfect Union: Six Essays on the Constitution* 145, 151–52 (1988); Christine A. Desan, "The Constitutional Commitment to Legislative Adjudication in the Early American Tradition," 111 *Harv. L. Rev.* 1381, 1470–71 (1998); Grey, supra note 3, at 852–53 (1978). A practice of blurring law, evolutionary custom, and reason was characteristic of certain strands in American jurisprudence throughout the nineteenth century. See Stephen A. Siegel, "Historicism in Late Nineteenth-Century Constitutional Thought," 1990 *Wisc. L. Rev.* 1431.

13. Nathan Fiske, *The Importance of Righteousness to the Happiness, and the Tendency of Oppression to the Misery of a People* 31 (Boston, John Kneeland, 1774).

14. Gough, supra note 1, at 1, 175–76; Grey, supra note 3, at 862–65; Richard L. Bushman, *King and People in Provincial Massachusetts* 4–5 (1985).

15. *Candid Observations on Two Pamphlets Lately Published* 26–31 (Barbados, 1766), quoted in Jack P. Greene, *Peripheries and Center: Constitutional Development in the Extended Polities of the British Empire and the United States* 85–86 (1986).

16. Richard Wooddeson, *Elements of Jurisprudence Treated in the Preliminary Part of a Course of Lectures on the Laws of England* 35 (Dublin, H. Fitzpatrick, 1792).

17. See Gough, supra note 1, at 160–202; Shannon Stimson, *The American Revolution in the Law* 15–22 (1990); Lois G. Schwoerer, "The Bill of Rights: Epitome of the Revolution of 1688–89," in J. G. A. Pocock, ed., *Three British Revolutions: 1641, 1688, 1776* at 224–37 (1980); Grey, supra note 3, at 850, 860–65. In the colonies, charters were also considered a source of constitutional law.

18. The classic cite here is, of course, J. G. A. Pocock, *The Ancient Constitution and the Feudal Law*, supra note 2, and especially the "retrospect" included in the 1987 edition at pp. 255–305.

19. See 3 John Reid, *Constitutional History of the American Revolution: The Authority to Legislate* 17–33 (1991) [hereinafter cited as Reid, *Authority to Legislate*]; Reid, "Jurisprudence of Liberty," supra note 2, *passim*.

20. Reid, "Jurisprudence of Liberty," supra note 2, at 156.

21. See Theodore F. T. Plucknett, *A Concise History of the Common Law* 157–69 (5th ed. 1956); J. H. Baker, *The Law's Two Bodies* 4–9 (1999).

22. J. M. Sosin, *The Aristocracy of the Long Robe* 53–93 (1989). Courts did address issues of fundamental law that dealt with the legal process itself. See, e.g., *Bushell's Case*, 124 Eng. Rep. 1006, 1009 (C.P. 1670) (holding that jurors cannot be punished for acquitting against the court's instructions); see Thomas Andrew Green, *Verdict According to Conscience: Perspectives on the English Trial Jury 1200–1600* (1985).

23. John Phillip Reid, "In a Defensive Rage: The Uses of the Mob, the Justification in Law, and the Coming of the American Revolution," 49 *N.Y.U. L. Rev.* 1043, 1087 (1974) [hereinafter Reid, "Defensive Rage"].

24. Sylvia Snowiss, *Judicial Review and the Law of the Constitution* 6 (1990).

25. See Edward Coke, *Reports of Sir Edward Coke* (preface to the reader) (London, John Streater et al., 1672).

26. Matthew Hale, *The History of the Common Law of England* 40 (Charles M. Gray, ed., 1971) (1739).

27. John Reeves, *Thoughts on the English Government. Addressed to the Quiet Good Sense of the People of England. In a Series of Letters. Letter the Second*, 65–66 (London, J. Owens, 1799).

28. It was, for example, at this time that Locke began writing his *Two Treatises of Government*. See Peter Laslett, "Two Treatises of Government and the Revolution of 1688," 12 *Cambridge Hist. J.* 40 (1956).

29. See Edmund Morgan, *Inventing the People* 107–21 (1988).

30. See David Lovejoy, *The Glorious Revolution in America* 235–70 (1972); J. M. Sosin, *English America and the Revolution of 1688* (1982).

31. Lovejoy, supra note 30, at 271–93; Desan, supra note 12, at 1399–1400.

32. Lovejoy, supra note 30, at 378; Greene, supra note 15, at 43–54. On the successful efforts of colonials to wrest control of their governments from imperial authorities generally, see Jack P. Greene, *The Quest for Power: The Lower Houses of Assembly in the Southern Royal Colonies, 1689–1763* (1963); Leonard W. Labaree, *Royal Government in America: A Study of the British Colonial System before 1783* (1930).

33. Thomas Rutherforth, *Institutes of Natural Law; Being the Substance of a Course of Lectures on Grotius' de Jure Belli ac Pacis* (2d ed., Baltimore, 1832)(1754–56), quoted in Greene, supra note 15, at 39.

34. See Reid, *Authority to Legislate*, supra note 19, at 211–12; for a general analysis of the role of precedent in shaping fundamental law, see John Reid, "In an Inherited Way: English Constitutional Rights, The Stamp Act Debates, and the Coming of the American Revolution," 49 *S. Cal. L. Rev.* 1109 (1976).

35. Jonathan Sewall, *A Cure for the Spleen* (1775), reprinted in 20 *Magazine of History* 119, 130 (1922).

36. John Adams, "Novanglus," reprinted in *The American Colonial Crisis: The Daniel Leonard–John Adams Letters to the Press 1774–1775*, at 99, 207 (Bernard Mason, ed., 1972); see Bushman, supra note 14, at 12.

37. John Dickinson, *Letters from a Farmer in Pennsylvania, to the Inhabitants of the British Colonies* (1768), reprinted in *The Writings of John Dickinson: Political Writings 1764–1774*, at 305, 312–15 (Paul Leicester Ford, ed., 1895).

38. Resolves of New Shoreham (Mar. 2, 1774), in 7 *Records of the Colony of Rhode Island and Providence Plantations in New England* 277 (John Russell Bartlett, ed., 1856–65).

39. Letter from Governor William Pitkin to William Samuel Johnson (June 6, 1768), in 9 *The Trumbull Papers* 277, 282 (Mass. Hist. Soc'y, 5th ser. 1885).

40. Letter from William Samuel Johnson to Governor Jonathon Trumbull (Feb. 3, 1770), in id. at 406.

41. Petition from the House of Burgesses to the King (June 27, 1770), in 2 *Documents of the American Revolution, 1770–1783*, at 129 (K. G. Davies, ed., 1972–81).

42. See Reid, *Authority to Legislate*, supra note 19, at 293–99.

43. See Gough, supra note 1, at 180–84.

44. See Reid, *Authority to Legislate*, supra note 19, at 79–86; William E. Nelson, *Marbury v. Madison: The Origins and Legacy of Judicial Review* 35–36 (2000); Grey, supra note 3, at 867. It is now generally accepted that legislative sovereignty was by no means a foregone conclusion at the time of the Glorious Revolution, but rather emerged slowly over the next century and was just becoming an orthodoxy in England in the 1760s, at the beginning of the American Revolution. Jennifer Carter, "The Revolution and the Constitution," in Geoffrey Holmes, ed., *Britain after the Glorious Revolution* 39–40, 47, 55 (1969); Greene, supra note 15, at 57–58. Jeffrey Goldsworthy has more recently argued that parliamentary sovereignty was established as early as the Henrician Reformation of the 1530s, but he uses a technical definition of sovereignty whose idiosyncrasy takes it out of this debate. Jeffrey Goldsworthy, *The Sovereignty of Parliament* 7, 9–21 (1999).

45. *Dr. Bonham's Case*, 8 Co. Rep. 113b, 118b, 77 Eng. Rep. 644, 652 (1610).

46. S. E. Thorne, "Dr. Bonham's Case," 54 *Law Q. Rev.* 543, 548–49 (1938); see also Goldsworthy, supra note 44, at 6, 109–24, 197–204; Baker, supra note 21, at 27–28. Glenn Burgess concludes that Coke had in mind a power of statutory interpretation, but one so broad as to approach a concept of judicial review. Glenn Burgess, *Absolute Monarchy and the Stuart Constitution* 193 (1996).

47. Thorne's argument was based mainly on Coke's opinion in *Dr. Bonham's Case* and his subsequent writings. Other scholars have similarly analyzed Coke's later writing, including Gough, supra note 1, at 39–42; Edward Corwin, "The 'Higher Law' Background of American Constitutional Law," 42 *Harv. L. Rev.* 367, 374 n.32 (1929); and Goldsworthy, supra note 44, at 113–14. The

implausibility of the judicial review reading given contemporaneous political theory is developed by Gough, supra note 1, at 30–47. Charles Gray found an alternative manuscript version of the opinion, based apparently on what Coke said from the bench (as opposed to the version Coke subsequently published in his reports, which was drafted after the fact). Charles M. Gray, "Bonham's Case Revisited," 116 *Proc. Am. Phil. Soc'y* 35 (1972). The manuscript shows Coke clearly making an argument based on statutory construction, and it suggests that Coke added the famous judicial review passage later. Gray concluded that Coke did not go beyond a statutory argument in court, but he hypothesized that "when [Coke] came to write his report, he fell to thinking about the transcendent power and excellence of the common law and became interested in showing the most that could be made of the authorities he had used in Bonham's case." Id. at 49. It seems more plausible, however, to conclude that in adding his famous language Coke was merely elaborating the same argument he had made in open court, particularly since—as numerous scholars have observed—Coke's authorities "provide scant basis for 'judicial review' and amount only to examples of strict construction applied to especially unmanageable statutes." Id. at 46. The classic discussion of Coke's authorities is Theodore F. T. Plucknett, "Bonham's Case and Judicial Review," 40 *Harv. L. Rev.* 30 (1927).

48. See Gough, supra note 1, at 105–39.

49. See *City of London v. Wood*, 12 Mod. 669 (1701); *Ship's Money Case*, 3 Howell's State Trials 825, 1235 (1637). According to Philip Hamburger, the report in *City of London v. Wood* is unreliable and Chief Justice Holt actually held the opposite view. Philip Hamburger, "Revolution and Judicial Review: Chief Justice Holt's Opinion in *City of London v. Wood*," 94 *Colum. L. Rev.* 2091, 2135–48 (1994). On the other hand, the *Ship's Money Case* suggests that Charles I thought it at least politically useful to get a judicial declaration supporting his authority over Parliament, though the judges who decided in his favor were promptly impeached for so doing. Goldsworthy, supra note 44, at 128–29.

50. See 19 Viner's Abridgments 512–13, "Statutes" (E.6) (1744); 4 Bacon's Abridgments 649, "Statutes" (E) (1759); 4 Comyn's Digest 340, "Parliament" (R. 10) (1766).

51. See Blackstone, supra note 8, at *91.

52. Grey, supra note 3, at 868; Haines, supra note 7, at 51–53, 72. This argument, assumed or made by many writers on judicial review, is developed most fully by Raoul Berger, *Congress v. The Supreme Court* 23–28, 349–68 (1969).

53. *Giddings v. Browne* (1657), in 2 *Hutchinson Papers* 1, 6 (Franklin series #131, 1967) (1st ed., Boston, 1769).

54. Id. at 11.

55. Berger, supra note 52, at 25.

56. See John Adams, *Contemporaneous Notes of the Writs of Assistance Hearing in February 1761*, reprinted in M. H. Smith, *The Writs of Assistance Case*, app., at 543 (1978).

57. Id. app., at 544. We have only Adams's notes for this argument, as Josiah Quincy was apparently not in the courtroom that particular day.

58. See Grey, supra note 3, at 869; Grey, *Six Essays*, supra note 12, at 150; Berger, supra note 52, at 25 and n. 87.

59. See Letter from John Adams to William Tudor (Mar. 29, 1817), in 10 *The Works of John Adams* 244, 247–48 (Charles Francis Adams, ed., 1856). From 1816–18, Adams sent some thirty letters to Tudor, which are collected in volume 10 of *The Works of John Adams*; the ones pertaining to the *Writs of Assistance Case* are discussed in Smith, supra note 56, at 379–84.

60. See O. M. Dickerson, "Writs of Assistance as a Cause of the Revolution," in Richard B. Morris, ed., *The Era of the American Revolution* 40, 43 (1939); Smith, supra note 56, at 415–17.

61. See Peter Shaw, *The Character of John Adams* 305–07 (1976); Akhil Reed Amar, "The Fourth Amendment, Boston, and the Writs of Assistance," 30 *Suffolk L. Rev.* 53, 76 (1996).

62. Smith, supra note 56, at 383.

63. Id. at 359.

64. See id. at 333, 359, 368.

65. Three years after arguing against general writs of assistance, Otis published a pamphlet protesting parliamentary taxation. See James Otis, *The Rights of the British Colonies Asserted and Proved*, reprinted in 1 *Pamphlets of the American Revolution 1750–1776*, at 419 (Bernard Bailyn with Jane N. Garret, eds., 1965). Otis's performance in this work was, as other historians have observed, possibly confused and definitely confusing. See, e.g., id. at 409–17 (introduction to the pamphlet by Bernard Bailyn); Robert Middlekauff, *The Glorious Cause* 120–22 (1982).

66. In *Robin v. Hardaway*, 1 Jeff. 109, 113–14 (Va. 1772), Mason argued (among other things) that a 1682 statute permitting the enslavement of Native American women was "void in itself, because it was contrary to natural right," citing *Dr. Bonham's Case*. The court ignored the argument but ruled in Mason's favor on the ground that the statute had been repealed in 1705, before the plaintiffs were born. Id. at 123.

67. If we are to make sense of constitutional thinking before the Revolution, an important distinction needs to be kept in mind between (a) the belief that a fundamental law existed and limited what government could do, which both Englishmen and Americans most assuredly held; and (b) the idea that courts were responsible for interpreting and enforcing it, which we have seen was not a significant part of their thinking. *Dr. Bonham's Case* was sometimes invoked in support of the former proposition without the latter one, which is how royalists used it against Parliament in the years leading up to the English Civil War. Some Americans cited the case this way, too, as part of their argument justifying extralegal interference with the Stamp Act. See Plucknett, supra note 47, at 63 (quoting Lieutenant-Governor Thomas Hutchinson sneering of the Stamp Act protesters that "our friends to liberty take the advantage of

a maxim they find in Lord Coke that an Act of Parliament against Magna Carta or the peculiar rights of Englishmen is *ipso facto* void").

68. The earliest cases and pamphlets to discuss judicial review are considered in the next chapter. Most of these make no mention or use whatever of Coke or *Dr. Bonham's Case*. The only references that show any direct influence are to Blackstone's interpretation of Coke as having articulated a limited rule of statutory interpretation. In this form, the argument became the basis of James Duane's opinion in *Rutgers v. Waddington* (picking up on an argument made in a brief submitted by Alexander Hamilton), see 1 *The Law Practice of Alexander Hamilton* 382, 415 (Julius Goebel et al., eds., 1964), and was cited by James Varnum in his argument to the court in *Trevett v. Weeden*, see James Varnum, *The Case, Trevett Against Weeden* 30, 33 (Providence, 1787). Indeed, the only direct reference to *Bonham's Case* in connection with judicial review of which I am aware is found in the notes of a law student at the Litchfield Law School in the mid-1790s. According to Asa Bacon's notes, Tapping Reeve gave a lecture on Blackstone in November 1794 in which he stated that the judiciary might declare an unconstitutional statute void, citing *Bonham* and other English cases. Curiously, this appears to be the only time Reeve made this claim, for the notes of other students from the same lectures in later years contain no references to judicial review. Donald F. Melhorn, Jr., "A Moot Court Exercise: Debating Judicial Review Prior to *Marbury v. Madison*," 12 *Const. Comm.* 327, 333-36 (1995).

69. 1 Julius Goebel, Jr., *The Other Wendell Holmes Devise—History of the Supreme Court: Antecedents and Beginnings to 1801*, at 50-95 (1971).

70. Gough, supra note 1, at 207; Gordon S. Wood, "Judicial Review in the Era of the Founding," in Robert A. Licht, ed., *Is the Supreme Court the Guardian of the Constitution?* 153, 160 (1993).

71. See "Jurisprudential Preface" to John Phillip Reid, *Constitutional History of the American Revolution*, at xviii-xx (abr.ed. 1995).

72. Reid, *Authority to Legislate*, supra note 19, at 28-29; see Daniel J. Hulsebosch, *Constituting Empire: New York and the Transformation of Constitutionalism in the Atlantic World* (forthcoming) (mss. at 195-96); Desan, supra note 12, at 1483.

73. The quotes are from several pamphleteers writing in the 1740s and 1750s, quoted in Greene, supra note 15, at 72.

74. John Dickinson, supra note 37, at Letter VI.

75. On the legality, role, and activities of resistance to unconstitutional laws, see Pauline Maier, *From Resistance to Revolution* 348 (1972); John Phillip Reid, "In a Defensive Rage: The Uses of the Mob, the Justification in Law, and the Coming of the American Revolution," 49 *N.Y.U. L. Rev.* 1043 (1974) [hereinafter Reid, "In a Defensive Rage"]; Richard M. Brown, "Violence and the American Revolution," in Stephen G. Kurtz and James H. Hutson, eds., *Essays on the American Revolution* 81 (1973).

76. See Desan, supra note 12, at 1484.

77. See Morgan, supra note 29, at 223–30; Desan, supra note 12, at 1486; Bushman, supra note 14, at 46–54. On the right of assembly, which seems only to have emerged as a formally articulated "right" in the 1770s, see Marc Harris, "The Right of Assembly and State Constitutionalism" (paper presented at the 2003 Annual Meeting of the Society for Historians of the Early American Republic).

78. See Reid, *Authority of Rights*, supra note 4, at 21–23; Raymond C. Bailey, *Popular Influence upon Public Policy: Petitioning in Eighteenth-Century America* 23–67 (1979); Ruth Bogin, "Petitioning and the New Moral Economy of Post-Revolutionary America," 45 *Wm. & Mary Q.* 391, 397–420 (3d ser. 1988); Gregory A. Mark, "The Vestigial Constitution: The History and Significance of the Right to Petition," 66 *Fordham L. Rev.* 2153, 2161–94 (1998).

79. Reid, *Authority of Rights*, supra note 4, at 22 (quoting I *A New and Impartial Collection of Interesting Letters, from the Public Papers* 64 (London, 1767)).

80. Edmund S. Morgan and Helen M. Morgan, *The Stamp Act Crisis: Prologue to Revolution* 54–74 (1995). In its memorial to the American people, the Continental Congress included among its grievances that "Humble and reasonable petitions from the Representatives of the people have been frequently treated with contempt." Memorial to the Inhabitants of the British American Colonies (Oct. 21, 1774), in *Extracts from the Votes and Proceedings of the American Continental Congress, held at Philadelphia, 5th Sept., 1774*, at 30, 41 (New York, H. Gaine, 1774).

81. See, e.g., The Confederation Congress and the Constitution, in 13 *The Documentary History of the Ratification of the Constitution* 229, 239 (John P. Kaminsky and Gaspare Saladino, eds., (1981) (amendments proposed by Richard Henry Lee, Sept. 27, 1787) [hereinafter cited as *DHRC*]; Amendments of the Minority of the Maryland Convention, in 17 *DHRC* at 236, 245; Federal Farmer: An Additional Number of Letters to the Republican, in id. at 265, 274; Virginia Convention Amendments, in 18 *DHRC* at 199, 202; New York Ratifies the Constitution, in id. at 294, 299.

82. See Mark, supra note 78, at 2212–29; William C. diGiacomantonio, "Petitioners and Their Grievances: A View from the First Federal Congress," in Kenneth R. Bowling and Donald R. Kennon, eds., *The House and the Senate in the 1790s*, at 29, 30–31 (2002); Christine A. Desan, "Contesting the Character of the Political Economy in the Early Republic: Rights and Remedies in *Chisholm v. Georgia*," in id. at 178, 201.

83. Marc L. Harris, "Civil Society in Post-Revolutionary America," in Eliga H. Gould and Peter S. Onuf, eds., *Empire and Nation: The American Revolution in the Atlantic World* (2004).

84. See Maier, supra note 75, at 16–17; Nelson, supra note 44, at 12–13; Douglas Greenberg, *Crime and Law Enforcement in the Colony of New York, 1691–1776* (1974).

85. Letter from Joseph Hawley, *Boston Evening-Post*, July 13, 1767, at 2, col. 1.

86. Thomas Hutchinson, *The History of the Province of Massachusetts Bay, from 1749–1774*, at 262 (1828).
87. See John Phillip Reid, *In a Defiant Stance: The Conditions of Law in Massachusetts Bay, the Irish Comparison, and the Coming of the American Revolution* 52 (1977).
88. See Maier, supra note 75, at 74–75, 114–38, 251–53.
89. Letter from Thomas Hutchinson to Viscount Hillsborough (Nov. 11, 1769), quoted in id. at 133.
90. See Kimberly K. Smith, *The Dominion of Voice: Riot, Reason, and Romance in Antebellum Politics* 11–50 (1999); George Rude, *The Crowd in History: A Study of Popular Disturbances in France and England, 1730–1848* (1964); E. P. Thompson, "The Moral Economy of the Crowd in the Eighteenth Century," 51 *Past and Present* 76 (1971); Maier, supra note 75, at 3–26.
91. See John Adams, "Novanglus," in 4 *Works of Adams*, supra note 59, at 79–83.
92. Natalie Zemon Davis, "The Reasons of Misrule: Youth Groups and Charivari in Sixteenth-Century France," 50 *Past and Present* 41 (1971); David Underdown, *Revel, Riot, and Rebellion: Popular Politics and Culture in England, 1603–1660*, at 99–103 (1985); E. P. Thompson, *Customs in Common: Studies in Traditional Popular Culture* ch. 8 (1993).
93. See William Pencak, Matthew Dennis, and Simon P. Newman, eds., *Riot and Revelry in Early America* (2002), esp. the introductory essay by Pencak and the essays by Steven J. Stewart (on the middle and New England colonies), Brendan McConville (on New Jersey), and Thomas J. Humphrey (on New York).
94. See Thomas J. Humphrey, "Crowd and Court: Rough Music and Popular Justice in Colonial New York," in *Riot and Revelry*, supra note 93, at 108; Smith, supra note 90, at 20–25; Maier, supra note 75, at 12–13; Rude, supra note 90, at 204–05. Historians remain divided over who actually controlled Revolution era mobs. Many historians still accept Pauline Maier's view of the mobs as largely nonviolent and controlled by gentry, but her thesis has been strongly challenged by New Left historians whose mobs are both more violent and more independent. See Alfred F. Young, "American Historians Confront 'The Transforming Hand of Revolution,'" in Ronald Hoffman and Peter J. Albert, eds., *The Transforming Hand of Revolution: Reconsidering the American Revolution as a Social Movement* 346–493 (1995). For present purposes, it does not matter who is closer to the truth beyond noting, as William Pencak has done, that Maier's view reflects that held by the elite colonial leaders themselves. William Pencak, "A Historical Perspective," in *Riot and Revelry*, supra note 93, at 4.
95. Maier; supra note 75, at 13; Rude, supra note 90, at 253. For studies of particular mob actions, see John K. Alexander, "The Fort Wilson Incident of 1779: A Case Study of the Revolutionary Crowd," 31 *Wm. & Mary Q.* 589 (3d ser. 1974); Jesse Lemisch, "Jack Tar in the Streets: Merchant Seamen in the Politics of Revolutionary America," 25 *Wm. & Mary Q.* 371 (3d ser. 1968).

96. "An Impartial Observer," *Boston Evening-Post*, Dec. 20, 1773, at p. 2, col. 3.

97. See Smith, supra note 90, at 20–28; Reid, *In a Defiant Stance*, supra note 87, at 85–91; Reid, "In a Defensive Rage," supra note 75, *passim*. For a succinct summary of these rules, see Maier, supra note 75, at 32–34.

98. Rude, supra note 90, at 255–57.

99. William Pencak, "A Historical Perspective," in *Riot and Revelry*, supra note 93, at 8; Gordon S. Wood, "A Note on Mobs in the American Revolution," 23 *Wm. & Mary Q.* 635, 639–40 (3d ser. 1966).

100. "Vote of the Abington Town Meeting, Mar. 19, 1770," in *Boston Gazette*, Apr. 2, 1770, at p. 3, col. 1. The reference is to the Townsend duties, as described in the seventh of a series of resolutions agreed to by the town.

101. Id.

102. See Reid, "In a Defensive Rage," supra note 75, at 1050–62.

103. See supra note 68.

104. 1 Bay 93, 96, 98 (S. Car. 1789).

105. See Stimson, supra note 17, at 5–6, 48, 56–60, 70–71, 78–81.

106. See William E. Nelson, *The Americanization of the Common Law* 13–35 (1975); William E. Nelson, "The Eighteenth-Century Background of John Marshall's Constitutional Jurisprudence," 76 *Mich. L. Rev.* 893, 904 (1978).

107. Adams's Diary Notes on the Rights of Juries, in 1 *Legal Papers of John Adams* 228, 230 (L. Kinvin Wroth and Hiller B. Zobel, eds., 1965).

108. 3 *Works of Adams*, supra note 59, at 481.

109. 1 *Legal Papers of Adams*, supra note 107, at 229.

110. Id. at 230; see also Diary Entry (Feb. 7, 1771), in 2 *The Diary and Autobiography of John Adams* 2, 4 (L. H. Butterfield, ed., 1961).

111. Stimson, supra note 17, at 52–55.

112. *Kamper v. Hawkins*, 1 Va. Cases 20, 24 (1793).

113. Desan, supra note 12, at 1463. Desan's careful and nuanced re-creation of this culture focuses on the practice of legislative adjudication in the early eighteenth century but remains apt.

114. Id.

115. Reid first developed the idea of Whig law in Reid, *In a Defiant Stance*, supra note 87. For one prominent historian's skepticism, see Barbara Black, Review, 24 *Am. J. Legal Hist.* 367 (1980).

116. Reid, "In a Defensive Rage," supra note 75, at 1087 (quoted supra text accompanying note 23).

117. The phrase, which made its way to America via James Harrington's influential *Oceana*, was a commonplace in the Founding generation, as it still is today. See James Harrington, *The Commonwealth of Oceana*, in *The Political Works of James Harrington* 170 (J. G. A. Popock, ed., 1977); "Novanglus" Letter No. VII, in 2 *The Papers of John Adams* 314 (R. Taylor, ed., 1977); *Marbury v. Madison*, 1 Cranch (5 U.S.) 137, 163 (1803).

118. H. L. A. Hart, *The Concept of Law* 144–50 (1961); Ronald Dworkin, *Law's Empire* 1–113 (1986).

119. *The Federalist No. 49*, at 340 (Jacob E. Cooke, ed., 1961).

120. Jack N. Rakove, *Original Meanings: Politics and Ideas in the Making of the Constitution* 208–14 (1996); John Phillip Reid, *The Concept of Representation in the Age of the American Revolution* (1989).

121. See Lewis Namier and John Brooke, *The House of Commons, 1754–1790*, at 183–84 (1964).

122. P. D. G. Thomas, *The House of Commons in the Eighteenth Century* 46–47 (1971).

123. Jack N. Rakove, *The Origins of Judicial Review: A Plea for New Contexts* 1055 (1997).

124. Rakove, *Original Meanings*, supra note 120, at 209.

125. Bailyn, supra note 3, at 26–27; Alan Taylor, "From Fathers to Friends of the People: Political Personas in the Early Republic," 11 *J. Early Republic* 465 (1987); Bushman, supra note 14, at 59–60.

126. For a sampling of the complexities surrounding this issue, see "Round Table Discussion: Deference or Defiance in Eighteenth-Century America," 85 *J. Amer. Hist.* 13–97 (1998) (essays by Michael Zuckerman, Aaron S. Fogelman, Kathleen M. Brown, John M. Murrin, and Robert A. Gross); Andrew W. Robertson, "Voting Rites Revisited: Electioneering Ritual, 1790–1820," in Jeffrey L. Pasley, Andrew W. Robertson, and David Waldstreicher, eds., *Beyond the Founders: New Approaches to the Political History of the Early American Republic* (2004).

127. See John M. Murrin, "Political Development," in Jack P. Greene and J. R. Pole, eds., *Colonial British America: Essays in the New History of the Early Modern Era* 442–45 (1984).

128. Jack P. Greene, "Changing Interpretations of American Politics," in Ray A. Billington, ed., *The Reinterpretation of American History* 171 (1966); see also J. R. Pole, "Historians and the Problem of Early American Democracy," 67 *Am. Hist. Rev.* 626 (1962); Roy Lokken, "The Concept of Democracy in Colonial Political Thought," 16 *Wm. & Mary Q.* 568 (3d ser. 1959); Richard Buel, "Democracy and the American Revolution: A Frame of Reference," 21 *Wm. & Mary Q.* 178 (3d ser. 1964).

129. See authorities cited, supra note 126; Smith, supra note 90, at 16–25; Allan Tully, "Constituent–Representative Relationships in Early America," 11 *Canadian J. Hist.* 139 (1976); John B. Kirby, "Early American Politics—The Search for Ideology: An Historical Analysis and Critique of the Concept of 'Deference,'" 32 *J. Politics* 808 (1970).

130. On contested elections, see Mark A. Kishlansky, Parliamentary Selection: Social and Political Choice in Early Modern England 105–223 (1986); on the politics and ideologies of Tories and Whigs and the radicalism of the Real Whigs, see Isaac Kramnick, *Bolingbroke and His Circle: Politics and Nostalgia in the Age of Walpole* (1968); Caroline Robbins, *The Eighteenth Century Commonwealthman* (1959).

131. On the relative importance of these radical voices in England and America, see Bailyn, supra note 3, at 27–57.
132. Morgan, supra note 29, at 13–14.
133. Don Herzog, *Happy Slaves: A Critique of Consent Theory* 23 (1989).

CHAPTER 2

1. See Jack P. Greene, *Peripheries and Center: Constitutional Development in the Extended Polities of the British Empire and the United States, 1607–1788*, at 7–150 (1986); John Phillip Reid, *In Defiance of the Law: The Standing-Army Controversy, the Two Constitutions, and the Coming of the American Revolution* 32–34 (1981); Christine A. Desan, "The Constitutional Commitment to Legislative Adjudication in the Early American Tradition," 111 *Harv. L. Rev.* 1381, 1392–1408 (1998).
2. 1 William Blackstone, *Commentaries on the Laws of England* *156–57 (1765). Most scholars date the beginning of this change with enactment of the Septennial Act in 1716. See J. W. Gough, *Fundamental Law in English Constitutional History* 160–213 (1955); Gordon S. Wood, *The Creation of the American Republic* 260–61 (1969).
3. See Gough, supra note 2, at 180–86; Jennifer Carter, "The Revolution and the Constitution," in Geoffrey Holmes, ed., *Britain after the Glorious Revolution* 39–40, 47, 55 (1969); Greene, supra note 1, at 57–58.
4. Jeffrey Goldsworthy, *The Sovereignty of Parliament* 192–97 (1999).
5. David S. Lovejoy, *The Glorious Revolution in America* 378 (1972); Greene, supra note 1, at 43–54; Desan, supra note 1, at 1403–04.
6. The general story of these years is told in Greene, supra note 1, at 18–76; see also Richard L. Bushman, *King and People in Provincial Massachusetts* 88–132 (1985).
7. Robert Middlekauff, *The Glorious Cause* 56–58 (1982); Lawrence Henry Gipson, *The Triumphant Empire: Thunder Clouds Gather in the West, 1763–1766*, at 181–99 (1961).
8. Edmund S. Morgan and Helen M. Morgan, *The Stamp Act Crisis: Prologue to Revolution* 21–27 (1995); Allen S. Johnson, "The Passage of the Sugar Act," 16 *Wm. & Mary Q.* 507, 511 (3d ser. 1959).
9. This point is established—to a degree that is well nigh incontrovertible—in John Reid's impressive four-volume *Constitutional History of the American Revolution*, which stands (in the apt words of one reviewer) "unmatched in the sheer weight of the erudition it brings to bear in the old cause." Stephan A. Conrad, "The Constitutionalism of 'the Common-Law Mind,'" 13 *Law & Soc. Inquiry* 619, 621 (1988). Other commentators have reached the same conclusion about the legal basis of the American Revolution. See Greene, supra note 1, at 79–150; Thomas C. Grey, "Origins of the Unwritten Constitution:

Fundamental Law in American Revolutionary Thought," 30 *Stan. L. Rev.* 843, 892 (1978); Barbara A. Black, "The Constitution of Empire: The Case for the Colonists," 124 *U. Pa. L. Rev.* 1157 (1976); Russell L. Hanson, "'Commons' and 'Commonwealth' at the American Founding: Democratic Republicanism as the New American Hybrid," in Terence Ball and J. G. A. Pocock, eds., *Conceptual Change and the Constitution* 165, 169 (1988). It would, of course, be unforgivable, not to include mention of Charles Howard McIlwain's great early effort, *The American Revolution: A Constitutional Interpretation* (1923).

10. Letter from Thomas Jefferson to Major John Cartwright (June 5, 1824), in 4 *Memoirs, Correspondence and Miscellanies from the Papers of Thomas Jefferson* 393, 394 (Thomas Jefferson Randolph, ed., 1829).

11. Thomas Jefferson, *A Summary View of the Rights of British America. Set Forth in Some Resolutions Intended for the Inspection of the Present Delegates of the People of Virginia Now in Convention*, in 1 *The Writings of Thomas Jefferson* 427–47 (Paul Leicester Ford, ed., 1892).

12. John Phillip Reid, *Constitutional History of the American Revolution* 14 (abr. ed. 1995). See also Daniel Boorstin, *The Genius of American Politics* 84 (1953) (Declaration of Independence was "a bill of indictment against the king, written in the language of British constitutionalism"); Thomas C. Grey, "The Original Understanding and the Unwritten Constitution," in *Toward a More Perfect Union: Six Essays on the Constitution* 145, 150 (1988).

13. James Varnum, *The Case, Trevett against Weedon* 28 (Providence, 1787).

14. A few hopeful reformers, including Massachusetts governor Sir Francis Bernard, toyed with the idea of allowing Americans to send representatives to Parliament, but this suggestion met with little enthusiasm on either side of the Atlantic. See Morgan and Morgan, supra note 8, at 12–20; Bernard Bailyn, *The Ordeal of Thomas Hutchinson* 86–96 (1974).

15. In an unusual twist, John Adams challenged the jurisdiction of a vice-admiralty court on the ground that a proceeding in admiralty deprived the defendant of his constitutional right to argue to a jury that a statute was unconstitutional and should not be enforced. Shannon C. Stimson, *The American Revolution in the Law* 78 (1990).

16. Quoted in Charles A. Barker, *The Background of the Revolution in Maryland* 309 (1940). See Morgan and Morgan, supra note 8, at 185; Grey, supra note 9, at 879.

17. See Morgan and Morgan, supra note 8, at 126, 145–49, 175–86.

18. John Adams, Address to the Council Chamber of Massachusetts (Dec. 1765), in *Reports of Cases Argued and Adjudged in the Superior Court of Judicature of the Province of Massachusetts Bay* 200, 201 (Josiah Quincy Jr., ed., Boston, 1865).

19. Id. at 206 (statement of Governor Francis Bernard summarizing the argument). See also Theodore F. T. Plucknett, "Bonham's Case and Judicial Review," 40 *Harv. L. Rev.* 30, 63 (1927) (quoting Thomas Hutchinson's report that the Massachusetts Assembly resolved that courts should remain open because the Stamp Act was null and void).

20. Pauline Maier, *From Resistance to Revolution* 98–99 (1991); Morgan and Morgan, supra note 8, at 179–85.

21. Although some courts in Massachusetts remained open, only in Rhode Island did courts continue to do business without interruption. Courts in New Hampshire, Maryland, and Delaware closed temporarily, but reopened before news of the Stamp Act's repeal reached the colonies. See Morgan and Morgan, supra note 8, at 180–84. Bear in mind that patriots in many communities were more than happy to see the courts close, since this allowed debtors and other potential defendants to avoid judgment. Id. at 175–78.

22. Letter from Edward Shippen, Jr., to Edward Shippen (Oct. 17, 1765), quoted in id. at 180.

23. American constitutional theory held that there were multiple constitutions governing the different parts of the empire. England had a constitution of its own, establishing the powers of king and Parliament over the people of England. Each colony had a similar constitution, typically embodied in a royal charter. Finally, the imperial constitution regulated relations between England and the colonies as well as among the colonies. See Greene, supra note 1, at 67–68. The essential character of all these constitutions was the same, though their particular terms differed, reflecting their different domains. Of course, English authorities were having none of this: in their eyes, there was but one constitution for the British empire, and it made Parliament (or, more precisely, the king-in-Parliament) sovereign.

24. Letter from Caesar Rodney to John Haslet (May 17, 1776), in *Letters to and from Caesar Rodney, 1756–1784*, at 80 (George Herbert Ryden, ed., 1933).

25. 4 *Journals of the Continental Congress, 1774–1789*, at 342, 357–58 (Worthington C. Ford et al., eds., 1904–37).

26. Only six states created formal bills of rights: Virginia, Delaware, Pennsylvania, Maryland, North Carolina, and Massachusetts. The territory of Vermont, still fighting for its own independence from New York and New Hampshire, copied the Pennsylvania declaration (along with the rest of Pennsylvania's handiwork) in its state constitution. In states that neither wrote a bill of rights nor embedded rights in the body of their constitutions, the legislatures sometimes adopted lists of rights by ordinary legislative means. See Marc W. Kruman, *Between Authority and Liberty: State Constitution Making in Revolutionary America* 37 (1997); Willi Paul Adams, *The First American Constitutions: Republican Ideology and the Making of State Constitutions in the Revolutionary Era* 144 n. 58 (expanded ed. 2001).

27. Compare Gordon S. Wood, *The Creation of the American Republic, 1776–1787* (1969) (arguing that the new American science of politics emerged only in 1789), with Kruman, supra note 26 (arguing that much or most of this was fully developed at the beginning of the Revolution). For a detailed portrait of the intellectual process that is generally consistent with Wood's account, see Jack N. Rakove, *Original Meanings: Politics and Ideas in the Making of the Constitution* (1996).

28. Kruman, supra note 26, at 7–8; Daniel J. Hulsebosch, *Constituting Empire: New York and the Transformation of Constitutionalism in the Atlantic World* (forthcoming) (mss. at 250–51).

29. See Adams, supra note 26, at 64–65.

30. The opinion in this case was delivered orally and was not contemporaneously reported. The principal record is a recounting in *State v. Parkhurst*, 9 N.J.L. 427, 444 (1802). See Wayne D. Moore, "Written and Unwritten Constitutional Law in the Early Founding Period: The Early New Jersey Cases," 7 *Const. Commentary* 341 (1990); Austin Scott, "*Holmes v. Walton*: The New Jersey Precedent," 4 *Am. Hist. Rev.* 456, 458–60 (1899).

31. Once again, there is no official report, and the main record of the case is from a pamphlet published by Weeden's attorney, Revolutionary leader James Varnum, after the fact. See Varnum, supra note 13, at 8.

32. Id. at 25.

33. Id. at 15.

34. *Bowman v. Middleton*, 1 Bay 252, 254–55 (S. Car. 1792); see also *Ham v. McLaws*, 1 Bay 93, 96–98 (1789); *Lindsay v. Commissioners*, 2 Bay 38, 57, 61–62 (1796).

35. 2 *The Records of the Federal Convention* 376 (Max Farrand, ed., 1966) (Madison's notes, Aug. 22, 1787).

36. Id.

37. See William Michael Treanor, "The Case of the Prisoners and the Origins of Judicial Review," 143 *U. Pa. L. Rev.* 491 (1995); William Michael Treanor, "Judicial Review in State Courts before *Marbury*" (unpublished manuscript on file with author); William Michael Treanor, "Judicial Review in the Federal Courts before *Marbury*" (unpublished manuscript on file with author).

38. See Mark A. Graber, "Naked Land Transfers and American Constitutional Development," 53 *Vanderbilt L. Rev.* 73 (2000); Grey, supra note 12, at 148–49, 167–68; David P. Currie, *The Constitution in the Supreme Court: The First Hundred Years* 47–48 (1994).

39. See Grey, supra note 12, at 146–49.

40. *Calder v. Bull*, 3 U.S. (3 Dall.) 386, 388 (1798).

41. Id. at 398.

42. Id. at 399.

43. John Hart Ely, *Democracy and Distrust: A Theory of Judicial Review* 210–11 (1980).

44. See Currie, supra note 38, at 46–47; for a sophisticated exposition of Chase's jurisprudence, albeit one that grounds his position in natural law, see Stephen B. Presser, *The Original Misunderstanding: The English, the Americans, and the Dialectic of Federalist Jurisprudence* 37–46 (1991).

45. See John Phillip Reid, *Constitutional History of the American Revolution: The Authority of Rights* 87–95 (1986) [hereinafter Reid, *Authority of Rights*]; Rakove, supra note 27, at 290–93.

46. *Calder v. Bull*, 3 U.S. (3 Dall.) at 388–89.

47. See, e.g., Paul Brest et al., *Processes of Constitutional Decisionmaking* 113 (4th ed. 2000). For a general collection of essays revealing today's uncertainty about what to make of the Ninth Amendment, see Randy Barnett, ed., *The Rights Retained by the People: The History and Meaning of the Ninth Amendment* (2 vols., 1989, 1993).

48. Reid lists ten separate sources of rights relied upon by Americans in their quarrels with England. Reid, *Authority of Rights*, supra note 45, at 293.

49. Cf. Grey, supra note 12, at 162–66.

50. James Wilson, "Lectures on Law," in 1 *The Works of James Wilson* 186 (Robert Green McCloskey, ed., 1967).

51. Nor was organized popular resistance confined to constitutional matters, for the radical impulses unleashed by the Revolution challenged the tradition of deference that had dominated colonial politics, and voters became more assertive about controlling what their representatives did in office. The story of these years is recounted with typical elegance and power in Gordon S. Wood, *The Radicalism of the American Revolution* 95–286 (1991).

52. See 8 Va. (4 Call) 141–47 (1788). The Remonstrance is also reprinted as an appendix to the opinion in *Kamper v. Hawkins*, 3 Va. (1 Va. Cases) 20, 99–108 (1793), in which the same court faced another question regarding the legislature's power to regulate the courts, this time choosing to address it through the newly developing concept of judicial review.

53. 1 Va. Cases at 108.

54. Charles T. Cullen, *St. George Tucker and Law in Virginia* 76–81 (1987). The legislature's response failed to meet the judges concern, leading eventually to *Kamper v. Hawkins*. See Margaret V. Nelson, "The Cases of the Judges," 31 *Va. L. Rev.* 243, 246–50 (1945).

55. Draught of a Fundamental Constitution for the Commonwealth of Virginia (1783), in Thomas Jefferson, *Notes on the State of Virginia* 209, 221 (William Peden, ed., 1954) (1787) (emphasis added).

56. I am indebted to Jack Rakove both for pointing out the importance of *Federalist 49–50* and, though our views are somewhat different, for helping me to understand Madison's thinking. Rakove's interpretation of Madison's argument is found in Rakove, supra note 27, at 140–42, 280–82.

57. *The Federalist No. 49*, at 340, 342–43 (Jacob E. Cooke, ed., 1961).

58. See Ralph Ketchum, *James Madison: A Biography* 158–73 (1990); Irving Brant, *James Madison: The Nationalist, 1780–1787*, at 306–87 (1948).

59. Letter to George Washington (Dec. 9, 1785), in 8 *The Papers of Madison* 439 (Robert A. Rutland, ed., 1973); Letter to Thomas Jefferson (Aug. 20, 1785), in id. at 346.

60. See David J. Siemers, *Ratifying the Republic: Antifederalists and Federalists in Constitutional Time* 89–121 (2002); John Ferejohn, "Madisonian Separation of Powers," in Samuel Kernell, ed., *James Madison: The Theory and Practice of Republican Government* (Stanford Press, 2003).

61. *The Federalist No. 49*, supra note 57, at 339.

62. *The Federalist No. 51*, id. at 347–48.
63. Rakove, *Original Meanings*, supra note 27, at 282.
64. *The Federalist No. 49*, supra note 57, at 339.
65. See Gordon S. Wood, "Interests and Disinterestedness in the Making of the Constitution," in Richard Beeman, Stephen Botein, and Edward C. Carter, III, eds., *Beyond Confederation* 69 (1987); Saul Cornell, *The Other Founders: Anti-Federalism and the Dissenting Tradition in America* 147–52 (1999); Rakove, supra note 27, at 214–27.
66. *The Federalist No. 51*, supra note 57, at 349.
67. Comments on the Removal Power of the President (June 17, 1789), reprinted in 12 *Papers of Madison*, supra note 59, at 238.
68. See Christopher Wolfe, *The Rise of Modern Judicial Review* 95 (rev. ed. 1994).
69. *The Federalist No. 49*, supra note 57, at 339.
70. *The Federalist No. 48*, id. at 333 (Madison).
71. *The Federalist No. 46*, id. at 316 (Madison); see Larry Kramer, "Putting the Politics Back into the Political Safeguards of Federalism," 100 *Colum. L. Rev.* 215, 257–65 (2000).
72. Speech by James Wilson to the Pennsylvania Ratifying Convention (Nov. 24, 1787), in 2 *Documentary History of the Ratification of the Constitution* 350, 362 (Merrill Jensen et al., eds., 1976) (version reported by Thomas Lloyd) [hereinafter cited as *DHRC*].
73. 11 *Annals of Congress* 660 (Feb, 1802).
74. Id. at 661.
75. Veto Message (Jan. 30, 1815), in 1 *A Compilation of the Messages and Papers of the Presidents* 555 (James D. Richardson, ed., 1900). Madison vetoed the bill on policy grounds, but a year later signed into law another bill for chartering a bank that answered his objections. See Drew R. McCoy, *The Last of the Fathers: James Madison and the Republican Legacy* 81 (1989).
76. Letter from Thomas Jefferson to Spencer Roane (Sept. 6, 1819), in 10 *Writings of Jefferson*, supra note 11, at 140. Daniel Sisson speaks of Jefferson's commitment to "revolutionary" rather than "constitutional" principles, but he is referring to the same thing: the fundamental principles that constitute the society and government. Daniel Sisson, *The American Revolution of 1800*, at 21 (1974).
77. Letter from Thomas Jefferson to Spencer Roane, supra note 76, at 140.
78. The best study of the problems of national government during the Confederation period is Jack N. Rakove, *The Beginnings of National Politics: An Interpretive History of the Continental Congress* (1979). Other works covering this period include Richard B. Morris, *The Forging of the Union: 1781–1789* (1987), which tends to celebrate the Federalists a bit too much; and Merrill Jensen, *The New Nation: A History of the United States during the Confederation* (1950), which tilts in the opposite direction and shows excessive traces of Charles Beard's continuing influence. Despite considerable recent work challenging its major premises, Gordon Wood, *Creation of the American Republic*, supra

note 27, remains essential reading to understand the intellectual and social forces shaping the period.

79. Wood, *Radicalism*, supra note 51, at 187–88. Compare with this William Nelson's description of the tasks of colonial legislatures, which, he says, "usually consisted of mere administration: raising and appropriating small amounts of money, distributing the even smaller amounts of government largess, and legislating as necessary to keep the few governmental institutions functioning." William E. Nelson, "The Eighteenth-Century Background of John Marshall's Constitutional Jurisprudence," 76 *Mich. L. Rev.* 893, 922 (1978).

80. *Vices of the Political System of the United States*, in 9 *Papers of Madison*, supra note 59, at 345, 353.

81. See Gordon S. Wood, "The Origins of Judicial Review," 22 *Suffolk L. Rev.* 1293, 1296 (1988); Gerald Stourzh, "Constitution: Changing Meanings of the Term from the Early Seventeenth to the Late Eighteenth Century," in *Conceptual Change and the Constitution* 35, 46–47 (Terence Ball and J. G. A. Pocock, eds., 1988); Sylvia Snowiss, *Judicial Review and the Law of the Constitution* 23–30 (1990).

82. See also Daniel J. Hulsebosch, *Constituting Empire: New York and the Transformation of Constitutionalism in the Atlantic World* (forthcoming) (mss. at 13).

83. 3 Va. (1 Va. Cases) 20, 78 (1793).

84. 2 U.S. (2 Dall.) 304, 308 (C.C.A. 1795). See also Letter from James Iredell to Richard Spaight (Aug. 26, 1787), in 2 Griffith J. McRee, *Life and Correspondence of James Iredell* 172, 174 (1857) (the Constitution is not "a mere imaginary thing, about which ten thousand different opinions may be formed, but a written document to which all may have recourse, and to which, therefore, the judges cannot wilfully blind themselves.").

85. My discussion of amendments has benefited greatly from Richard B. Bernstein, with Jerome Agel, *Amending America* 3–30 (1993). See also Kruman, supra note 26, at 53–59; Adams, supra note 26, at 136–42; John R. Vile, *The Constitutional Amending Process in American Political Thought* 1–42 (1992); Charles Borgeaud, *Adoption and Amendment of Constitutions in Europe and America* 3–20, 131–45 (Charles D. Hazen, trans., 1895).

86. Vile, supra note 85, at 1–17; see J. G. A. Pocock, *The Machiavellian Moment: Florentine Political Thought and the Atlantic Republican Tradition* (1975).

87. No one had anticipated this problem, and many people missed it at first. Fewer than half of the states had adopted amending procedures by 1780, for example, and five (Virginia, North Carolina, New York, Connecticut, and Rhode Island) still had no formal process in place as late as 1787, when the Federal Convention met. See Bernstein, supra note 85, at 8–9; Kruman, supra note 26, at 55; Adams, supra note 26, at 138–39. Nevertheless, awareness of the problem was widespread by the mid-1780s.

88. 1 Farrand, supra note 35, at 122 (Madison's notes, June 5, 1787).

89. Id. at 121.

90. *Massachusetts, Colony to Commonwealth: Documents on the Formation of Its Constitution, 1775–1780*, at 67–68 (Robert J. Taylor, ed., 1961).
91. 1 Farrand, supra note 35, at 202–03 (Madison's notes, June 11, 1787).
92. Letter from James Madison to Thomas Jefferson (Feb. 4, 1790), in 13 *Papers of Madison*, supra note 59, at 19. Madison is responding to the famous letter in which Jefferson proclaimed "that the earth belongs in usufruct to the living." Letter from Thomas Jefferson to James Madison (Sept. 6, 1789), in 5 *Writings of Jefferson*, supra note 11, at 115.
93. See Bernstein, supra note 85, at 4–13; Kruman, supra note 26, at 54–59; Adams, supra note 26, at 137–42.
94. See Wood, *Radicalism*, supra note 51, 229–325; Edward Countryman, *A People in Revolution* 193–251 (1981); Alfred E. Young, ed., *The American Revolution: Explorations in the History of American Radicalism* (1976).
95. See Morris, supra note 78, at 130–61. Merrill Jensen paints a rosier picture of the same period. Jensen, supra note 78, at 179–257. On problems of public finance, see E. James Ferguson, *The Power of the Purse* 220–50 (1961).
96. Letter from Alexander Hamilton to Robert R. Livingston (Aug. 13, 1783), in 3 *The Papers of Alexander Hamilton* 431 (Harold G. Syrett and Jacob E. Cooke, eds., 1962). See Jensen, supra note 78, at 261–81; Snowiss, supra note 81, at 35.
97. See Wood, supra note 27, at 46–124; a more succinct version is presented in Wood, *Radicalism*, supra note 51, at 169–89. Many aspects of Wood's argument have been challenged since he first advanced it in 1969, and there is still controversy and uncertainty about what the Founding generation meant by "republicanism." But Wood is clearly right about the outburst of enthusiasm for republicanism understood in its most stripped-down form—a government in which authority derives explicitly and exclusively from the people.
98. Stourzh, supra note 81, at 47; see Snowiss, supra note 81, at 30–33; William E. Nelson, *Marbury v. Madison: The Origins and Legacy of Judicial Review* 37–38 (2000); Stimson, supra note 15, at 47–48.
99. John Adams, *Thoughts on Government* (Boston, 1776), in 1 *American Political Writing during the Founding Era, 1760–1805*, at 401, 408–09 (Charles S. Hyneman and Donald S. Lutz, eds., 1983).
100. See Kruman, supra note 26, at 17–19.
101. Id. at 53–55 has an excellent discussion of the new progressivism expressed in provisions for changing a constitution. In contrast, Adams, supra note 26, at 140–42, emphasizes the conservative side of the same provisions.
102. Letter from Thomas Jefferson to Edmund Pendleton (Aug. 13, 1776), in 1 *The Papers of Thomas Jefferson* 492 (Julian Boyd, ed., 1952).
103. North Carolina Declaration of Rights; see also Virginia Declaration of Rights, § 15 (June 12, 1776) ("That no free government, or the blessings of liberty, can be preserved to any people, but by a firm adherence to justice, moderation, temperance, frugality, and virtue, and by frequent recurrence to fundamental principles"). On the significance of this political concept generally, see Ger-

ald Stourzh, *Alexander Hamilton and the Idea of Republican Government* ch. 1 (1970).

104. Address to the Convention, March 1780, in *The Popular Sources of Political Authority: Documents on the Massachusetts Constitution of 1780*, at 435 (Oscar Handlin and Mary Handlin, eds., 1966).

105. See Donald H. Meyer, *The Democratic Enlightenment* 97–168 (1976).

106. *The Federalist No. 14*, supra note 57, at 88–89.

107. Rakove, *Original Meanings*, supra note 27, at 96–108.

108. See id. at 97; see also Adams, supra note 26, at 61–90 (state-by-state description of process).

109. See Jefferson, *Notes on the State of Virginia*, supra note 55, at 121–25 (the existing Virginia constitution "is alterable by the ordinary legislature"); John Adams, *Thoughts on Government*, supra note 99, at 406 ("if by experiment [the constitution's provisions for electing officers] should be found inconvenient, the legislature may, at its leisure, devise other methods of creating them"). These were minority views. Indeed, the main issue in *Kamper v. Hawkins*, 1 Va. Cases 20 (1793), often cited for its discussion of judicial review, was to refute Jefferson on this point and make clear that the Virginia constitution was properly deemed supreme, fundamental law; each of the judges addressed this issue at length in his opinion.

110. See *Vices of the Political System of the United States*, supra note 80, at 348–49; Letter from James Madison to Thomas Jefferson (Oct. 17, 1788), in 11 *Papers of Madison*, supra note 59, at 295, 297.

111. See Wood, supra note 65.

112. *Commonwealth v. Caton*, 8 Va. (4 Call) 5, 17 (1782).

113. *Kamper v. Hawkins*, 3 Va. (1 Va. Cases) 20, 30 (1793).

114. Id. at 77 (noting that some writers "affirm, that the constitution of a state is a rule to the *legislature only*, and not to the *judiciary*, or the *executive*: the legislature being bound not to transgress it; but that neither the executive nor the judiciary can resort to it to enquire whether they do transgress it, or not"). Tucker rejected the argument as a "sophism," relying on the theory described below.

115. See infra notes 147–70 and accompanying text; Gordon S. Wood, "The Origins of Judicial Review Revisited, or How the Marshall Court Made More Out of Less," 56 *Wash. & Lee L. Rev.* 787, 795–97 (1999).

116. Letter from Richard Dobbs Spaight to James Iredell (Aug. 12, 1787), in 2 *Correspondence of Iredell*, supra note 84, at 168, 169. Writing from Philadelphia where he was a delegate to the Federal Convention, Spaight found the argument for judicial review incomprehensible, "as [the judges] would have operated as an absolute negative on the proceedings of the Legislature, which no judiciary ought ever to possess: and the State, instead of being governed by the representatives in general Assembly, would be subject to the will of three individuals. . . ." Id.

117. Id. at 169–70.

118. [Anonymous], *Four Letters on Interesting Subjects* (Philadelphia, 1776), reprinted in Hyneman and Lutz, supra note 99, at 368, 389.

119. See Adams, supra note 26, at 267–68; Charles Grove Haines, *The American Doctrine of Judicial Supremacy* 124–33 (1914); 1 Julius Goebel, Jr., *The Oliver Wendell Holmes Devise—History of the Supreme Court: Antecedents and Beginnings to 1801*, at 102–03 (1971).

120. See Haines, supra note 119, at 133–38; Kruman, supra note 26, at 125; William A. Polf, *The New York Constitution of 1777* (1977).

121. See Letter from James Madison to Caleb Wallace (Aug. 23, 1785), in *James Madison: Writings* 39, 41 (Jack N. Rakove, ed., 1999) [hereinafter *Madison: Writings*].

122. See Madison's Observations on Jefferson's Proposed Revision of the Virginia Constitution, in 6 *Papers of Jefferson*, supra note 102, at 308, 315.

123. See 1 Farrand, supra note 35, at 21 (8th resolution of the Virginia Plan) (Madison's notes, May 29, 1787); id. at 97–104, 138–40 (Madison's notes, June 4, 6, 1787) (debate on council of revision); 2 id. at 73–80 (Madison's notes, July 21, 1787) (same); Rakove, *Original Meanings*, supra note 27, at 261–62.

124. *The Federalist No. 10*, supra note 57, at 59. See Larry D. Kramer, "Madison's Audience," 112 *Harv. L. Rev.* 611, 628–36, 656 (1999); on the uncomprehending reactions of others to Madison's novel arguments, see id. at 637–78.

125. Instructions to Chowan County Representatives (Sept. 1783), in 2 *The Papers of James Iredell* 446, 449 (Don Higginbotham, ed., 1976) (urging the state legislature to provide judges with "liberal Salaries" in 1783 so they could serve faithfully as "guardians and protectors" of the state's constitution); Gouverneur Morris, *An Address on the Bank of North America* (1785), in 3 *The Life of Gouverneur Morris with Selections from His Correspondence and Miscellaneous Papers* 438 (Jared Sparks, ed., 1832) (noting that the legislature is not omnipotent and cannot change the constitution and that "[a] law was once passed in New Jersey, which the judges pronounced to be unconstitutional, and therefore void").

126. *Bayard v. Singleton*, 1 N.C. (Mart.) 48 (1787). It is unclear whether Iredell was representing the plaintiffs or serving as a "friend of the court." See Willis P. Whichard, *Justice James Iredell* 10–11 (2000).

127. An Elector, "To the Public," in 2 *Correspondence of Iredell*, supra note 84, at 145, 148.

128. Id. at 145–46.

129. Id. at 147.

130. Id. The remainder of the quotes in this paragraph are from the same page.

131. Id. at 148. As mentioned earlier, supra note 125, Iredell had previously recognized that courts might have a role to play in enforcing the constitution.

132. These cases are surveyed in Treanor, "Judicial Review in State Courts before Marbury," supra note 37, at 4–37; Robert Lowry Clinton, *Marbury v. Madison and Judicial Review* 48–55 (1989); and J. M. Sosin, *The Aristocracy of the Long*

Robe 203–26 (1989). Different scholars count the cases differently; the literature includes estimates as high as nine cases and as low as four.

133. The first published law reports of a state did not appear until Ephraim Kirby published a volume of Connecticut decisions in 1789, followed by Alexander Dallas for Pennsylvania in 1790. Sosin, supra note 132, at 203–04.

134. 8 Va. (4 Call) 5, 17 (1782).

135. Wood, supra note 115, at 792–93.

136. See Snowiss, supra note 81, at 50.

137. See Varnum, supra note 13, at 26. See also Letter from Edmund Randolph to James Madison (Oct. 26, 1782), in 5 *Papers of Madison*, supra note 59, at 217, 218 (favoring judicial review because "without an accommodation fou[n]ded upon a reasonable construction of the constitution, the appeal must be made to the people").

138. Wood, supra note 115, at 798.

139. See supra notes 16–22 and accompanying text.

140. See Treanor, "The Case of the Prisoners," supra note 37, at 511–12.

141. Id. at 512.

142. Edmund Randolph, Rough Draft of Argument in *Respondent v. Lamb*, quoted in id. at 512.

143. *Commonwealth v. Caton*, 8 Va. (4 Call) 5, 8 (1782). In fairness to Wythe, this awful, purple prose may not be his. The report of the case was published by Daniel Call in 1827, some forty-five years after the fact, when everyone connected with the case—including the judges whose opinions Call reported—was dead. See Sosin, supra note 132, at 207. Significant reasons exist to doubt the reliability of Call's reporting. See 1 Louis B. Boudin, *Government by Judiciary* 533–34 (1932). Having said that, Wythe's fellow judge, Edmund Pendleton kept his own notes of the case, and while these are brief, they support the same general interpretation of Wythe's analysis. Pendleton records Wythe urging "several strong and sensible reasons of the nature of those used by Lord Abblington" in favor of treating the law as void. Edmund Pendleton, Pendleton's Account of "The Case of the Prisoners," in 2 *The Letters and Papers of Edmund Pendleton, 1734–1803*, at 426 (David J. Mays, ed., 1967). As William Treanor explains:

> Lord Abingdon's 1777 *Thoughts on the Letter of Edmund Burke to the Sheriffs of Bristol on Affairs in America* argued that no duty of obedience existed to laws inconsistent with the constitution. Thus, there is at least a possibility that the actual opinion delivered by Wythe reflected a notion of judicial review that was based on the older English-based notion of constitutionality. . . . Under the older view, the citizen had no obligation to obey the unconstitutional statute because that statute violated the compact between governed and governors; disobedience was justified, but it was also tantamount to an act of rebellion.

Treanor, supra note 37, at 534.

144. Wood, supra note 115, at 796.
145. Gordon S. Wood, "Judicial Review in the Era of the Founding," in Is the Supreme Court the Gurdian of the Constitution? 153, 158 (Robert A. Licht, ed., 1993).
146. Letter from James Monroe to James Madison (Nov. 22, 1788), in 1 *The Writings of James Monroe* 196 (Stanislaus Murray Hamilton, ed., 1898).
147. Letter from James Iredell to Richard Dobbs Spaight (Aug. 26, 1787), in 2 *Correspondence of Iredell*, supra note 84, at 172, 175.
148. If the law violated either the treaty or the law of nations, Hamilton wrote, citing *Bonham's Case*, "the *act is void* . . .—But let us see whether there are not rules of construction which [render] this extremity unnecessary." 1 *The Law Practice of Alexander Hamilton* 382 (Julius Goebel et al., eds., 1964).
149. There is no official report of the case, which can be found in id. at 393–419. The language quoted in text is at page 415. Compare Duane's recitation to Blackstone's tenth rule of construction, of which it is a paraphrase. See 1 Blackstone, supra note 2, at *91.
150. New York Assembly Journal, 8th Assembly, 1st meeting, at 33 (Nov. 2, 1784), quoted in *Law Practice of Hamilton*, supra note 148, at 312.
151. *The New York Packet and the American Advertiser*, Nov. 4, 1784, quoted in id. at 313–14. This letter had been written earlier, at a meeting in a tavern held in September, at which time it was sent to the legislature. Id. at 313 n. 85.
152. The name of the case is unknown, as there was no opinion or official report. Knowledge of the proceedings is based on contemporaneous newspaper accounts. See Clinton, supra note 132, at 53–54.
153. See 2 William Winslow Crosskey, *Politics and the Constitution in the History of the United States* 970 (1953); Sosin, supra note 132, at 211–12.
154. See id.
155. See Timothy A. Lawrie, "Interpretation and Authority: Separation of Powers and the Judiciary's Battle for Independence in New Hampshire, 1786–1818," 39 *Am. J. Leg. Hist.* 310 (1995); John Phillip Reid, "Controlling the Law: Legal Politics in Early National New Hampshire" (draft on file with author). The cases that finally succeeded in confirming the judiciary's review power were *Dartmouth College v. Woodward*, 17 U.S. (4 Wheat.) 518 (1819), and *Merrill v. Sherburne*, 1 N.H. Reports 203 (1818), though this became clear only in retrospect.
156. 1 Martin 42 (N.C. 1787).
157. 2 Crosskey, supra note 153, at 971–72.
158. These efforts are described in Martin's report of the case. 1 Martin at 49.
159. Id.
160. Haines, supra note 119, at 206; 2 Crosskey, supra note 153, at 972; Whichard, supra note 126, at 13.
161. See Varnum, supra note 13, at 15–18, 38–39 ("The plea of the defendant, in a matter of mere surplussage, mentions the act of the General Assembly as

'unconstitutional, and so void'; but the judgment of the Court simply is, 'that the information is not cognizable before them'").

162. Id. at 38.

163. Id. at 45.

164. Sosin, supra note 132, at 217–18.

165. See Treanor, "Case of the Prisoners," supra note 37, at 499–500.

166. 8 Va. (4 Call) 5 (1782).

167. See Letter from Edmund Pendleton to James Madison (Nov. 8, 1782), in 5 *Papers of Madison*, supra note 59, at 260, 261 (describing the resolution of "[t]he great constitutional question, as it was called in our papers"); Treanor, "Case of the Prisoners," supra note 37, at 504–05.

168. For an exceptionally useful and enlightening discussion of the case, see id. at 500–540.

169. Id. at 539–40.

170. See supra note 146 and accompanying text.

171. See Treanor, "Judicial Review in the State Courts before Marbury," supra note 37, at 4; Sosin, supra note 132, at 222; Michael J. Klarman, "How Great Were the 'Great' Marshall Court Decisions," 87 *Va. L. Rev.* 1111, 1121 (2001); Leonard W. Levy, "Judicial Review, History, and Democracy: An Introduction," in *Judicial Review and the Supreme Court* 1, 11 (Leonard W. Levy, ed., 1967); Louis Boudin, "Government by Judiciary," 26 *Pol. Sci. Q.* 238, 254–55 (1911).

172. The cases are *Holmes v. Walton* in New Jersey, the so-called Ten Pound Act cases in New Hampshire, *Trevett v. Weeden* in Rhode Island, and *Bayard v. Singleton* in North Carolina. There is some question about whether *Bayard* should be classified as a jury case. The law at issue in the case did more than deprive a class of plaintiffs of their right to a jury: it stripped the state court of power to hear their cases altogether. Nevertheless, the judges based their ruling on the argument that "by the constitution every citizen had undoubtedly a right to a decision of his property by a trial by jury," apparently referring to the jury guarantee of the North Carolina constitution. See *Bayard v. Singleton*, 1 Martin 42, 49 (N.C. 1787).

173. 1 Farrand, supra note 35, at 97 (Madison's notes, June 4, 1787).

174. 2 id. at 73 (Madison's notes, July 21, 1787).

175. I made this argument myself in earlier work. See Larry Kramer, "The Supreme Court, 2000 Term—Foreword: We the Court," 115 *Harv. L. Rev.* 4, 59–60 (2001).

176. John Adams, Diary Notes on the Right of Juries (Feb. 12, 1771), in 1 *Legal Papers of John Adams* 229 (L. Kinvin Wroth and Hiller B. Zobel, eds., 1965).

177. Id. at 228–29.

178. Id.

179. Both Luther Martin and George Mason suggested that judicial review would guard against unconstitutional laws generally, disagreeing only about the desirability of a Council for additional protection against unwise ones. See

2 Farrand, supra note 35, at 76 (Madison's notes, July 21, 1787) (remarks of Luther Martin); id. at 78 (remarks of George Mason).
180. See James Wilson, Speech at the Pennsylvania Convention (Dec. 1, 1787), in 2 *DHRC*, supra note 72, at 450–51.

CHAPTER 3

1. Gouverneur Morris spoke to the issue at least three times, the most of any supporter. See 2 *The Records of the Federal Convention* 28 (Max Farrand, ed., 1966) (Madison's notes, July 17, 1787) [hereinafter cited as Farrand]; id. at 92 (Madison's notes, July 23, 1787); id. at 299 (Madison's notes, Aug. 15, 1787). Other delegates who made comments suggesting that they either supported or accepted judicial review include Roger Sherman, id. at 27 (Madison's notes, July 17, 1787); George Mason, id. at 78 (Madison's notes, July 21, 1787); and Hugh Williamson, id. at 376 (Madison's notes, Aug. 22, 1787). Madison's notes also include several instances in which he himself made comments that seem directly or indirectly to recognize judicial review. See id. at 27 (July 17, 1787); id. at 93 (July 23, 1787); id. at 440 (Aug. 28, 1787). But Madison was not exactly a supporter of judicial review, and as with most things his thinking on the subject is complex and nuanced. (Madison's views on judicial review are discussed separately in chapters 4 and 6.) In addition, William Pierce records Rufus King describing what appears to be the Blackstonian/Cokean position that "the Judges will have the expounding of those Laws when they come before them; and they will no doubt stop the operation of such as shall appear repugnant to the constitution." 1 id. at 109 (Pierce's notes, June 4, 1787); see also id. at 98 (Madison's notes reporting King simply as "observing that the Judges ought to be able to expound the law as it should come before them"); id. at 105 (Yate's notes reporting King discussing whether judges will "be biased in the interpretation" of laws if they failed to veto them on a Council of Revision).

    Raoul Berger has compiled a detailed catalog of remarks about judicial review made at the Convention, both pro and con. See Raoul Berger, *Congress v. The Supreme Court* 47–81 (1969). But Berger's account of the discussions is unreliable as a guide. In the main, so determined was he to show broad support for the practice that he misstated or misunderstood the meaning of much of what was said, especially as respects the Council of Revision. While some delegates did refer to judicial review in these discussions, see infra notes 24–28 and accompanying text, the role contemplated for judges as part of the Council was legislative in nature and so cut along different dimensions than judicial review. The same is true for remarks about judicial power to "expound" the law, the significance of which Berger also consistently overread.

2. See Speech by John Francis Mercer, 2 Farrand, supra note 1, at 298 (Madison's notes, Aug. 15, 1787); see also Speech by Gunning Bedford, 1 id. at 100 (Mad-

ison's notes, June 4, 1787). Richard Dobbs Spaight made his opposition clear not on the floor of the convention, but in a letter he wrote home to his friend James Iredell after hearing about the decision in *Bayard v. Singleton*. Letter from Richard Dobbs Spaight to James Iredell (Aug. 12, 1787), in 2 *Life and Correspondence of James Iredell* 168 (Griffith J. McRee, ed., 1949).

3. See Speech by John Dickinson, 1 Farrand, supra note 1, at 299.

4. Letter from James Madison to Thomas Jefferson (Oct. 24, 1787), in 13 *The Documentary History of the Ratification of the Constitution* 445 (John P. Kaminski and Gaspare J. Saladino, eds., 1981) [hereinafter cited as *DHRC*].

5. *Vices of the Political System of the United States*, in 9 *The Papers of James Madison* 348 (Robert A. Rutland et al., eds., 1975).

6. See Letter from James Madison to Thomas Jefferson, dated Mar. 19, 1787, in 9 *Papers of Madison*, supra note 5, at 384. The leading study of Madison's proposed negative remains Charles H. Hobson, "The Negative on State Laws: James Madison and the Crisis of Republican Government," 36 *Wm. & Mary Q.* 215 (3d ser. 1979).

7. The Virginia Plan or Randolph Resolutions, reprinted in 3 Farrand, supra note 1, at 593.

8. 2 id. at 245.

9. Jack N. Rakove, "The Origins of Judicial Review: A Plea for New Contexts," 49 *Stan. L. Rev.* 1031, 1046–47 (1997).

10. Id. The New Jersey Plan's version of the Supremacy Clause was unacceptable in two respects: it failed to mention the national Constitution as a source of law superior to state law, and it omitted state constitutions from the final clause resolving conflicts of law in favor of the national authority. Id. at 1047 n. 69.

11. 1 Farrand, supra note 1, at 164–68 (Madison's notes, June 8, 1787). See Larry Kramer, "Madison's Audience," 112 *Harv. L. Rev.* 611, 649–53 (1999).

12. 2 Farrand, supra note 1, at 27 (Madison's notes).

13. Id.

14. Morris opened that day's debate on the negative by stating that he opposed the power "as likely to be terrible to the States, and not necessary, if sufficient Legislative authority should be given to the Genl. Government." Id. at 27.

15. Id. at 28.

16. Madison explained why a judicial check was regarded as inferior to a legislative one in a letter to Jefferson written soon after the Convention. To those who say that "the Judicial authority . . . will keep the States within their proper limits, and supply the place of a negative on their laws," Madison explained:

> The answer is, that it is more convenient to prevent the passage of a law, than to declare it void after it is passed; that this will be particularly the case, where the law aggrieves individuals, who may be unable to support an appeal agst. a State to the supreme Judiciary; that a State which would violate the Legislative rights of the Union, would not be very ready to obey a Judicial decree in support of them, and that a recurrence

to force, which in the event of disobedience would be necessary, is an evil which the new Constitution meant to exclude as far as possible. Letter from James Madison to Thomas Jefferson (Oct. 24, 1788), in 10 *Papers of Madison*, supra note 5, at 206, 211. See Jack N. Rakove, "Judicial Power in the Constitutional Theory of James Madison," 43 *Wm. & Mary L. Rev.* 1513, 1524–25 (2002).

17. See, e.g., Speech of James Madison in 2 Farrand, supra note 1, at 440 (Madison's notes, Aug. 19, 1787) (asking whether the Ex Post Facto Clause, "which will oblige the Judges to declare [retrospective] interferences null & void" makes the Contract Clause unnecessary).

18. The exchange of letters on judicial review between Iredell and Spaight occurred while Spaight was in Philadelphia at the Convention, leading one commentator to hypothesize that Iredell's letter explaining his position may have been shown to some of the delegates. See Sylvia Snowiss, *Judicial Review and the Law of the Constitution* 46 (1990). But Iredell's letter is dated Aug. 26, and, given the slowness of the mail, one has to wonder whether the letter arrived in time to do any good before the Convention broke up on Sept. 17.

19. 1 Farrand, supra note 1, at 21 (Madison's notes, May 29, 1787) (8th resolution).

20. Comments of John Dickinson, in id. at 140 (Madison's notes, June 6); see Comments of Elbridge Gerry, in id. at 98 (Madison's notes, June 4); Comments of Charles Pinckney, in id. at 139 (Madison's notes, June 6).

21. Comments of Rufus King, in id. at 98 (Madison's notes, June 4, 1787).

22. Comments of Elbridge Gerry, in id. at 97, discussed in chapter 2 at pages 172–81.

23. See, e.g., Comments of James Madison, 1 Farrand, supra note 1, at 138 (Madison's notes, June 6, 1787); Comments of James Wilson, 2 id. at 79 (Madison's notes, July 21, 1787). The vote, on June 4, was 8–2 in favor. Id. at 104. Wilson and Madison moved the issue again on June 6, but were defeated by a vote of 8–3. Id. at 140.

24. Comments of James Wilson, in 2 Farrand, supra note 1, at 73 (Madison's notes, July 21).

25. For a catalogue of objections to the Council, see Rakove, supra note 9, at 1058.

26. Comments of Luther Martin, in 2 Farrand, supra note 1, at 76 (Madison's notes, July 21).

27. Comments of George Mason, in id. at 78.

28. Comments of Elbridge Gerry, in id. at 98. For Madison, though not it seems anyone else, the extensive size of the Republic itself provided an additional check. See Kramer, supra note 11.

29. See also the final discussion of this issue on Aug. 23, during which John Francis Mercer expressed opposition to judicial review, Gouverneur Morris reiterated his support, and John Dickenson expressed uncertainty; other delegates raised still different issues, and the veto was left with the executive alone. 2 Farrand, supra note 1, at 298–302 (Madison's notes, Aug. 23, 1787).

30. William E. Nelson, *Marbury v. Madison: The Origins and Legacy of Judicial Review* 1–2 (2000).

31. James Madison, Speech on the Jay Treaty in the Fourth Congress (April 6, 1796), in 6 *The Writings of James Madison* 263, 272 (Galliard Hunt, ed., 1906). This was not a new position for Madison, who made the same point in *Federalist 40* in response to charges that the Convention had exceeded its mandate. See *The Federalist No. 40*, at 263–64 (Jacob E. Cooke, ed., 1961); see also Speech by James Wilson in the Pennsylvania Ratification Convention (Dec. 4, 1787), in 2 *DHRC*, supra note 4, at 483–84.

32. See Larry Kramer, "Fidelity to History—And Through It," 65 *Fordham L. Rev.* 1627, 1642–51 (1997); Charles A. Lofgren, "The Original Understanding of Original Intent," 5 *Const. Commentary* 77 (1988).

33. Brutus XV, *New York Journal*, Mar. 20, 1788, in 16 *DHRC*, supra note 4, at 434; see also Brutus XI, *New York Journal*, Jan. 31, 1788, in 15 id. at 512–17; Brutus XII, *New York Journal*, Feb. 7 and 14, 1788, in 16 id. at 72–75, 120–22. Brutus's discussion of judicial review is part of a larger critique of the federal judiciary that encompassed his final five essays.

34. Brutus XV, *New York Journal*, Mar. 20, 1788, in 16 *DHRC*, supra note 4, at 433; Brutus XI, *New York Journal*, Jan. 31, 1788, in 15 id. at 515.

35. Brutus XV, in 16 *DHRC*, supra note 4, at 434. The Federal Farmer made a similar observation about the threat posed to states by the authority to decide cases "in equity," though he did not explicitly tie his point to the power of judicial review. See Federal Farmer: An Additional Number of Letters to the Republican (Letter XV), in 17 *DHRC*, supra note 4, at 265, 341.

36. *The Federalist No. 78*, supra note 31, at 521.

37. Snowiss, supra note 18, at 77.

38. *The Federalist No. 78*, supra note 31, at 524, 525 (emphasis added).

39. Id. at 527.

40. Id. at 528.

41. *The Federalist No. 10*, supra note 31, at 65.

42. *The Federalist No. 78*, supra note 31, at 527.

43. Brutus XI and XII were not reprinted; Brutus XV was reprinted in the Boston *American Herald* (after Massachusetts had ratified) and in the Providence *United States Chronicle*. See 15 *DHRC*, supra note 4, at 517 n. 1; 16 id. at 75 n. 1, and 435 n. 1. Reprinting was a crucial mechanism for disseminating ideas and serves as a useful proxy for contemporary pertinence and importance. See Preface, in 13 id. at xviii; William H. Riker, *The Strategy of Rhetoric: Campaigning for the American Constitution* 26–28 (1996). In this light, compare Brutus's poor record of reprintings with that of such influential items as James Wilson's November 24 Speech in the Pennsylvania Ratifying Convention (80 reprintings), or Elbridge Gerry's objections to the Constitution (43 reprintings). 13 *DHRC*, supra note 4, at 595; 14 id. at 532; see Saul A. Cornell, *The Other Founders: Anti-Federalism and the Dissenting Tradition in America* 25–26 (1999).

44. Only 24 numbers of *The Federalist* were reprinted at all outside New York City, and these in but few places each. See Editorial Note to Publius, *The Federalist No. 1*, in 13 *DHRC*, supra note 4, at 486, 490; Elaine F. Crane, "Publius in the Provinces: Where Was The Federalist Reprinted Outside New York City?" 21 *Wm. & Mary Q.* (3d ser.) 589, 592 (1964).

45. Publius's final eight essays (nos. 78–85) were written to cover issues that had not been reached or had been overlooked in the newspaper series, and they appeared for the first time in a printed volume published on May 28, 1788. *Federalist 78* was subsequently reprinted in the New York *Independent Journal* on June 14 and in the *New York Packet* on June 17, though these were its only reprintings.

46. The power of judicial review was also referred to by a few Anti-Federalists in addition to Brutus. See Speech of Patrick Henry at the Virginia Ratifying Convention, 10 *DHRC*, supra note 4, at 1219 (questioning whether federal judges would have the same "fortitude" to oppose unconstitutional laws as had been demonstrated by judges in Virginia); Speech of George Mason at the Virginia Ratifying Convention, in id. at 1361 (arguing that the new Congress would be unable to pay off debts incurred under the old government because this would require Congress to devalue outstanding notes, something the Supreme Court would not allow under the Ex Post Facto Clause); Luther Martin, Genuine Information X, in 16 id. at 8 (suggesting that whether laws passed by Congress are contrary to the Constitution "rests *only* with the judges, who are *appointed* by Congress" and so cannot be trusted to protect state interests); Speech by William Grayson at the Virginia Ratifying Convention, in id. at 1448 (arguing that the Constitution *requires* allowing states to be sued in federal court and that Congress could not repeal the jurisdiction because "[t]he Judges are to defend it.").

47. Fabius IV, *Pennsylvania Mercury*, Apr. 19, 1788, in 17 *DHRC*, supra note 4, at 182. See also Aristedes, Remarks on the Proposed Plan of a Federal Government, Jan. 31–Mar. 27, 1788, in 15 id. at 531 (arguing that those who fear Congress "may reflect, however, that every judge in the union, whether of federal or state appointment, (and some persons would say every jury) will have a right to reject any act, handed to him as a law, which he may conceive repugnant to the constitution"); Speech by George Nicholas at the Virginia Ratifying Convention, 10 id. at 1327 ("If they exceed these powers, the Judiciary will declare it void"); Speech by John Steele, in 4 *The Debates in the Several State Conventions on the Adoption of the Federal Constitution* 71 (Jonathan Elliot, ed., 1888 ed.) (dismissing Anti-Federalist charges that Congress will make elections inconvenient and noting that, if they do, "[t]he judicial power . . . is so well constructed as to be a check").

48. Speech of James Wilson at the Pennsylvania Ratifying Convention, in 2 *DHRC*, supra note 4, at 450–51. See also id. at 517 (Wilson repeating that "[i]f a law should be made inconsistent with those powers vested by this instrument in Congress, the judges, as a consequence of their independence, and

the particular powers of government being defined, will declare such law to be null and void.") Wilson's speech actually provoked a response from the opposition—the only instance in any of the recorded debates—and an unnamed speaker apparently suggested that any judge who dared to do such a thing would be impeached. "The judges are to be impeached because they decide an act null and void that was made in defiance of the Constitution!" cried an indignant Wilson, "What House of Representatives would dare to impeach, or Senate to commit judges for the performance of their duty?" Id. at 492. The exchange received a brief mention in the *Pennsylvania Herald* and was reprinted in eleven other papers, again the only apparent example of newspaper coverage of an exchange on judicial review. Id. at 524–25 and n. 1.

49. Speech by John Marshall at the Virginia Ratifying Convention, in 10 *DHRC*, supra note 4, at 1431. Marshall referred back to the point a moment later in explaining why the provision conferring jurisdiction on federal courts in cases arising under the Constitution reflected no disrespect to state courts. He emphasized that courts may act in order to avoid bloodshed. "To what quarter will you look for protection from an infringement of the Constitution, if you will not give the power to the judiciary? There is no other body that can afford such a protection." Id. at 1432.

50. See Americanus VII, *New York Daily Advertiser*, Jan. 21, 1788, in 2 *The Debate on the Constitution* 60 (Bernard Bailyn, ed., 1993)("the Constitution itself is a *supreme law of the land*, unrepealable by any *subsequent law*: every law that is not made in conformity to *that*, is in itself nugatory, and the Judges, who by their oath, are bound to support the Constitution as the *supreme law of the land* must determine accordingly"); Speech by Oliver Ellsworth at the Connecticut Ratifying Convention, in 3 *DHRC*, supra note 4, at 553 ("If the United States go beyond their powers, if they make a law which the Constitution does not authorize, it is void; and the judicial power, that national judges, who are to secure their impartiality made independent, will declare it to be void."); Speech by Samuel Adams, in 6 id. at 131 (approving a proposed amendment to prohibit Congress from exercising powers not expressly granted on the ground that, with such an amendment, if Congress were to overreach "it will be an errour, and adjudged by the courts of law to be void").

51. Speech by William R. Davie at the North Carolina Ratifying Convention, in 4 Elliot, supra note 47, at 156–57.

52. Letter from George Washington to Sir Edward Newenham (Dec. 25, 1787), in 15 *DHRC*, supra note 4, at 91.

53. Letter from William Grayson to William Short (Nov. 10, 1787), in 14 *DHRC*, supra note 4, at 81.

54. Cf. Riker, supra note 43, at app. (cataloguing the various arguments and how frequently they were made).

55. John Stevens, Oliver Ellsworth, and George Nicholas similarly followed their references to judicial review by immediately emphasizing that power and responsibility to resolve disputes between the general and the particular gov-

ernments ultimately rested with the people. See Americanus VII, in 2 Bailyn, supra note 50, at 60; Speech by Oliver Ellsworth at the Connecticut Ratifying Convention, in 2 *DHRC*, supra note 4, at 553; Speech by George Nicholas at the Virginia Ratifying Convention, in 10 id. at 1327.

56. Speech by John Steele, in 4 Elliot, supra note 47, at 71.

57. A Jerseyman, To the Citizens of New Jersey, *Trenton Mercury*, Nov. 6, 1787, in 3 *DHRC*, supra note 4, at 148.

58. Letter from George Washington to Bushrod Washington (Nov. 10, 1787), in 8 id. at 154.

59. Publicola, An Address to the Freemen of North Carolina, *State Gazette of North Carolina*, in 16 *DHRC*, supra note 4, at 437.

60. For additional examples of this argument, see Notes of Anthony Wayne at the Pennsylvania Ratifying Convention, in 2 id. at 411; Speech by Thomas McKean at the Pennsylvania Ratifying Convention, in id. at 414; Speech by James Wilson at the Pennsylvania Ratifying Convention, in id. at 515; Speech by Thomas McKean at the Pennsylvania Ratifying Convention, in id. at 538; Philanthrop, To the People, *American Mercury*, Nov. 19, 1787, in 3 id. at 468; A Citizen of New Haven, *Connecticut Courant*, Jan. 7, 1788, in 3 id. at 524; The Republican, To the People, *Connecticut Courant*, Jan. 7, 1788, in id. at 528; Speech by Oliver Ellsworth at the Connecticut Ratifying Convention, in id. at 553; Cassius VI, *Mass. Gazette*, Dec. 25, 1787, in 5 id. at 512; Remarker, *Indep. Chronicle*, Dec. 27, 1787, in 5 id. at 529; A.B., *Hampshire Gazette*, Jan. 9, 1788, in 5 id. at 671; *Massachusetts Centinel*, Jan. 26, 1787, in 5 id. at 805; Speech by J. C. Jones at the Massachusetts Ratifying Convention, in 6 id. at 1219; Speech by Increase Sumner at the Massachusetts Ratifying Convention, in 6 id. at 1298; Speech by Christopher Gore at the Massachusetts Ratifying Convention, in 6 id. at 1299; Speech by James Bowdoin at the Massachusetts Ratifying Convention, in 6 id. at 1321–23; Speech by Theophilus Parsons at the Massachusetts Ratifying Convention, in 6 id. at 1328; Speech by Josiah Smith at the Massachusetts Ratifying Convention, in 6 id. at 1347; Speech by Samuel Stillman at the Massachusetts Ratifying Convention, in 6 id. at 1458; *Virginia Independent Chronicle*, Nov. 28, 1787, in 8 id. at 179; An Impartial Citizen VI, *Petersburg Virginia Gazette*, Mar. 13, 1788, in 8 id. at 497; Speech by George Nicholas at the Virginia Ratifying Convention, in 9 id. at 927–28; Speech by Edmund Randolph at the Virginia Ratifying Convention, in 9 id. at 1024–25; Speech by James Madison at the Virginia Ratifying Convention, in 9 id. at 1149; Speech by Edmund Pendleton at the Virginia Ratifying Convention, in 10 id. at 1197; Speech by George Nicholas at the Virginia Ratifying Convention, in 10 id. at 1327; *Poughkeepsie Country Journal*, Oct. 3, 1787, in 13 id. at 309; Letter from Edmund Pendleton to James Madison (Oct. 8, 1787), in id. at 355; A Citizen of Philadelphia, The Weaknesses of Brutus Exposed, in 14 id. at 68–69; Uncus, *Maryland Journal*, Nov. 9, 1787, in id. at 79; A Countryman II, *New Haven Gazette*, Nov. 22, 1787, in id. at 173–174; Letter from Timothy Pickering to Charles Tillinghast (Dec. 24, 1787), in id. at 196, 201, 203; A

Landholder IV, *Connecticut Courant*, Nov. 26, 1787, in id. at 234; A Landholder V, *Connecticut Courant*, Dec. 3, 1787, in id. at 337; A Countryman IV, *New Haven Gazette*, Dec. 6, 1787, in id. at 356–57; Draft Letter from Roger Sherman (Dec. 8, 1787), in id. at 386–87; America, *New York Daily Advertizer*, Dec. 31, 1787, in 15 id. at 195–97; Report of Speech at Edenton by Hugh Williamson, *New York Daily Advertiser*, Feb. 25–27, 1788, in 16 id. at 203; Fabius IV, *Pennsylvania Mercury*, Apr. 19, 1788, in 17 id. at 181; Fabius IX, *Pennsylvania Mercury*, May 1, 1788, in id. at 263–64; A Patriotic Citizen, *Pennsylvania Mercury*, May 10, 1788, in 18 id. at 10; Speech by Alexander Hamilton at the New York Ratifying Convention, in 2 Elliot, supra note 47, at 252; Speech by James Iredell at the North Carolina Ratifying Convention, in 4 id. at 98; Speech by Archibald Maclaine at the North Carolina Ratifying Convention, in id. at 161–62, 172.

61. Federal Farmer, Letters to the Republican (Letter I), in 14 *DHRC*, supra note 4, at 24; Jack N. Rakove, *Original Meanings: Politics and Ideas in the Making of the Constitution* 181–88 (1996); Rakove, supra note 9, at 1049–50.

62. Riker, supra note 43, at 32; John P. Kaminski, "From Impotence to Omnipotence: The Debate over Structuring Congress under the New Federal Constitution of 1787," in Kenneth R. Bowling and Donald R. Kennon, eds., *The House and Senate in the 1790s* 1, 9 (2002).

63. Speech by Increase Sumner in the Massachusetts Ratifying Convention, in 6 *DHRC*, supra note 4, at 1298.

64. Herbert Wechsler, "The Political Safeguards of Federalism: The Role of the States in the Composition and Selection of the National Government," 54 *Colum. L. Rev.* 543 (1954).

65. See Speech by James Wilson at the Pennsylvania Ratifying Convention, in 2 *DHRC*, supra note 4, at 400–405. The quotations from Wilson in the remainder of this paragraph all come from this speech.

66. See Wat Tyler, A Proclamation, *Pennsylvania Herald*, Oct. 24, 1787, in 2 *DHRC*, supra note 4, at 203 (satire); Speech by Thomas McKean at the Pennsylvania Ratifying Convention, id. at 412; Demonsthenes Minor, *Gazette of the State of Georgia*, Nov. 22, 1787, in 3 id. at 246; Speech by Oliver Wolcott at the Connecticut Ratifying Convention, id. at 557–58; Speech by Richard Law at the Connecticut Ratifying Convention, id. at 559; Poplicola, *Massachusetts Centinel*, Oct. 31, 1787, in 4 id. at 181; Speech by Francis Dana at the Massachusetts Convention, 6 id. at 1237–38; Speech by Gen. E. Brooks at the Massachusetts Ratifying Convention, 6 id. at 1339; Speech by Rev. Samuel Stillman at the Massachusetts Ratifying Convention, 6 id. at 1459; *Virginia Independent Chronicle*, Nov. 28, 1787, in 8 id. at 177–78; Speech by Henry Lee at the Virginia Ratifying Convention, in 9 id. at 948; Speech by James Madison at the Virginia Ratifying Convention, in id. at 1150–51; Speech by Edmund Pendleton at the Virginia Ratifying Convention, in 10 id. at 1199; Speech by James Wilson at a Public Meeting in Philadelphia, Oct. 6, 1787, in 13 id. at 341–42; An American Citizen IV: On the Federal Government, in id. at 436–37; Letter from James Madison to Thomas Jefferson (Oct. 24, 1787), in id. at

445–46; Letter from Timothy Pickering to Charles Tillinghast (Dec. 24, 1787), in 14 id. at 196; A Landholder IV, in id. at 234; The New Roof, *Pennsylvania Packet*, Dec. 29, 1787, in 15 id. at 184–85; A Freeman I, *Pennsylvania Gazette*, Jan. 23, 1788, in id. at 457–58; Aristedes, Remarks on the Proposed Plan of a Federal Government, Jan. 31–Mar. 27, 1788, in id. at 545; Fabius IV, in 17 id. at 182; Speech by James Iredell at the North Carolina Ratifying Convention, 4 Elliot, supra note 47, at 53; Speech by William Davie at the North Carolina Ratifying Convention, id. at 58–59; Speech by Archibald Maclaine at the North Carolina Ratifying Convention, id. at 180–81.

67. See Speech by Oliver Wolcott at the Connecticut Ratifying Convention, in 3 *DHRC*, supra note 4, at 557–58; Speech by Theophilus Parsons at the Massachusetts Ratifying Convention, 6 id. at 1217; Speech by Fisher Ames at the Massachusetts Ratifying Convention, in 6 id. at 1256; Speech by Rufus King at the Massachusetts Convention, in 6 id. at 1257; Americanus II, in 8 id. at 247; Ezra Stiles Diary, in 15 id. at 57, 58; A Freeman II, id. at 510; A Freeman III, 16 id. at 50–51; Letter from George Cabot to Theophilus Parsons (Feb. 28, 1788), in id. at 249–50; *Gazette of the State of Georgia*, Mar. 20, 1788, in id. at 445; Fabius II, in 17 id. at 122; Fabius VIII, in id. at 248–49; Letter from Edmund Pendleton to Richard Henry Lee (June 14, 1788), in 18 id. at 181; Speech by James Iredell at the North Carolina Ratifying Convention, in 4 Elliot, supra note 47, at 38; Speech by William Davie at the North Carolina Ratifying Convention, in id. at 42–43; *The Federalist*, supra note 31, at Nos. 59 (Hamilton), 62 (Madison).

68. See Larry Kramer, "Putting the Politics Back into the Political Safeguards of Federalism," 100 *Colum. L. Rev.* 215, 256–57 (2000).

69. Speech by Edmund Randolph at the Virginia Ratifying Convention, in 9 *DHRC*, supra note 4, at 1102.

70. See Kramer, supra note 11 (arguing that almost no one understood, much less accepted, Madison's argument about faction in *The Federalist No. 10*).

71. My discussion of *The Federalist* on federalism has benefited greatly from Jack Rakove's insightful analysis of the subject. See Rakove, supra note 61, at ch. 7.

72. *The Federalist No. 39*, supra note 31, at 257.

73. *The Federalist No. 45*, supra note 31, at 308. Madison had adverted briefly to this question in number 39, and then again near the end of number 44, where he noted that the success of any federal usurpation "[i]n the first instance . . . will depend on the executive and judiciary departments, which are to expound and give effect to the legislative acts; and in the last resort, a remedy must be obtained from the people, who can by the election of more faithful representatives, annul the acts of the usurpers." *The Federalist No. 44*, id. at 305; *The Federalist No. 39*, id. at 256–57. This is consistent with Madison's "departmental" position, discussed in chapter 4, and his general desire to resolve problems without needing explicitly to appeal for popular support.

74. See Rakove, supra note 61, at 193–201.

75. *The Federalist No. 45*, supra note 31, at 311.
76. *The Federalist No. 46*, id. at 315–16.
77. *The Federalist No. 45*, id. at 311.
78. *The Federalist Nos. 45–46*, id. at 312–23. The quoted language is at page 315.
79. See *The Federalist No. 45*, id. at 312.
80. Id. at 313.
81. *The Federalist No. 46*, id. at 316.
82. *The Federalist No. 45*, id. at 313.
83. Id.
84. *The Federalist No. 46*, id. at 316.
85. Id. at 316.
86. Id. at 319.
87. Id.
88. Id. at 319–20.
89. Id. at 320.
90. Id.
91. Id. at 320–22.
92. Id. at 322. While *Federalist 45–46* constitute the most elaborate presentation of the argument that states would control the federal government less through their role in its selection and composition than by outside agitation, it was a pervasive theme in the writings of Publius. Arguments along the same lines feature prominently in *Federalist 17, 25, 26, 28, 31, 32, 55,* and *84*.
93. Speech by Alexander Hamilton at the New York Ratifying Convention, in 2 Elliot, supra note 47, at 304.
94. Id. at 304–05. This argument was a particular favorite of Hamilton's, and he pressed it repeatedly both in his essays as Publius and at the New York Ratifying Convention. See *The Federalist Nos. 17, 25, 26, 28, 31, 84*. Speech by Alexander Hamilton at the New York Ratifying Convention, in 2 Elliot, supra note 47, at 253; Speech by Alexander Hamilton at the New York Ratifying Convention, in id. at 353–55.

For examples of others making the same arguments, see A Citizen of New Haven, *Connecticut Courant*, Jan. 7, 1788, in 3 *DHRC*, supra note 4, at 525; Responses to An Old Whig I, *Massachusetts Centinel*, Oct. 31, 1787, in 4 id. at 181; *Massachusetts Centinel*, Jan. 26, 1788, in 5 id. at 805; Speech by Thomas Thacher at the Massachusetts Ratifying Convention, in 6 id. at 1419; An Independent Freeholder, *Winchester Virginia Gazette*, Jan. 25, 1788, in 8 id. at 326–28; Alexander White, *Winchester Virginia Gazette*, Feb. 22, 1788, in id. at 405–06; Alexander White, *Winchester Virginia Gazette*, Feb. 29, 1788, in id. at 439; An Impartial Citizen VI, *Petersburg Virginia Gazette*, March 13, 1788, in id. at 497–500; Speech by George Nicholas at the Virginia Ratifying Convention, in 9 id. at 926–27; Speech by James Madison at the Virginia Ratifying Convention, in id. at 997–98; Speech by James Madison at the Virginia Ratifying Convention, in id. at 1151–52; An American Citizen VI: On the Federal Government, in 13 id. at 436–37; *Virginia Independent Chronicle*, Nov. 28, 1787, in 14 id. at 244; Draft Letter from Roger Sherman (Dec. 8, 1787), in id. at 387; Speech by Charles Pinckney in the South Carolina Legislature, in 4 Elliot, supra note 47, at 259.

CHAPTER 4

1. Stanley Elkins and Eric McKitrick, *The Age of Federalism: The Early American Republic, 1788–1800*, at 441 (1993); Drew R. McCoy, *The Elusive Republic: Political Economy in Jeffersonian America* 166 (1980).
2. Douglass C. North, *The Economic Growth of the United States, 1790–1860*, at 36–38, 221, 229 (1961); Donald R. Adams, Jr., "Wage Rates in the Early National Period: Philadelphia, 1785–1830," 28 *J. Econ. Hist.* 404–26 (1968).
3. James Roger Sharp, *American Politics in the Early Republic: The New Nation in Crisis* 5 (1993); Richard H. Kohn, *Eagle and Sword: The Federalists and the Creation of the Military Establishment in America, 1783–1802*, at 195 (1975).
4. Letter from Thomas Jefferson to John Adams (June 15, 1813), in *The Adams–Jefferson Letters: The Complete Correspondence between Thomas Jefferson and Abigail and John Adams* 331 (Lester J. Cappon, ed., 1987); Letter from John Adams to Thomas Jefferson (June 30, 1813), in id. at 346, 347–48.
5. James Madison, *Vices of the Political System of the United States*, in 9 *The Papers of James Madison* 357 (Robert A. Rutland et al., eds., 1975); see Jack N. Rakove, "The Structure of Politics at the Accession of George Washington," in Richard Beeman, Stephen Botein, and Edward C. Carter, III, eds., *Beyond Confederation* 261, 285 (1987).
6. Noble Cunningham, *The Jeffersonian Republicans: The Formation of Party Organization, 1789–1801* (1957), carefully delineates the early gropings for organizational form. Useful collections of essays on the first American political parties are found in William Nisbet Chambers, ed., *The First Party System: Federalists and Republicans* (1972); and Paul Goodman, ed., *The Federalists vs. The Jeffersonian Republicans* (1967).
7. See Joanne B. Freeman, "'The Art and Address of Ministerial Management': Secretary of the Treasury Alexander Hamilton and Congress," in Kenneth R. Bowling and Donald R. Kennon, eds., *Neither Separate Nor Equal: Congress in the 1790s*, at 269–93 (2000).
8. See Larry Kramer, "Putting the Politics Back into the Political Safeguards of Federalism," 100 *Colum. L. Rev.* 215, 274–78 (2000).
9. Some of the better known, and better, political histories of the 1790s include: Elkins and McKitrick, supra note 1; Sharp, supra note 3; John C. Miller, *The Federalist Era* (1960); Stephen G. Kurtz, *The Presidency of John Adams* (1957); Manning J. Dauer, *The Adams Federalists* (1953).
10. See William R. Casto, *The Supreme Court in the Early Republic: The Chief Justiceships of John Jay and Oliver Ellsworth* 213–14 (1995); David P. Currie, *The Constitution in the Supreme Court: The First Hundred Years* 4–5 (1985).

11. *Hylton v. United States*, 3 U.S. (3 Dall.) 171 (1796).

12. *Chisholm v. Georgia*, 2 U.S. (2 Dall.) 419 (1793).

13. See Maeva Marcus, "Judicial Review in the Early Republic," in Ronald J. Hoffman and Peter J. Albert, eds., *Launching the "Extended Republic": The Federalist Era* 25 (1996); William Michael Treanor, "Judicial Review in State Courts before *Marbury*" 37 (unpublished manuscript on file with author); William Michael Treanor, "Judicial Review in Federal Courts before *Marbury*" (unpublished manuscript on file with author).

14. Act of Mar. 23, 1792, ch. 11, 1 Stat. 243 (1792).

15. See Maeva Marcus and Robert Teir, "Hayburn's Case: A Misinterpretation of Precedent," 1988 *Wisc. L. Rev.* 527, 529–34.

16. See Editors' Introduction to *Hayburn's Case* in 6 *The Documentary History of the Supreme Court of the United States* 33–37 (Maeva Marcus, ed., 1998) [hereinafter cited as *DHSC*].

17. Letter from James Wilson, John Blair, and Richard Peters to George Washington (Apr. 18, 1792), in 6 *DHSC*, supra note 16, at 53.

18. A number of the Justices found a way around their constitutional objections by interpreting the statute to appoint them as commissioners in a nonjudicial capacity. Justice Wilson, at least, refused to go through a charade and declined to hear any petitions. See Casto, supra note 10, at 176–77.

19. Marcus and Teir, supra note 15, at 534–42. The Court avoided a decision formally striking down the Invalid Pensions Act in two subsequent cases, *Ex parte Chandler* and *United States v. Yale Todd*. See 6 *DHSC*, supra note 16, at 41–45, 284–95, 370–86; Currie, supra note 10, at 9–11.

20. Letter from Fisher Ames to Thomas Dwight (Apr. 25, 1792), in 2 *Works of Fisher Ames* 942 (W. B. Allen, ed., Liberty Press, 1983).

21. Letter from William Vans Murray to [John Gwinn] (Apr. 15, 1792), in 6 *DHSC*, supra note 16, at 50–51.

22. *Gazette of the United States*, May 9, 1792, in id. at 58.

23. *National Gazette*, Apr. 16, 1792, in id. at 51, 52; see also *National Gazette*, May 10, 1792, in id. at 59 (exercise of judicial review "may be contemplated under some very pleasing aspects").

24. *General Advertiser*, Apr. 13, 1792, in id. at 48.

25. *General Advertiser*, Apr. 20, 1792, in id. at 54; Camden, *General Advertiser*, Apr. 21, 1792, in id. at 55.

26. There is no official report. The case is described in Charles Warren, "Earliest Cases of Judicial Review by Federal Court," 32 *Yale L.J.* 15, 26–28 (1922). See also Julius S. Goebel, 1 *The Oliver Wendell Holmes Devise—History of the Supreme Court of the United States: Antecedents and Beginnings to 1801*, at 589 (1971).

27. *Providence Gazette and Country Journal*, June 23, 1792, quoted in Warren, supra note 26, at 28.

28. *Maryland Journal* (Baltimore), May 17, 1791, quoted in 6 *DHSC*, supra note 16, at 123.

29. *Columbian Centinel* (Boston), May 11, 1791, quoted in id. n. 6.
30. See Treanor, "Judicial Review in State Courts before *Marbury*," supra note 13, at 37, 43, 49. Most of the federal cases involved questions pertaining to the supremacy of federal over state law and so were easy under the Supremacy Clause—though only four decisions went against state law. The only federal laws called into question were the Invalid Pension Act at issue in *Hayburn's Case*, 2 U.S. (2 Dall.) 409 (C.C.D. Pa.1792), and the carriage tax addressed in *Hylton v. United States*, 3 U.S. (3 Dall.) 171 (1796).
31. See Marcus, supra note 13, at 33–35.
32. See 11 *Documentary History of the First Federal Congress* 842–939 (Charles Bangs Bickford, Kenneth R. Bowling, and Helen E. Veit, eds., 1992) [hereinafter cited as *DHFFC*] (debates in the House of Representatives, June 16–17, 1789), see esp. comments by William Smith at 849, 876, 935–36; Alexander White at 873, 957; Elbridge Gerry at 879, 931, 976, 1022; Fisher Ames at 884; Michael Jenifer Stone at 893, 918; John Laurence at 911; Theodore Sedgwick at 946; Abraham Baldwin at 996, 1007–08; Peter Silvester at 1010.
33. Amendments to the Constitution, in 12 *Papers of Madison*, supra note 5, at 196, 207 (Speech to the House of Representatives, June 8, 1789); see Letter from Thomas Jefferson to James Madison (Mar. 15, 1789), in id. at 13.
34. Speech to the House of Representatives, Mar. 18, 1790, quoted in Marcus, supra note 13, at 34.
35. See, e.g., Speech by John Laurance, Feb. 4, 1791, in 14 *DHFFC*, supra note 32, at 404; Speech by Michael Jenifer Stone, Feb. 5, 1791, in id. at 431; Speech by Elias Boudinot, Feb. 5, 1791, in id. at 440–41.
36. See quotations collected in Charles Warren, *Congress, the Constitution, and the Supreme Court* 105–18 (1935).
37. E.g., Speech of John Breckenridge, 11 *Annals of Congress* 178–80 (Feb. 1802); Speech of Philip R. Thompson, in id. at 552–53; Speech of John Randolph, in id. at 661; see David P. Currie, *The Constitution in Congress: The Jeffersonians* 16–17 (2001); Richard E. Ellis, *The Jeffersonian Crisis: Courts and Politics in the Young Republic* 58 (1971).
38. See, e.g., Speech of Stevens Thomas Mason, in 11 *Annals of Congress*, supra note 37, at 59; Speech of Josiah Smith, in id. at 698–99.
39. Speech of John Bacon, in id. at 983.
40. See, e.g., Goebel, supra note 26, at 589–92; Currie, supra note 10, at 33, 39–41.
41. See Introduction to 1 *The Works of James Wilson* 37–40 (Robert Green McCloskey, ed., 1967); Page Smith, *James Wilson: Founding Father* (1956).
42. 1 *Works of Wilson*, supra note 41, at 329.
43. Id.
44. Id. at 329–30.
45. Id. at 330.
46. Id.
47. See Charles Grove Haines, *The American Doctrine of Judicial Supremacy* 104 (1914). This influence was due in no small measure to the fact that the

opinions in *Kamper* were quickly published in pamphlet form and thus more accessible than other opinions in an age before official reports were common. Id.; Margaret V. Nelson, "The Cases of the Judges: Fact or Fiction?" 31 *Va. L. Rev.* 243, 251 (1945).

48. *Kamper v. Hawkins*, 3 Va. (1 Va. Cases) 20, 21 (1793).

49. Judge James Henry disagreed with his brethren in this respect, finding that "the legislature were fully authorized by the form of government, to appoint the district judges to exercise a chancery jurisdiction," but that the appointments had not been made according to the proper procedure. Id. at 52–53.

50. Id. at 71.

51. Id. at 78, 79 (emphasis added).

52. Id. at 81.

53. Id. at 79.

54. Id. at 38–39.

55. Id. at 39.

56. Id. at 59.

57. Id. at 61.

58. Id. at 65–66.

59. Id. at 61.

60. See Casto, supra note 10, at 222–30; Sylvia Snowiss, *Judicial Review and the Law of the Constitution* 59–63 (1990); Haines, supra note 47, at 176–78.

61. See, e.g., *Respublica v. Duquet*, 2 Yeates 493, 498 (Pa. 1799) ("we must be satisfied beyond doubt, before we can declare a law void").

62. Recollections of James Iredell, quoted in Casto, supra note 10, at 223; *Ravara* is found at 2 U.S. (2 Dall.) 297 (C.C.D. Pa. 1793).

63. 3 U.S. (3 Dall.) 386, 395 (1798).

64. 3 U.S. (3 Dall.) 171, 173, 175 (1796).

65. 4 U.S. (4 Dall.) 14, 18 (1800).

66. Id. at 19.

67. 3 U.S. (3 Dall.) 171 (1796).

68. The only case in which the Court held a state law unconstitutional was *Ware v. Hylton*, 3 U.S. (3 Dall.) 199 (1796), and it stretched pretty far to avoid doing so in *Calder v. Bull*, 3 U.S. (3 Dall.) 386 (1798).

69. The story of this case is recounted in detail in 4 *The Law Practice of Alexander Hamilton* 297–340 (J. Goebel and J. Smith, eds., 1980) and Robert P. Frankel, Jr., "Before *Marbury*: *Hylton v. United States* and the Origins of Judicial Review," 28 *J. Sup. Ct. Hist.* 1 (2003); Casto, supra note 10, at 101–05.

70. Letter from William Bradford to Alexander Hamilton (July 3, 1795), in 18 *The Papers of Alexander Hamilton* 393, 396 (Harold C. Syrett, ed., 1973).

71. First, Hylton stipulated that he had failed to pay taxes on 125 carriages, when in fact he owned only one. This was necessary to satisfy the amount in controversy required for the Supreme Court to exercise appellate jurisdiction, though Hylton went along only after the government agreed that any judgment against him could be discharged for $16—the tax and penalty on a single

carriage. Second, even this phony pleading made the amount in controversy exactly $2,000 (125 carriages at $16 per carriage), whereas the Judiciary Act conferred jurisdiction only if "the matter in dispute *exceeds* the sum or value of two thousand dollars." Judiciary Act of 1789, ch. 20, § 22, 1 Stat. 73, 84 (emphasis added). Third, the court below had been evenly divided and so had not decided the case, meaning there was no "final judgment" to review—a problem the parties sought to avoid by having the defendant "confess[ ] judgment." 3 U.S. (3 Dall.) at 172. Fourth, even if Hylton's confession were treated as creating a reviewable judgment, a party cannot ordinarily appeal from a judgment to which it consented. Fifth, the government paid Hylton's attorney's fees and costs, presumably destroying the necessary adversarial relationship. Not only did the Court reach the merits despite these impediments—in striking contrast to its behavior in, for example, *Hayburn's Case*, 2 U.S. (2 Dall.) 409 (1792)—but none of the Justices bothered even to mention them. See Currie, supra note 10, at 32.

72. See Currie, supra note 10, at 33–37; Casto, supra note 10, at 104–05. For a defense of the decision, see Bruce Ackerman, "Taxation and the Constitution," 99 *Colum. L. Rev.* 1, 20–24 (1999).

73. 3 U.S. (3 Dall.) at 183–84.

74. See, e.g., *Kamper v. Hawkins*, 3 Va. (1 Va. Cases), at 39 (opinion of Judge Roane); *Vanhorne's Lessee v. Dorrance*, 2 U.S. (2 Dall.) 304, 309 (1795); *Marbury v. Madison*, 5 U.S. (1 Cranch) 137, 179 (1803). See Michael J. Klarman, "How Great Were the 'Great' Marshall Court Decisions?" 87 *Va. L. Rev.* 1111, 1121–22 (2001).

75. James Iredell's Charge to the Grand Jury of the circuit court for the district of Georgia, Oct. 17, 1791, in 2 *DHSC*, supra note 16, at 219.

76. 2 U.S. (2 Dall.) 304, 308–09 (1795).

77. Cf. James Wilson, "Lectures on Law," in 1 *Works of Wilson*, supra note 41, at 186 (explaining that "whoever would be obliged to obey a constitutional law, is justified in refusing to obey an unconstitutional act of legislature" and that "everyone who is called to act, has a right to judge").

78. See chapter 5.

79. 1 Zephaniah Smith, *A System of the Laws of the State of Connecticut* 51–52 (1795) (repr. Arno Press, 1972).

80. Id. at 52–53.

81. See also Donald F. Melhorn, "A Moot Court Exercise: Debating Judicial Review Prior to *Marbury v. Madison*," 12 *Const. Comm.* 327, 346–52 (1995), describing a moot court held at the Litchfield Law School in 1797 in which an array of arguments were presented for and against judicial review. The moot court voted 2–1 that courts should have no such power.

82. Madison's Observations on Jefferson's Draft of a Constitution for Virginia, in 6 *The Papers of Thomas Jefferson* 308, 315 (Julian P. Boyd, ed., 1952). Though Jefferson prepared his draft in 1783 and sent it to Madison at that time,

Madison did not sit down to make extensive comments until after the Federal Convention in 1788. See Editorial Note, in id. at 282–83.

83. 1 William Blackstone, *Commentaries on the Laws of England* *91 (1765).

84. See Robert Lowry Clinton, *Marbury v. Madison and Judicial Review* 24 (1989); Shannon C. Stimson, *The American Revolution in the Law* 100–104 (1990); Michael Stokes Paulsen, "The Most Dangerous Branch: Executive Power to Say What the Law Is," 83 *Geo. L.J.* 217, 228–29 (1994).

85. Speech by James Madison to the House of Representatives on the Removal Power of the President (June 17, 1789), in 12 *Papers of Madison*, supra note 5, at 232, 238. See also James Madison, "Helvidius" Number 2 (Aug. 31, 1793), in 15 *Papers of Madison*, id. at 80, 83.

86. See David N. Mayer, *The Constitutional Thought of Thomas Jefferson* 257–94 (1994). As Mayer explains, Jefferson's emphasis shifted over time—from an early confidence in the reliability of courts to a late-life belief that federal judges were an irresponsible "corps of sappers and miners" working to undermine the Constitution's careful balancing act. Letter from Thomas Jefferson to Thomas Ritchie (Dec. 25, 1820), in 10 *The Writings of Thomas Jefferson* 169–70 (Paul Leicester Ford, ed., 1898). But these were changes in tone that occurred within the same departmentalist framework, a framework Jefferson restated on numerous occasions over the course of three decades. See Letter from Thomas Jefferson to Mrs. Adams (Sept. 11, 1804), in 4 *Memoirs, Correspondence and Miscellanies from the Papers of Thomas Jefferson* 26, 27 (Thomas Jefferson Randolph, ed., 1829); Letter from Thomas Jefferson to George Hay (June 2, 1807), in id. at 75, 75; Letter from Thomas Jefferson to W. H. Torrance (June 11, 1815), in 9 *The Writings of Thomas Jefferson*, supra, at 516, 517–18; Letter from Thomas Jefferson to Spencer Roane (Sept. 6, 1819), in 10 id. at 140, 141–42; Letter from Thomas Jefferson to William Jarvis Short (Sept. 28, 1820), in id. at 160, 160–61.

87. Letter from Thomas Jefferson to Spencer Roane (Sept. 6, 1819), in 10 *The Writings of Jefferson*, supra note 84, at 140, 142.

88. Snowiss, supra note 60, at 98; see also Louis Fisher, *Constitutional Dialogues: Interpretation as Political Process* 238–39 (1988) ("The problem with Jefferson's doctrine is that he neglects to identify those questions [as to which each branch is to be final].")

89. Clinton, supra note 84, at 25.

90. See Scott E. Gant, "Judicial Supremacy and Nonjudicial Interpretation of the Constitution," 24 *Hastings Const. L.Q.* 359 (1997); David A. Strauss, "Presidential Interpretation of the Constitution," 15 *Cardozo L. Rev.* 113 (1993); Edward A. Hartnett, "A Matter of Judgment, Not a Matter of Opinion," 74 *N.Y.U. L. Rev.* 123 (1999); Mark Tushnet, "Two Versions of Judicial Supremacy," 39 *Wm. & Mary L. Rev.* 945 (1998); "Symposium: The Crisis in Legal Theory and the Revival of Classical Jurisprudence," 73 *Cornell L. Rev.* 281 (essays by John Harrison, Burt Neuborne, Robert Nagel, and Steven Ross); Paulsen, supra note

84; Christopher Eisgruber, "The Most Competent Branch: A Response to Professor Paulsen," 83 *Geo. L.J.* 347 (1994); Sanford Levinson, "Constitutional Protestantism in Theory and Practice," 83 *Geo. L.J.* 373 (1994); Frank H. Easterbrook, "Presidential Review," 40 *Case W. Res. L. Rev.* 905, 926 (1990); Neal Devins and Louis Fisher, "Judicial Exclusivity and Political Instability," 84 *Va. L. Rev.* 83 (1998).

91. Speech by Stevens Thomas Mason, in 11 *Annals of Congress*, supra note 37, at 59.

92. Mayer, supra note 86, at 270. The quoted passage is from Jefferson's notes for his First Inaugural Address. He deleted the passage because, in context, it pertained to his plans to pardon those convicted under the Sedition Act, and this was a politically controversial step that Jefferson wanted to downplay in the interest of striking a conciliatory tone. See id. at 269. See also Letter from Thomas Jefferson to W. H. Torrance (June 11, 1815), in 9 *The Writings of Thomas Jefferson*, supra note 86, at 518.

93. The *locus classicus* of this principle is, of course, Madison's *Federalist 51*. James Wilson makes the point equally well, however, in his "Lectures on Law." See *Works of Wilson*, supra note 41, at 300.

94. Speech to the House of Representatives on the President's Removal Power, in 12 *Papers of Madison*, supra note 5, at 238.

95. Letter from Thomas Jefferson to William Charles Jarvis (Sept. 28, 1820), in 10 *Writings of Jefferson*, supra note 86, at 160, 162.

96. Speech by John Breckinridge, in 11 *Annals of Congress*, supra note 37, at 179–80.

97. See Stimson, supra note 84, at 100.

98. On the public sphere generally, see Jürgen Habermas, *The Structural Transformation of the Public Sphere* (Thomas Burger with Frederick Lawrence, trans., 1989); John L. Brooke, "Reason and Passion in the Public Sphere: Habermas and the Cultural Historians," 29 *J. Interdisciplinary Stud.* 43 (1998); William E. Forbath, "Review Essay: Habermas's *Constitution: A History, Guide, and Critique*," 23 *Law & Soc. Inquiry* 969, 981–84 (1998). On its development in eighteenth-century America, see Saul Cornell, *The Other Founders* 19–143 (1999); Christopher Grasso, *A Speaking Aristocracy: Transforming Discourse in Eighteenth-Century Connecticut* 279–485 (1999); Michael Warner, *Letters of the Republic: Publication and the Public Sphere in Eighteenth-Century America* (1990); John L. Brooke, "Ancient Lodges and Self-Created Societies: Freemasonry and the Public Sphere in the Early Republic," in Ronald Hoffman and Peter J. Albert, eds., *The Beginnings of the "Extended Republic": The Federalist Era* 273 (1996).

99. See Alexander Keyssar, *The Right to Vote* 8–52 (2000); Robert J. Dinkin, *Voting in Revolutionary America* 27–44, 107–30 (1982).

100. See David Waldstreicher, *In the Midst of Perpetual Fetes: The Making of American Nationalism* (1997); Simon P. Newman, *Parades and the Politics of the Streets: Festive Culture in the Early Republic* (1997); Margaret H. McAleer, "In

NOTES TO PAGES 109–10

Defense of Civil Society: Irish Radicals in Philadelphia during the 1790s," 1 *Early Amer. Stud.* 176 (2003).

101. See Cornell, supra note 98, at 147–218; John L. Brooke, "To Be 'Read by the Whole People': Press, Party, and Public Sphere in the United States, 1789–1840," 110 *Proc. Amer. Antiquarian Soc'y* 41, 58–79 (2002).

102. Waldstreicher, supra note 99, at 3. The often subtle and sometimes not so subtle ways in which women, blacks, and poor whites found a voice, albeit one that usually remained subordinate, is a theme in both Waldstreicher's and Newman's books. See also Susan G. Davis, *Parades and Power: Street Theater in the Nineteenth Century* (1986); William Pencak, Matthew Dennis, and Simon P. Newman, *Riot and Revelry in Early America* 12–13 (2002) and esp. the essays by Thomas J. Humphrey at pp. 107–19, and by Susan Branson and Simon P. Newman at 229–48.

103. See Gordon S. Wood, *The Radicalism of the American Revolution* 229–305 (1991); Gordon S. Wood, "Interests and Disinterestedness in the Making of the Constitution," in Richard Beeman, Stephen Botein, and Edward C. Carter, III, eds., *Beyond Confederation* 69 (1987).

104. David J. Siemers, *Ratifying the Republic: Antifederalists and Federalists in Constitutional Time* 135–63 (2002).

105. Newman, supra note 100, at 7.

106. Suzette Hemberger, "A Government Based on Representations," 10 *Stud. in Amer. Pol. Dev.* 289, 290, 326–32 (1996).

107. Letter from Samuel Adams to Noah Webster (Apr. 30, 1784), in 4 *The Writings of Samuel Adams* 305 (Harry A. Cushing, ed., 1968). On Adams's activities in the years before Independence, see Bernard Bailyn, *The Ordeal of Thomas Hutchinson* (1974).

108. Siemers, supra note 104, at 13; Michael Lienesch, "Reinterpreting Rebellion: The Influence of Shays's Rebellion on American Political Thought," in Robert A. Gross, ed., *In Debt to Shays* 161–82 (1993); Leonard L. Richards, *Shays's Rebellion: The American Revolution's Final Battle* 117–38 (2002). It was in this connection, for instance, that Jefferson made his famous remark about how "a little rebellion now and then is a good thing, and as necessary in the political world as storms in the physical." Letter from Thomas Jefferson to James Madison (Jan. 30, 1787), in 11 *Papers of Jefferson*, supra note 82, at 93.

109. *Riot and Revelry*, supra note 102, at 9. On the Whiskey Rebellion, see Hemberger, supra note 106, at 315–32 (esp. 323–24); Thomas P. Slaughter, *The Whiskey Rebellion: Frontier Epilogue to the American Revolution* (1986); on regulator activity, see Alan Taylor, "Agrarian Independence: Northern Land Rioters after the Revolution," in Alfred F. Young, ed., *Beyond the American Revolution: Explorations in the History of American Radicalism* 221 (1993); on Fries Rebellion, see Robert H. Churchill, "Popular Nullification, Fries' Rebellion, and the Waning of Radical Republicanism," 67 *Penn. Hist.* 105 (2000); on Jay's Treaty and the Alien and Sedition Acts, see Sharp, supra note 3, at 117–37, 187–225;

on the Baltimore riots, see Paul A. Gilje, "The Baltimore Riots of 1812 and the Breakdown of the Anglo-American Mob Tradition," 13 *J. Soc. Hist.* 547 (1980).

110. Letter from Thomas Jefferson to Edmund Pendleton (Feb. 14, 1799), in 7 *Writings of Jefferson*, supra note 86, at 356.

111. See Churchill, supra note 109, at 129–33; Kimberly K. Smith, *The Dominion of Voice: Riot, Reason, and Romance in Antebellum Politics* 39–45 (1999).

112. See Alan Taylor, "From Fathers to Friends of the People: Political Personas in the Early Republic," 11 *J. Early Republic* 465 (1987); Roy Lokken, "The Concept of Democracy in Colonial Political Thought," 16 *Wm. & Mary Q.* 568 (1959); Allan Tully, "Constituent–Representative Relationships in Early America," 11 *Canadian J. Hist.* 139 (1976); John B. Kirby, "Early American Politics—The Search for Ideology: An Historical Analysis and Critique of the Concept of 'Deference,'" 32 *J. Politics* 808 (1970).

113. James Madison, For the *National Gazette*: Public Opinion (Dec. 19, 1791), in 14 *Papers of Madison*, supra note 5, at 170.

114. "[A]s FORCE is always on the side of the governed," Hume wrote, "the governors have nothing to support them but opinion. It is therefore, on opinion only that government is founded; and this maxim extends to the most despotic and most military governments, as well as to the most free and most popular." David Hume, "Of the First Principles of Government," in *Essays: Moral, Political and Literary* (Eugene F. Miller, ed., rev. ed. 1985).

115. James Madison, For the *National Gazette*: Who Are the Best Keepers of the People's Liberties? (Dec. 20, 1792), in 14 *Papers of Madison*, supra note 5, at 426. See Colleen A. Sheehan, "Madison and the French Enlightenment: The Authority of Public Opinion," 59 *Wm. & Mary Q.* 925, 947–48, 954–56 (2002).

116. Sheehan , supra note 115, at 948.

117. Thomas Jefferson, First Inaugural Address (Mar. 4, 1801), in 1 *A Compilation of the Messages and Papers of the Presidents* 321, 322–23 (J. Richardson, ed., 1897).

118. Notes for the *National Gazette* Essays (ca. Dec. 19, 1791–Mar. 3, 1793), in 14 *Papers of Madison*, supra note 5, at 157, 168.

119. For the *National Gazette*: Public Opinion, in 14 *Papers of Madison*, supra note 5, at 170.

120. Grasso, supra note 98, at 282, 448–51.

121. Sheehan, supra note 115, at 953–54. See also Colleen A. Sheehan, "The Politics of Public Opinion: James Madison's 'Notes on Government,'" 49 *Wm. & Mary Q.* 609 (1992); Colleen A. Sheehan, "Madison's Party Press Essays," 17 *Interpretation* 355 (1990).

122. Sheehan, supra note 115, at 948.

123. For the *National Gazette*: Government (Dec. 31, 1791), in 14 *Papers of Madison*, supra note 5, at 179.

124. Robert G. McCloskey, *The American Supreme Court* 40 (1960).

125. Alexander Bickel, *The Least Dangerous Branch: The Supreme Court at the Bar of Politics* 1 (1962).

126. In addition to the sources discussed below, significant works rethinking the importance of *Marbury* include: Christopher Wolfe, *The Rise of Modern Judicial Review* (rev. ed. 1994); J. M. Sosin, *The Aristocracy of the Long Robe* (1989); Clinton, supra note 84. Paul Kahn's *The Reign of Law: Marbury v. Madison and the Construction of America* (1997) is an exception to this general trend.

127. Klarman, supra note 74, at 1126.

128. James O'Fallon, "*Marbury*," 44 *Stan. L. Rev.* 219, 260 (1992) (citing Joyce Appleby, "The American Heritage: The Heirs and the Disinherited," 74 *J. Am. Hist.* 798, 803 (1987)).

129. Mark A. Graber, "The Problematic Establishment of Judicial Review," in Howard Gillman and Clayton Cornell, eds., *The Supreme Court in American Politics* 28, 29 (1999).

130. 4 U.S. (4 Dall.) at 19.

131. Id.

132. For example, although Republicans had a large majority among voters state-wide in Pennsylvania, a legislative deadlock over the enactment of rules for selecting electors led to a last-minute compromise whereby the vote was split 8–7 (in favor of Jefferson). See Harry Marlin Tinckom, *The Republicans and Federalists in Pennsylvania, 1790–1801*, at 245–53 (1950).

133. See Dauer, supra note 9, at 273, 274 tbls. 21 and 22. We should note, however, that these numbers are skewed in Jefferson's favor by the 3/5 clause, which gave the Southern states where Jefferson was strongest a disproportionate number of seats relative to their actual voting population. (I thank Akhil Amar for drawing this point to my attention.)

134. See, e.g., 1790 Report of Attorney General Randolph, in 1 *American State Papers—Miscellaneous* 23–24 (1832); memorials of the Chief Justice and Associate Justices of the Supreme Court to Congress dated Nov. 7, 1792, and Feb. 19, 1794, in id. at 52, 77–78; Kathryn Turner, "Federalist Policy and the Judiciary Act of 1801," 22 *Wm. & Mary Q.* 3, 5–9 (1965); George Lee Haskins and Herbert A. Johnson, 2 *The Oliver Wendell Holmes Devise History of the Supreme Court: Foundations of Power: John Marshall, 1801–15*, at 110–22 (1981).

135. See Dean Alfange, Jr., "*Marbury v. Madison* and Original Understandings of Judicial Review: In Defense of Traditional Wisdom," 1993 *Sup. Ct. Rev.* 329, 351–52; Turner, supra note 134, at 15–21.

136. Letter from Gouverneur Morris to Robert R. Livingston (Feb. 20, 1801), in 3 *The Life of Gouverneur Morris* 153, 154 (Jared Sparks, ed., 1832).

137. See Judiciary Act of 1801, ch. 4, §§ 6–7, 2 Stat. 90.

138. The story of how these appointments were made is recounted in Kathryn Turner, "The Midnight Judges," 109 *U. Pa. L. Rev.* 494 (1961).

139. Act of Feb. 27, 1801, § 3, 2 Stat. 103, 104.

140. See Turner, supra note 138, at 522. Albert Beveridge calls this "an absurd tale." 2 Albert J. Beveridge, *The Life of John Marshall* 561 n. 2 (1916). While Beveridge's account of Marshall's life veers more toward hagiography than biography, he is probably right about this one.

141. See James Morton Smith, *Freedom's Fetters: The Alien and Sedition Laws and American Civil Liberties* (1966); John C. Miller, *Crisis in Freedom: The Alien and Sedition Acts* (1951); Elkins and McKitrick, supra note 1, at 694–711.

142. Letter from Thomas Jefferson to Edmund Randolph (Aug. 18, 1799), in 7 *Writings of Jefferson*, supra note 86, at 383, 384.

143. See Letter from Thomas Jefferson to Abigail Adams (June 13, 1804), in 8 id. at 307.

144. See Dumas Malone, *Jefferson the President: First Term, 1801–1805*, at 17–28, 69–89, 144 (1970); Noble E. Cunningham, *The Jeffersonian Republicans in Power: Party Operations, 1801–1809*, at 12–70 (1963). A recent article on William Marbury appears to suggest that this number may have been lower, perhaps twenty-two. David F. Forte, "Marbury's Travail: Federalist Politics and William Marbury's Appointment as Justice of the Peace," 45 *Catholic L. Rev.* 349, 400–402 and n. 271 (1996).

145. See Haskins and Johnson, supra note 134, at 152–53; Alfange, supra note 135, at 354–55.

146. First Annual Message (Dec. 8, 1801), in 8 *Writings of Jefferson*, supra note 86, at 108, 123.

147. See, e.g., Haskins and Johnson, supra note 134, at 152; 3 Beveridge, supra note 140, at 18–22.

148. See, e.g., 1 Charles Warren, *The Supreme Court in United States History* 204 (1922); Malone, supra note 144, at 115–16; Ellis, supra note 37, at 34–35, 41–43; Alfange, supra note 135, at 355–56.

149. See 1 Warren, supra note 148, at 194–98; Ellis, supra note 37, at 40.

150. *National Intelligencer*, Dec. 21, 1801.

151. Ellis, supra note 37, at 44.

152. Id.; O'Fallon, supra note 128, at 238, 242; Alfange, supra note 135, at 354, 358.

153. Federalists "have retired into the Judiciary as a stronghold," an incensed Jefferson wrote to John Dickinson the day after Marshall issued his order, "and from that battery all the works of Republicanism are to be beaten down and erased." Letter from Thomas Jefferson to John Dickinson (Dec. 18, 1801), in 10 *The Writings of Thomas Jefferson* 302 (Andrew A. Lipscomb, ed., 1904).

154. Letter from Stevens Thomas Mason to James Madison (Dec. 21, 1801), quoted in Ellis, supra note 37, at 44.

155. Speech by James A. Bayard, 11 *Annals of Congress*, supra note 37, at 650.

156. See, e.g., Speech by James A. Bayard, in id. at 614–15; Speech by John Randolph, in id. at 661; Speech by Samuel W. Dana, in id. at 903–06.

157. See, e.g., Speech by Stevens Thomas Mason, in id. at 59; Speech by John Breckinridge, in id. at 178–80; Speech by John Randolph, in id. at 661; Speech by Nathaniel Macon, in id. at 710, 717–20.

158. The Senate had voted for repeal a month earlier by the uncomfortably close margin of a single vote—a by-product of the fact that only one-third of the Senate turned over in any given election. Also following party lines, the House vote more accurately reflected the Republicans' control of Congress and was 59–32. Id. at 982.

159. Ellis, supra note 37, at 60–62.

160. Letter from Thomas Jefferson to Joel Barlow (May 3, 1802), in 8 *Writings of Jefferson*, supra note 86, at 148, 149.

161. See Linda K. Kerber, "Oliver Wolcott: Midnight Judge," 32 *Conn. Hist. Soc'y Bulletin* 25 (1967).

162. On the popularity of repeal, see Haskins and Johnson, supra note 134, at 156–63.

163. O'Fallon, supra note 128, at 240–41; Ellis, supra note 37, at 64. The petitioners managed to establish the existence of their commissions at trial only with great difficulty. After unsuccessfully examining clerks in the State Department and Attorney General Levi, they offered an affidavit from James Marshall, the Chief Justice's brother, who had been helping to deliver commissions and who testified that he saw the commissions in the office of the Secretary of State. See Jean Edward Smith, *John Marshall: Definer of a Nation* 315–18 (1996). An even better witness was present in court, of course, but Marbury's lawyer was understandably reluctant to call the Chief Justice himself.

164. Ellis, supra note 37, at 58–59.

165. See id. at 62–63; Smith, supra note 163, at 310–11.

166. Id. (The quote is from a letter by Levi Lincoln to Jefferson.)

167. *Stuart v. Laird*, 5 U.S. (1 Cranch) 299, 309 (1803).

168. Id.

169. See Linda K. Kerber, *Federalists in Dissent: Imagery and Ideology in Jeffersonian America* (1980); James M. Banner, Jr., *To the Hartford Convention* (1970); David Hackett Fischer, *The Revolution of American Conservatism: The Federalist Party in the Era of Jeffersonian Democracy* 1–49 (1965); David Waldstreicher, "Federalism, the Style of Politics, and the Politics of Style," in Doron Ben-Atar and Barbara G. Oberg, eds., *Federalists Reconsidered* 99 (1998). On Republican interpretations and reactions, see McCoy, supra note 1.

170. 11 *Annals of Congress*, supra note 37, at 41.

171. Id. at 76.

172. Jefferson's message, dated Feb. 3, 1803, was received by the House of Representatives on Feb. 4, just prior to the commencement of the Court's long-delayed term. See *Annals of Congress*, 7th Cong., 2d Sess. c 460 (1803); Malone, supra note 144, at 147–48.

173. Alfange, supra note 135, at 364–65.

174. Id. at 363–64.

175. Smith, supra note 163, at 319.

176. Although no contemporaneous commentary by Jefferson has been found, that the case rankled him is clear from a letter he wrote to George Hay in 1807, in

connection with Burr's trial for treason. "I observe that the case of Marbury v. Madison has been cited," Jefferson complained, "and I think it material to stop at the threshold the citing that case as authority, and to have it denied to be law." Urging that Marshall's opinion was both "extrajudicial, and as such of no authority" and "against law," Jefferson closed: "I have long wished for a proper occasion to have the gratuitous opinion in Marbury v. Madison brought before the public, and denounced as not law: and I think the present a fortunate one, because it occupies such a place in the public attention." Letter from Thomas Jefferson to George Hay (June 2, 1807), in 4 *Miscellanies from the Papers of Jefferson*, supra note 86, at 75, 76.

177. Among other things, Marshall assumed without explanation that justices of the peace were not removable at will by the Executive, contrary to the rule established in 1789. He also held that the petitioners acquired a property right in their office once their commissions were signed by the President, whereas most historians agree with Jefferson that delivery was essential to make the commissions valid. See United States Senate, *The Constitution of the United States of America, 82d Cong., 2d Sess.* 454 (Edward S. Corwin, ed., 1953) (Jefferson's "is probably the correct doctrine"); Malone, supra note 144, at 144 ("But for the distortions of partisan politics [Jefferson's] supposition would probably have been generally accepted at the time as natural and reasonable").

178. Ellis, supra note 37, at 67.

179. See Malone, supra note 144, at 151; Smith, supra note 163, at 325.

180. See Currie, supra note 10, at 67–68.

181. See id. at 68–69; O'Fallon, supra note 128, at 255–56; R. Kent Newmyer, *John Marshall and the Heroic Age of the Supreme Court* 167–70 (2001).

182. See Newmyer, supra note 181, at 167; Ellis, supra note 37, at 58; 1 Warren, supra note 148, at 215–16.

183. Alfange, supra note 135, at 367–68; see also Malone, supra note 144, at 147.

184. McCloskey, supra note 124, at 40.

185. See chapter 5, at pp. 00–00.

186. See, e.g., Speech by Gouverneur Morris, 11 *Annals of Congress*, supra note 37, at 82–83, 90, 180–81; Speech by John Rutledge, in id. at 739–43, 754–55, 760; Speech by Samuel W. Dana, in id. at 920–33.

187. 5 U.S. (1 Cranch) 137, 176 (1803).

188. Id. at 176–77 (quotes at p. 177).

189. Id.

190. Id.

191. Id.

192. Id. at 177–78.

193. U.S. Const., Art. III, § 2.

194. 5 U.S. (1 Cranch) at 179.

195. Id.

196. Id. at 179–80 (emphasis added).

197. Id. at 180 (emphasis added).
198. See Snowiss, supra note 60, at 125, 139.
199. 5 U.S. (1 Cranch) at 176.
200. See Bickel, supra note 125, at 1.

CHAPTER 5

1. The label "judicial supremacy" was being used with familiarity in the first years of the nineteenth century. See Barry Friedman, "The History of the Counter-majoritarian Difficulty, Part One: The Road to Judicial Supremacy," 73 N.Y.U. L. Rev. 333, 375 (1998) (quoting George Mason worrying about whether the independence of the judiciary will "soon become something like supremacy" in 1802, and Caesar Rodney warning in 1803 that "[j]udicial supremacy may be made to bow before the strong arm of Legislative authority").

2. See David Hackett Fischer, The Revolution of American Conservatism 2–17 (1965); David Waldstreicher, "Federalism, the Styles of Politics, and the Politics of Style," in Doron Ben Atar and Barbara B. Oberg, eds., Federalists Reconsidered 99, 109–111 (1998); Gordon S. Wood, "Interests and Disinterestedness in the Making of the Constitution," in Richard Beeman, Stephen Botein, and Edward C. Carter, III, eds., Beyond Confederation 69 (1987).

3. Wood, "Interests and Disinterestedness," supra note 2, at 83; James P. Martin, "When Repression is Democratic and Constitutional: The Federalist Theory of Representation and the Sedition Act of 1798," 66 U. Chi. L. Rev. 117, 130–76 (1999); Michael Les Benedict, "The Jeffersonian Republicans and Civil Liberty," in Essays in the History of Liberty 23 (1988).

4. Benjamin Rush, "On the Defects of the Confederation" (1787), in The Selected Writings of Benjamin Rush 26, 28 (Dagobert D. Runes, ed., 1947); see Martin, supra note 3, at 142, 166–69.

5. See Alan Taylor, "From Fathers to Friends of the People: Political Personae in the Early Republic," in Doron Ben-Atar and Barbara B. Oldberg, eds., Federalists Reconsidered 225, 225–26 (1998).

6. 2 The Diary of Landon Carter, 1752–1778, at 1008–09 (Jack P. Greene, ed., 1965) (confessing he was turned out of office for failing to "familiarize myself among the People"); Douglas Adair, ed., "James Madison's Autobiography," 2 Wm. & Mary Q. 199 (1945) (recalling his distaste at having to "recommend" himself to voters by "personal solicitation"); Robert Munford, The Candidates; or, the Humours of a Virginia Election 34 (William & Mary reprint, 1949) (1770) (Sir John Toddy is liked by plain folk in this farce because he "wont turn his back upon a poor man, but will take a chearful cup with one as well as another"). The analogy between eighteenth-century elections and medieval carnival—characterized by a temporary upending of normal social relations—is made in Edmund Morgan, Inventing the People 174–208 (1988) and in Andrew W. Robertson, "Voting Rites Revisited: Electioneering Ritual,

1790–1820," in Jeffrey L. Pasley, Andrew W. Robertson, and David Waldstreicher, eds., *Beyond the Founders: New Approaches to the Political History of the
Early American Republic* (2004). General studies of elections in this period
may be found in Robert J. Dinkin, *Voting in Provincial America* (1977); Robert
J. Dinkin, *Voting in Revolutionary America* (1982); and Courtland F. Bishop,
History of Elections in the American Colonies (1893). A narrative account of
election practices and changes is found in Alan Taylor, *William Cooper's Town*
229–55 (1995).

7. "Order," *Columbian Centinel* 1 (Sept. 3, 1794).

8. Waldstreicher, supra note 2, at 101, 109; Martin, supra note 3, at 143–52; Benedict, supra note 3, at 26–29.

9. Waldstreicher, supra note 2, at 101–11, 132. The Democratic-Republican societies flourished briefly from 1793 to 1796, until they were publicly condemned
by George Washington and lost credibility. See Eugene Perry Link, *The
Democratic-Republican Societies* 175–209 (1942); James Roger Sharp, *American
Politics in the Early Republic: The New Nation in Crisis* 100–104 (1993); Stanley
Elkins and Eric McKitrick, *The Age of Federalism: The Early American Republic, 1788–1800*, at 487 (1993).

10. *Gazette of the United States*, May 5, 1796 (Philadelphia), at 3.

11. Id.

12. Seth Cotlar, "The Federalists' Transatlantic Cultural Offensive of 1798 and
the Moderation of American Democratic Discourse," in Pasley, Robertson,
and Waldstreicher, supra note 6; Martin, supra note 3, at 160–66.

13. Samuel Kendal, *A Sermon Delivered on the Day of National Thanksgiving* 30
(Samuel Hall, 1795).

14. "To the Vigil," *Gazette of the United States* 2 (Dec. 6, 1794).

15. Kendal, supra note 13, at 30.

16. Quoted in 1 *Memoirs of the Administrations of Washington and John Adams* 178,
179 (George Gibbs, ed., 1846) (Oliver Wolcott, Mar. 26, 1795).

17. Nathaniel Emmons, *A Discourse Delivered on the National Fast* (1799), in 2
American Political Writing during the Founding Era 1023, 1027 (Charles S.
Hyneman and Donald S. Lutz, eds., 1983).

18. See Speech of Alexander White (June 16, 1789), in 11 *Documentary History
of the First Federal Congress* 873 (Charles Bangs Bickford, Kenneth R. Bowling, and Helen E. Veit, eds., 1992) [hereinafter cited as *DHFFC*]; Speech of
Fisher Ames (June 16, 1789), in id. at 884; Speech of Abraham Baldwin (June
17, 1789), in id. at 996.

19. Speech of William Smith (June 16, 1789), in id. at 876.

20. Speech of Peter Silvester (June 19, 1787), in id. at 1010.

21. James T. Horton, *James Kent: A Study in Conservatism* 63, 85–87 (1939).

22. Id. at 95.

23. See editor's introduction to James Kent, "An Introductory Lecture to a Court
of Law Lectures," in 2 Hyneman and Lutz, supra note 17, at 936.

24. See Daniel J. Hulsebosch, *Constituting Empire: New York and the Transformation of Constitutionalism in the Atlantic World* (forthcoming) [ms. at 389–90].

25. Kent, "Introductory Lecture," supra note 23, at 941.

26. The only previous writer to make anything of the point was Alexander Hamilton in *Federalist 78*, though even he offered it as a secondary justification, after protecting the people from "legislative encroachments." *The Federalist No. 78*, at 527–28 (Jacob Cooke, ed., 1961).

27. Kent, "Introductory Lecture," supra note 23, at 942.

28. See David Waldstreicher, *In the Midst of Perpetual Fetes: The Making of American Nationalism* (1997); Simon P. Newman, *Parades and the Politics of the Streets: Festive Culture in the Early Republic* (1997); Saul A. Cornell, *The Other Founders: Anti-Federalism and the Dissenting Tradition in America* (1999); Gordon S. Wood, *The Radicalism of the American Revolution* 229–305 (1991).

29. *The Federalist No. 10*, supra note 26, at 64.

30. Kent, "Introductory Lecture," supra note 23, at 942.

31. Id. at 942–43.

32. Id. at 944.

33. Cotlar, supra note 12.

34. See, e.g., The Federalist (Trenton, N.J., Apr. 8, 1799), in 3 *The Documentary History of the Supreme Court of the United States, 1780–1800*, at 328, 330 (Maeva Marcus, ed., 1990) [hereinafter cited as *DHSC*]: "It is happy for the United States, that they have judges so conspicuous for wisdom, and venerable for integrity! It is the province of the judiciary to decide on the *constitutionality* of the laws."

35. Francis Wharton, *State Trials of the United States during the Administrations of Washington and Adams* 336 (1849).

36. Samuel Chase's Charge to the Grand Jury of the Circuit Court for the District of Pennsylvania (Apr. 12, 1800), in 3 *DHSC*, supra note 34, at 408, 412.

37. See Wharton, *State Trials*, supra note 35, at 637–38; Elkins and McKitrick, supra note 9, at 696–99.

38. See 3 *DHSC*, supra note 34, at 405; James Haw, *Stormy Patriot: The Life of Samuel Chase* 203–06 (1980). Even while telling Callendar's counsel, William Wirt, that "it is not competent to the jury to decide on this point [of constitutionality]," Chase conceded the jury's general "right to decide the law," *United States v. Callendar*, 25 F.Cas. 239, 253, 255 (C.C.D. Va. 1800) (No. 14,709)—evidence that, as suggested below, Chase's actions were less a shift in judicial philosophy than an overreaction to fears that Republicans wanted to import the French Revolution to America.

39. Aurora, Nov. 9, 1798 (Philadelphia); 3 *DHSC*, supra note 34, at 236 n. 24.

40. See Manning J. Dauer, *The Adams Federalists* 198–211 (1953); Stephen G. Kurtz, *The Presidency of John Adams: The Collapse of Federalism* 310–13 (1957); Richard H. Kohn, *Eagle and Sword: The Federalists and the Creation of the Military Establishment in America, 1783–1802*, at 195 (1975).

41. See Adrienne Koch, *Jefferson and Madison: The Great Collaboration* 174–211 (1950).

42. See Larry Kramer, "Putting the Politics Back into the Political Safeguards of Federalism," 100 *Colum. L. Rev.* 215, 257–65 (2000).

43. On Pennsylvania and the excise tax, see Thomas P. Slaughter, *The Whiskey Rebellion: Frontier Epilogue to the American Revolution* 97–98 (1986); on Virginia and assumption, see John C. Miller, *The Federalist Era* 52 (1960); on Virginia and the Jay Treaty, see Thomas J. Farnham, "The Virginia Amendments of 1795: An Episode in Opposition to Jay's Treaty," 75 *Va. Mag. Hist. & Bio.* 75 (1967).

44. See The Kentucky Resolutions of 1798 and 1799, in 4 Jonathan Elliot, *The Debates in the Several State Conventions on the Adoption of the Federal Constitution* 540, 542, 544 (1888 ed.). Jefferson's original draft was more radical, but someone along the way—either Jefferson's messenger John Breckinridge or the Kentucky legislature itself—deleted the passages that appeared to endorse resistance by individual states to federal authority. See Koch, supra note 41, at 188–89; Ethelbert D. Warfield, *The Kentucky Resolutions of 1798: An Historical Study* 180–85 (1894); H. Jefferson Powell, "The Principles of '98: An Essay in Historical Retrieval," 80 *Va. L. Rev.* 689, 719–21 (1994).

45. Cotlar, supra note 12.

46. See Elkins and McKitrick, supra note 9, at 726; Sharp, supra note 9, at 200.

47. For Delaware, see Answers of the Several State Legislatures—Delaware, in 4 Elliot, supra note 44, at 532; for Connecticut, see id. at 538; for Massachusetts, see id. at 533–37.

48. Id. at 538, 539.

49. Id. at 533.

50. Id. at 539.

51. Report on the Alien and Sedition Acts (Jan. 7, 1800), in *James Madison: Writings* 608, 613 (Library of America, Jack Rakove, ed., 1999).

52. Id. Madison refers to "the ultimate right of the parties to the constitution" rather than to the people, which many contemporary and some modern commentators have misread as a reference to state governments. Madison was clear, however, that when he referred to "states" he meant "the people composing those political societies, in their highest sovereign capacity." Id. at 610.

53. Report on the Alien and Sedition Acts, in *Madison: Writings*, supra note 51, at 613–14.

54. Id. at 614.

55. On the disillusionment of these first-generation Federalists after 1800, see Linda K. Kerber, *Federalists in Dissent: Imagery and Ideology in Jeffersonian America* (1970). David Hackett Fisher and, more recently, Marshall Foletta have, in different ways, described the efforts of next generation Federalists to reinvent themselves—Fisher in politics, where they had little success, and Foletta in intellectual pursuits, where their impact was somewhat greater.

David Hackett Fischer, *The Revolution of American Conservatism: The Federalist Party in the Era of Jeffersonian Democracy* (1965); Marshall Foletta, *Coming to Terms with Democracy: Federalist Intellectuals and the Shaping of an American Culture* (2001). Daniel Hulsebosch depicts the later Federalists' quite substantial success in changing the legal profession and practice of law. See Daniel J. Hulsebosch, *Constituting Empire: New York and the Transformation of Federalism in the Atlantic World* chs. 7–8 (forthcoming) (manuscript on file with author).

56. The decline of the Federalist party was by no means smooth. The advent of new leadership within the party combined with Jefferson's unpopular embargo and other problems with England brought a brief resurgence of Federalist fortunes in 1808 and again in 1814, though the party never came close to unseating the Republicans nationally. See Shaw Livermore, *The Twilight of Liberalism: The Disintegration of the Federalist Party, 1815–1830* (1962); Winfred E. A. Bernhard, ed., *Political Parties in American History, 1789–1828* (1973).

57. Speech by Uriah Tracy, 11 *Annals of Congress* 56 (Jan. 1802).

58. Speech by Samuel W. Dana, in id. at 931; see also Speech by John Stanley, in id. at 574 (observing that without judicial review, Americans would be left, "as under the despotism of a monarch, to seek redress through the throes and convulsions of a revolution").

59. Speech by Roger Griswold, in id. at 783.

60. Id. at 743.

61. Id. at 83, 90.

62. Id. at 41.

63. Speech of John Breckinridge, in id. at 179.

64. See, e.g., Speech by Calvin Goddard, in id. at 727; Speech by Roger Griswold, in id. at 783; Speech by Samuel Dana, in id. at 920–26.

65. Speech of Gouverneur Morris, in id. at 180.

66. Speech of Samuel Dana, in id. at 920; Speech of Roger Griswold, in id. at 783; see also, e.g., Speech of Joseph Hemphill, in id. at 542; Speech of Calvin Goddard, in id. at 727–28.

67. Speech of Joseph Hemphill, in id. at 543.

68. Speech of Calvin Goddard, in id. at 728.

69. Speech of John Stanley, in id. at 578.

70. Speech by Gouverneur Morris, in id. at 38.

71. Speech by John Rutledge, in id. at 743.

72. Id.

73. Speech of James Jackson, in id. at 49.

74. Speech of Nathanial Macon, in id. at 710.

75. Id. at 717.

76. Id. at 720.

77. Speech by William Cocke, in id. at 75.

78. Speech by James Jackson, in id. at 48.

79. Speech by John Randolph, in id. at 661.
80. Id.
81. Id.
82. See, e.g., Speech by John Breckinridge, in id. at 178–80; Speech by John Randolph, in id. at 661.
83. Speech by Philip R. Thompson, in id. at 553.
84. Speech by John Bacon, in id. at 983.
85. See Richard E. Ellis, *The Jeffersonian Crisis: Courts and Politics in the Young Republic* 47–51 (1971).
86. See 11 *Annals of Congress*, supra note 57, at 982 (repeal approved by a vote of 59–32).
87. See Dumas Malone, *Jefferson the President: First Term, 1801–1805*, at 140–41 (1970).

CHAPTER 6

1. The phrase is from Drew R. McCoy, *The Last of the Fathers: James Madison and the Republican Legacy* (1989).
2. Letter from James Madison to Mr. ———— (1834), in 4 *Letters and Other Writings of James Madison* 349, 349–50 (1884).
3. Letter from James Madison to Caleb Wallace (Aug. 23, 1785), in 8 *The Papers of Madison* 350, 355–56 (Robert A. Rutland, ed., 1973) (discussing ways to review the constitution, including Jefferson's proposal to permit two of the three branches to call a convention for an alleged violation of the third).
4. Observations on Jefferson's Draft of a Constitution for Virginia, in 6 *The Papers of Thomas Jefferson* 308, 315 (Julian Boyd, ed., 1952).
5. Removal Power of the President (June 17, 1789), in 12 *Papers of Madison*, supra note 3, at 238.
6. Report on the Alien and Sedition Acts (Jan. 7, 1800), in *James Madison: Writings* 608, 613 (Jack N. Rakove, ed., 1999).
7. 1 Joseph Story, *Commentaries on the Constitution of the United States* 347 (1833).
8. Id. at 357.
9. See Stephen M. Griffin, *American Constitutionalism* 42–46 (1996) (refuting the so-called gatekeeper thesis that judicial interpretation has been the primary means of constitutional development).
10. William E. Nelson, "Changing Conceptions of Judicial Review: The Evolution of Constitutional Theory in the States, 1790–1860," 120 *U. Pa. L. Rev.* 1166, 1169–70 (1972) (quoting *Moore v. Houston*, 3 Serg. & Rawle 169, 178 (Pa. 1817)).
11. *Eakin v. Raub*, 2 Serg. & Rawle 330, 1825 WL 1913, *13 (1825) (Gibson, J., dissenting).
12. See Nelson, supra note 10, at 1170–72.

13. *Cohen v. Hoff*, 2 Treadway 657, 658, 3 Brev. 500, 501 (S.C. 1814); see *Bristoe v. Evans*, 2 Tenn. 341, 346 (1815); *Grimball v. Ross*, T. Charlt. 175, 176 (Ga. 1808); *Whittington v. Polk*, 1 Harr. & J. 236, 242 (Md. 1802); *Merrill v. Sherburne*, 1 H.H. 199, 201 (1818).

14. *Rutherford v. M'Faddon* (Ohio 1807), in *Ohio Unreported Judicial Decisions—Prior to 1823*, at 71, 73 (E. Pollack, ed., 1952).

15. Id.; *Whittington v. Polk*, 1 Harr. & J. 236, 242 (Md. 1802); *Bristoe v. Evans*, 2 Tenn. 341, 346 (1815); *Emerick v. Harris*, 1 Binn. 416, 420 (Pa. 1808).

16. See Sylvia Snowiss, *Judicial Review and the Law of the Constitution* 121–61 (1990); Charles F. Hobson, *The Great Chief Justice: John Marshall and the Rule of Law* 199 (1996).

17. 17 U.S. (4 Wheat.) 120, 202 (1819); see also *Cohens v. Virginia*, 19 U.S. (6 Wheat.) 264, 380 (1821).

18. *M'Culloch v. Maryland*, 17 U.S. (4 Wheat.) 315, 413, 416 (1819); *Sturgis*, 17 U.S. (4 Wheat.) at 205.

19. *M'Culloch*, 17 U.S. (4 Wheat.) at 418. See generally Akhil Amar, "Foreword—The Document and the Doctrine," 114 *Harv. L. Rev.* 26 (2000); Akhil Amar, "Intratextualism," 112 *Harv. L. Rev.* 747 (1999).

20. G. Edward White, *The Marshall Court and Cultural Change, 1815–1835*, at 119 (abr. ed. 1988).

21. Id. at 155.

22. Daniel J. Hulsebosch, *Constituting Empire: New York and the Transformation of Constitutionalism in the Atlantic World* (forthcoming) (ms. at 370).

23. See Robert Lowry Clinton, *Marbury v. Madison and Judicial Review* 117–18 (1989).

24. See Morton J. Horwitz, *The Transformation of American Law, 1780–1860* (1977).

25. Nelson, supra note 10, at 1173–76; William E. Nelson, *Marbury v. Madison* 73–82 (2000); Gordon S. Wood, "The Origins of Judicial Review Revisited, or How the Marshall Court Made More out of Less," 56 *Wash. & Lee L. Rev.* 787, 805 (1999); Mark Graber, "The Problematic Establishment of Judicial Review," in *The Supreme Court in American Politics* 28, 29–34 (Howard Gillman and Cornell Clayton, eds., 1999).

26. Nelson, supra note 10, at 1176.

27. See Snowiss, supra note 16, at 161; Wood, supra note 25, at 805; Barry Friedman, "The History of the Countermajoritarian Difficulty, Part One: The Road to Judicial Supremacy," 73 *N.Y.U. L. Rev.* 333, 390–91 (1998).

28. *Eakin v. Raub*, 2 Serg. & Rawle 330, 354 (1825). See Nelson, supra note 25, at 85; Snowiss, supra note 16, at 73–75, 106–08, 177–83; J. M. Sosin, *The Aristocracy of the Long Robe: The Origins of Judicial Review in America* 326–30 (1989); Clinton, supra note 23, at 128–38.

29. *Rutherford v. M'Faddon*, in *Ohio Unreported Decisions*, supra note 14, at 71. See Donald F. Melhorn, *"Lest We Be Marshall'd": Judicial Powers and Politics in Ohio, 1806–1812* (2003).

30. Articles of Impeachment against George Tod, Ohio Senate, Seventh General Assembly, Journal at 52–54 (1809), reprinted in Melhorn, supra note 29, at app. C.
31. Circular Letter of Members of the Ohio Bar, *Chillicothe Scioto Gazette* (Feb. 13, 1809), reprinted in id. at app. D. Ohio lawyers apparently followed through on this promise. Id. at 115.
32. See Theodore W. Ruger, "'The Question which Convulses a Nation': The Early Republic's Greatest Debate About the Judicial Review Power," 117 *Harvard Law Review* (2004); Arndt M. Stickles, *The Critical Court Struggle in Kentucky, 1819–1829* (1929); B. J. Benthurum, "Old and New Court Controversy," 6 *Ky. L.J.* 173 (1918); Philip Lindsley, "The Old and the New Court: A Kentucky Judicial Episode," 16 *Green Bag* 520 (1904).
33. *Blair v. Williams*, 14 Kent. (4 Litt.) 33 (1823); *Lapsley v. Brashears*, 14 Kent. (4 Litt.) 41 (1823).
34. Ruger, supra note 32, at 27; see 1824–1825 Ky. Acts 44, 48 (Dec. 24, 1824).
35. See Ruger, supra note 32, at 3 ("What is less ambiguous . . . is that the *kind* of judicial review that Kentuckians voted to reestablish was significantly more modest than the current doctrine, leaving meaningful interpretive authority with the public and the elected branches of government"); Melhorn, supra note 29, at 118 (if events in Ohio "had proven anything for certain, it was that judicial supremacy had been overwhelmingly rejected as a doctrine of Ohio constitutional law, whatever might be left of the courts' claim to the power of judicial review."). There was also a brief conflict in Georgia in 1815 after a state superior court declared debtor relief legislation unconstitutional. The Georgia House of Representatives responded with a resolution denying that the judges had authority to hold conferences and for several years there were none. See Albert B. Saye, *A Constitutional History of Georgia, 1732–1968*, at 190–91 (rev. ed. 1970); William E. Nelson, *The Roots of American Bureaucracy, 1830–1900*, at 37 (1982).
36. See Leslie Friedman Goldstein, *Constituting Federal Sovereignty: The European Union in Comparative Context* 23–29 (2001).
37. See Dwight Wiley Jessup, *Reaction and Accommodation: The United States Supreme Court and Political Conflict, 1809–1835*, at 425–28 (1987).
38. For participants, the issue turned on whether one conceived the United States as a compact of sovereign states, a national government constituted by a single people, or some mix of the two. G. Edward White explores the various alternatives with great sensitivity to the nuances of this complex (if ultimately fruitless) debate. White, supra note 20, at 485–594.
39. Quoted in Jessup, supra note 37, at 359.
40. John Taylor, *Tyranny Unmasked* 202 (F. Thornton Miller, ed., 1992) (1822).
41. Id. at 203.
42. See *Norris v. Clymer*, 2 Pa. 277, 1845 Pa. Lexis 332, *11 (1845); Charles Grove Haines, *The American Doctrine of Judicial Supremacy* 246 (1914).

43. See, e.g., William E. Dodd, "Chief Justice Marshall and Virginia," 12 *Amer. Hist. Rev.* 776, 780 (1907).

44. Hampden III, *Richmond Enquirer* (June 18, 1819), reprinted in Gerald Gunther, *John Marshall's Defense of McCulloch v. Maryland* 138 (1969). See also Amphycton I, *Richmond Enquirer* (Mar. 30, 1819), in id. at 54–55; Letter from James Madison to Spencer Roane (Sept. 2, 1819), in *James Madison: Writings*, supra note 25, at 733, 734 ("Does not the Court also relinquish by their doctrine, all controul on the Legislative exercise of unconstitutional powers?").

45. See Goldstein, supra note 36, at 32 ("Supreme Court authority to declare void state law, was accepted as legitimate, in almost all the states, almost all the time, and on almost all issues.")

46. *M'Culloch*, 17 U.S. (4 Wheat.) at 407; see Snowiss, supra note 16, at 170.

47. *M'Culloch*, 17 U.S. (4 Wheat.) at 401.

48. Hampden IV, *Richmond Enquirer* (June 22, 1819), in Gunther, supra note 44, at 138.

49. A Friend of the Constitution IX, *Alexandria Gazette* (July 15, 1819), in id. at 208.

50. See id. at 11; Jessup, supra note 37, at 198–200; Jean Edward Smith, *John Marshall, Definer of a Nation* 450–52 (1996).

51. See Thomas Sergeant, *Constitutional Law: Being a View of the Practice and Jurisdiction of the Courts of the United States and of Constitutional Points Decided* 412–13 (1830); William Rawle, *A View of the Constitution of the United States of America* 216–17, 267–70 (1825); Peter S. Du Ponceau, *A Dissertation on the Nature and Extent of Jurisdiction of the Courts of the United States* (1824); J. M Goodenow, *Historical Sketches of the Principles and Maxims of American Jurisprudence* (1819). Virginia Supreme Court Justice St. George Tucker touched on the power of courts to address unconstitutional statutes at several points in his essay *A View of the Constitution of the United States*, which was appended to Tucker's annotated 1803 edition of Blackstone. A good Republican, Tucker largely adhered to Jefferson's departmental view, though he emphasized that, in the nature of things, this approach would make the judiciary the particular guardian of individual rights. See St. George Tucker, *A View of the Constitution of the United States, with Selected Writings* 103, 293 (Liberty Fund ed. 1999) (1803). On the emergence of this new legal commentary generally, see White, supra note 20, at 86–95; Hulsebosch, supra note 22, at chs. 7–8.

52. See Paul A. Gilje, *Rioting in America* 12–20 (1996); Paul A. Gilje, *The Road to Mobocracy: Popular Disorder in New York City, 1763–1834*, at 5–35 (1987); George Rude, *The Crowd in History* (1964).

53. See Gilje, *Rioting in America*, supra note 52, at 24–34.

54. See Christine A. Desan, "The Constitutional Commitment to Legislative Adjudication in the Early American Tradition," 111 *Harv. L. Rev.* 1381 (1998); Timothy A. Lawrie, "Interpretation and Authority: Separation of Powers and

the Judiciary's Battle for Independence in New Hampshire, 1786–1818," 39 *Am. J. Leg. Hist.* 310 (1995).

55. William Nelson, *Americanization of the Common Law* 21 (1975). Numerous commentators have made the same point, though none examined primary sources to the same extent as Nelson. See, e.g., Mark DeWolfe Howe, "Juries as Judges of Criminal Law," 52 *Harv. L. Rev.* 582 (1939); Jeffrey Abramson, *We, the Jury: The Jury System and the Ideal of Democracy* 30–31, 37, 63–64, 75–76 (1994); David J. Bodenhamer, *Fair Trial: Rights of the Accused in American History* 61 (1992); Forrest McDonald, *Novus Ordo Seclorum: The Intellectual Origins of the Constitution* 40–41 (1985); Shannon C. Stimson, *The American Revolution in the Law* (1990). Additional authorities are cited in Stanton D. Krauss, "An Inquiry into the Right of Criminal Juries to Determine the Law in Colonial America," 89 *Nw. U. L. Rev.* 111, 119–21 n. 43 (1998). Krauss challenges the claim that juries in criminal cases had the legal right to find law, though his argument does not extend to civil juries and does not gainsay Nelson's main point, which was that the procedural system was structured in a way that ensured the jury's control as a practical matter.

56. Jack N. Rakove, "The Origins of Judicial Review: A Plea for New Contexts," 49 *Stan. L. Rev.* 1031, 1064 (1997).

57. See Jack N. Rakove, *Original Meanings: Politics and Ideas in the Making of the Constitution* 318–25 (1996); William H. Riker, *The Strategy of Rhetoric: Campaigning for the American Constitution* 85–90, 104 (1996).

58. Rakove, supra note 56, at 1064.

59. Richard E. Ellis, *The Jeffersonian Crisis: Courts and Politics in the Young Republic* 111 (1971).

60. See Maxwell Bloomfield, *American Lawyers in a Changing Society, 1776–1876*, at 139 (1976); Lawrence M. Friedman, *A History of American Law* 99, 315–16 (1973); Alfred Z. Reed, *Training for the Public Profession of the Law* 67–103 (1921).

61. See Friedman, supra note 60, at 97–98; Charles R. McKirdy, "The Lawyer as Apprentice: Legal Education in Eighteenth Century Massachusetts," 28 *J. Legal Educ.* 124 (1976); Hoyt P. Canady, "Legal Education in Colonial South Carolina," in *South Carolina Legal History* 101 (Herbert Johnson, ed., 1980).

62. Ellis, supra note 59, at 115; Friedman, supra note 60, at 124–27.

63. William Plumer, Jr., *Life of William Plumer* 183 (1857); see John Phillip Reid, *Controlling the Law: Legal Politics in Early National New Hampshire* 71–82 (2004).

64. See Plumer, supra note 63, at 236; Nelson, supra note 55, at 26; Reid, supra note 63, at 108.

65. Id. See also Plumer, supra note 63, at 158.

66. See Nelson, supra note 55, at 21–28; Friedman, supra note 60, at 152–56.

67. See Reid, supra note 63, at ch. 11.

68. Friedman, supra note 60, at 102–04.

69. See J. M. Sosin, *The Aristocracy of the Long Robe* 203 (1989).

70. See Ellis, supra note 59, at 118–19; Alan V. Briceland, "Ephraim Kirby: Pioneer of American Law Reporting," 16 *Amer. J. Legal Hist.* 210–11 (1972); Edward Dumbauld, "Legal Records in English and American Courts," 36 *American Archivist* 28–29 (1973).

71. See Reid, supra note 63, at ch. 12. Their reviews were published in *The Monthly Anthology and Boston Review.* Later, other distinguished lawyers—including not only Webster, but also Caleb Cushing, Joseph Story, and Henry Wheaton—reviewed volumes of judicial reports in *The North American Review*, the leading monthly journal of its kind. Id.

72. See Friedman, supra note 60, at 107–13.

73. John H. Morison, *Life of the Hon. Jeremiah Smith* 174 (1845).

74. See Reid, supra note 63, at ch. 2.

75. Jesse Higgins, *Sampson against the Philistines, or the Reformation of Lawsuits; and Justice Made Cheap, Speedy, and Brought Home to Every Man's Door: Agreeably to the Principles of the Ancient Trial by Jury, before the Same was Innovated by Judges and Lawyers. Compiled for the Honest Citizens of the United States* 24–25 (2d. ed, Philadelphia, 1805).

76. See White, supra note 20, at 77–78; Ellis, supra note 59, at 114; Gerard W. Gawalt, *The Promise of Power: The Legal Profession in Massachusetts, 1760–1840*, at 81–118 (1979); Christopher Grasso, *A Speaking Aristocracy: Transforming Public Discourse in Eighteenth-Century Connecticut* 436 (1999).

77. Reid, supra note 63, at 24.

78. *Hall v. Perkins*, 3 Wend. 626, 629–30 (N.Y. 1829).

79. See Reid, supra note 63, at 25–26.

80. John Reid, "From Common Sense to Common Law to Charles Doe: The Evolution of Pleading in New Hampshire," 1 *New Hampshire Bar Journal* 27, 29 (1959); Charles R. Corning, "The Highest Courts of Law in New Hampshire—Colonial, Provincial, and State," 2 *Greenbag* 469, 471 (1890).

81. William Plumer, Jr., "The Constitution of New Hampshire," 4 *Historical Magazine* 172, 182 (1868).

82. Reid, supra note 63, at 25.

83. Plumer, supra note 63, at 153–55. In recounting this speech, the author sneered that he "made the judge speak good English, which he did not often do." Id. at 155.

84. Ellis, supra note 59, at 111–16.

85. See Perry Miller, *The Life of the Mind in America from the Revolution to the Civil War* 96–265 (1965); William P. LaPiana, *Logic and Experience: The Origin of Modern Legal Education* 37–38 (1994).

86. Reid, supra note 63, at 141. For the curious, "agistment" is an ancient law term referring to a person—an agister—who takes in animals for feeding or pasturing; it is a species of bailment.

87. See R. Kent Newmyer, "Harvard Law School, New England Legal Culture, and the Antebellum Origins of American Jurisprudence," 74 *J. Amer. Hist.* 814, 822 (1987).

88. Letter from James Kent to Thomas Washington (Oct. 6, 1828), in 1 *Select Essays in Anglo-American Legal History* 843 (1907).

89. A Friend to Justice, "On the Judicial Act," *Portsmouth Oracle*, July 17, 1813, at p. 2, col. 1.

90. Charles H. Bell, *The Bench and Bar of New Hampshire* 37 (1894).

91. For studies of the politics of legal reform in the early Republic, see Ellis, supra note 59, at 111–229 (Kentucky, Pennsylvania, and Massachusetts); Reid, supra note 63 (New Hampshire); Gawalt, supra note 76 (Massachusetts); A. G. Roeber, *Faithful Magistrates and Republican Lawyers: Creators of Virginia Legal Culture, 1680–1810*, at 160–261 (1981). In addition, G. Edward White touches on some of the broader themes in introducing the legal culture of the Marshall Court. See White, supra note 20, at 76–156.

92. John H. Langbein, "Chancellor Kent and the History of Legal Literature," 93 *Col. L. Rev.* 547, 566 (1993).

93. See Gawalt, supra note 76, at 95–96.

94. See Reid, supra note 63, at ch. 3.

95. 1 William Blackstone, *Commentaries on the Laws of England* *4 (Univ. of Chicago ed., 1979) (1765).

96. See White, supra note 20, at 79–83; LaPiana, supra note 85, at 29–38; Gawalt, supra note 76, at 81–82.

97. See White, supra note 20, at 86–95; LaPiana, supra note 85, at 40–41; Hulsebosch, supra note 22, at 394, 397; Daniel J. Hulsebosch, "Writs to Rights: Navigability and the Transformation of the Common Law in the Nineteenth Century," 23 *Cardozo L. Rev.* 1049 (2002). According to Hulsebosch, the writers of these treatises and proponents of change were also concerned with creating a unifying national law to replace piecemeal state adjudication, thus adding an important element of federalism to the push for legal reform.

98. See LaPiana, supra note 85, at 29–78; Newmyer, supra note 87; see generally Anton-Hermann Chroust, *The Rise of the Legal Profession in America: The Revolutionary and Post-Revolutionary Era* (1965).

99. See White, supra note 20, at 86, 94.

100. See Gawalt, supra note 76, at 98–99, 105–07; Reid, supra note 63, at ch. 9; Nelson, supra note 55, at 165–74.

101. Ellis, supra note 59, at 163–64, quoting 1 David Paul Brown, *The Forum: or Forty Years Full Practice at the Philadelphia Bar* 344–55 (1856).

102. Unless otherwise indicated, the points in this paragraph and the next are drawn from Ellis, supra note 59, at 111–266, who describes the politics of judicial reform in a number of states; and Reid, supra note 63, *passim*, who closely studies one state (New Hampshire). The broad framework suggested by these authors, particularly Reid, is supported by William Nelson's and Gerard Gawalt's studies of Massachusetts and by A. G. Roeber's study of Virginia. See Nelson, supra note 55; Gawalt, supra note 76; Roeber, supra not 91. See also White, supra note 20, at ch. 2; Bloomfield, supra note 60, at chs. 2–3; Friedman, supra note 60. It is unfortunate that we lack equally intensive

studies of other states, though the sporadic evidence that exists suggests a process that was similar nationally in its essentials.

103. See Bloomfield, supra note 60, at 84; Gawalt, supra note 76, at 182–83; Charles M. Cook, *The American Codification Movement: A Study of Antebellum Legal Reform* (1981); Miller, supra note 85, at 239–65; Robert Gordon, Book Review, 36 *Vand. L. Rev.* 431 (1983) (reviewing Cook).

104. Friedman, supra note 60, at 371.

105. See 1 Louis Boudin, *Government by Judiciary* 317–405 (1968); Friedman, supra note 60, at 126–27, 371–73; James Willard Hurst, *The Growth of American Law: The Law Makers* 140 (1950).

106. See Clinton Rossiter, *Politics and Parties in America* 1 (1960); E. E. Schattschneider, *Party Government* 1 (1942); William Nisbet Chambers, *Political Parties in a New Nation: The American Experience, 1776–1809* (1963).

107. See *The Antifederalists* xxxix (Cecelia M. Kenyon, ed., 1985); Herbert J. Storing, *What the Anti-Federalists Were For* 15 (1981).

108. See, e.g., Luther Martin, "The Genuine Information IV," *Baltimore Maryland Gazette*, Jan. 8, 1788, in 15 *The Documentary History of the Ratification of the Constitution* 296, 300 (John P. Kaminski and Gaspare J. Saladino, eds., 1984) [hereinafter cited as *DHRC*]; The Federal Farmer, An Additional Number of Letters to the Republican (letter VII), in 17 *DHRC* at 265, 281–82.

109. See, e.g., Brutus I, *New York Journal*, Oct. 18, 1787, in 13 *DHRC*, supra note 108, at 411, 420; Brutus IV, *New York Journal*, Nov. 29, 1787, in 14 id. at 299–300; The Impartial Examiner III, *Virginia Independent Chronicle*, June 4, 1788, in 10 id. at 1576; Cato III, *New York Journal*, Oct. 25, 1787, in 13 id. at 476; Federal Farmer, Letters to the Republican (Letter II), in 14 id. at 29; Speech by Patrick Henry at the Virginia Ratifying Convention, June 12, 1788, in 10 id. at 1217; Letter from Thomas Tudor Tucker to St. George Tucker (Dec. 28, 1787), in 15 id. at 143, 144; John DeWitt I, *American Herald*, Oct.–Dec., 1787, in 4 *The Complete Anti-Federalist* 27 (Herbert J. Storing, ed., 1981).

110. See, e.g., Luther Martin, The Genuine Information IV, *Baltimore Maryland Gazette*, Jan. 8, 1788, in 15 *DHRC*, supra note 108, at 300–301; Federal Farmer, Letters to the Republican (Letter III), in 14 id. at 32.

111. "I believe it may be laid down as a general rule," Alexander Hamilton wrote in *Federalist 27*, that the people's "confidence in and obedience to a government, will commonly be proportioned to the goodness or badness of its administration." The *Federalist No. 27*, at 172 (Jacob Cooke, ed., 1961); see also *The Federalist No. 68*, id. 61 (Hamilton) ("the true test of a good government is its aptitude and tendency to produce a good administration"); Letter from George Washington to John Armstrong, Sr. (Apr. 25, 1788), in 9 *DHRC*, supra note 108, at 758, 759.

112. See William Nisbet Chambers, "Party Development and Party Action," in *The First Party System* 41–42, 48–53 (William Nisbet Chambers, ed., 1972); John Zvesper, *Political Philosophy and Rhetoric: A Study of the Origins of American Political Parties* 75 (1977).

113. David J. Siemers, *Ratifying the Republic: Antifederalists and Federalists in Constitutional Time* 135–63 (2002); J. R. Pole, "Political Parties and the Right to Vote," in *The Federalists vs. The Jeffersonian Republicans* 82–87 (Paul Goodman, ed., 1967); Michael Wallace, "Changing Concepts of Party in the United States: New York, 1815–1828," 74 *Am. Hist. Rev.* 453, 455 and n. 5 (1968) (citing authorities).

114. Id.; Noble E. Cunningham, Jr., "John Beckley: An Early American Party Manager," 13 *Wm. & Mary Q.* 40 (1956); Roland M. Baumann, "Philadelphia's Manufacturers and the Excise Tax of 1794: The Forging of the Jeffersonian Coalition," 106 *Penn. Mag. Hist. & Bio.* 3 (1982).

115. See Noble E. Cunningham, *The Jeffersonian Republicans: The Formation of Party Organization, 1789–1801* (1957).

116. See David Waldstreicher and Stephen R. Grossbart, "Abraham Bishop's Vocation; or the Mediation of Jeffersonian Politics," 18 *J. Early Republic* 617, 624, 641 (1998).

117. Andrew W. Robertson, "Voting Rites Revisited: Electioneering Ritual, 1790–1820," in Jeffrey L. Pasley, Andrew W. Robertson, and David Waldstreicher, eds., *Beyond the Founders: New Approaches to the Political History of the Early American Republic* (2004); Cunningham, supra note 115, at 252–55; David Waldstreicher, *In the Midst of Perpetual Fetes: The Making of American Nationalism* 201 (1997); Richard P. McCormick, *The Second American Party System* (1966); John H. Aldritch, *Why Parties? The Origin and Transformation of Political Parties in America* 97–125 (1995); William G. Shade, "Political Pluralism and Party Development: The Creation of a Modern Party System: 1815–1852," in *The Evolution of American Electoral Systems* 77 (Paul Kleppner et al., eds., 1981).

118. This thesis is most famously associated with William Nesbit Chamber, in particular with his classic, *Political Parties in a New Nation: The American Experience, 1776–1809* (1963); for other elaborations on this idea, see Rossiter, supra note 106; V. O. Key, *Politics, Parties, and Pressure Groups* (1942); *The First Party System: Federalists and Republicans* (William Nisbet Chambers, ed., 1972); and *The Federalists vs. The Jeffersonian Republicans* 61–64 (Paul Goodman, ed., 1967).

119. See Ronald Formisano, "Federalists and Republicans: Parties Yes—System, No," in *The Evolution of American Electoral Systems,* supra note 117, at 33–35; Ronald Formisano, "Deferential-Participant Politics: The Early Republic's Political Culture, 1789–1840," 68 *Am. Pol. Sci. Rev.* 473 (1974).

120. See Joanne B. Freeman, *Affairs of Honor: National Politics in the New Republic* 199–261 (2001).

121. See McCormick, supra note 117, *passim.*

122. Jeffrey L. Pasley, "The Cheese and the Words: Popular Political Culture and Participatory Democracy in the Early American Republic," in Pasley, Robertson, and Waldstreicher, supra note 117; Robertson, supra note 117.

123. See Gilje, *Rioting in America*, supra note 52, at 67; Gilje, *Road to Mobocracy*, supra note 52; David Grimsted, *American Mobbing, 1828–1861: Toward Civil War* (1998); Kimberly K. Smith, *The Dominion of Voice: Riot, Reason, and Romance in Antebellum Politics* 51–83 (1999); Mary P. Ryan, *Civic Wars* 129–31 (1997).

124. Reeve Huston, "Popular Movements and Party Rule: The New York Anti-Rent Wars and the Jacksonian Political Order," in Pasley, Robertson, and Waldstreicher, supra note 117.

CHAPTER 7

1. Letter from Timothy Pickering to William Coleman (Apr. 30, 1827), quoted in James McClellan, *Joseph Story and the American Constitution* 40–43 and n.143 (1971).

2. Id. On Story's embrace of Federalism, see R. Kent Newmyer, *Supreme Court Justice Joseph Story: Statesman of the Old Republic* 127 (1985).

3. Letter from Joseph Story to John Marshall (June 27, 1821), quoted in Charles Warren, "The Story–Marshall Correspondence (1819–1831)," 21 *Wm. & Mary Q.* 1, 7 (2d ser. 1941). The remaining quotes in this paragraph are taken from the same letter.

4. William Charles Jarvis, *The Republican: A Series of Essays on the Principles and Policy of Free States; having a Particular Reference to the United States of American and the Individual States* (1820).

5. Letter from Thomas Jefferson to William Charles Jarvis (Sept. 28, 1820), in 10 *The Writings of Thomas Jefferson* 160 (Paul Leicester Ford, ed., 1899).

6. Id.

7. Letter from William Jarvis to Thomas Jefferson, reprinted in Warren, supra note 3, at 9–10.

8. Cf. H. Jefferson Powell, "The Principles of '98: An Essay in Historical Retrieval," 80 *Va. L. Rev.* 689, 693–96 (1994) (discussing how the Jeffersonian principles of '98 were still conventional wisdom in the early 1830s).

9. Letter from Thomas Jefferson to Phillip Mazzei (Apr. 24, 1796), in 7 *Writings of Jefferson*, supra note 5, at 75.

10. See Letter from Thomas Jefferson to Thomas Pinckney (Dec. 3, 1792), in 6 *Writings of Jefferson*, supra note 5, at 143; James Roger Sharp, *American Politics in the Early Republic: The New Nation in Crisis* 182 (1993).

11. "A Candid State of Parties," *National Gazette*, Sept. 22, 1792, in 14 *The Papers of James Madison* 372 (Robert A. Rutland et al., eds., 1983).

12. See Dumas Malone, *Jefferson the President: First Term, 1801–1805*, at 110–56, 458–85 (1970); Richard E. Ellis, *The Jeffersonian Crisis: Courts and Politics in the Young Republic* 69–107 (1971); Keith E. Whittington, *Constitutional Construction: Divided Power and Constitutional Meaning* 20–71 (1999).

13. Bradford Perkins, *Prologue to War: England and the United States , 1805-1812*, at 165-74 (1961); Walter Lefeber, "Jefferson and American Foreign Policy," in *Jeffersonian Legacies* 340, 384-85 (Peter S. Onuf, ed., 1993).

14. Leonard W. Levy, *Jefferson and Civil Liberties* 93-141 (1963); Perkins, supra note 13, at 159-65.

15. Dumas Malone, *Jefferson the President: Second Term, 1805-1809*, at 641-57 (1974); H. V. Ames, ed., *State Documents on Federal Relations: The States and the U.S.* 34-44 (1900).

16. Connecticut Resolutions of Mar. 1, 1809, in Ames, supra note 15, at 40-42.

17. See generally Leslie Friedman Goldstein, *Constituting Federal Sovereignty* 14-42 (2001); Dwight Wiley Jessup, *Reaction and Accommodation: The United States Supreme Court and Political Conflict, 1809-1835* (1987).

18. *United States v. Peters*, 9 U.S. (5 Cranch) 115 (1809). See Jessup, supra note 17, at 140-48; William Douglas, "Interposition and the Peters Case," 9 *Stan. L. Rev.* 1, 3-12 (1957); Sanford W. Higginbotham, *The Keystone in the Democratic Arch: Pennsylvania Politics, 1800-1816*, at 177-204 (1952).

19. 14 U.S. (1 Wheat.) 304 (1816).

20. 19 U.S. (6 Wheat.) 264 (1821).

21. 21 U.S. (8 Wheat.) 1 (1823). See Jessup, supra note 17, at 216-31; Paul W. Gates, "Tenants of the Log Cabin," 51 *Miss. Valley Hist. Rev.* 3 (1967).

22. 17 U.S. (4 Wheat.) 316 (1819).

23. 22 U.S. (9 Wheat.) 738 (1824). See Jessup, supra note 17, at 231-44; John D. Aiello, "Ohio's War upon the Bank of the United States, 1817-1824" (Ph.D. dissertation, Ohio State Univ. 1972).

24. Ralph Ketcham, *James Madison: A Biography* 536-38, 592-93 (1990); J. C. A. Staggs, *Mr. Madison's War* 253-69 (1983).

25. Ketcham, supra note 24, at 477-83; James M. Banner, Jr., *To the Hartford Convention: The Federalists and the Origins of Party Politics in Massachusetts, 1789-1815* (1970).

26. Ketcham, supra note 24, at 599-612; Merrill D. Peterson, *The Great Triumvirate: Webster, Clay, and Calhoun* 43-50 (1987).

27. See Peterson, supra note 26, at 68-84; Robert V. Remini, *Henry Clay: Statesman for the Union* 133-53, 210-33 (1991); George Dangerfield, *The Era of Good Feelings* 119-20 (1952).

28. Speech of James Madison in 1 *The Records of the Federal Convention of 1787*, at 486 (Max Farrand, ed., rev. ed. 1937) (Madison's notes, June 30, 1787).

29. See Glover Moore, *The Missouri Compromise, 1819-1821* (1953); Peterson, supra note 26, at 59-66; George Dangerfield, *The Era of Good Feelings* 217-45 (1952).

30. Dangerfield, supra note 29, at 243.

31. See, e.g., G. Edward White, *The Marshall Court and Cultural Change, 1815-1835*, at 656-57, 764 (abr. ed. 1988); R. Kent Newmyer, *The Supreme Court under Marshall and Taney* 81-88 (1968); Benjamin Wright, *The Contract Clause of the Constitution* 50-56 (1938); Edwin Corwin, *John Marshall and the Constitution*

190–91 (1919); Stuart S. Nagel, "Court Curbing Periods in American History," 18 *Vanderbilt L. Rev.* 925–44 (1965).

32. See, e.g., 4 Albert J. Beveridge, *The Life of John Marshall* 321–584 (1919); Felix Frankfurter, *The Commerce Clause under Marshall, Taney, and Waite* 18–45 (1937); Robert J. Steamer, *The Supreme Court in Crisis: A History of Conflict* 24–53 (1971).

33. See Jessup, supra note 17, at 283–338.

34. See id. at 329–30.

35. See Foreword to Herman Belz, ed., *The Webster–Hayne Debate on the Nature of the Union* x (2000) [hereinafter *Webster–Hayne Debate*].

36. Register of Debates in Congress, 1st Cong., 1st Sess. at 24 (Jan. 19, 1830).

37. See Peterson, supra note 26, at 170–71.

38. Id. at 179–80.

39. Foreword to *Webster–Hayne Debate*, supra note 35, at xii; Peterson, supra note 26, at 180.

40. Speech of Daniel Webster (Jan. 26–27, 1830), in *Webster–Hayne Debate*, supra note 35, at 126, 135.

41. Id. at 136–37.

42. Id. at 142.

43. Id. at 136–37.

44. Id. at 137.

45. See William W. Freehling, *Prelude to Civil War: The Nullification Controversy in South Carolina, 1816–1836*, at 89–133 (1965).

46. *Charleston Mercury*, July 18–21, 1827.

47. See Peterson, supra note 26, at 159–61.

48. See Freehling, supra note 45, at 134–76. There was, of course, more to the theory of nullification than these two short sentences convey. In its most intelligible form—articulated by John C. Calhoun—the distinction between constitution-making and lawmaking was carefully preserved, as was the doctrine of popular sovereignty. See *Union and Liberty: The Political Philosophy of John C. Calhoun* 311–66, 367–400 (Ross M. Lence, ed., 1992) (South Carolina "Exposition and Protest" and Fort Hill Address); Letter to Governor James Hamilton, Jr., in 11 *The Papers of John C. Calhoun* 613–49 (W. Edwin Hemphill, Robert L. Meriwether, and Clyde Wilson, eds., 1959–84). But such distinctions counted for little in public discussion, and the debate over nullification was treated as presenting a stark choice between institutions to resolve conflicts between the state and federal governments: either the federal courts had final say or the states themselves did.

49. Speech of Robert Hayne (Jan. 27, 1830), in *Webster–Hayne Debate*, supra note 35, at 169, 170.

50. Id. at 170.

51. Id.

52. Speech of John Rowan (Feb. 4, 1830), in id. at 286–87.

53. Id. at 287.

54. Id. at 285–86.
55. Speech of William Smith (Feb. 25, 1830), in id. at 329. This was not the same William Smith as the one who, in 1789, had argued for judicial supremacy because "[a] great deal of mischief has arisen in the several states, by the legislature undertaking to decide constitutional questions." See chapter 5.
56. Id. at 330.
57. Speech of Daniel Webster (Jan. 26–27), in id. at 139.
58. Id. at 141.
59. Speech of John Clayton (Mar. 4, 1830), in id. at 361.
60. Id. at 363.
61. See Foreword, in id. at xiii; Peterson, supra note 26, at 179–80.
62. On the tariff of 1832, see Freehling, supra note 45, at 247–50 (arguing that the 1832 bill did in fact ease the burden on Southern planters, but that it was misstated and misunderstood in the South anyway). As for Calhoun, he had secretly authored the South Carolina "Exposition and Protest" in 1829; while this was a more or less open secret, it was not until his Fort Hill Address on July 26, 1831, that Calhoun openly declared his support for nullification. Calhoun resigned as Vice President on December 28, 1832. See John Niven, *John C. Calhoun and the Price of Union* 158–70, 181–84, 193 (1988).
63. South Carolina Ordinance of Nullification (Nov. 19, 1832), in *State Papers on Nullification* 29–31 (1834).
64. Proclamation of Dec. 10, 1832, in 3 *A Compilation of the Messages and Papers of the Presidents* 1203–19 (James Richardson, ed., 1907).
65. Force Bill Message (Jan. 16, 1833), in id. at 1174–95.
66. For the points in this paragraph, see Richard Ellis, *The Union at Risk: Jacksonian Democracy, States' Rights, and the Nullification Crisis* 83–91, 129–32, 158–77 (1987); Merrill D. Peterson, *The Olive Branch and Sword: The Compromise of 1833* (1982); Freehling, supra note 45, at 260–97.
67. Diary of John Floyd, quoted in Ellis, supra note 66, at 130.
68. See Jessup, supra note 17, at 348–51; Charles Warren, *The Supreme Court and Sovereign States* 39–40 (1924); James Parker, "A Brief History of the Boundary Disputes between New York and New Jersey," 8 *Proceedings of the New Jersey Historical Soc'y* 107–13 (ser. 1, 1859).
69. See Tim Alan Garrison, *The Legal Ideology of Removal: The Southern Judiciary and the Sovereignty of Native American Nations* (2002); Jill Norgren, *The Cherokee Cases: The Confrontation of Law and Politics* (1996). The Supreme Court's decisions and John Marshall's thinking are carefully analyzed in R. Kent Newmyer, "Chief Justice John Marshall's Last Campaign: Georgia, Jackson, and the Cherokee Cases," 23 *J. Sup. Ct. Hist.* 76 (1999).
70. Garrison, supra note 69, at 103–24; Norgren, supra note 69, at 95–98.
71. The Marshall Court dismissed *Cherokee Nation v. Georgia*, 30 U.S. (5 Pet.) 1, 20 (1831), for lack of jurisdiction, but invited the Indians to try again in a "proper case with the proper parties." The Alabama supreme court responded

with a clear repudiation in *Caldwell v. Alabama*, 6 Stew. & P. 327 (Ala. 1831). Garrison, supra note 69, at 151–68.

72. Garrison, supra note 69, at 169–97; Jessup, supra note 17, at 369–71; 1 Charles Warren, *The Supreme Court in United States History* 756–61 (1922); Richard P. Longaker, "Andrew Jackson and the Judiciary," 71 *Pol. Sci. Q.* 345–46 (1956). For an interesting critique of the politics of Marshall's opinion, see Gerard N. Magliocca, "Preemptive Opinions: The Secret History of *Worcester v. Georgia* and *Dred Scott*," 63 *U. Pitt. L. Rev.* 487, 510–53 (2002).

73. Norgren, supra note 69, at 130–33. In 1834 Georgia and the Supreme Court replayed the Tassels episode when Georgia ignored another show cause order and executed James Graves, a Cherokee Indian convicted of murder under state law. See id. at 132–33.

74. See *Tennessee v. Forman*, 16 Tenn. (8 Yerg.) 256 (1835); Garrison, supra note 69, at 198–245.

75. See Michael F. Holt, *The Rise and Fall of the American Whig Party* 15–16 (1999).

76. Andrew Jackson, Veto Message (July 10, 1832), in 2 Richardson, supra note 64, at 576, 582.

77. For Webster, see "The Presidential Veto of the United States Bank Bill," in 3 Daniel Webster, *The Works of Daniel Webster* 416, 432–35 (1851); Clay is quoted in Peterson, supra note 26, at 211.

78. Remini, supra note 27, at 402–11; Samuel R. Gammon, Jr., *The Presidential Campaign of 1832* (1922).

79. See Remini, supra note 27, at 444–47; Bray Hammond, *Banks and Politics in America* 412–38 (1957).

80. Hammond, supra note 79, at 432.

81. See Jackson's "Protest" to the Senate (Apr. 15, 1834), in 2 Richardson, supra note 64, at 69, 90–93; Robert C. Byrd, "The Senate Censures Andrew Jackson, 1833–1837," in 1 *The Senate, 1789–1989* (1988).

82. See Robert V. Remini, *Andrew Jackson and the Bank War* (1968); Hammond, supra note 79, at 405–50; for a brief and highly readable account, see Robert V. Remini, *The Life of Andrew Jackson* 326–32, 261–77, 328–30 (1988).

83. For examples, see Jessup, supra note 17, *passim*; and White, supra note 31, at 741–78.

84. See 1 Joseph Story, *Commentaries on the Constitution of the United States* 352–53 (1833). Indeed, Story's discussion of "who is final judge" is found in chapter IV of book III, immediately after Story's discussion of the compact theory.

85. Id. at 358–59.

86. See chapter 2, at pp. 00–00.

87. For a more detailed discussion of this subject, see Jack N. Rakove, "Judicial Power in the Constitutional Theory of James Madison," 43 *Wm. & Mary L. Rev.* 1513, 1534–47 (2002). While basically consistent with my account, Rakove believes that Madison put more stock in judicial enforcement at the beginning and so believes that the change in Madison's views over time was somewhat

smaller than I do. Rakove bases this mainly on the brief reference to judicial review in *Federalist 39*, but his argument ignores Madison's speech in the 1789 removal debate, his *National Gazette* essays of 1791–92, and his Report of 1800 on the Virginia Resolves—all of which strongly support Madison's skepticism and concern when it came to the judicial power and his firm commitment to popular constitutionalism.

88. Letter from James Madison to Spencer Roane (May 6, 1821), in *Madison: Writings* 772, 774 (Jack N. Rakove, ed., 1999).

89. Letter from James Madison to Spencer Roane (June 29, 1821), in id. at 777, 778–79.

90. Letter from James Madison to Thomas Jefferson (June 27, 1823), in id. at 798, 800.

91. Id.

92. Id. at 801.

93. Id.

94. Id.

95. *The Federalist No 39*, at 256 (Jacob Cooke, ed., 1961).

96. Letter from James Madison to Edward Everett (Aug. 28, 1830), in *Madison: Writings*, supra note 88, at 842, 845.

97. Id.

98. Id.

99. Id. at 845–46.

100. James Madison, Report on the Alien and Sedition Acts, quoted in chapter 5, at p. oo.

101. Letter from James Madison to Edward Everett, in *Madison: Writings*, supra note 88, at 847.

102. Id. at 848.

103. Id.

104. Letter from James Madison (1834), in 4 *Letters and Other Writings of James Madison* 349, 350 (1865.

105. While theorists differ substantially in how they think the Court should go about its business, mistrust of popular majorities lies at the heart of virtually every modern defense or justification of judicial review. See, e.g., Ronald Dworkin, *Law's Empire* 355–99 (1986); Cass R. Sunstein, *The Partial Constitution* 17–194 (1993); John Hart Ely, *Democracy and Distrust* (1980); Christopher L. Eisgruber, *Constitutional Self-Government* (2001).

106. See, e.g., Larry Alexander and Frederick Schauer, "On Extrajudicial Constitutional Interpretation," 110 *Harv. L. Rev.* 1359 (1997).

107. White, supra note 31, at 594.

108. Andrew Jackson, Veto Message (July 10, 1832), in 2 Richardson, supra note 64, at 582.

109. Id. at 581–82. This was, in effect, the same position Madison had taken when he signed the bank into law in 1816, but consistent opposition to the bank since that time led Jackson to interpret popular views differently.

110. "The Supreme Court of the United States: Its Judges and Jurisdiction," 1 *Democratic Rev.* 143, 166 (1838).

111. See Remini, supra note 27, at 402–11.

112. See U.S. Dept. of Commerce, *Historical Statistics of the United States: Colonial Times to 1970*, at tables A1–5 (1975).

113. Id. at A43–56.

114. Kerby A. Miller, *Emigrants and Exiles: Ireland and the Irish Exile to North America* 193–279 (1985).

115. See Gordon S. Wood, *The Radicalism of the American Revolution* 305–11 (1991).

116. See generally Susan Previant Lee and Peter Passell, *A New Economic View of American History* (1979); Diane Lindstrom, "American Economic Growth before 1840: New Evidence and New Directions," 39 *J. Econ. Hist.* 289 (1979); Douglass C. North, *The Economic Growth of the United States, 1790–1860* (1961).

117. Charles Sellers, *The Market Revolution: Jacksonian America, 1815–1876*, at 20 (1991).

118. Id. at 21; see also Harry L. Watson, *Liberty and Power: The Politics of Jacksonian America* 17–41 (1990).

119. See Wood, supra note 115, at 325–34.

120. Alexis de Tocqueville, *Democracy in America* 512 (J. P. Mayer, ed., 1969); Wood, supra note 115, at 328.

121. See Mary P. Ryan, *Civic Wars: Democracy and Public Life in the American City of the Nineteenth Century* 120–24 (1997); Alexander Keyssar, *The Right to Vote: The Contested History of Democracy in the United States* 54–60 (2000).

122. Keyssar, supra note 121, at 26–42; Watson, supra note 118, at 49–52; Ryan, supra note 121, at 114–20.

123. Watson, supra note 118, at 232.

124. Keyssar, supra note 121, at 42–52; Wood, supra note 115, at 229–325.

125. Quoted in Ryan, supra note 121, at 116–17.

126. Elias Smith, *The Loving Kindness of God Displayed in the Triumph of Republicanism in America* 14–15 (n.p., 1809), quoted in Wood, supra note 115, at 232.

127. Gerald Leonard, *The Invention of Party Politics* 5, 30, 175 (2002).

128. See Paul A. Gilje, *Rioting in America* 63 (1996); Paul Gilje, *The Road to Mobocracy* (1987); David Grimsted, *American Mobbing, 1828–1861: Toward Civil War* (1998); Ryan, supra note 121, at 129–31 (1997).

129. Ryan, supra note 121, at 124.

130. Samuel Johnson, *A Dictionary of the English Language* (12th ed. 1802), quoted in Gordon S. Wood, "Conspiracy and the Paranoid Style: Causality and Deceit in the Eighteenth Century," 39 *Wm. & Mary Q.* 401, 409 (3d ser. 1982).

131. Wood, supra note 130, at 407–20; Richard Hofstadter, *The Paranoid Style in American Politics and Other Essays* 27, 32, 36 (1965).

132. James Madison, "A Candid State of Parties," *National Gazette* (Sept. 22, 1792), in 14 *Papers of Madison*, supra note 11, at 370.

133. Martin Van Buren, *Inquiry into the Origins and Course of Political Parties in the United States* 7 (1867).

134. Substance of Mr. Van Buren's Observations in the Senate of the United States, on Mr. Foote's Amendment (Feb. 12, 1828), quoted in Michael Wallace, "Changing Concepts of Party in the United States: New York, 1815–1828," 74 *Am. Hist. Rev.* 453, 483 (1968).

135. "A Candid State of Parties," supra note 132, at 372.

136. Van Buren, supra note 133, at 5.

137. Harry Ammon, *James Monroe: The Quest for National Identity* 371 (1990).

138. Leonard, supra note 127, at 34.

139. Van Buren, supra note 133, at 3–5.

140. Id. at 42–43.

141. Leonard, supra note 127, at 6.

142. Albany Argus, May 28, 1824. See Leonard, supra note 127, at 72; Wallace, supra note 134, at 487–90.

143. Leonard, supra note 127, at 3.

144. Id. at 12, 47.

145. Id. at 35–36.

146. Id. at 118.

147. Id. at 14.

148. Wallace, supra note 134, at 457–58; Ralph Ketcham, *Presidents above Party* 141 (1984); Gerald Leonard, "Party as a 'Political Safeguard of Federalism': Martin Van Buren and the Constitutional Theory of Party Politics," 54 *Rutgers L. Rev.* 221, 256–57 (2001).

149. Wallace, supra note 134, at 470.

150. Leonard, supra note 148, at 256–57.

151. *Chicago Democrat*, July 8, 1835.

152. Leonard, supra note 127, at 12, 189–90; Leonard, supra note 148, at 250–59.

153. See Jeffrey L. Pasley, *The Tyranny of Printers: Newspaper Politics in the Early American Republic* 348–99 (2001).

154. See Watson, supra note 118, at 73–95; Peterson, supra note 26, at 113–64; Remini, supra note 27, at 234–72.

155. Leonard, supra note 127, at 37.

156. Speech of Fisher Ames, 4 *Annals of Cong.* (H.R.) 3d Cong., 2d Sess. 923 (Nov. 1794).

157. The classic remains Richard P. McCormick, *The Second Party System: Party Formation in the Jacksonian Era* (1966). For useful studies of particular states—each, however, with a central focus on something other than political history and the mechanics of party formation—see Leonard, supra note 127 (Illinois), and Harry L. Watson, *Jacksonian Politics and Community Conflict: The Emergence of the Second American Party System in Cumberland County North Carolina* (1981).

158. McCormick, supra note 157, at 343–51.

159. Ryan, supra note 121, at 109.

160. Bruce Ackerman, *We the People: Foundations* 6–7, 230–94 (1991).

161. McCormick, supra note 157, at 30, 349–50; Gil Troy, *See How They Ran: The Changing Role of the Presidential Candidate* 16–38 (rev. ed. 1996).

162. Apologies for such a short aside on such a huge topic. Don Herzog incisively criticizes the view that democratic debate should be "a relentlessly disinterested discussion of issues of principle" in *Poisoning the Minds of the Lower Orders* 146–52 (1998). A short quote will convey the basic point:

> It's easy enough to deride the whimsical irrationalities that infect democratic debate. Yet it doesn't follow that a public debate without passion would be desirable. Take appeals to the sympathies and compassion of one's audience, intensely evocative sketches of the suffering of the subordinate and pariahs. Or take the attempt to summon up simmering resentment, even boiling rage, at some injustice. Or the gleeful adolescent pursuit of puncturing the bloated bubbles of complacency, hypocrisy, and pomposity. Do we really want a politics purged of such appeals to affection?

Id. at 150. Even if we wanted it, we could not have it—a fact abundantly clear to anyone who has experienced the anger of those who defend a politics of reason when challenged.

163. Ryan, supra note 121, at 95; Glenn C. Altschuler and Stuart M. Blumin, *Rude Republic: Americans and Their Politics in the Nineteenth Century* 14–46 (2000); William Pencak, "A Historical Perspective," in *Riot and Revelry in Early America* 11 (William Pencak, Matthew Davis, and Simon P. Newman, eds., 2002).

164. Ryan, supra note 121, at 109.

165. See *Illinois Advocate*, May 6, 1835; *Chicago American*, July 30, 1839; *Kingston Democratic Journal*, May 5, 1852; Leonard, supra note 127, at 127–28; Altschuler and Blumin, supra note 163, at 49–50.

166. Ryan, supra note 121, at 111–12.

167. *Chicago Democrat*, Dec. 2, 1835.

168. See McCormick, supra note 157, at 94–95, 168, 346–47, 349; Donald J. Ratcliffe, *Party Spirit in a Frontier Republic: Democratic Politics in Ohio, 1793–1821*, at 125–27 (1998); Altschuler and Blumin, supra note 163, at 19–20; Leonard, supra note 127, at 119; Leonard, supra note 148, at 256–57.

169. Letter from Caspar Thiell to Mahlon Greed in *Belleville Advocate*, Aug. 29 and Sept. 19, 1840.

170. Wallace, supra note 134, at 460–68; Richard Hofstadter, *The Idea of a Party System* 244–46 (1969).

171. *Black Rock Beacon*, quoted in *Albany Argus*, Feb. 17, 1824.

172. Leonard, supra note 148, at 256–57; Hofstader, supra note 170, at 244–48.

173. Quoted in Hofstader, supra note 170, at 245.

174. Van Buren, supra note 133, at 352.

175. On codification, see Charles M. Cook, *The American Codification Movement* (1981); Perry Miller, *The Life of the Mind in America: From the Revolution to*

the Civil War 239–65 (1965); Robert Gordon, "Book Review, *The American Codification Movement: A Study in Antebellum Legal Reform*," 36 *Vand. L. Rev.* 431 (1983). On judicial elections, see Lawrence Friedman, *A History of American Law* 127, 371–73 (2d ed. 1985); 1 Louis B. Boudin, *Government by Judiciary* 317–405 (Russell & Russell, 2d ed. 1968); J. Willard Hurst, *The Growth of American Law: The Law Makers* 140 (1950).

176. Van Buren, supra note 133, at 348.

177. Id. at 329.

178. Id. at 329–30.

179. Id. at 330.

180. Id. at 352.

181. Id.

182. On the Whig party and its formation, see Holt, supra note 75, at 1–121; Daniel Walker Howe, *The Political Culture of the American Whigs* (1980).

183. Leonard, supra note 127, at 235–44; Holt, supra note 75, at 10.

184. Condition of the Party, *Sangamo Journal*, May 26, 1838.

185. Holt, supra note 75, at 17.

186. Id. at 25–30.

187. See, e.g., Robert V. Remini, "The Election of 1832," in 1 *History of American Presidential Elections* (Arthur M. Schlesinger, Jr. and Fred Israel, eds., 1971).

188. Resolutions of Marshall County, in *Sangamo Journal*, Sept. 6, 1839.

189. See Leonard, supra note 127, at 196–204.

190. Holt, supra note 75, at 15–121; Ryan, supra note 121, at 113.

191. Altschuler and Blumin, supra note 163, at 270.

192. John L. Brooke, "To be 'Read by the Whole People': Press, Party, and Public Sphere in the United States, 1789–1840," 110 *Amer. Antiquarian Soc'y* 41, 116 (2002).

193. Many historians have emphasized the enthusiasm of party rank and file for politics. See, e.g., William E. Gienapp, "Politics Seems to Enter into Everything: Political Culture in the North, 1840–1860," in Stephen E. Maizlish and John J. Kushman, eds., *Essays on Antebellum American Politics, 1840–1860* (1982); Watson, supra note 118; Watson, supra note 157; Joel H. Silbey, *The American Political Nation, 1838–1893* (1991).

194. Altschuler and Blumin, supra note 163, at 273.

195. Edmund Morgan, *Inventing the People: The Rise of Popular Sovereignty in England and America* 14 (1988).

196. See chapter 1.

197. See also Don Herzog, *Happy Slaves: A Critique of Consent Theory* 5–38 (1989).

198. Reeve Huston, "Popular Movements and Party Rule: The New York Anti-Rent Wars and the Jacksonian Political Order," in Jeffrey L. Pasley, Andrew W. Robertson, and David Waldstreicher, eds., *Beyond the Founders: New Approaches to the Political History of the Early American Republic* (2004).

199. Letter from Joseph Story to Ezekial Bacon (Apr. 12, 1845), in 2 *Life and Letters of Joseph Story* 527–28 (William W. Story, ed., 1851).

CHAPTER 8

1. For a useful analysis of the political dynamic that typically provokes these outbursts, see Keith E. Whittington, "The Politics of Constitutional Meaning" (unpublished manuscript on file with author); Stephen Skowronek, *The Politics Presidents Make* (1993): Thomas E. Cronin and Michael A. Genovese, *The Paradoxes of the American Presidency* 224–72 (1998).

2. H. Jefferson Powell, "Enslaved to Judicial Supremacy?" 106 *Harv. L. Rev.* 1197, 1197 (1993). This view is especially widespread among constitutional lawyers and theorists. See, e.g., Ronald Dworkin, *Freedom's Law* 34–35 (1996) ("interpretive authority is already distributed by history" which "shows that our judges have final interpretive authority"); Kathleen M. Sullivan, "The Nonsupreme Court," 91 *Mich. L. Rev.* 1121, 1124 (1993) ("The judicial supremacist vision of the Court . . . has prevailed ever since Hamilton in *Federalist 78* first located the Supreme Court atop a 'hierarchical pyramid' within the national government"). There are, of course, exceptions. See, e.g., Michael Stokes Paulsen, "The Most Dangerous Branch: Executive Power to Say What the Law Is," 83 *Geo. L.J.* 217 (1994); Christopher L. Eisgruber, "The Most Competent Branches: A Response to Professor Paulsen," 83 *Geo. L.J.* 347 (1994).

3. The phrase is from the letter quoted at the beginning of chapter 6. See Letter from James Madison to ——— (1834), in 4 *Letters and Other Writings of James Madison* 349, 350 (1865).

4. See Symposium, "The Bicentennial and the Rediscovery of Constitutional History, Part II: Rights Consciousness in American History," 74 *J. Amer. Hist.* 665, 793–1034 (1987) (including articles by Ellen C. DuBois, Eric Foner, Staughton Lynd, Martha Minow, and Hendrik Hartog discussing different historical instances).

5. See Morton J. Horwitz, *The Transformation of American Law, 1780–1860*, at 253–56 (1977).

6. See Richard Drew, "Bringing the State Courts Back In: Party Politics and the Antebellum Surge in American Judicial Power" (unpublished manuscript on file with author).

7. 1 Joseph Story, *Commentaries on the Constitution of the United States* 346, 347 (1833).

8. Id. at 346.

9. Id. Compare this to the vanishingly small category recognized by the current Supreme Court. See Rachel Barkow, "More Supreme than Court? The Fall of the Political Question Doctrine and the Rise of Judicial Supremacy," 102 *Colum. L. Rev.* 237, 263–73 (2002).

10. Story, supra note 7, at 346–47.

11. See David P. Currie, *The Constitution in the Supreme Court: The First Hundred Years, 1789–1888*, at 201–81 (1985).

12. 2 Charles Warren, *The Supreme Court in United States History* 212 (1926) (quoting Vermont Whig George P. Marsh). For further discussion, see id. at

206–17; Keith E. Whittington, "The Road Not Taken: Dred Scott, Judicial Authority, and Political Questions," 63 *J. Pol.* 365, 377–78 (2001).

13. 60 U.S. (19 How.) 393 (1857).

14. Mark Graber, "Desperately Ducking Slavery: Dred Scott and Contemporary Constitutional Theory," 14 *Const. Comm.* 271, 283–93 (1997).

15. See Don E. Fehrenbacher, *The Dred Scott Case: Its Significance in American Law and Politics* 417–48 (1978); Barry Friedman, "The History of the Countermajoritarian Difficulty, Part One: The Road to Judicial Supremacy," 73 *N.Y.U. L. Rev.* 333, 416–18 (1998). Friedman finds that *Dred Scott* "continued to be a significant blot on [the Court's] record" well after the Civil War and that it was "referred to frequently as a basis for doubting the Court." Barry Friedman, "The History of the Countermajoritarian Difficulty, Part Two: Reconstruction's Political Court," 91 *Geo. L.J.* 1, 20 (2002).

16. See Fehrenbacher, supra note 15, at 440–43; *New York Tribune*, Mar. 7, 9–12, 16–17, 19–21, 25 (1857).

17. *New York Evening Post*, Mar. 14 (1857).

18. *New York Tribune*, Mar. 12, 16 (1857).

19. Fehrenbacher, supra note 15, at 427.

20. Martin Van Buren, *Inquiry into the Origin and Course of Political Parties in the United States* 376 (1867).

21. Thomas Hart Benton, *A Review of the Decision of the Supreme Court of the United States in the Dred Scott Case* (Louisville, 1857); other contemporaneous books and articles are discussed in Fehrenbacher, supra note 15, at 423–28.

22. See James M. McPherson, *Battle Cry of Freedom: The Civil War Era* 176–79 (1988); David M. Potter, *The Impending Crisis, 1848–1861*, at 291–93 (1976); Fehrenbacher, supra note 15, at 423–48.

23. See, e.g., Abraham Lincoln, The *Dred Scott* Decision: Speech at Springfield, Illinois (June 26, 1857), in *Abraham Lincoln: His Speeches and Writings* 352, 355–57 (Roy P. Basler, ed., paperback ed. 1946).

24. Abraham Lincoln, First Inaugural Address (Mar. 4, 1861), in id. at 579, 585–86.

25. On coastal shipping, see 10 Op. Att'y Gen. 382, 412 (1862); on passports, see 5 *The Works of Charles Sumner* 497–98 (1880); on patents, see 6 id. at 144; on abolition, see 12 Stat. 432 (1862) (territories), and 12 Stat. 376 (District of Columbia). See generally Keith E. Whittington, "Extrajudicial Constitutional Interpretation: Three Objections and Responses," 80 *N. Car. L. Rev.* 773, 785 (2002).

26. Lincoln had been equally careful in his earlier public statements about *Dred Scott*. In his important speech in Springfield on June 26, 1857, for example, he took the position that *Dred Scott* could be challenged because it had not been unanimous, because it was consistent with neither "legal public expectation" nor past political practice, and because it was the first time the Court had addressed the issue. Were things otherwise, he mused, "it then might be,

perhaps would be, factious, nay, even revolutionary, not to acquiesce in it as a precedent." *Lincoln: Speeches and Writings*, supra note 23, at 355.

27. Robert H. Jackson, *The Struggle for Judicial Supremacy: A Study of a Crisis in American Power Politics* (1941).

28. Robert A. Burt, *The Constitution in Conflict* 232–53 (1992); Stephen M. Griffin, *American Constitutionalism* 99–100 (1996).

29. Congressional Research Service, *The Constitution of the United States of America: Analysis and Interpretation* (1998). Mark Graber has argued that this standard count leaves out a handful of cases from the early and middle decades of the nineteenth century in which the Supreme Court found federal land grants unconstitutional. Mark A. Graber, "Naked Land Transfers and American Constitutional Development," 53 *Vanderbilt L. Rev.* 73 (2000). But these cases involved what amounted to "personal" bills and so presented a different problem than that posed by general legislation.

30. See Robert Lowry Clinton, *Marbury v. Madison and Judicial Review* 162 (1989); Morton J. Horwitz, *The Transformation of American Law, 1870–1960: The Crisis of Legal Orthodoxy* 19 (1992); Christopher Wolfe, *The Rise of Modern Judicial Review* 4 (rev. ed. 1994); Griffin, supra note 28, at 91; John Brigham, *The Cult of the Court* 43 (1987).

31. See Allan J. Lichtman and Ken DeCell, *The Thirteen Keys to the Presidency* 145–81 (1990); Rafael Gely and Pablo T. Spiller, "The Political Economy of Supreme Court Constitution Decisions: The Case of Roosevelt's Court-Packing Plan," 12 *Int'l Rev. L. & Econ.* 45 (1992); Mark Ramseyer, "The Puzzling (In)Dependence of Courts: A Comparative Analysis," 23 *J. Legal Stud.* 741 (1994).

32. See William E. Forbath, "The Ambiguities of Free Labor: Labor and Law in the Gilded Age," 1985 *Wisc. L. Rev.* 767, 786–801; Eric Foner, *Politics and Ideology in the Age of the Civil War* 97–200 (1980).

33. See Burt, supra note 28, at 244.

34. David Brewer, "The Nation's Safeguard," *Proceedings of the N.Y. State Bar Ass'n* 47 (1893).

35. John F. Dillon, "Address of the President," in *Report of the Fifteenth Annual Meeting of the American Bar Association* 167, 203, 206 (1892).

36. Horwitz, supra note 30, at 273 n.1.

37. Id. at 10–31. See also William E. Nelson, *The Roots of American Bureaucracy, 1830–1900*, at 82–112, 133–55 (1982).

38. See Barry Friedman, "The History of the Countermajoritarian Difficulty, Part Three: The Lesson of Lochner," 76 *N.Y.U. L. Rev.* 1383 (2001).

39. The literature is immense. Among the more significant recent contributions are Horowitz, supra note 30; 2 Bruce Ackerman, *We the People: Transformations* (1998); G. Edward White, *The Constitution and the New Deal* (2000); Edward A. Purcell, Jr., *Brandeis and the Progressive Constitution* (2000); Barry Cushman, *Rethinking the New Deal Court* (1998). Barry Friedman discusses

both the politics of judicial review and the literature in "The History of the Countermajoritarian Difficulty, Part Three," supra note 38, and "The History of the Countermajoritarian Difficulty, Part Four: Law's Politics," 148 *U. Penn. L. Rev.* 971 (2000).

40. See, e.g., Hendrik Hartog, "The Constitution of Aspiration and 'The Rights That Belong to Us All,'" 74 *J. Amer. Hist.* 1013 (1987); Ellen C. DuBois, "Outgrowing the Compact of the Fathers: Equal Rights, Woman Suffrage, and the United States Constitution, 1820–1878," 74 *Amer. J. Hist.* 836 (1987); Martha Minow, "We, the Family: Constitutional Rights and American Families," 74 *J. Amer. Hist.* 959 (1987); William E. Forbath, "Caste, Class, and Equal Citizenship," 98 *Mich. L. Rev.* 1 (1999); James Gray Pope, "Labor's Constitution of Freedom," 106 *Yale L.J.* 941 (1997); James Gray Pope, "The Thirteenth Amendment Versus the Commerce Clause: Labor and the Shaping of American Constitutional Law, 1921–1957," 102 *Colum. L. Rev.* 1 (2002); Reva B. Siegel, "Text in Contest: Gender and the Constitution from a Social Movement Perspective," 150 *U. Pa. L. Rev.* 297 (2001); Michele Landis Daubert, *Helping Ourselves: Disaster Relief and the Origins of the American Welfare State* ch. 3 (forthcoming).

41. See Stephen Skowronek, *Building a New American State: The Expansion of Administrative Capacities, 1877–1920* (1982).

42. See William Forbath, "Democracy and the Constitution: Revisiting the Progressives" (unpublished manuscript on file with author); Peter G. Fish, *The Politics of Federal Judicial Administration* 18 (1973).

43. See Walter Dean Burnham, "The System of 1896: An Analysis," in *The Evolution of American Electoral Systems* 147, 166–69 (1981).

44. Platform of the Progressive Party (Aug. 7, 1912).

45. Friedman, "The History of the Countermajoritarian Difficulty, Part Three," supra note 38, at 1436–44; William G. Ross, *A Muted Fury: Populists, Progressives, and Labor Unions Confront the Courts, 1890–1937* (1994).

46. 1912 Platform of the Progressive Party, supra note 44.

47. Theodore Roosevelt, A Charter of Democracy—Address before the Ohio Constitutional Convention at Columbus, Ohio, Feb. 21, 1912, in *Social Justice and Popular Rule: Essays, Addresses, and Public Statements Relating to the Progressive Movement* 119, 141–42 (1926).

48. Id. at 142.

49. Theodore Roosevelt, Introduction to T. J. Ransom, *The Judiciary and Majority Rule* (1912); see Forbath, supra note 42. On Roosevelt's views about judicial recall, see Theodore Roosevelt, The Right of the People to Rule—Address at Carnegie Hall, Mar. 20, 1912, in *Social Justice and Popular Rule*, supra note 47, at 151, 154–55.

50. Roosevelt, Charter of Democracy, supra note 47, at 140.

51. Id. at 122. See also Theodore Roosevelt, The Recall of Judicial Decisions—Address at Philadelphia, Pa., Apr. 10, 1912, in *Social Justice and Popular Rule*, supra note 47, at 190–203.

52. Created by Congress in 1910 to hear appeals from railroad rate decisions of the Interstate Commerce Commission, the judges of this court managed in an incredibly short time to alienate everyone with an interest in its business, and Congress put the court out of business in 1913. George Dix, "Death of the Commerce Court: A Study in Institutional Weakness," 8 *Am. J. Legal Hist.* 238, 244–52 (1964); Charles G. Geyh, "Judicial Independence, Judicial Accountability, and the Role of Constitutional Norms in Congressional Regulation of Courts," 78 *Ind. L.J.* 153, 190–94 (2003).

53. Friedman, "The History of the Countermajoritarian Difficulty, Part Three," supra note 38, at 1444–47; Ross, supra note 45.

54. See Ackerman, supra note 39, at 279–382.

55. William E. Forbath, "The New Deal Constitution in Exile," 51 *Duke L.J.* 165, 181 (2001); see also Forbath, supra note 40, at 75. Nor was the New Dealers' vision of the Constitution the only example of popular constitutionalism contending for authority. As James Gray Pope has shown, there were elements in the labor movement with a very different vision, albeit one that shared the premise that authority to construe the Constitution rested with the people. Pope, supra note 40.

56. Franklin D. Roosevelt, Address on Constitution Day, Washington, D.C., Sept. 17, 1937, in 6 *The Public Papers and Addresses of Franklin D. Roosevelt* 359, 362–63, 365 (Samuel I. Rosenman, ed., 1941).

57. 79 Cong. Rec. 13, 910 (1935) (statement of Rep. Lewis).

58. Id.

59. Id. at 13, 916.

60. Forbath, supra note 55, at 179–80.

61. See Horwitz, supra note 30, at 258–68.

62. *United States v. Carolene Prods. Co.*, 304 U.S. 144, 152–53 n.4 (1938).

63. The single exception in this period was the Court's unexpected 1976 decision in *National League of Cities v. Usery*, 469 U.S. 528 (1976), which tried to articulate limits on Congress's power to regulate the instrumentalities of state government. Within less than a decade, however, after a series of opinions upheld federal laws and revealed how difficult the principle was to implement, the Court overruled *Usery*. *Garcia v. San Antonio Metropolitan Transit Auth.*, 469 U.S. 528 (1985).

64. 358 U.S. 1, 18 (1958). The Court made similarly explicit pronouncements in three other cases: *Baker v. Carr*, 369 U.S. 186 (1962); *Powell v. McCormack*, 395 U.S. 486 (1969); and *United States v. Nixon*, 418 U.S. 683 (1974).

65. See Barry Friedman, "Birth of an Academic Obsession: The History of the Countermajoritarian Difficulty, Part Five," 112 *Yale L.J.* 153, 185–202 (2002).

66. Susan R. Burgess, *Contest for Constitutional Authority: The Abortion and War Powers Debates* 7–9 (1992).

67. Meese's speech is reprinted as "The Law of the Constitution," 61 *Tulane L. Rev.* 979, 983 (1987).

68. Anthony Lewis, "Law or Power?" *N.Y. Times*, Oct. 27, 1986, at A23; see also Ronald J. Ostrow, "Meese's View that Court Doesn't Make Laws Scored," *L.A. Times*, Oct. 24, 1986, at I13 (quoting Ira Glasser describing Meese's speech as an "invitation to lawlessness").

69. Edwin Meese III, "The Tulane Speech: What I Meant," *Wash. Post*, Nov. 13, 1986, at A21.

70. See Richard A. Primus, *The American Language of Rights* (1999).

71. Joseph A. Schumpeter, *Capitalism, Socialism and Democracy* (1942); Robert Dahl, *A Preface to Democratic Theory* (1956).

72. Robert H. Bork, "The Supreme Court Needs a New Philosophy," *Fortune*, Dec. 1968, at 140.

73. Burgess, supra note 66, at 7–9.

74. Edward A. Purcell, *The Crisis of Democratic Theory: Scientific Naturalism and the Problem of Value* (1973); Horwitz, supra note 30, at 247–72; Laura Kalman, *The Strange Career of Legal Liberalism* 1–131 (1996); Friedman, "The History of the Countermajoritarian Difficulty, Part V," supra note 65.

75. Morton Horwitz, "The Warren Court and the Pursuit of Justice," 50 *Wash. & Lee L. Rev.* 5, 10 (1993).

76. John Hart Ely, *Democracy and Distrust: A Theory of Judicial Review* (1980).

77. 369 U.S. 186, 217 (1962).

78. Herbert Wechsler, "The Political Safeguards of Federalism: The Role of the States in the Composition and Selection of the National Government," 54 *Colum. L. Rev.* 543 (1954).

79. See Burgess, supra note 66, at 7–12; Whittington, supra note 25, at 777 and n. 21 (reporting polls showing 60% of respondents identifying the Supreme Court as having the final say on constitutional matters); Scott E. Gant, "Judicial Supremacy and Nonjudicial Interpretation of the Constitution," 24 *Hastings Const. L.Q.* 359, 362 (1997); David A. Strauss, "Presidential Interpretation of the Constitution," 15 *Cardozo L. Rev.* 113, 119–20 (1993); Robert Nagel, "The Role of the Legislative and Executive Branches in Interpreting the Constitution," 73 *Cornell L. Rev.* 380, 381–82 (1988).

80. Insightful and useful analyses of the Court's doctrine include: Louis D. Bilionis, "The New Scrutiny," 51 *Emory L.J.* 481, 485 (2002); Robert C. Post and Reva B. Siegel, "Equal Protection by Law: Federal Antidiscrimination after Morrison and Kimel," 110 *Yale L.J.* 441 (2000); Robert C. Post and Reva B. Siegel, "Protecting the Constitution from the People: Juriscentric Restrictions on Section Five Power," 78 *Ind. L.J.* (2003); Evan H. Caminker, "'Appropriate' Means-Ends Constraints on Section 5 Powers," 53 *Stan. L. Rev.* 1127 (2001); John C. Yoo, "The Judicial Safeguards of Federalism," 70 *S. Cal. L. Rev.* 1311 (1997). My own critique of the Court's recent jurisprudence is found in Larry D. Kramer, "The Supreme Court, 2000 Term—Foreword: We the Court," 115 *Harv. L. Rev.* 4, 130–58 (2001).

81. *United States v. Morrison*, 120 S. Ct. 1740, 1753 n.7 (2000).

CHAPTER 9

1. Charles G. Geyh, "Judicial Independence, Judicial Accountability, and the Role of Constitutional Norms in Congressional Regulation of Courts," 78 *Ind. L.J.* 153, 155, 159 (2003).

2. See Patrick Leahy, The Supreme Court's Decision in Board of Trustees v. Garrett, Cong. Rec. S1671–73 (Feb. 28, 2001).

3. "Who Are the Best Keeper's of the People's Liberties?" *National Gazette* (Dec. 22, 1792), in 14 *The Papers of James Madison* 427 (Robert A. Rutland et al., eds., 1983).

4. See Barry Friedman and Anna L. Harvey, "Electing the Supreme Court," 78 *Ind. L.J.* 123 (2003); Thomas W. Merrill, "The Making of the Second Rehnquist Court: A Preliminary Analysis," 47 *St. Louis U. L.J.* 569 (2003).

5. See David Easton, "A Re-Assessment of the Concept of Political Support," 5 *Brit. J. Pol. Sci.* 435 (1975); Walter F. Murphy, Joseph Tanenhaus, and Daniel Kastner, *Public Evaluations of Constitutional Courts: Alternative Explanations* (1973); Gregory A. Caldiera, and James L. Gibson, "The Etiology of Public Support for the Supreme Court," 36 *Am. J. Pol. Sci.* 635 (1992).

6. Caldiera and Gibson, supra note 5, at 660.

7. See James L. Gibson, Gregory A. Caldeira, and Lester Kenyatta Spence, "The Supreme Court and the U.S. Presidential Election of 2000: Wounds, Self-Inflicts or Otherwise?" 33 *Brit. J. Pol. Sci.* 535 (2003) ("the weak effect" of the election on the Court's standing among Americans "is most likely due to pre-existing attitudes towards the Court that blunted the impact of disapproval of the Court's involvement in the case"); Barry Friedman, "Mediated Popular Constitutionalism," 101 *Mich. L. Rev.* 2595 (2003).

8. James L. Gibson, Gregory A. Caldeira, and Lester Kenyatta Spence, "Public Knowledge of the United States Supreme Court, 2001" (unpublished manuscript on file with author); Ruth Marcus, "Constitution Confuses Most Americans," *Wash. Post*, Feb. 15, 1987, at A13.

9. Cf. Joseph Tanenhaus and Walter F. Murphy, "Patterns of Public Support for the Supreme Court: A Panel Study," 43 *J. Pol.* 24 (1981); James L. Gibson, Gregory A. Caldeira, and Vanessa A. Baird, "On the Legitimacy of National High Courts," 92 *Am. Pol. Sci. Rev.* 343, 345 (1998) (it is "the slow accretion of positive messages about courts and law that leads to legitimacy," because "diffuse support is an attitude that evolves over time").

10. *United States v. Dougherty*, 473 U.S. 1113, 1134 (D.C. Cir. 1972); Mortimer R. Kadish and Stanley H. Kadish, *Discretion to Disobey* 61 (1973); Rachel E. Barkow, "Recharging the Jury: The Criminal Jury's Constitutional Role in an Era of Mandatory Sentencing," 152 *U. Pa. L. Rev.* (2003).

11. Michael McCann, "How the Supreme Court Matters in American Politics: New Institutionalist Perspectives," in *The Supreme Court in American Politics: New Institutionalist Interpretations* 63, 80 (Howard Gillman and Cornell

Clayton, eds., 1999); Michael McCann, "Reform Litigation on Trial," 17 *L. & Soc. Inquiry* 715, 733 (1993).

12. Martin Van Buren, *Inquiry into the Origin and Course of Political Parties in the United States* 376 (1867).

13. The leading article making this argument is Larry Alexander and Frederick Schauer, "On Extrajudicial Constitutional Interpretation," 110 *Harv. L. Rev.* 1359 (1997). Susan R. Burgess collects other examples in *Contest for Constitutional Authority: The Abortion and War Powers Debates* 20, 112–14 (1992).

14. Barry Friedman, "Birth of an Academic Obsession: The History of the Countermajoritarian Difficulty, Part Five," 112 *Yale L.J.* 153 (2002).

15. Keith E. Whittington, "Extrajudicial Constitutional Interpretation: Three Objections and Responses," 80 *N. Car. L. Rev.* 773, 789 (2002).

16. Mark Tushnet, *Taking the Constitution Away from the Courts* 28 (1999).

17. Whittington, supra note 15, at 806–07; for case studies, see Keith E. Whittington, *Constitutional Construction* (1999); Donald G. Morgan, *Congress and the Constitution: A Study of Responsibility* (1966).

18. Thomas H. Hammond and Gary J. Miller, "The Core of the Constitution," 81 *Am. Pol. Sci. Rev.* 1155, 1157–63 (1987); Keith Krehbiel, *Pivotal Politics: A Theory of U.S. Lawmaking* 230–31 (1998); Tushnet, supra note 16, at 52.

19. Murphy, Tanenhaus, and Kastner, supra note 5; Caldiera and Gibson, supra note 5.

20. Letter from James Madison to Mr. ———— (1834), in 4 *Letters and Other Writings of James Madison* 349, 350 (1865).

21. See *Brown v. Allen*, 344 U.S. 443, 540 (1953) (Jackson, J., concurring) ("We are not final because we are infallible, but we are infallible only because we are final.")

22. Jeremy Waldron, *Law and Disagreement* 268 (1999). Amy Gutmann and Dennis Thompson similarly emphasize the significance of unavoidable disagreement in thinking about democracy, though they have no particular interest in the problem of courts and judicial review. See Amy Gutmann and Dennis Thompson, *Democracy and Disagreement* (1996).

23. Waldron, supra note 22, at 12.

24. Id. at 181.

25. Id. at 253.

26. Id. at 185.

27. Whittington, supra note 15, at 821. For useful reconstructions of some of these debates, see Burgess, supra note 13, at 28–108; Morgan, supra note 17, at 163–330.

28. Tushnet, supra note 16, at 57.

29. Id. at 55. Tushnet describes some particular ways in which the judicial overhang works id. at 57–65.

30. Id. at 65–66; see Richard L. Hall, *Participation in Congress* (1996).

31. See John R. Wright, *Interest Groups and Congress* (1996); John Mark Hansen, *Gaining Access* (1991); Jeffrey M. Berry, *The New Liberalism* 87–118 (1999);

Richard A. Smith, "Advocacy, Interpretation, and Influence in the U.S. Congress," 78 *Am. Pol. Sci. Rev.* 44 (1984).

32. John W. Kingdon, *Congressmen's Voting Decisions* 47–54 (3d ed. 1989); R. Douglas Arnold, *The Logic of Congressional Action* 64–87 (1990); Richard F. Fenno, Jr., *Home Style: House Members in Their Districts* 141–57 (1978).

33. Tushnet, supra note 16, at 106.

34. Richard Parker, *"Here, the People Rule"* 4 (1994).

35. Id. at 56.

36. Id. at 58. The preceding few sentences are drawn from Parker's list of contrasting elite and non-elite characteristics, which is lengthier and more elaborate. Id. at 57–58.

37. Id. at 69–70.

38. Tushnet, supra note 16, at 177.

39. J. M. Balkin, "Populism and Progressivism as Constitutional Categories," 104 *Yale L.J.* 1935, 1951 (1995).

40. Roberto Mangbeira Unger, *What Should Legal Analysis Become?* 72 (1996).

41. Id. at 73.

42. John Brigham, *The Cult of the Court* (1987).

43. "Supreme Court Term: Beyond Bush v. Gore," *N.Y. Times*, July 2, 2001, at A1.

44. Richard A. Posner, *Breaking the Deadlock: The 2000 Election, the Constitution, and the Courts* 145 (2001).

45. Burgess, supra note 13, at 7–10.

46. See, e.g., Cass R. Sunstein et al., "Predictably Incoherent Judgments," 54 *Stan. L. Rev.* 1153 (2002); Cass R. Sunstein, "Book Review: *The Perception of Risk* by Paul Slovic," 115 *Harv. L. Rev.* 1119 (2002).

47. Parker, supra note 34, at 92.

48. Balkin, supra note 39, at 1948–49.

49. Waldron, supra note 22, at 13.

50. Van Buren, supra note 12, at 352; see Gerald Leonard, *The Invention of Party Politics* 35–50 (2002).

51. Sanford Levinson, *Constitutional Faith* (1988).

52. Franklin D. Roosevelt, Address on Constitution Day, Washington, D.C., Sept. 17, 1937, in 6 *The Public Papers and Addresses of Franklin D. Roosevelt* 359, 362–63, 365 (Samuel I. Rosenman, ed., 1941).

NOTES TO THE EPILOGUE

1. Larry Kramer, "The Supreme Court, 2000 Term—Foreword: We the Court," 115 *Harv. L. Rev.* 4, 169 (2001).

2. See Hans Kelsen, "Judicial Review of Legislation: A Comparative Study of the Austrian and the American Constitution, 4 *J. Pol.* 183 (1942); Louis Favoreu, "Constitutional Review in Europe," in Louis Henkin and Albert J.

Rosenthal, eds., *Constitutionalism and Rights: The Influence of the United States Constitution Abroad* 38, 40–59 (1990).

3. See the country-by-country surveys in Vicki C. Jackson and Mark Tushnet, *Comparative Constitutional Law* 489–91 (1999); and Alec Stone Sweet, "Constitutional Adjudication and Parliamentary Democracy," in *Governing with Judges: Constitutional Politics in Europe*, at table 2.3 (2000).

4. The most obvious example is the decision of the Federal Constitutional Court of Germany concerning the display of a crucifix in the classroom, 93 BVerfGE 1 (1995), which Donald Kommers reports has "tarnished the court's reputation in the eyes of many Germans and raised questions . . . about the legitimacy of judicial review"—questions that are common in the United States but until now have been "a rare occurrence in Germany." Donald Kommers, *The Constitutional Jurisprudence of the Federal Republic of Germany* xiv (2d ed. 1997). Similar concerns are beginning to percolate in other countries as well.

5. Alexander Hamilton's *Federalist 78* is an exception—another instance where Publius understood things differently and with greater sophistication than others. As we have seen, however, Hamilton's argument was ignored during ratification, and when the issue came into focus for the broader public in the late 1790s, his High Federalist position on the judiciary's role was politically repudiated.

6. See John A. Ferejohn and Larry D. Kramer, "Independent Judges, Dependent Judiciary: Institutionalizing Judicial Restraint," 77 *N.Y.U. L. Rev.* 962, 1037–39 (2002).

7. See Donald S. Lutz, "Toward a Theory of Constitutional Amendment," in Sanford Levinson, ed., *Responding to Imperfection* 237 (1995); Stephen Holmes and Cass R. Sunstein, "The Politics of Constitutional Revision in Eastern Europe," in id. at 275.

8. See James L. Gibson, Gregory A. Caldeira, and Vanessa A. Baird, "On the Legitimacy of High National Courts," 92 *Am. Pol. Sci. Rev.* 343, 356 (1998); Gregory A. Caldeira and James L. Gibson, "The Etiology of Public Support for the Supreme Court," 36 *Am. J. Pol. Sci.* 635, 636 (1992); Gregory A. Caldeira, "Neither the Purse nor the Sword: The Dynamics of Public Confidence in the United States Supreme Court," 80 *Am. Pol. Sci. Rev.* 1209 (1986); Joseph Tanenhaus and Walter F. Murphy, "Patterns of Public Support for the Supreme Court: A Panel Study," 43 *J. Pol.* 24 (1981); Roger Handberg, "Public Opinion and the United States Supreme Court, 1935–1981," 59 *International Social Sci. Rev.* 3 (1984); David Adamny and Joel Grossman, "Support for the Supreme Court as a National Policymaker," 5 *Law & Pol. Q.* 405 (1983).

9. Letter from James Madison to Mr. —— (1834), in 4 *Letters and Other Writings of James Madison* 349, 349–50 (1865). See James L. Gibson, Gregory A. Caldeira, and Lester Kenyatta Spence, "The Supreme Court and the U.S. Presidential Election of 2000: Wounds, Self-Inflicted or Otherwise?" 33 *Brit. J. Pol. Sci.* 535 (2003) ("When courts become salient, people become exposed to the symbolic trappings of judicial power—'the marble temple, the high

bench, the purple curtain, the black robes.' . . . Thus, the effect of displeasure with a particular court decision may be muted by contact with these legitimating symbols. To know courts is indeed to love them. . . .")

10. Barry Friedman, "Mediating Popular Constitutionalism," 101 *Mich. L. Rev.* 295 (2003).

11. As evidenced, for example, by the ambivalent public reaction to FDR's Court-packing plan. See Greg Caldeira, "Public Opinion and the U.S. Supreme Court: FDR's Court-Packing Plan," 81 *Am. Pol. Sci. Rev.* 1139 (1987); Bruce Ackerman, *We the People: Transformations* 324–28 (1998); Barry Cushman, "Mr. Dooley and Mr. Gallup: Public Opinion and Constitutional Change in the 1930s," 50 *Buffalo L. Rev.* 7 (2002). See Gibson, Caldeira, and Baird, supra note 8, at 356–57; Caldeira and Gibson, "Etiology", supra note 8, at 659–60.

12. Gibson, Caldeira, and Baird, supra note 8, at 356–57; Caldeira and Gibson, "Etiology," supra note 8, at 659–60.

Index